CompTIA®
Cybersecurity Analyst (CSA+™)
Study Guide

CompTIA®
Cybersecurity Analyst (CSA+™)
Study Guide
Exam CS0-001

Mike Chapple

David Seidl

SYBEX®
A Wiley Brand

Senior Acquisitions Editor: Kenyon Brown
Development Editor: David Clark
Technical Editor: Robin Abernathy
Production Editor: Rebecca Anderson
Copy Editor: Elizabeth Welch
Editorial Manager: Mary Beth Wakefield
Production Manager: Kathleen Wisor
Executive Editor: Jim Minatel
Book Designers: Judy Fung and Bill Gibson
Proofreader: Kim Wimpsett
Indexer: Ted Laux
Project Coordinator, Cover: Brent Savage
Cover Designer: Wiley
Cover Image: ©Getty Images Inc./Jeremy Woodhouse

Copyright © 2017 by John Wiley & Sons, Inc., Indianapolis, Indiana

Published simultaneously in Canada

ISBN: 978-1-119-34897-9
ISBN: 978-1-119-34991-4 (ebk.)
ISBN: 978-1-119-34988-4 (ebk.)

Manufactured in the United States of America

For general information on our other products and services or to obtain technical support, please contact our Customer Care Department within the U.S. at (877) 762-2974, outside the U.S. at (317) 572-3993 or fax (317) 572-4002.

Wiley publishes in a variety of print and electronic formats and by print-on-demand. Some material included with standard print versions of this book may not be included in e-books or in print-on-demand. If this book refers to media such as a CD or DVD that is not included in the version you purchased, you may download this material at http://booksupport.wiley.com. For more information about Wiley products, visit www.wiley.com.

Library of Congress Control Number: 2017935704

10 9 8 7 6 5 4 3 2 1

I dedicate this book to my father, who was a role model of the value of hard work, commitment to family, and the importance of doing the right thing. Rest in peace, Dad.
—Mike Chapple

This book is dedicated to Ric Williams, my friend, mentor, and partner in crime through my first forays into the commercial IT world. Thanks for making my job as a "network janitor" one of the best experiences of my life.
—David Seidl

Acknowledgments

Books like this involve work from many people, and as authors, we truly appreciate the hard work and dedication that the team at Wiley shows. We would especially like to thank senior acquisitions editor Kenyon Brown. We have worked with Ken on multiple projects and consistently enjoy our work with him.

We also greatly appreciated the editing and production team for the book, including David Clark, our developmental editor, who brought years of experience and great talent to the project, Robin Abernathy, our technical editor, who provided insightful advice and gave wonderful feedback throughout the book, and Becca Anderson, our production editor, who guided us through layouts, formatting, and final cleanup to produce a great book. We would also like to thank the many behind-the-scenes contributors, including the graphics, production, and technical teams who make the book and companion materials into a finished product.

Our agent, Carole Jelen of Waterside Productions, continues to provide us with wonderful opportunities, advice, and assistance throughout our writing careers.

Finally, we would like to thank our families and significant others who support us through the late evenings, busy weekends, and long hours that a book like this requires to write, edit, and get to press.

About the Authors

Mike Chapple, Ph.D., CSA+, is author of the best-selling *CISSP (ISC)² Certified Information Systems Security Professional Official Study Guide* (Sybex, 2015) and the *CISSP (ISC)² Official Practice Tests* (Sybex 2016). He is an information security professional with two decades of experience in higher education, the private sector, and government.

Mike currently serves as senior director for IT Service Delivery at the University of Notre Dame. In this role, he oversees the information security, data governance, IT architecture, project management, strategic planning, and product management functions for Notre Dame. Mike also serves as Associate Teaching Professor in the university's IT, Analytics, and Operations department, where he teaches undergraduate and graduate courses on cybersecurity, data management, and business analytics.

Before returning to Notre Dame, Mike served as executive vice president and chief information officer of the Brand Institute, a Miami-based marketing consultancy. Mike also spent four years in the information security research group at the National Security Agency and served as an active duty intelligence officer in the U.S. Air Force.

Mike is technical editor for *Information Security Magazine* and has written more than 25 books. He earned both his B.S. and Ph.D. degrees from Notre Dame in computer science and engineering. Mike also holds an M.S. in computer science from the University of Idaho and an MBA from Auburn University. Mike holds the Cybersecurity Analyst+ (CSA+), Security+, and Certified Information Systems Security Professional (CISSP) certifications.

David Seidl is the senior director for Campus Technology Services at the University of Notre Dame. As the senior director for CTS, David is responsible for central platform and operating system support, database administration and services, identity and access management, application services, email and digital signage, and document management.

During his over 20 years in information technology, he has served in a variety of leadership, technical, and information security roles, including leading Notre Dame's information security team as Notre Dame's director of information security. He currently teaches a popular course on networking and security for Notre Dame's Mendoza College of Business and has written books on security certification and cyberwarfare, including co-authoring *CISSP (ISC)² Official Practice Tests* (Sybex 2016).

David holds a bachelor's degree in communication technology and a master's degree in information security from Eastern Michigan University, as well as CISSP, GPEN, and GCIH certifications.

Contents at a Glance

Contents

CompTIA.

Becoming a CompTIA Certified IT Professional is Easy

It's also the best way to reach greater professional opportunities and rewards.

Why Get CompTIA Certified?

Growing Demand

Labor estimates predict some technology fields will experience growth of over 20% by the year 2020.* CompTIA certification qualifies the skills required to join this workforce.

Higher Salaries

IT professionals with certifications on their resume command better jobs, earn higher salaries and have more doors open to new multi-industry opportunities.

Verified Strengths

91% of hiring managers indicate CompTIA certifications are valuable in validating IT expertise, making certification the best way to demonstrate your competency and knowledge to employers.**

Universal Skills

CompTIA certifications are vendor neutral—which means that certified professionals can proficiently work with an extensive variety of hardware and software found in most organizations.

 Learn  Certify  Work

Learn more about what the exam covers by reviewing the following:

- Exam objectives for key study points.

- Sample questions for a general overview of what to expect on the exam and examples of question format.

- Visit online forums, like LinkedIn, to see what other IT professionals say about CompTIA exams.

Purchase a voucher at a Pearson VUE testing center or at CompTIAstore.com.

- Register for your exam at a Pearson VUE testing center:

- Visit pearsonvue.com/CompTIA to find the closest testing center to you.

- Schedule the exam online. You will be required to enter your voucher number or provide payment information at registration.

- Take your certification exam.

Congratulations on your CompTIA certification!

- Make sure to add your certification to your resume.

- Check out the CompTIA Certification Roadmap to plan your next career move.

Learn more: Certification.CompTIA.org/certifications/cybersecurity-analyst

* Source: CompTIA 9th Annual Information Security Trends study: 500 U.S. IT and Business Executives Responsible for Security
** Source: CompTIA Employer Perceptions of IT Training and Certification

Introduction

CompTIA Cybersecurity Analyst (CSA+) Study Guide provides accessible explanations and real-world knowledge about the exam objectives that make up the Cybersecurity Analyst+ certification. This book will help you to assess your knowledge before taking the exam, as well as provide a stepping-stone to further learning in areas where you may want to expand your skillset or expertise.

Before you tackle the CSA+, you should already be a security practitioner. CompTIA suggests that test takers have between 3 and 4 years of existing hands-on information security experience. You should also be familiar with at least some of the tools and techniques described in this book. You don't need to know every tool, but understanding how to approach a new scenario, tool, or technology that you may not know using existing experience is critical to passing the CSA+ exam.

 For up-to-the-minute updates covering additions or modifications to the CompTIA certification exams, as well as additional study tools, videos, practice questions, and bonus material, be sure to visit the Sybex website and forum at www.sybex.com.

CompTIA

CompTIA is a nonprofit trade organization that offers certification in a variety of IT areas, ranging from the skills that a PC support technical needs, which are covered in the A+ exam, to advanced certifications like the CompTIA Advanced Security Practitioner, or CASP certification. CompTIA divides its exams into four different categories based on the skill level required for the exam and what topics it covers, as shown in the following table:

Foundational	Professional	Specialty	Mastery
IT Fundamentals	A+	CDIA+	CASP
	Cloud+ with Virtualization	CTT+	
	CSA+	Cloud Essentials	
	Linux+	Healthcare IT Tech	
	Mobility+		
	Network+		
	Security+		
	Project+		
	Server+		

CompTIA recommends that practitioners follow a cybersecurity career path as shown here:

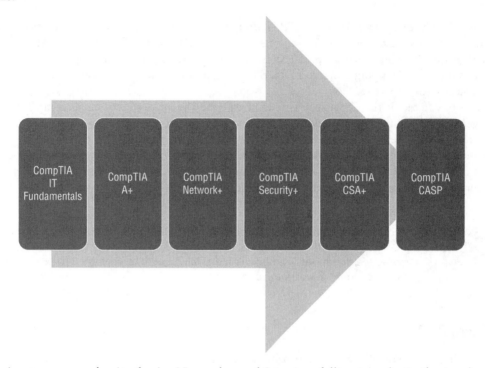

As you can see, despite the A+, Network+, and Security+ falling into the Professional certification category, the Cybersecurity Analyst+ exam is a more advanced exam, intended for professionals with hands-on experience and who possess the knowledge covered by the prior exams.

CompTIA certifications are ISO and ANSI accredited, and they are used throughout multiple industries as a measure of technical skill and knowledge. In addition, CompTIA certifications, including the Security+ and the CASP, have been approved by the U.S. government as Information Assuance baseline certifications and are included in the State Department's Skills Incentive Program.

The Cybersecurity Analyst+ Exam

The Cybersecurity Analyst+ exam, which CompTIA refers to as the CSA+, is designed to be a vendor-neutral certification for cybersecurity, threat, and vulnerability analysts. The CSA+ certification is designed for security analysts and engineers as well as Security Operations Center (SOC) staff, vulnerability analysts, and threat intelligence analysts. It focuses on security analytics and practical use of security tools in real-world scenarios. It covers four major domains: Threat Management, Vulnerability Management, Cyber

Incident Response, and Security Architecture and Tool Sets. These four areas include a range of topics, from reconnaissance to incident response and forensics, while focusing heavily on scenario-based learning.

The CSA+ exam fits between the entry-level Security+ exam and the CompTIA Advanced Security Practitioner (CASP) certification, providing a mid-career certification for those who are seeking the next step in their certification and career path.

The CSA+ exam is conducted in a format that CompTIA calls "performance-based assessment." This means that the exam uses hands-on simulations using actual security tools and scenarios to perform tasks that match those found in the daily work of a security practitioner. Exam questions may include multiple types of questions such as multiple-choice, fill-in-the-blank, multiple-response, drag-and-drop, and image-based problems.

CompTIA recommends that test takers have 3–4 years of information security–related experience before taking this exam. The exam costs $320 in the United States, with roughly equivalent prices in other locations around the globe. More details about the CSA+ exam and how to take it can be found at https://certification.comptia.org/certifications/cybersecurity-analyst.

Study and Exam Preparation Tips

A test preparation book like this cannot teach you every possible security software package, scenario, or specific technology that may appear on the exam. Instead, you should focus on whether you are familiar with the type or category of technology, tool, process, or scenario as you read the book. If you identify a gap, you may want to find additional tools to help you learn more about those topics.

CompTIA recommends the use of NetWars-style simulations, penetration testing and defensive cybersecurity simulations, and incident response training to prepare for the CSA+.

Additional resources for hands-on exercises include the following:

- Exploit-Exercises.com provides virtual machines, documentation, and challenges covering a wide range of security issues at https://exploit-exercises.com/.

- Hacking-Lab provides Capture the Flag (CTF) exercises in a variety of fields at https://www.hacking-lab.com/index.html.

- The OWASP Hacking Lab provides excellent web application–focused exercises at https://www.owasp.org/index.php/OWASP_Hacking_Lab.

- PentesterLab provides a subscription-based access to penetration testing exercises at https://www.pentesterlab.com/exercises/.

- The InfoSec Institute provides online capture-the-flag activities with bounties for written explanations of successful hacks at http://ctf.infosecinstitute.com/.

Since the exam uses scenario-based learning, expect the questions to involve analysis and thought, rather than relying on simple memorization. As you might expect, it is impossible to replicate that experience in a book, so the questions here are intended to help you be confident that you know the topic well enough to think through hands-on exercises.

Taking the Exam

Once you are fully prepared to take the exam, you can visit the CompTIA website to purchase your exam voucher:

    www.comptiastore.com/Articles.asp?ID=265&category=vouchers

CompTIA partners with Pearson VUE's testing centers, so your next step will be to locate a testing center near you. In the United States, you can do this based on your address or your ZIP code, while non-U.S. test takers may find it easier to enter their city and country. You can search for a test center near you at the Pearson Vue website, where you will need to navigate to "Find a test center."

    http://www.pearsonvue.com/comptia/

Now that you know where you'd like to take the exam, simply set up a Pearson VUE testing account and schedule an exam:

    https://certification.comptia.org/testing/schedule-exam

On the day of the test, take two forms of identification, and make sure to show up with plenty of time before the exam starts. Remember that you will not be able to take your notes, electronic devices (including smartphones and watches), or other materials in with you.

After the Cybersecurity Analyst+ Exam

Once you have taken the exam, you will be notified of your score immediately, so you'll know if you passed the test right away. You should keep track of your score report with your exam registration records and the email address you used to register for the exam.

Maintaining Your Certification

CompTIA certifications must be renewed on a periodic basis. To renew your certification, you can either pass the most current version of the exam, earn a qualifying higher-level CompTIA or industry certification, or complete sufficient continuing education activities to earn enough continuing education units (CEUs) to renew it.

CompTIA provides information on renewals via their website at

    https://certification.comptia.org/continuing-education/how-to-renew

When you sign up to renew your certification, you will be asked to agree to the CE program's Code of Ethics, to pay a renewal fee, and to submit the materials required for your chosen renewal method.

A full list of the industry certifications you can use to acquire CEUs toward renewing the CSA+ can be found at

    https://certification.comptia.org/continuing-education/renewothers/renewing-csa

What Does This Book Cover?

This book is designed to cover the four domains included in the CSA+:

Chapter 1: Defending Against Cybersecurity Threats   The book starts by teaching you how to assess cybersecurity threats, as well as how to evaluate and select controls to keep your networks and systems secure.

Chapter 2: Reconnaissance and Intelligence Gathering   Gathering information about an organization and its systems is one of the things that both attackers and defenders do. In this chapter, you will learn how to acquire intelligence about an organization using popular tools and techniques. You will also learn how to limit the impact of intelligence gathering performed against your own organization.

Chapter 3: Designing a Vulnerability Management Program   Managing vulnerabilities helps to keep your systems secure. In this chapter you will learn how to identify, prioritize, and remediate vulnerabilities using a well-defined workflow and continuous assessment methodologies.

Chapter 4: Analyzing Vulnerability Scans   Vulnerability reports can contain huge amounts of data about potential problems with systems. In this chapter you will learn how to read and analyze a vulnerability scan report, what CVSS scoring is and what it means, as well as how to choose the appropriate actions to remediate the issues you have found. Along the way, you will explore common types of vulnerabilities and their impact on systems and networks.

Chapter 5: Building an Incident Response Program   This chapter focuses on building a formal incident response handling program and team. You will learn the details of each stage of incident handling from preparation, to detection and analysis, to containment, eradication, and recovery, to the final post-incident recovery, as well as how to classify incidents and communicate about them.

Chapter 6: Analyzing Symptoms for Incident Response   Responding appropriately to an incident requires understanding how incidents occur and what symptoms may indicate that an event has occurred. To do that, you also need the right tools and techniques. In this chapter, you will learn about three major categories of symptoms. First, you will learn about network events, including malware beaconing, unexpected traffic, and link failures, as well as network attacks. Next, you will explore host issues, ranging from system resource consumption issues to malware defense and unauthorized changes. Finally, you will learn about service- and application-related problems.

Chapter 7: Performing Forensic Analysis   Understanding what occurred on a system, device, or network, either as part of an incident or for other purposes, frequently involves forensic analysis. In this chapter you will learn how to build a forensic capability and how the key tools in a forensic toolkit are used.

Chapter 8: Recovery and Post-Incident Analysis   Once an incident has occurred and the initial phases of incident response have taken place, you will need to work on recovering from it. That process involves containing the incident to ensure no further issues occur and then working on eradicating malware, rootkits, and other elements of a compromise. Once the incident has been cleaned up, the recovery stage can start, including reporting and preparation for future issues.

Chapter 9: Policy and Compliance   Policy provides the foundation of any cybersecurity program, and building an effective set of policies is critical to a successful program. In this chapter you will acquire the tools to build a standards-based set of security policies, standards, and procedures. You will also learn how to leverage industry best practices by using guidelines and benchmarks from industry experts.

Chapter 10: Defense-in-Depth Security Architectures   A strong security architecture requires layered security procedures, technology, and processes to provide defense in depth, ensuring that a single failure won't lead to a failure. In this chapter you will learn how to design a layered security architecture and how to analyze security designs for flaws, including single points of failure and gaps.

Chapter 11: Identity and Access Management Security   The identities that we rely on to authenticate and authorize users, services, and systems are a critical layer in a defense-in-depth architecture. This chapter explains identity, authentication, and authorization concepts and systems. You will learn about the major threats to identity and identity systems as well as how to use identity as a defensive layer.

Chapter 12: Software Development Security   Creating, testing, and maintaining secure software, from simple scripts to complex applications, is critical for security analysts. In this chapter you will learn about the software development life cycle, including different methodologies, testing and review techniques, and how secure software is created. In addition, you will learn about industry standards for secure software to provide you with the foundation you need to help keep applications and services secure.

Chapter 13: Cybersecurity Toolkit   This chapter provides a survey-style view of the many tools that you may encounter while performing threat and vulnerability management as well as incident response. We review tools, what they do, and where to get them.

Practice Exam   Once you have completed your studies, the practice exam will provide you with a chance to test your knowledge. Use this exam to find places where you may need to study more or to verify that you are ready to tackle the exam. We'll be rooting for you!

Appendix A: Answers to Review Questions   The appendix has answers to the review questions you will find at the end of each chapter.

Objective Mapping

The following listing shows how the four Cybersecurity Analyst Exam objectives map to the chapters in this book. If you want to study a specific domain, this mapping can help you identify where to focus your reading.

Threat Management: Chapters 1, 2

Vulnerability Management: Chapters 3, 4

Cyber Incident Response: Chapters 5, 6, 7, 8

Security Architecture and Tools Sets: Chapters 7, 9, 10, 11, 12, 13

The book is written to build your knowledge as you progress through it, so starting at the beginning is a good idea. Each chapter includes notes on important content and 20 questions to help you test your knowledge. Once you are ready, a complete practice test is provided to assess your knowledge.

Study Guide Elements

This study guide uses a number of common elements to help you prepare. These include the following:

Summaries   The summary section of each chapter briefly explains the chapter, allowing you to easily understand what it covers.

Exam Essentials   The exam essentials focus on major exam topics and critical knowledge that you should take into the test. The exam essentials focus on the exam objectives provided by CompTIA.

Chapter Review Questions   A set of questions at the end of each chapter will help you assess your knowledge and if you are ready to take the exam based on your knowledge of that chapter's topics.

Written Labs   The written labs provide more in-depth practice opportunities to expand your skills and to better prepare for performance-based testing on the Cybersecurity Analyst+ exam.

Real-World Scenarios   The real-world scenarios included in each chapter tell stories and provide examples of how topics in the chapter look from the point of view of a security professional. They include current events, personal experience, and approaches to actual problems.

Additional Study Tools

This book comes with a number of additional study tools to help you prepare for the exam. They include the following.

Go to www.wiley.com/go/Sybextestprep to register and gain access to this interactive online learning environment and test bank with study tools.

Sybex Test Preparation Software

Sybex's test preparation software lets you prepare with electronic test versions of the review questions from each chapter, the practice exam, and the bonus exam that are included in this book. You can build and take tests on specific domains, by chapter, or cover the entire set of Cybersecurity Analyst+ exam objectives using randomized tests.

Electronic Flashcards

Our electronic flashcards are designed to help you prepare for the exam. Over 100 flash-cards will ensure that you know critical terms and concepts.

Glossary of Terms

Sybex provides a full glossary of terms in PDF format, allowing quick searches and easy reference to materials in this book.

Bonus Practice Exam

In addition to the practice questions for each chapter, this book includes both a full 90-question practice exam and a 50-question bonus exam. We recommend that you use them both to test your preparedness for the certification exam.

Objectives Map for CompTIA Cybersecurity Analyst (CSA+) Exam CS0-001

The following objective map for the CompTIA Cybersecurity Analyst (CSA+) certification exam will enable you to find the chapter in this book, which covers each objective for the exam.

Objectives Map

Objective	Chapter
1.0 Threat Management	
1.1 Given a scenario, apply environmental reconnaissance techniques using appropriate tools and processes.	Chapter 2
Procedures/common tasks including Topology discovery, OS fingerprinting, Service discovery, Packet capture, Log review, Router/firewall ACLs review, Email harvesting, Social media profiling, Social engineering, DNS harvesting, Phishing; Variables including Wireless vs. wired, virtual vs. physical, internal vs. external, and on-premises vs. cloud; Tools including NMAP, Host scanning, Network mapping, netstat, packet analyzers, IDS/IPS, HIDS/NIDS, Firewall rule-based and logs, Syslog, Vulnerability scanners	

Objective	Chapter
1.2 Given a scenario, analyze the results of a network reconnaissance.	Chapter 2

Point-in-time data analysis including Packet analysis, Protocol analysis, Traffic analysis, Netflow analysis, Wireless analysis; Data correlation and analytics including Anomaly analysis, Trend analysis, Availability analysis, Heuristic analysis, Behavioral analysis; Data output including Firewall logs, Packet captures, NMAP scan results, Event logs, Syslogs, IDS reports; Tools including SIEM, Packet analyzers, IDS/IPS, Resource monitoring tools, Netflow analyzer

1.3 Given a network-based threat, implement or recommend the appropriate response and countermeasure.	Chapter 1

Network segmentation, system isolation, jump boxes and bastion hosts, Honeypots and honeynets, Endpoint security, Group policies, ACLs, Sinkholes, Hardening, Mandatory Access Control (MAC), Compensating controls, Blocking unused ports/services, Patching, Network Access Control (NAC) policies including time-based, rule-based, role-based, and location-based

1.4 Explain the purpose of practices used to secure a corporate environment.	Chapter 1

Penetration testing, Rules of engagement: timing, scope. Authorization, exploitation, communication, and reporting. Reverse engineering, Isolation/sandboxing, Hardware concerns including source authenticity of hardware, trusted foundry, and OEM documentation. Software/malware, Fingerprinting/hashing, Decomposition, Training and exercises, Red teams, Blue teams, and White teams. Risk evaluation, Technical control review, Operational control review, Technical impact and likelihood and rating: High, Medium, and Low

2.0 Vulnerability Management

2.1 Given a scenario, implement an information security vulnerability management process.	Chapter 3

Identification of requirements, Regulatory environments, Corporate policy, Data classification, Asset inventory including critical and non-critical assets. Establishing scanning frequency based on risk appetite, regulatory requirements, technical constraints, and workflow. Configure tools to perform scans according to specification, Determining scanning criteria, setting sensitivity levels, vulnerability feeds, scan scope, credentialed vs. non-credentialed, types of data, and server-based vs. agent-based scanning. Tool updates/plug-ins, SCAP, Permissions and access, How to execute scanning and generate reports, Automated vs. manual distribution, remediation, prioritizing response based on criticality and difficulty of implementation. Communication/change control, Sandboxing/testing, Inhibitors to remediation: MOUs, SLAs, organizational governance, business process interruption, and degrading functionality. Ongoing scanning and continuous monitoring

Objective	Chapter
2.2 Given a scenario, analyze the output resulting from a vulnerability scan.	Chapter 4
Analyze reports from a vulnerability scan, Review and interpret scan results, Identify false positives, Identify exceptions, Prioritize response actions, Validate results and correlate other data points, Compare to best practices or compliance, Reconcile results, Review related logs and/or other data sources, Determine trends	
2.3 Compare and contrast common vulnerabilities found in the following targets within an organization.	Chapter 4
Servers, Endpoints, Network infrastructure, Network appliances, Virtual infrastructure, Virtual hosts, Virtual networks, Management interfaces, Mobile devices, Interconnected networks, Virtual private networks (VPNs), Industrial Control Systems (ICSs), SCADA devices	

3.0 Cyber Incident Response

3.1 Given a scenario, distinguish threat data or behavior to determine the impact of an incident	Chapter 5
Threat classification: known threats vs. unknown threats, Zero day, and advanced persistent threats. Factors contributing to incident severity and prioritization: scope of impact, downtime, recovery time. data integrity, economic impact, system process criticality. Types of data: Personally Identifiable Information (PII), Personal Health Information (PHI), payment card information, intellectual property, corporate confidential, accounting data. mergers and acquisitions	
3.2 Given a scenario, prepare a toolkit and use appropriate forensics tools during an investigation.	Chapter 7
Forensics kits, Digital forensics workstations, Write blockers, Cables, Drive adapters, Wiped removable media, Cameras, o Crime tape, Tamper-proof seals, Documentation/forms, Chain of custody forms, Incident response plan, Incident forms, Call list/escalation lists. Forensic investigation suites, Imaging utilities, Analysis utilities, Chain of custody, Hashing utilities, OS and process analysis, Mobile device forensics, Password crackers, Cryptography tools, Log viewers	
3.3 Explain the importance of communication during the incident response process.	Chapter 5
Stakeholders: HR, legal, marketing, and management. Purpose of communication processes: Limiting communication to trusted parties, disclosure based on regulatory/legislative requirements, o Preventing inadvertent release of information, secure method of communication. Role-based responsibilities: technical, management, law enforcement, and retaining an incident response provider	

Objective	Chapter
3.4 Given a scenario, analyze common symptoms to select the best course of action to support incident response.	Chapter 6

Common network-related symptoms: bandwidth consumption, beaconing, irregular peer-to-peer communication, rogue devices on the network, scan sweeps, and unusual traffic spikes. Common host-related symptoms: processor (CPU) consumption, memory consumption, drive capacity consumption, unauthorized software, malicious processes, unauthorized changes, unauthorized privileges, data exfiltration. Common application-related symptoms: anomalous activity, introduction of new accounts, unexpected output, unexpected outbound communication, service interruption, memory overflows

3.5 Summarize the incident recovery and post-incident response process.	Chapter 8

Containment techniques: segmentation, isolation, removal, and reverse engineering. Eradication techniques: sanitization, reconstruction/reimage, secure disposal, validation, patching, permissions, scanning, and verifying logging/communication to security monitoring. Corrective actions, Lessons learned reports, Change control process, Updating incident response plans, Incident summary reports

4.0 Security Architecture and Tool Sets

4.1 Explain the relationship between frameworks, common policies, controls, and procedures.	Chapter 9

Regulatory compliance, Frameworks: NIST, ISO, COBIT, SABSA, TOGAF, ITIL. Policies: password policy, acceptable use policy, data ownership policy, data retention policy, account management policy, and data classification policies. Controls, Control selection based on criteria, Organizationally defined parameters, Physical controls, Logical controls, Administrative controls, Procedures: continuous monitoring, evidence production, patching, compensating control development, control testing procedures, managing exceptions, developing and executing remediation plans. Verifications and quality control, Audits, Evaluations, Assessments, Maturity models, Certification

4.2 Given a scenario, use data to recommend remediation of security issues related to identity and access management.	Chapter 11

Security issues associated with context-based authentication based on time, location, frequency, behavioral patterns. Security issues associated with identities: personnel, endpoints, servers, services, roles, applications. Security issues associated with identity repositories, Directory services, TACACS+, RADIUS, Security issues associated with federation and single sign-on: o Manual vs. automatic provisioning/deprovisioning and self-service password reset. Exploits: impersonation, man-in-the-middle attacks, session hijacking, cross-site scripting, privilege escalation, and rootkits.

Objective	Chapter
4.3 Given a scenario, review security architecture and make recommendations to implement compensating controls.	Chapter 10

Security data analytics using data aggregation and correlation, trend analysis, and historical analysis. Manual review of firewall logs, syslogs, authentication logs, and event logs. Defense in depth concepts. Personnel security: training, dual control, separation of duties, third party/consultants, cross training, mandatory vacation, succession planning. Defense in depth related processes: continual improvement, scheduled reviews, and retirement of processes. Technologies: automated reporting, security appliances. security suites, outsourcing, Security as a Service (SaaS), and cryptography. Other security concepts: network design and network segmentation

Objective	Chapter
4.4 Given a scenario, use application security best practices while participating in the Software Development Life Cycle (SDLC).	Chapter 12

Best practices during software development, Security requirements definition, Security testing phases, Static code analysis, Web app vulnerability scanning, Fuzzing, Use of interception proxies to crawl applications, Manual peer reviews, User acceptance testing, Stress testing applications, Security regression testing, Input validation, Secure coding best practices from OWASP, SANS, Center for Internet Security. System design recommendations and benchmarks

Objective	Chapter
4.5 Compare and contrast the general purpose and reasons for using various cybersecurity tools and technologies.	Chapter 13

Preventative tools, including IPS: Sourcefire, Snort, Bro, HIPS, Firewalls: Cisco, Palo Alto, Check Point. Antivirus and Anti-malware, EMET, Web proxies, Web Application Firewall (WAF) systems: ModSecurity, NAXSI, Imperva.

Collective tools, including SIEMs: ArcSight, QRadar, Splunk, AlienVault, OSSIM, Kiwi Syslog. Network scanning tool with NMAP, Vulnerability scanning using Qualys, Nessus, OpenVAS, Nexpose, Nikto, and the Microsoft Baseline Security Analyzer. o Packet capture using Wireshark, tcpdump, Network General, and Aircrack-ng. Command line/IP utilities: netstat, ping, tracert/ traceroute, ipconfig/ifconfig, nslookup/dig, the Sysinternals suite, OpenSSL. IDS/HIDS: Bro.

Analytical tools, including Vulnerability scanning including Qualys, Nessus, OpenVAS, Nexpose, Nikto, and the Microsoft Baseline Security Analyzer. Monitoring tools: MRTG, Nagios, SolarWinds, Cacti, NetFlow Analyzer. Interception proxies: Burp Suite, Zap, and Vega.

Exploit tools, including Interception proxies: Burp Suite, Zap, and Vega. o Exploit framework: Metasploit and Nexpose. Fuzzers: Untidy, Peach Fuzzer, Microsoft SDL File/Regex Fuzzer.

Forensics tools, including Forensic suites: EnCase, FTK, Helix, Sysinternals, and Cellebrite. Hashing tools: MD5sum, SHAsum. Password cracking tools; John the Ripper, Cain & Abel. Imaging using DD

Assessment Test

If you're considering taking the Cybersecurity Analyst+ exam, you should have already taken and passed the CompTIA Security+ and Network+ exams and should have 3–4 years of experience in the field. You may also already hold other equivalent certifications. The following assessment test help to make sure that you have the knowledge that you should have before you tackle the Cybersecurity Analyst+ certification and will help you determine where you may want to spend the most time with this book.

1. After running an nmap scan of a system, you receive scan data that indicates the following three ports are open:

    22/TCP

    443/TCP

    1521/TCP

    What services commonly run on these ports?

    A. SMTP, NetBIOS, MySQL

    B. SSH, Microsoft DS, WINS

    C. · SSH, HTTPS, Oracle

    D. FTP, HTTPS, MS-SQL

2. Which of the following tools is best suited to querying data provided by organizations like the American Registry for Internet Numbers (ARIN) as part of a footprinting or reconnaissance exercise?

    A. nmap

    B. traceroute

    C. regmon

    D. whois

3. What type of system allows attackers to believe they have succeeded with their attack, thus providing defenders with information about their attack methods and tools?

    A. A honeypot

    B. A sinkhole

    C. A crackpot

    D. A darknet

4. What cybersecurity objective could be achieved by running your organization's web servers in redundant, geographically separate datacenters?

    A. Confidentiality

    B. Integrity

    C. Immutability

    D. Availability

5. Which of the following vulnerability scanning methods will provide the most accurate detail during a scan?

    A. Black box

    B. Authenticated

    C. Internal view

    D. External view

6. In early 2017, a flaw was discovered in the Chakra JavaScript scripting engine in Microsoft's Edge browser that could allow remote execution or denial of service via a specifically crafted website. The CVSS 3.0 score for this reads

    `CVSS:3.0/AV:N/AC:H/PR:N/UI:R/S:U/C:H/I:H/A:H`

    What is the attack vector and the impact to integrity based on this rating?

    A. System, 9, 8

    B. Browser, High

    C. Network, High

    D. None, High

7. Alice is a security engineer tasked with performing vulnerability scans for her organization. She encounters a false positive error in one of her scans. What should she do about this?

    A. Verify that it is a false positive, and then document the exception

    B. Implement a workaround

    C. Update the vulnerability scanner

    D. Use an authenticated scan, and then document the vulnerability

8. Which phase of the incident response process is most likely to include gathering additional evidence such as information that would support legal action?

    A. Preparation

    B. Detection and Analysis

    C. Containment, Eradication, and Recovery

    D. Post-Incident Activity and Reporting

9. Which of the following descriptions explains an integrity loss?

    A. Systems were taken offline, resulting in a loss of business income.

    B. Sensitive or proprietary information was changed or deleted.

    C. Protected information was accessed or exfiltrated.

    D. Sensitive personally identifiable information was accessed or exfiltrated.

10. Which of the following techniques is an example of active monitoring?

    A. Ping

    B. RMON

    C. Netflows

    D. A network tap

11. Ben's monitoring detects regular traffic sent from a system that is suspected to be compromised and participating in a botnet to a set of remote IP addresses. What is this called?

    A. Anomalous pings

    B. Probing

    C. Zombie chatter

    D. Beaconing

12. Which of the following tools is not useful for monitoring memory usage in Linux?

    A. df

    B. top

    C. ps

    D. free

13. Which of the following tools cannot be used to make a forensic disk image?

    A. xcopy

    B. FTK

    C. dd

    D. EnCase

14. During a forensic investigation, Shelly is told to look for information in slack space on the drive. Where should she look, and what is she likely to find?

    A. She should look at unallocated space, and she is likely to find file fragments from deleted files.

    B. She should look at unused space where files were deleted, and she is likely to find complete files hidden there by the individual being investigated.

    C. She should look in the space reserved on the drive for spare blocks, and she is likely to find complete files duplicated there.

    D. She should look at unused space left when a file is written, and she is likely to find file fragments from deleted files.

15. What type of system is used to contain an attacker to allow them to be monitored?

    A. A white box

    B. A sandbox

    C. A network jail

    D. A VLAN

16. Bob's manager has asked him to ensure that a compromised system has been completely purged of the compromise. What is Bob's best course of action?

    A. Use an antivirus tool to remove any associated malware

    B. Use an antimalware tool to completely scan and clean the system

    C. Wipe and rebuild the system

    D. Restore a recent backup

17. What level of secure media disposition as defined by NIST SP-800-88 is best suited to a hard drive from a high-security system that will be reused in the same company by an employee of a different level or job type?

    A. Clear

    B. Purge

    C. Destroy

    D. Reinstall

18. Which of the following actions is not a common activity during the recovery phase of an incident response process?

    A. Reviewing accounts and adding new privileges

    B. Validating that only authorized user accounts are on the systems

    C. Verifying that all systems are logging properly

    D. Performing vulnerability scans of all systems

19. A statement like "Windows workstations must have the current security configuration template applied to them before being deployed" is most likely to be part of which document?

    A. Policies

    B. Standards

    C. Procedures

    D. Guidelines

20. Jim is concerned with complying with the U.S. federal law covering student educational records. Which of the following laws is he attempting to comply with?

    A. HIPAA

    B. GLBA

    C. SOX

    D. FERPA

21. A fire suppression system is an example of what type of control?

    A. Logical

    B. Physical

    C. Administrative

    D. Operational

22. Lauren is concerned that Danielle and Alex are conspiring to use their access to defraud their organization. What personnel control will allow Lauren to review their actions to find any issues?

    A. Dual control

    B. Separation of duties

    C. Background checks

    D. Cross training

23. Joe wants to implement an authentication protocol that is well suited to untrusted networks. Which of the following options is best suited to his needs in its default state?

   A. Kerberos

   B. RADIUS

   C. LDAP

   D. TACACS+

24. Which software development life cycle model uses linear development concepts in an iterative, four-phase process?

   A. Waterfall

   B. Agile

   C. RAD

   D. Spiral

Answer to the Assessment Test

1. **C.** These three TCP ports are associated with SSH (22), HTTPS (443), and Oracle databases (1521). Other ports mentioned in the potential answers are SMTP (25), NetBIOS (137–139), MySQL (3306), WINS (1512), FTP (20 and 21), and MS-SQL (1433/1434).

2. **D.** Regional Internet registries like ARIN are best queried either via their websites or using tools like Whois. Nmap is a useful port scanning utility, traceroute is used for testing the path packets take to a remote system, and regmon is an outdated Windows Registry tool that has been supplanted by Process Monitor.

3. **A.** Honeypots are systems that are designed to look like attractive targets. When they are attacked, they simulate a compromise, providing defenders with a chance to see how attackers operate and what tools they use. DNS sinkholes provide false information to malicious software, redirecting queries about command and control systems to allow remediation. Darknets are segments of unused network space that are monitored to detect traffic—since legitimate traffic should never be aimed at the darknet, this can be used to detect attacks and other unwanted traffic. Crackpots are eccentric people—not a system you'll run into on a network.

4. **D.** Redundant systems, particularly when run in multiple locations and with other protections to ensure uptime, can help provide availability.

5. **B.** An authenticated, or credentialed, scan provides the most detailed view of the system. Black-box assessments presume no knowledge of a system and would not have credentials or an agent to work with on the system. Internal views typically provide more detail than external views, but neither provides the same level of detail that credentials can allow.

6. **C.** When reading the CVSS 3.0 score, AV is the attack vector. Here, N means network. Confidentiality (C), Integrity (I), and Availability (A) are listed at the end of the listing, and all three are rated as High in this CVSS rating.

7. **A.** When Alice encounters a false positive error in her scans, her first action should be to verify it. This may involve running a more in-depth scan like an authenticated scan, but could also involve getting assistance from system administrators, checking documentation, or other validation actions. Once she is done, she should document the exception so that it is properly tracked. Implementing a workaround is not necessary for false positive vulnerabilities, and updating the scanner should be done before every vulnerability scan. Using an authenticated scan might help but does not cover all of the possibilities for validation she may need to use.

8. **C.** The Containment, Eradication, and Recovery phase of an incident includes steps to limit damage and document what occurred, including potentially identifying the attacker and tools used for the attack. This means that information useful to legal actions is most likely to be gathered during this phase.

9. **B.** Integrity breaches involve data being modified or deleted. Systems being taken offline is an availability issue, protected information being accessed might be classified as a breach of proprietary information, and sensitive personally identifiable information breaches would typically be classified as privacy breaches.

10. C. Active monitoring sends traffic like pings to remote devices as part of the monitoring process. RMON and netflows are both examples of router-based monitoring, whereas network taps allow passive monitoring.

11. C. Regular traffic from compromised systems to command and control nodes is known as beaconing. Anomalous pings could describe unexpected pings, but they are not typically part of botnet behavior, zombie chatter is a made-up term, and probing is part of scanning behavior in some cases.

12. C. The df command is used to show the amount of free and used disk space. Each of the other commands can show information about memory usage in Linux.

13. A. FTK, EnCase, and dd all provide options that support their use for forensic disk image creation. Since xcopy cannot create a bitwise image of a drive, it should not be used to create forensic images.

14. D. Slack space is the space left when a file is written. Since the space may have previously been filled by another file, file fragments are likely to exist and be recoverable. Unallocated space is space that has not been partitioned and could contain data, but looking there isn't part of Shelly's task. The reserved space maintained by drives for wear leveling (for SSDs) or to replace bad blocks (for spinning disks) may contain data, but again, this was not part of her task.

15. B. Sandboxes are used to isolate attackers, malicious code, and other untrusted applications. They allow defenders to monitor and study behavior in the sandbox without exposing systems or networks to potential attacks or compromise.

16. C. The most foolproof means of ensuring that a system does not remain compromised is to wipe and rebuild it. Without full knowledge of when the compromise occurred, restoring a backup may not help, and both antimalware and antivirus software packages cannot always ensure that no remnant of the compromise remains, particularly if the attacker created accounts or otherwise made changes that wouldn't be detected as malicious software.

17. B. NIST SP 800-88 defines three levels of action of increasing severity: clear, purge, and destroy. In this case, purging, which uses technical means to make data infeasible to recover, is appropriate for a high-security device. Destruction might be preferable, but the reuse element of the question rules this out. Reinstallation is not an option in the NIST guidelines, and clearing is less secure.

18. A. The recovery phase does not typically seek to add new privileges. Validating that only legitimate accounts exist, that the systems are all logging properly, and that systems have been vulnerability scanned are all common parts of an incident response recovery phase.

19. B. This statement is most likely to be part of a standard. Policies contain high-level statements of management intent; standards provide mandatory requirements for how policies are carried out, including statements like that provided in the question. A procedure would include the step-by-step process, and a guideline describes a best practice or recommendation.

20. D. The Family Educational Rights and Privacy Act (FERPA) requires educational institutions to implement security and privacy controls for student educational records. HIPAA covers security and privacy for healthcare providers, health insurers, and health information clearinghouses; GLBA covers financial institutions; and SOX applies to financial records of publicly traded companies.

21. B. Fire suppression systems are physical controls. Logical controls are technical controls that enforce confidentiality, integrity, and availability. Administrative controls are procedural controls, and operational controls are not a type of security control as used in security design.

22. B. Lauren should implement separation of duties in a way that ensures that Danielle and Alex cannot abuse their rights without a third party being involved. This will allow review of their actions and should result in any issues being discovered.

23. A. Kerberos is designed to run on untrusted networks and encrypts authentication traffic by default. LDAP and RADIUS can be encrypted but are not necessarily encrypted by default (and LDAP has limitations as an authentication mechanism). It is recommended that TACACS+ be run only on isolated administrative networks.

24. D. The Spiral model uses linear development concepts like those used in Waterfall but repeats four phases through its life cycle: requirements gathering, design, build, and evaluation.

CompTIA®
Cybersecurity Analyst (CSA+™)
Study Guide

Chapter

1

Defending Against Cybersecurity Threats

THE COMPTIA CYBERSECURITY ANALYST+ EXAM OBJECTIVES COVERED IN THIS CHAPTER INCLUDE:

Domain 1: Threat Management

✓ **1.3 Given a network-based threat, implement or recommend the appropriate response and countermeasure.**

✓ **1.4 Explain the purpose of practices used to secure a corporate environment.**

Cybersecurity analysts are responsible for protecting the confidentiality, integrity, and availability of information and information systems used by their organizations. Fulfilling this responsibility requires a commitment to a defense-in-depth approach to information security that uses multiple, overlapping security controls to achieve each cybersecurity objective. It also requires that analysts have a strong understanding of the threat environment facing their organization in order to develop a set of controls capable of rising to the occasion and answering those threats.

In the first section of this chapter, you will learn how to assess the cybersecurity threats facing your organization and determine the risk that they pose to the confidentiality, integrity, and availability of your operations. In the sections that follow, you will learn about some of the controls that you can put in place to secure networks and endpoints and evaluate the effectiveness of those controls over time.

Cybersecurity Objectives

When most people think of cybersecurity, they imagine hackers trying to break into an organization's system and steal sensitive information, ranging from Social Security numbers and credit cards to top-secret military information. Although protecting sensitive information from unauthorized disclosure is certainly one element of a cybersecurity program, it is important to understand that cybersecurity actually has three complementary objectives, as shown in Figure 1.1.

FIGURE 1.1 The three key objectives of cybersecurity programs are confidentiality, integrity, and availability.

- Confidentiality ensures that unauthorized individuals are not able to gain access to sensitive information. Cybersecurity professionals develop and implement security controls, including firewalls, access control lists, and encryption, to prevent unauthorized access to information. Attackers may seek to undermine confidentiality controls to achieve one of their goals: the unauthorized disclosure of sensitive information.

- Integrity ensures that there are no unauthorized modifications to information or systems, either intentionally or unintentionally. Integrity controls, such as hashing and integrity monitoring solutions, seek to enforce this requirement. Integrity threats may come from attackers seeking the alteration of information without authorization or nonmalicious sources, such as a power spike causing the corruption of information.

- Availability ensures that information and systems are ready to meet the needs of legitimate users at the time those users request them. Availability controls, such as fault tolerance, clustering, and backups, seek to ensure that legitimate users may gain access as needed. Similar to integrity threats, availability threats may come either from attackers seeking the disruption of access or nonmalicious sources, such as a fire destroying a datacenter that contains valuable information or services.

Cybersecurity analysts often refer to these three goals, known as the CIA Triad, when performing their work. They often characterize risks, attacks, and security controls as meeting one or more of the three CIA Triad goals when describing them.

Evaluating Security Risks

Cybersecurity risk analysis is the cornerstone of any information security program. Analysts must take the time to thoroughly understand their own technology environments and the external threats that jeopardize their information security. A well-rounded cybersecurity risk assessment combines information about internal and external factors to help analysts understand the threats facing their organization and then design an appropriate set of controls to meet those threats.

Before diving into the world of risk assessment, we must begin with a common vocabulary. You must know three important terms to communicate clearly with other risk analysts: vulnerabilities, threats, and risks.

A vulnerability is a weakness in a device, system, application, or process that might allow an attack to take place. Vulnerabilities are internal factors that may be controlled by cybersecurity professionals. For example, a web server that is running an outdated version of the Apache service may contain a vulnerability that would allow an attacker to conduct a denial-of-service (DoS) attack against the websites hosted on that server, jeopardizing their availability. Cybersecurity professionals within the organization have the ability to remediate this vulnerability by upgrading the Apache service to the most recent version that is not susceptible to the DoS attack.

A threat in the world of cybersecurity is an outside force that may exploit a vulnerability. For example, a hacker who would like to conduct a DoS attack against a website and knows about an Apache vulnerability poses a clear cybersecurity threat. Although many threats are malicious in nature, this is not necessarily the case. For example, an earthquake may also disrupt the availability of a website by damaging the datacenter containing the web servers. Earthquakes clearly do not have malicious intent. In most cases, cybersecurity professionals cannot do much to eliminate a threat. Hackers will hack and earthquakes will strike whether we like it or not.

A risk is the combination of a threat and a corresponding vulnerability. Both of these factors must be present before a situation poses a risk to the security of an organization. For example, if a hacker targets an organization's web server with a DoS attack but the server was patched so that it is not vulnerable to that attack, there is no risk because even though a threat is present (the hacker), there is no vulnerability. Similarly, a datacenter may be vulnerable to earthquakes because the walls are not built to withstand the extreme movements present during an earthquake, but it may be located in a region of the world where earthquakes do not occur. The datacenter may be vulnerable to earthquakes but there is little to no threat of earthquake in its location, so there is no risk.

The relationship between risks, threats, and vulnerabilities is an important one, and it is often represented by this equation:

$$\text{Risk} = \text{Threat} \times \text{Vulnerability}$$

This is not meant to be a literal equation where you would actually plug in values. Instead, it is meant to demonstrate the fact that risks exist only when there is both a threat and a corresponding vulnerability that the threat might exploit. If either the threat or vulnerability is zero, the risk is also zero. Figure 1.2 shows this in another way: risks are the intersection of threats and vulnerabilities.

FIGURE 1.2   Risks exist at the intersection of threats and vulnerabilities. If either the threat or vulnerability is missing, there is no risk.

Organizations should routinely conduct risk assessments to take stock of their existing risk landscape. The National Institute of Standards and Technology (NIST) publishes a guide for conducting risk assessments that is widely used throughout the cybersecurity field as a foundation for risk assessments. The document, designated NIST Special Publication (SP) 800-30, suggests the risk assessment process shown in Figure 1.3.

FIGURE 1.3 The NIST SP 800-30 risk assessment process suggests that an organization should identify threats and vulnerabilities and then use that information to determine the level of risk posed by the combination of those threats and vulnerabilities.

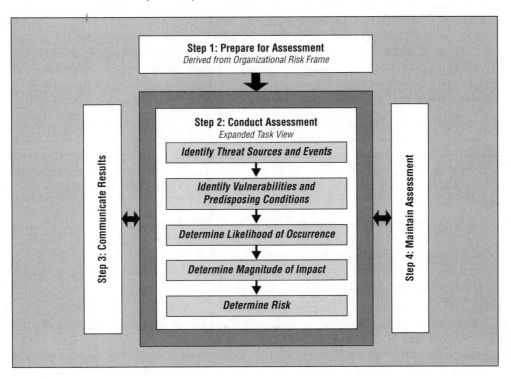

Source: NIST SP 800-30

Identify Threats

Organizations begin the risk assessment process by identifying the types of threats that exist in their threat environment. Although some threats, such as malware and spam, affect all organizations, other threats are targeted against specific types of organizations. For example, government-sponsored advanced persistent threat (APT) attackers typically target government agencies, military organizations, and companies that operate in related fields. It is unlikely that an APT attacker would target an elementary school.

NIST identifies four different categories of threats that an organization might face and should consider in its threat identification process:

- Adversarial threats are individuals, groups, and organizations that are attempting to deliberately undermine the security of an organization. Adversaries may include trusted insiders, competitors, suppliers, customers, business partners, or even nation-states. When evaluating an adversarial threat, cybersecurity analysts should consider the capability of the threat actor to engage in attacks, the intent of the threat actor, and the likelihood that the threat will target the organization.

- Accidental threats occur when individuals doing their routine work mistakenly perform an action that undermines security. For example, a system administrator might accidentally delete a critical disk volume, causing a loss of availability. When evaluating an accidental threat, cybersecurity analysts should consider the possible range of effects that the threat might have on the organization.

- Structural threats occur when equipment, software, or environmental controls fail due to the exhaustion of resources (such as running out of gas), exceeding their operational capability (such as operating in extreme heat), or simply failing due to age. Structural threats may come from IT components (such as storage, servers, and network devices), environmental controls (such as power and cooling infrastructure), and software (such as operating systems and applications). When evaluating a structural threat, cybersecurity analysts should consider the possible range of effects that the threat might have on the organization.

- Environmental threats occur when natural or man-made disasters occur that are outside the control of the organization. These might include fires, flooding, severe storms, power failures, or widespread telecommunications disruptions. When evaluating a  ~~structural~~ threat, cybersecurity analysts should consider the possible range of effects that the threat might have on the organization.

The nature and scope of the threats in each of these categories will vary depending on the nature of the organization, the composition of its technology infrastructure, and many other situation-specific circumstances. That said, it may be helpful to obtain copies of the risk assessments performed by other, similar, organizations as a starting point for an organization's own risk assessment or to use as a quality assessment check during various stages of the organization's assessment.

The Insider Threat

When performing a threat analysis, cybersecurity professionals must remember that threats come from both external and internal sources. In addition to the hackers, natural disasters, and other threats that begin outside the organization, rouge employees, disgruntled team members, and incompetent administrators also pose a significant threat to enterprise cybersecurity. As an organization designs controls, it must consider both internal and external threats.

 NIST SP 800-30 provides a great deal of additional information to help organizations conduct risk assessments, including detailed tasks associated with each of these steps. This information is outside the scope of the Cybersecurity Analyst+ exam, but organizations preparing to conduct risk assessments should download and read the entire publication.

Identify Vulnerabilities

During the threat identification phase of a risk assessment, cybersecurity analysts focus on the external factors likely to impact an organization's security efforts. After completing threat identification, the focus of the assessment turns inward, identifying the vulnerabilities that those threats might exploit to compromise an organization's confidentiality, integrity, or availability.

Chapters 3 and 4 of this book focus extensively on the identification and management of vulnerabilities.

Determine Likelihood, Impact, and Risk

After identifying the threats and vulnerabilities facing an organization, risk assessors next seek out combinations of threat and vulnerability that pose a risk to the confidentiality, integrity, or availability of enterprise information and systems. This requires assessing both the likelihood that a risk will materialize and the impact that the risk will have on the organization if it does occur.

When determining the likelihood of a risk occurring, analysts should consider two factors. First, they should assess the likelihood that the threat source will initiate the risk. In the case of an adversarial threat source, this is the likelihood that the adversary will execute an attack against the organization. In the case of accidental, structural, or environmental threats, it is the likelihood that the threat will occur. The second factor that contributes is the likelihood that, if a risk occurs, it will actually have an adverse impact on the organization, given the state of the organization's security controls. After considering each of these criteria, risk assessors assign an overall likelihood rating. This may use categories, such as "low," "medium," and "high," to describe the likelihood qualitatively.

Risk assessors evaluate the impact of a risk using a similar rating scale. This evaluation should assume that a threat actually does take place and cause a risk to the organization and then attempt to identify the magnitude of the adverse impact that the risk will have on the organization. When evaluating this risk, it is helpful to refer to the three objectives of cybersecurity shown in Figure 1.1, confidentiality, integrity, and availability, and then assess the impact that the risk would have on each of these objectives.

The risk assessment process described here, using categories of "high," "medium," and "low," is an example of a qualitative risk assessment process. Risk assessments also may use quantitative techniques that numerically assess the likelihood and impact of risks. Quantitative risk assessments are beyond the scope of the Cybersecurity Analyst+ exam but are found on more advanced security exams, including the CompTIA Advanced Security Practitioner (CASP) and Certified Information Systems Security Professional (CISSP) exams.

After assessing the likelihood and impact of a risk, risk assessors then combine those two evaluations to determine an overall risk rating. This may be as simple as using a matrix similar to the one shown in Figure 1.4 that describes how the organization assigns overall ratings to risks. For example, an organization might decide that the likelihood of a hacker attack is medium whereas the impact would be high. Looking this combination up in Figure 1.4 reveals that it should be considered a high overall risk. Similarly, if an organization assesses the likelihood of a flood as medium and the impact as low, a flood scenario would have an overall risk of low.

FIGURE 1.4 Many organizations use a risk matrix to determine an overall risk rating based on likelihood and impact assessments.

Likelihood		Impact		
High	Medium	High	High
Medium	Low	Medium	High
Low	Low	Low	Medium
	Low	Medium	High

Reviewing Controls

Cybersecurity professionals use risk management strategies, such as risk acceptance, risk avoidance, risk mitigation, and risk transference, to reduce the likelihood and impact of risks identified during risk assessments. The most common way that organizations manage security risks is to develop sets of technical and operational security controls that mitigate those risks to acceptable levels.

Technical controls are systems, devices, software, and settings that work to enforce confidentiality, integrity, and/or availability requirements. Examples of technical controls include building a secure network and implementing endpoint security, two topics discussed later in this chapter. Operational controls are practices and procedures that bolster cybersecurity. Examples of operational controls include conducting penetration testing and using reverse engineering to analyze acquired software. These two topics are also discussed later in this chapter.

Building a Secure Network

Many threats to an organization's cybersecurity exploit vulnerabilities in the organization's network to gain initial access to systems and information. To help mitigate these risks, organizations should focus on building secure networks that keep attackers at bay.

Examples of the controls that an organization may use to contribute to building a secure network include network access control (NAC) solutions; network perimeter security controls, such as firewalls; network segmentation; and the use of deception as a defensive measure.

Network Access Control

One of the basic security objectives set forth by most organizations is controlling access to the organization's network. Network access control (NAC) solutions help security professionals achieve two cybersecurity objectives: limiting network access to authorized individuals and ensuring that systems accessing the organization's network meet basic security requirements.

The 802.1x protocol is a common standard used for NAC. When a new device wishes to gain access to a network, either by connecting to a wireless access point or plugging into a wired network port, the network challenges that device to authenticate using the 802.1x protocol. A special piece of software, known as a supplicant, resides on the device requesting to join the network. The supplicant communicates with a service known as the authenticator that runs on either the wireless access point or the network switch. The authenticator does not have the information necessary to validate the user itself, so it passes access requests along to an authentication server using the RADIUS protocol. If the user correctly authenticates and is authorized to access the network, the switch or access point then joins the user to the network. If the user does not successfully complete this process, the device is denied access to the network or may be assigned to a special quarantine network for remediation. Figure 1.5 shows the devices involved in 802.1x authentication.

FIGURE 1.5   In an 802.1x system, the device attempting to join the network runs a NAC supplicant, which communicates with an authenticator on the network switch or wireless access point. The authenticator uses RADIUS to communicate with an authentication server.

Supplicant   Authenticator

RADIUS Server

There are many different NAC solutions available on the market, and they differ in two major ways:

Agent-Based vs. Agentless   Agent-based solutions, such as 802.1x, require that the device requesting access to the network run special software designed to communicate with the NAC service. Agentless approaches to NAC conduct authentication in the web browser and do not require special software.

In-Band vs. Out-of-Band   In-band (or inline) NAC solutions use dedicated appliances that sit in between devices and the resources that they wish to access. They deny or limit network access to devices that do not pass the NAC authentication process. The "captive portal" NAC solutions found in hotels that hijack all web requests until the guest enters a room number are examples of in-band NAC. Out-of-band NAC solutions, such as 802.1x, leverage the existing network infrastructure and has network devices communicate with authentication servers and then reconfigure the network to grant or deny network access, as needed.

NAC solutions are often used simply to limit access to authorized users based on those users successfully authenticating, but they may also make network admission decisions based on other criteria. Some of the criteria used by NAC solutions include:

Time of Day   Users may be authorized to access the network only during specific time periods, such as during business hours.

Role   Users may be assigned to particular network segments based on their role in the organization. For example, a college might assign faculty and staff to an administrative network that may access administrative systems while assigning students to an academic network that does not allow such access.

Location   Users may be granted or denied access to network resources based on their physical location. For example, access to the datacenter network may be limited to systems physically present in the datacenter.

System Health   NAC solutions may use agents running on devices to obtain configuration information from the device. Devices that fail to meet minimum security standards, such as having incorrectly configured host firewalls, outdated virus definitions, or missing patches, may be either completely denied network access or placed on a special quarantine network where they are granted only the limited access required to update the system's security.

Administrators may create NAC rules that limit access based on any combination of these characteristics. NAC products provide the flexibility needed to implement the organization's specific security requirements for network admission.

> You'll sometimes see the acronym NAC expanded to "Network Admission Control" instead of "network access control." In both cases, people are referring to the same general technology. Network Admission Control is a proprietary name used by Cisco for its network access control solutions.

Firewalls and Network Perimeter Security

NAC solutions are designed to manage the systems that connect directly to an organization's wired or wireless network. They provide excellent protection against intruders who seek to gain access to the organization's information resources by physically accessing a facility and connecting a device to the physical network. They don't provide protection against intruders seeking to gain access over a network connection. That's where firewalls enter the picture.

Network firewalls sit at the boundaries between networks and provide perimeter security. Much like a security guard might control the physical perimeter of a building, the network firewall controls the electronic perimeter. Firewalls are typically configured in the

Research Cisco NAC Solutions

triple-homed fashion illustrated in Figure 1.6. Triple-homed simply means that the firewall connects to three different networks. The firewall in Figure 1.6 connects to the Internet, the internal network, and a special network known as the demilitarized zone (DMZ). Any traffic that wishes to pass from one zone to another, such as between the Internet and the internal network, must pass through the firewall.

FIGURE 1.6   A triple-homed firewall connects to three different networks, typically an internal network, a DMZ, and the Internet.

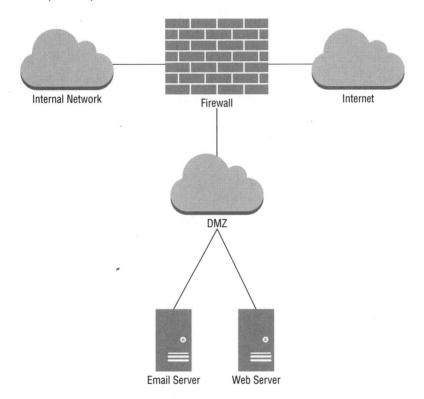

The DMZ is a special network zone designed to house systems that receive connections from the outside world, such as web and email servers. Sound firewall designs place these systems on an isolated network where, if they become compromised, they pose little threat to the internal network because connections between the DMZ and the internal network must still pass through the firewall and are subject to its security policy.

Whenever the firewall receives a connection request, it evaluates it according to the firewall's rule base. This rule base is an access control list (ACL) that identifies the types of traffic permitted to pass through the firewall. The rules used by the firewall typically specify the source and destination IP addresses for traffic as well as the destination port corresponding to the authorized service. A list of common ports appears in Table 1.1. Firewalls follow the default deny principle, which says that if there is no rule explicitly allowing a connection, the firewall will deny that connection.

Memorize Table!!!

TABLE 1.1 Common TCP ports

Port	Service
20,21	FTP
22	SSH
23	Telnet
25	SMTP
53	DNS
69	TFTP
80	HTTP
110	POP3
123	NTP
143	IMAP
161	SNMP
389	LDAP
443	HTTPS
1443	SQL Server
1521	Oracle
1720	H.323
1723	PPTP
3389	RDP

Several categories of firewalls are available on the market today, and they vary in both price and functionality:

- Packet filtering firewalls simply check the characteristics of each packet against the firewall rules without any additional intelligence. Packet filtering firewall capabilities are typically found in routers and other network devices and are very rudimentary firewalls.

- Stateful inspection firewalls go beyond packet filters and maintain information about the state of each connection passing through the firewall. These are the most basic firewalls sold as stand-alone products.

- Next-generation firewalls (NGFWs) incorporate even more information into their decision-making process, including contextual information about users, applications, and business processes. They are the current state-of-the-art in network firewall protection and are quite expensive compared to stateful inspection devices.

- Web application firewalls (WAFs) are specialized firewalls designed to protect against web application attacks, such as SQL injection and cross-site scripting. WAFs are discussed in more detail in Chapter 13, "Cybersecurity Toolkit."

Network Segmentation

Firewalls use a principle known as network segmentation to separate networks of differing security levels from each other. This principle certainly applies to the example shown in Figure 1.6, where the internal network, DMZ, and Internet all have differing security levels. The same principle may be applied to further segment the internal network into different zones of trust.

For example, imagine an organization that has several hundred employees and a large datacenter located in its corporate headquarters. The datacenter may house many sensitive systems, such as database servers that contain sensitive employee information, business plans, and other critical information assets. The corporate network may house employees, temporary contractors, visitors, and other people who aren't entirely trusted. In this common example, security professionals would want to segment the datacenter network so that it is not directly accessible by systems on the corporate network. This can be accomplished using a firewall, as shown in Figure 1.7.

The network shown in Figure 1.7 uses a triple-homed firewall, just as was used to control the network perimeter with the Internet in Figure 1.6. The concept is identical, except in this case the firewall is protecting the perimeter of the datacenter from the less trusted corporate network.

Notice that the network in Figure 1.7 also contains a DMZ with a server called the jump box. The purpose of this server is to act as a secure transition point between the corporate network and the datacenter network, providing a trusted path between the two zones. System administrators who need to access the datacenter network should not connect their laptops directly to the datacenter network but should instead initiate an administrative connection to the jump box, using secure shell (SSH), the Remote Desktop Protocol (RDP), or a similar secure remote administration protocol. After successfully authenticating to the jump box, they may then connect from the jump box to the datacenter network, providing some isolation between their own systems and the datacenter network. Connections to the jump box should be carefully controlled and protected with strong multifactor authentication technology.

Jump boxes may also be used to serve as a layer of insulation against systems that may only be partially trusted. For example, if you have contractors who bring equipment owned by their employer onto your network or employees bringing personally-owned devices, you might use a jump box to prevent those systems from directly connecting to your company's systems.

FIGURE 1.7 A triple-homed firewall may also be used to isolate internal network segments of varying trust levels.

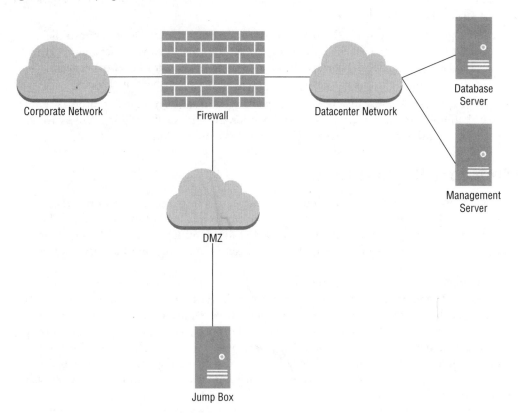

Defense through Deception

Cybersecurity professionals may wish to go beyond typical security controls and engage in active defensive measures that actually lure attackers to specific targets and seek to monitor their activity in a carefully controlled environment.

Honeypots are systems designed to appear to attackers as lucrative targets due to the services they run, vulnerabilities they contain, or sensitive information that they appear to host. The reality is that honeypots are designed by cybersecurity experts to falsely appear vulnerable and fool malicious individuals into attempting an attack against them. When an attacker tries to compromise a honeypot, the honeypot simulates a successful attack and then monitors the attacker's activity to learn more about his or her intentions. Honeypots may also be used to feed network blacklists, blocking all inbound activity from any IP address that attacks the honeypot.

DNS sinkholes feed false information to malicious software that works its way onto the enterprise network. When a compromised system attempts to obtain information from a DNS server about its command-and-control server, the DNS server detects the suspicious request and, instead of responding with the correct answer, responds with the IP address of a sinkhole system designed to detect and remediate the botnet-infected system.

Secure Endpoint Management

Laptop and desktop computers, tablets, smartphones, and other endpoint devices are a constant source of security threats on a network. These systems interact directly with end users and require careful configuration management to ensure that they remain secure and do not serve as the entry point for a security vulnerability on enterprise networks. Fortunately, by taking some simple security precautions, technology professionals can secure these devices against most attacks.

Hardening System Configurations

Operating systems are extremely complex pieces of software designed to perform thousands of different functions. The large code bases that make up modern operating systems are a frequent source of vulnerabilities, as evidenced by the frequent security patches issued by operating system vendors.

One of the most important ways that system administrators can protect endpoints is by hardening their configurations, making them as attack-resistant as possible. This includes disabling any unnecessary services or ports on the endpoints to reduce their susceptibility to attack, ensuring that secure configuration settings exist on devices and centrally controlling device security settings.

Patch Management

System administrators must maintain current security patch levels on all operating systems and applications under their care. Once the vendor releases a security patch, attackers are likely already aware of a vulnerability and may immediately begin preying on susceptible systems. The longer an organization waits to apply security patches, the more likely it becomes that they will fall victim to an attack. That said, enterprises should always test patches prior to deploying them on production systems and networks.

Fortunately, patch management software makes it easy to centrally distribute and monitor the patch level of systems throughout the enterprise. For example, Microsoft's System Center Configuration Manager (SCCM) allows administrators to quickly view the patch status of enterprise systems and remediate any systems with missing patches.

Thought:

Software title | version | Vendor | Purpose/Description

Security Patches

Compensating Controls

In some cases, security professionals may not be able to implement all of the desired security controls due to technical, operational, or financial reasons. For example, an organization may not be able to upgrade the operating system on retail point-of-sale terminals due to an incompatibility with the point-of-sale software. In these cases, security professionals should seek out compensating controls designed to provide a similar level of security using alternate means. In the point-of-sale example, administrators might place the point-of-sale terminals on a segmented, isolated network and use intrusion prevention systems to monitor network traffic for any attempt to exploit an unpatched vulnerability and block it from reaching the vulnerable host. This meets the same objective of protecting the point-of-sale terminal from compromise and serves as a compensating control.

Group Policies

Group Policies provide administrators with an efficient way to manage security and other system configuration settings across a large number of devices. Microsoft's Group Policy Object (GPO) mechanism allows administrators to define groups of security settings once and then apply those settings to either all systems in the enterprise or a group of systems based upon role.

For example, Figure 1.8 shows a GPO designed to enforce Windows Firewall settings on sensitive workstations. This GPO is configured to require the use of Windows Firewall and block all inbound connections.

FIGURE 1.8   Group Policy Objects (GPOs) may be used to apply settings to many different systems at the same time.

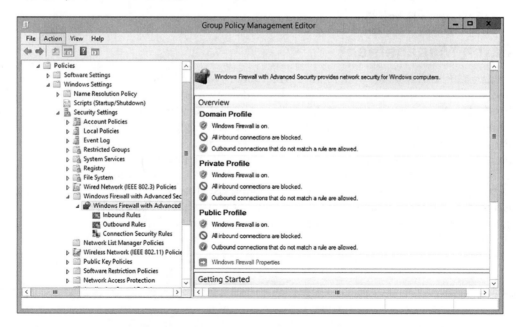

Administrators may use GPOs to control a wide variety of Windows settings and create different policies that apply to different classes of system.

Endpoint Security Software

Endpoint systems should also run specialized security software designed to enforce the organization's security objectives. At a minimum, this should include antivirus software designed to scan the system for signs of malicious software that might jeopardize the security of the endpoint. Administrators may also choose to install host firewall software that serves as a basic firewall for that individual system, complementing network-based firewall controls or host intrusion prevention systems (HIPSs) that block suspicious network activity. Endpoint security software should report its status to a centralized management system that allows security administrators to monitor the entire enterprise from a single location.

Mandatory Access Controls

In highly secure environments, administrators may opt to implement a mandatory access control (MAC) approach to security. In a MAC system, administrators set all security permissions, and end users cannot modify those permissions. This stands in contrast to the discretionary access control (DAC) model found in most modern operating systems where the owner of a file or resource controls the permissions on that resource and can delegate them at his or her discretion.

MAC systems are very unwieldy and, therefore, are rarely used outside of very sensitive government and military applications. Security Enhanced Linux (SE Linux), an operating system developed by the U.S. National Security Agency, is an example of a system that enforces mandatory access controls.

Penetration Testing

In addition to bearing responsibility for the design and implementation of security controls, cybersecurity analysts are responsible for monitoring the ongoing effectiveness of those controls. Penetration testing is one of the techniques they use to fulfill this obligation. During a penetration test, the testers simulate an attack against the organization using the same information, tools, and techniques available to real attackers. They seek to gain access to systems and information and then report their findings to management. The results of penetration tests may be used to bolster an organization's security controls.

Penetration tests may be performed by an organization's internal staff or by external consultants. In the case of internal tests, they require highly skilled individuals and are quite time-consuming. External tests mitigate these concerns but are often quite expensive to conduct. Despite these barriers to penetration tests, organizations should try to perform them periodically since a well-designed and well-executed penetration test is one of the best measures of an organization's cybersecurity posture.

NIST divides penetration testing into the four phases shown in Figure 1.9.

FIGURE 1.9   NIST divides penetration testing into four phases.

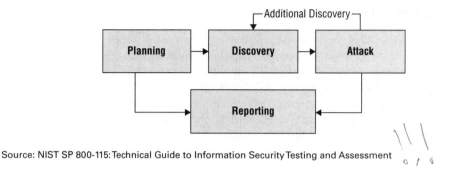

Source: NIST SP 800-115: Technical Guide to Information Security Testing and Assessment

Planning a Penetration Test

The planning phase of a penetration test lays the administrative groundwork for the test. No technical work is performed during the planning phase, but it is a critical component of any penetration test. There are three important rules of engagement to finalize during the planning phase:

Timing   When will the test take place? Will technology staff be informed of the test? Can it be timed to have as little impact on business operations as possible?

Scope   What is the agreed-upon scope of the penetration test? Are any systems, networks, personnel, or business processes off-limits to the testers?

Authorization   Who is authorizing the penetration test to take place? What should testers do if they are confronted by an employee or other individual who notices their suspicious activity?

These details are administrative in nature, but it is important to agree on them up front and in writing to avoid problems during and after the penetration test.

 WARNING   You should never conduct a penetration test without permission. Not only is an unauthorized test unethical, it may be illegal.

Conducting Discovery

The technical work of the penetration test begins during the discovery phase when attackers conduct reconnaissance and gather as much information as possible about the targeted network, systems, users, and applications. This may include conducting reviews of publicly available material, performing port scans of systems, using network vulnerability scanners and web application testers to probe for vulnerabilities, and performing other information gathering.

Vulnerability scanning is an important component of penetration testing. This topic is covered extensively in Chapters 3 and 4.

Executing a Penetration Test

During the attack phase, penetration testers seek to bypass the organization's security controls and gain access to systems and applications run by the organization. Testers often follow the NIST attack process shown in Figure 1.10.

FIGURE 1.10   The attack phase of a penetration test uses a cyclical process that gains a foothold and then uses it to expand access within the target organization.

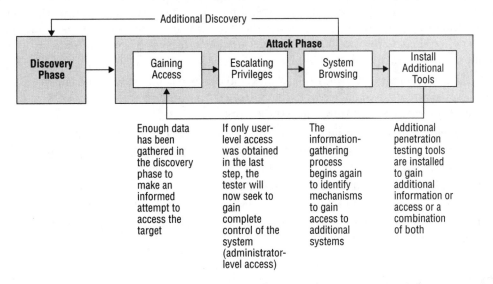

Source: NIST SP 800-115: Technical Guide to Information Security Testing and Assessment

In this process, attackers use the information gathered during the discovery phase to gain initial access to a system. Once they establish a foothold, they then seek to escalate their access until they gain complete administrative control of the system. From there, they can scan for additional system on the network, install additional penetration testing tools, and begin the cycle anew, seeking to expand their footprint within the targeted organization. They continue this cycle until they exhaust the possibilities or the time allotted for the test expires.

The attack phase of a penetration test is also known as the exploitation phase. Questions on the exam referring to test execution, the attack phase, and the exploitation phase are all referring to the same thing.

Communicating Penetration Test Results

At the conclusion of the penetration test, the testers prepare a detailed report communicating the access they were able to achieve and the vulnerabilities they exploited to gain this access. The results of penetration tests are valuable security planning tools, as they describe the actual vulnerabilities that an attacker might exploit to gain access to a network. Penetration testing reports typically contain detailed appendixes that include the results of various tests and may be shared with system administrators responsible for remediating issues.

Training and Exercises

In addition to performing penetration tests, some organizations choose to run wargame exercises that pit teams of security professionals against each other in a cyberdefense scenario. These exercises are typically performed in simulated environments, rather than on production networks, and seek to improve the skills of security professionals on both sides by exposing them to the tools and techniques used by attackers. Three teams are involved in most cybersecurity wargames:

- The red team plays the role of the attacker and uses reconnaissance and exploitation tools to attempt to gain access to the protected network. The red team's work is similar to that of the testers during a penetration test.

- The blue team is responsible for securing the targeted environment and keeping the red team out by building, maintaining, and monitoring a comprehensive set of security controls.

- The white team coordinates the exercise and serves as referees, arbitrating disputes between the team, maintaining the technical environment, and monitoring the results.

Cybersecurity wargames can be an effective way to educate security professionals on modern attack and defense tactics.

Reverse Engineering

In many cases, vendors do not release the details of how hardware and software work. Certainly, the authors of malicious software don't explain their work to the world. In these situations, security professionals may be in the dark about the security of their environments. Reverse engineering is a technique used to work backward from a finished product to figure out how it works. Security professionals sometimes use reverse engineering to learn the inner workings of suspicious software or inspect the integrity of hardware. Reverse engineering uses a philosophy known as decomposition where the reverse engineer starts with the finished product and works his or her way back to its component parts.

Isolation and Sandboxing

One of the most dangerous threats to the security of modern organizations is customized malware developed by APT actors who create specialized tools designed to penetrate a single target. Since they have never been used before, these tools are not detectable with the signature-detection technology used by traditional antivirus software.

Sandboxing is an approach used to detect malicious software based on its behavior rather than its signatures. Sandboxing systems watch systems and the network for unknown pieces of code and, when they detect an application that has not been seen before, immediately isolate that code in a special environment known as a sandbox where it does not have access to any other systems or applications. The sandboxing solution then executes the code and watches how it behaves, checking to see if it begins scanning the network for other systems, gathering sensitive information, communicating with a command-and-control server, or performing any other potentially malicious activity.

If the sandboxing solution identifies strange behavior, it blocks the code from entering the organization's network and flags it for administrator review. This process, also known as code detonation, is an example of an automated reverse engineering technique that takes action based on the observed behavior of software.

Reverse Engineering Software

In most programming languages, developers write software in a human-readable language such as C/C++, Java, Ruby, or Python. Depending on the programming language, the computer may process this code in one of two ways. In interpreted languages, such as Ruby and Python, the computer works directly from the source code. Reverse engineers seeking to analyze code written in interpreted languages can simply read through the code and often get a good idea of what the code is attempting to accomplish.

In compiled languages, such as Java and C/C++, the developer uses a tool called a compiler to convert the source code into binary code that is readable by the computer. This binary code is what is often distributed to users of the software, and it is very difficult, if not impossible, to examine binary code and determine what it is doing, making the reverse engineering of compiled languages much more difficult. Technologists seeking to reverse engineer compiled code have two options. First, they can attempt to use a specialized program known as a decompiler to convert the binary code back to source code. Unfortunately, however, this process usually does not work very well. Second, they can instrument a specialized environment and carefully monitor how software responds to different inputs in an attempt to discover its inner workings. In either case, reverse engineering compiled software is extremely difficult.

Real World Scenario

Fingerprinting Software

Although it is difficult to reverse engineer compiled code, technologists can easily detect whether two pieces of compiled code are identical or whether one has been modified. Hashing is a mathematical technique that analyzes a file and computes a unique finger-print, known as a message digest or hash, for that file. Analysts using hash functions, such as the Secure Hash Algorithm (SHA), can compute the hashes of two files and compare the output values. If the hashes are identical, the file contents are identical. If the hashes differ, the two files contain at least one difference. Hashing software is covered in more detail in Chapter 13, "Cybersecurity Toolkit."

Reverse Engineering Hardware

Reverse engineering hardware is even more difficult than reverse engineering software because the authenticity of hardware often rests in the invisible code embedded within integrated circuits and firmware contents. Although organizations may perform a physical inspection of hardware to detect tampering, it is important to verify that hardware has source authenticity, meaning that it comes from a trusted, reliable source, because it is simply too difficult to exhaustively test hardware.

The U.S. government recognizes the difficulty of ensuring source authenticity and operates a trusted foundry program for critical defense systems. The Department of Defense and National Security Agency (NSA) certify companies as trusted foundries that are approved to create sensitive integrated circuits for government use. Companies seeking trusted foundry status must show that they completely secure the production process, including design, prototyping, packing, assembly, and other elements of the process.

Reverse engineers seeking to determine the function of hardware use some of the same techniques used for compiled software, particularly when it comes to observing behavior. Operating a piece of hardware in a controlled environment and observing how it responds to different inputs provides clues to the functions performed in the hardware. Reverse engineers may also seek to obtain documentation from original equipment manufacturers (OEMs) that provide insight into how components of a piece of hardware function.

Real World Scenario

Compromising Cisco Routers

According to NSA documents released by Edward Snowden, the U.S. government has engaged in reverse engineering of hardware designed to circumvent security.

(TS//SI//NF) Left: Intercepted packages are opened carefully; Right: A "load station" implants a beacon

Source: "Spiegel supply chain interdiction: Stealthy techniques can crack some of sigints hardest targets" by eff.org licensed under CC By 3.0 US

In a process shown in this photo, NSA employees intercepted packages containing Cisco routers, switches, and other network gear after it left the factory and before it reached the customer. They then opened the packages and inserted covert firmware into the devices that facilitated government monitoring.

Summary

Cybersecurity professionals are responsible for ensuring the confidentiality, integrity, and availability of information and systems maintained by their organizations. Confidentiality ensures that unauthorized individuals are not able to gain access to sensitive information. Integrity ensures that there are no unauthorized modifications to information or systems, either intentionally or unintentionally. Availability ensures that information and systems are ready to meet the needs of legitimate users at the time those users request them. Together, these three goals are known as the CIA Triad.

As cybersecurity analysts seek to protect their organizations, they must evaluate risks to the CIA Triad. This includes identifying vulnerabilities, recognizing corresponding threats, and determining the level of risk that results from vulnerability and threat combinations. Analysts must then evaluate each risk and identify appropriate risk management strategies to mitigate or otherwise address the risk.

Cybersecurity analysts mitigate risks using security controls designed to reduce the likelihood or impact of a risk. Network security controls include network access control (NAC) systems, firewalls, and network segmentation. Secure endpoint controls include hardened system configurations, patch management, Group Policies, and endpoint security software.

Penetration tests and reverse engineering provide analysts with the reassurance that the controls they've implemented to mitigate risks are functioning properly. By following a careful risk analysis and control process, analysts significantly enhance the confidentiality, integrity, and availability of information and systems under their control.

Exam Essentials

The three objectives of cybersecurity are confidentiality, integrity, and availability. Confidentiality ensures that unauthorized individuals are not able to gain access to sensitive information. Integrity ensures that there are no unauthorized modifications to information or systems, either intentionally or unintentionally. Availability ensures that information and systems are ready to meet the needs of legitimate users at the time those users request them.

Cybersecurity risks result from the combination of a threat and a vulnerability. A vulnerability is a weakness in a device, system, application, or process that might allow an attack to take place. A threat in the world of cybersecurity is an outside force that may exploit a vulnerability.

Cybersecurity threats may be categorized as adversarial, accidental, structural, or environmental. Adversarial threats are individuals, groups, and organizations that are attempting to deliberately undermine the security of an organization. Accidental threats occur when individuals doing their routine work mistakenly perform an action that undermines security. Structural threats occur when equipment, software, or environmental controls fail due to the exhaustion of resources, exceeding their operational capability or simply failing due to age. Environmental threats occur when natural or man-made disasters occur that are outside the control of the organization.

Networks are made more secure through the use of network access control, firewalls, and segmentation. Network access control (NAC) solutions help security professionals achieve two cybersecurity objectives: limiting network access to authorized individuals and ensuring that systems accessing the organization's network meet basic security requirements. Network firewalls sit at the boundaries between networks and provide perimeter security. Network segmentation uses isolation to separate networks of differing security levels from each other.

Endpoints are made more secure through the use of hardened configurations, patch management, Group Policy, and endpoint security software. Hardening configurations includes disabling any unnecessary services on the endpoints to reduce their susceptibility to attack, ensuring that secure configuration settings exist on devices and centrally controlling device security settings. Patch management ensures that operating systems and applications are not susceptible to known vulnerabilities. Group Policy allows the application of security settings to many devices simultaneously, and endpoint security software protects against malicious software and other threats.

Penetration tests provide organizations with an attacker's perspective on their security. The NIST process for penetration testing divides tests into four phases: planning, discovery, attack, and reporting. The results of penetration tests are valuable security planning tools, since they describe the actual vulnerabilities that an attacker might exploit to gain access to a network.

Reverse engineering techniques attempt to determine how hardware and software functions internally. Sandboxing is an approach used to detect malicious software based on its behavior rather than its signatures. Other reverse engineering techniques are difficult to perform, are often unsuccessful, and are quite time-consuming.

Lab Exercises

Activity 1.1: Create an Inbound Firewall Rule

In this lab, you will verify that the Windows Firewall is enabled on a server and then create an inbound firewall rule that blocks file and printer sharing.

This lab requires access to a system running Windows Server 2012 or Windows Server 2012 R2.

Part 1: Verify that Windows Firewall is enabled

1. Open the Control Panel for your Windows Server.
2. Choose System And Security.
3. Under Windows Firewall, click Check Firewall Status.
4. Verify that the Windows Firewall state is set to On for Private networks. If it is not on, enable the firewall by using the "Turn Windows Firewall on or off" link on the left side of the window.

Part 2: Create an inbound firewall rule that blocks file and printer sharing

1. On the left side of the Windows Firewall control panel, click "Allow an app or feature through Windows Firewall."
2. Scroll down the list of applications and find File And Printer Sharing.
3. Uncheck the box to the left of that entry to block connections related to File And Printer Sharing.
4. Click OK to apply the setting.

   Note: You should perform this lab on a test system. Disabling file and printer sharing on a production system may have undesired consequences.

Activity 1.2: Create a Group Policy Object

In this lab, you will create a Group Policy Object and edit its contents to enforce an organization's password policy.

This lab requires access to a system running Windows Server 2012 or Windows Server 2012 R2 that is configured as a domain controller.

1. Open the Group Policy Management Console. (If you do not find this console on your Windows 2012 Server, it is likely that it is not configured as a domain controller.)
2. Expand the folder corresponding to your Active Directory forest.

3. Expand the Domains folder.

4. Expand the folder corresponding to your domain.

5. Right-click the Group Policy Objects folder and click New on the pop-up menu.

6. Name your new GPO **Password Policy** and click OK.

7. Right-click the new Password Policy GPO and choose Edit from the pop-up menu.

8. When Group Policy Editor opens, expand the Computer Configuration folder.

9. Expand the Policies folder.

10. Expand the Windows Settings folder.

11. Expand the Security Settings folder.

12. Expand the Account Policies folder.

13. Click on Password Policy.

14. Double-click Maximum password age.

15. In the pop-up window, select the Define This Policy Setting check box and set the expiration value to 90 days.

16. Click OK to close the window.

17. Click OK to accept the suggested change to the minimum password age.

18. Double-click the Minimum Password Length option.

19. As in the prior step, click the box to define the policy setting and set the minimum password length to 12 characters.

20. Click OK to close the window.

21. Double-click the Password Must Meet Complexity Requirements option.

22. Click the box to define the policy setting and change the value to Enabled.

23. Click OK to close the window.

24. Click the X to exit Group Policy Editor

You have now successfully created a Group Policy Object that enforces the organization's password policy. You may apply this GPO to users and/or groups as needed.

Activity 1.3: Write a Penetration Testing Plan

For this activity, design a penetration testing plan for a test against an organization of your choosing. If you are employed, you may choose to use your employer's network. If you are a student, you may choose to create a plan for a penetration test of your school. Otherwise, you may choose any organization, real or fictitious, of your choice.

Your penetration testing plan should cover the three main criteria required before initiating any penetration test:

▪ Timing

▪ Scope

▪ Authorization

One word of warning: You should not conduct a penetration test without permission of the network owner. This assignment only asks you to design the test on paper.

Activity 1.4: Security Tools

Match each of the security tools listed in this table with the correct description.

Firewall	Determines what clients may access a wired or wireless network
Decompiler	Creates a unique fingerprint of a file
Antivirus	Filters network connections based upon source, destination, and port
NAC	System intentionally created to appear vulnerable
GPO	Attempts to recover source code from binary code
Hash	Scans a system for malicious software
Honeypot	Protects against SQL injection attacks
WAF	Deploys configuration settings to multiple Windows systems

Review Questions

1. Which one of the following objectives is not one of the three main objectives that information security professionals must achieve to protect their organizations against cybersecurity threats?

   A. Integrity

   B. Nonrepudiation

   C. Availability

   D. Confidentiality

2. Tommy is assessing the security of several database servers in his datacenter and realizes that one of them is missing a critical Oracle security patch. What type of situation has Tommy detected?

   A. Risk

   B. Vulnerability

   C. Hacker

   D. Threat

3. Ben is preparing to conduct a cybersecurity risk assessment for his organization. If he chooses to follow the standard process proposed by NIST, which one of the following steps would come first?

   A. Determine likelihood

   B. Determine impact

   C. Identify threats

   D. Identify vulnerabilities

4. Cindy is conducting a cybersecurity risk assessment and is considering the impact that a failure of her city's power grid might have on the organization. What type of threat is she considering?

   A. Adversarial

   B. Accidental

   C. Structural

   D. Environmental

5. Which one of the following categories of threat requires that cybersecurity analysts consider the capability, intent, and targeting of the threat source?

   A. Adversarial

   B. Accidental

   C. Structural

   D. Environmental

6. Vincent is responding to a security incident that compromised one of his organization's web servers. He does not believe that the attackers modified or stole any information, but they did disrupt access to the organization's website. What cybersecurity objective did this attack violate?

   A. Confidentiality

   B. Nonrepudiation

   C. Integrity

   D. Availability

7. Which one of the following is an example of an operational security control?

   A. Encryption software

   B. Network firewall

   C. Antivirus software

   D. Penetration tests

8. Paul recently completed a risk assessment and determined that his network was vulnerable to hackers connecting to open ports on servers. He implemented a network firewall to reduce the likelihood of a successful attack. What risk management strategy did Paul choose to pursue?

   A. Risk mitigation

   B. Risk avoidance

   C. Risk transference

   D. Risk acceptance

9. Robert's organization has a Bring Your Own Device (BYOD) policy, and he would like to ensure that devices connected to the network under this policy have current antivirus software. What technology can best assist him with this goal?

   A. Network firewall

   B. Network access control

   C. Network segmentation

   D. Virtual private network

10. When performing 802.1x authentication, what protocol does the authenticator use to communicate with the authentication server?

   A. 802.11g

   B. EAP

   C. PEAP

   D. RADIUS

11. Juan is configuring a new device that will join his organization's wireless network. The wireless network uses 802.1x authentication. What type of agent must be running on the device for it to join this network?

A. Supplicant

B. Authenticator

C. Authentication server

D. Command and control

12. Rick is preparing a firewall rule that will allow network traffic from external systems to a web server running the HTTPS protocol. What TCP port must he allow to pass through the firewall?

A. 25

B. 80

C. 143

D. 443

13. What type of firewall provides the greatest degree of contextual information and can include information about users and applications in its decision-making process?

A. NGFW

B. WAF

C. Packet filter

D. Stateful inspection

14. Wayne is configuring a jump box server that system administrators will connect to from their laptops. Which one of the following ports should definitely not be open on the jump box?

A. 22

B. 23

C. 443

D. 3389

15. Tom would like to deploy consistent security settings to all of his Windows systems simultaneously. What technology can he use to achieve this goal?

A. GPO

B. HIPS

C. IPS

D. DNS

16. During what phase of a penetration test should the testers obtain written authorization to conduct the test?

   A. Planning

   B. Attack

   C. Discovery

   D. Reporting

17. Which step occurs first during the attack phase of a penetration test?

   A. Gaining access

   B. Escalating privileges

   C. System browsing

   D. Install additional tools

18. Barry is participating in a cybersecurity wargame exercise. His role is to attempt to break into adversary systems. What team is he on?

   A. Red team

   B. Blue team

   C. White team

   D. Black team

19. Which one of the following techniques might be used to automatically detect and block malicious software that does not match known malware signatures?

   A. MAC

   B. Hashing

   C. Decompiling

   D. Sandboxing

20. Kevin would like to implement a specialized firewall that can protect against SQL injection, cross-site scripting, and similar attacks. What technology should he choose?

   A. NGFW

   B. WAF

   C. Packet filter

   D. Stateful inspection

Chapter

2

Reconnaissance and Intelligence Gathering

THE COMPTIA CYBERSECURITY ANALYST+ EXAM OBJECTIVES COVERED IN THIS CHAPTER INCLUDE:

Domain 1: Threat Management

✓ 1.1 Given a scenario, apply environmental reconnaissance techniques using appropriate tools and processes

✓ 1.2 Given a scenario, analyze the results of a network reconnaissance

Security analysts, penetration testing professionals, vulnerability and threat analysts, and others who are tasked with understanding the security environment in which an organization operates need to know how to gather that information. This process is called reconnaissance or intelligence gathering.

Information gathering is often a requirement of information security standards and laws. For example, the PCI-DSS standard calls for vulnerability scanning in section 11.2, requiring both internal and external network vulnerability scans at least quarterly, and after any significant change. Gathering internal and external information about your own organization is typically considered a necessary part of understanding organizational risk, and implementing industry best practices to meet required due diligence requirements is likely to result in this type of work.

In this chapter, you will explore active intelligence gathering, including port scanning tools and how you can determine a network's topology from scan data. Then you will learn about passive intelligence gathering, including tools, techniques, and real-world experiences to help you understand your organization's footprint. Finally, you will learn how to limit a potential attacker's ability to gather information about your organization using the same techniques.

Footprinting

The first step when gathering organizational intelligence is to identify an organization's footprint. *Footprinting* is used to create a map of an organization's networks, systems, and other infrastructure. This is typically accomplished by combining information-gathering tools with manual research to identify the networks and systems that an organization uses.

Standards for penetration testing typically include footprinting and reconnaissance processes and guidelines. There are a number of publicly available resources, including the Open Source Security Testing Methodology Manual (OSSTMM), the Penetration Testing Execution Standard, and National Institute of Standards and Technology (NIST) Special Publication 800-115, the Technical Guide to Information Security Testing and Assessment:

- OSSTMM: www.isecom.org/research/

- Penetration Testing Execution Standard: www.pentest-standard.org/index.php/ Main_Page

- SP 800-115: http://csrc.nist.gov/publications/nistpubs/800-115/SP800-115.pdf

Active Reconnaissance

Information gathered during footprinting exercises is typically used to provide the targets for active reconnaissance. Active reconnaissance uses host scanning tools to gather information about systems, services, and vulnerabilities. It is important to note that reconnaissance does not involve exploitation but that it can provide information about vulnerabilities that can be exploited.

Permission and Executive Support

Scanning a network or systems can cause problems for the devices that are scanned. Some services may not tolerate scan traffic well, whereas others may fill their logs or set off security alarms when scanned. This means you should make sure you have permission from the appropriate authorities in your organization before conducting active reconnaissance. You'll likely hear approvals like this referred to as "Get out of jail free cards," as they help to ensure that you won't get into trouble for the scans. You may still want to make sure that you touch base with system and network administrators to make sure that the scans don't have an unintended impact.

Scanning systems belonging to others may also be illegal without permission or may be prohibited by the terms of use of your Internet service provider. For example, both Microsoft Azure and Amazon Web Services cloud computing platforms require users to complete a vulnerability or penetration testing request form before conducting scans using their infrastructure, and both apply limits to the types of systems and services that can be scanned.

Mapping Networks and Discovering Topology

Active scans can also provide information about network design and topology. As a scanning tool traverses a network range, it can assess information contained in the responses it receives. This can help a tester take an educated guess about the topology of the network based on the *TTL*, or time to live of the packets it receives; traceroute information; and responses from network and security devices. Figure 2.1 shows a scan of a simple example network. Routers or gateways are centrally connected to hosts and allow you to easily see where a group of hosts connect to. The system that nmap runs from becomes the center of the initial scan and shows its local loopback address 127.0.0.1. A number of hosts appear on a second network segment behind the 10.0.2.1 router. Nmap (and Zenmap, using nmap) may not discover all systems and network devices—firewalls or other security devices can stop scan traffic, resulting in missing systems or networks.

FIGURE 2.1 Zenmap topology view

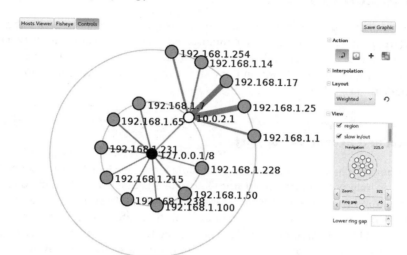

When you are performing network discovery and mapping, it is important to lay out the systems that are discovered based on their network addresses and time to live. These data points can help you assess their relative position in the network. Of course, if you can get actual network diagrams, you will have a much more accurate view of the network design than scans may provide.

The Zenmap graphical user interface to nmap provides a built-in topology discovery tool that provides a visual representation of the scanned network. Remember that this is a best guess and isn't necessarily a perfect match for the actual network!

The topology information gathered by a scanning tool is likely to have flaws and may not match the actual design of the target network. Security and network devices can cause differences in the TTL and traceroute information, resulting in incorrect or missing data. Firewalls can also make devices and systems effectively invisible to scans, resulting in segments of the network not showing up in the topology built from scan results.

In addition to challenges caused by security devices, you may have to account for variables, including differences between wired and wireless networks, virtual networks and virtual environments like VMware and Microsoft HyperV, and of course on-premises networks versus cloud-hosted services and infrastructure. If you are scanning networks that you or your organization control, you should be able to ensure that your scanning systems or devices are placed appropriately to gather the information that you need. If you are scanning as part of a penetration test or a zero-knowledge test, you may need to review your data to ensure that these variables haven't caused you to miss important information.

Real World Scenario

Mapping and Scanning VMs and the Cloud

Mapping networks, port scanning, service discovery, and many of the other techniques we discuss involve such variables as whether the networks are wired or wireless, whether systems and network devices are virtual or physical, or whether the systems and services are on-premises or in the cloud. This may mean that you need to use a tool that specifically targets wireless networks, or you may need to account for virtual systems that are not visible outside of a VMware host's firewall. You may also need to handle a service different, such as avoiding scanning a cloud service or system based on contracts or agreements. Remember to document what you know about the networks and systems you are scanning and to consider how these could impact both the data you gather and the techniques you use.

Port Scanning and Service Discovery Techniques and Tools

Port scanning tools are designed to send traffic to remote systems and then gather responses that provide information about the systems and the services they provide. They are one of the most frequently used tools when gathering information about a network and the devices that are connected to it. Due to this, port scans are often the first step in an active reconnaissance of an organization.

Port scanners have a number of common features, including

- Host discovery
- Port scanning and service identification
- Service version identification
- Operating system identification

 Real World Scenario

Ports Scanners: A Handy Swiss Army Knife

These capabilities also mean that port scanners are also useful for network inventory tasks, security audits to identify new systems and services, and of course testing security devices and systems by sending scanning traffic for them to alert on. Integrating a port scanner into your toolkit (and scripting it!) can be a powerful tool.

An important part of port scanning is an understanding of common ports and services. Ports from 0–1023 are known as *well-known ports* or *system ports*, but there are quite a few higher ports that are commonly of interest when conducting port scanning. Ports ranging from 1024 to 49151 are *registered ports* and are assigned by the Internet Assigned Numbers Authority (IANA) when requested. Many are also used arbitrarily for services. Since ports can be manually assigned, simply assuming that a service running on a given port matches the common usage isn't always a good idea. In particular, many SSH and HTTP/HTTPS servers are run on alternate ports, either to allow multiple web services to have unique ports or to avoid port scanning that only targets their normal port.

Analysis of scan data can be an art, but basic knowledge of how to read a scan is quite useful since scans can provide information about what hosts are on a network, what services they are running, and clues about whether they are vulnerable to attacks. In Figure 2.2, a vulnerable Linux system with a wide range of services available has been scanned. To read this scan, you can start at the top with the command used to run it. The nmap port scanner (which we will discuss in more depth in a few pages) was run with the -O option, resulting in an attempt at operating system identification. The -P0 flag tells nmap to skip pinging the system before scanning, and the -sS flag performed a TCP SYN scan, which sends connection attempts to each port. Finally, we see the IP address of the remote system. By default, nmap scans 1,000 common ports, and nmap discovered 23 open ports out of that list.

FIGURE 2.2   Nmap scan results

```
root@demo:~# nmap -O -P0 -sS 10.0.2.4

Starting Nmap 7.01 ( https://nmap.org ) at 2016-10-02 12:22 EDT
Nmap scan report for 10.0.2.4
Host is up (0.00017s latency).
Not shown: 977 closed ports
PORT      STATE SERVICE
21/tcp    open  ftp
22/tcp    open  ssh
23/tcp    open  telnet
25/tcp    open  smtp
53/tcp    open  domain
80/tcp    open  http
111/tcp   open  rpcbind
139/tcp   open  netbios-ssn
445/tcp   open  microsoft-ds
512/tcp   open  exec
513/tcp   open  login
514/tcp   open  shell
1099/tcp  open  rmiregistry
1524/tcp  open  ingreslock
2049/tcp  open  nfs
2121/tcp  open  ccproxy-ftp
3306/tcp  open  mysql
5432/tcp  open  postgresql
5900/tcp  open  vnc
6000/tcp  open  X11
6667/tcp  open  irc
8009/tcp  open  ajp13
8180/tcp  open  unknown
MAC Address: 08:00:27:92:5F:44 (Oracle VirtualBox virtual NIC)
Device type: general purpose
Running: Linux 2.6.X
OS CPE: cpe:/o:linux:linux_kernel:2.6
OS details: Linux 2.6.9 - 2.6.33
Network Distance: 1 hop

OS detection performed. Please report any incorrect results at https://nmap.org/
submit/ .
Nmap done: 1 IP address (1 host up) scanned in 1.77 seconds
```

Next, the scan shows us the ports it found open, whether they are TCP or UDP, their state (which can be open if the service is accessible, closed if it is not, or filtered if there is a firewall or similar protection in place), and its guess about what service the port is. Nmap service identification can be wrong—it's not as full featured as some vulnerability scanners, but the service list is a useful starting place.

Finally, after we see our services listed, we get the MAC address—in this case, indicating that the system is running as a VM under Oracle's VirtualBox virtualization tool and that it is running a 2.6 Linux kernel. This kernel is quite old as of the writing of this book and reached its end-of-life support date in February 2016, meaning that it's likely to be vulnerable.

The final things to note about this scan are the time it took to run and how many hops there are to the host. This scan completed in less than two seconds, which tells us that the host responded quickly and that the host was only one hop away—it was directly accessible from the scanning host. A more complex network path will show more hops, and scanning more hosts or additional security on the system or between the scanner and the remote target can slow things down.

The viewpoint of active reconnaissance can make a big difference in the data gathered. Internal scans from a trusted system or network will typically provide much more information than an external scan of a well-secured network. If you are attempting to replicate a specific scenario, such as scanning by an external attacker who has no access to an internal system, your scanning viewpoint should match.

Table 1.1 in the previous chapter included some of the most commonly used ports.

OS Fingerprinting

The ability to identify an operating system based on the network traffic that it sends is known as *operating system fingerprinting*, and it can provide useful information when performing reconnaissance. This is typically done using TCP/IP stack fingerprinting techniques that focus on comparing responses to TCP and UDP packets sent to remote hosts. Differences in how operating systems and even operating system versions respond, what TCP options they support, what order they send packets in, and a host of other details can provide a good guess at what OS the remote system is running.

Service and Version Identification

The ability to identify a service can provide useful information about potential vulnerabilities, as well as verify that the service that is responding on a given port matches the service that typically uses that port. Service identification is usually done in one of two ways: either by connecting and grabbing the *banner* or connection information provided by the service or by comparing its responses to the signatures of known services.

Figure 2.3 shows the same system scanned in Figure 2.1 with the nmap -sV flag used. The -sV flag grabs banners and performs other service version validation steps to capture additional information, which it checks against a database of services.

FIGURE 2.3   Nmap service and version detection

```
Starting Nmap 7.01 ( https://nmap.org ) at 2016-10-02 12:41 EDT
Nmap scan report for 10.0.2.4
Host is up (0.00022s latency).
Not shown: 977 closed ports
PORT      STATE SERVICE     VERSION
21/tcp    open  ftp         vsftpd 2.3.4
22/tcp    open  ssh         OpenSSH 4.7p1 Debian 8ubuntu1 (protocol 2.0)
23/tcp    open  telnet      Linux telnetd
25/tcp    open  smtp        Postfix smtpd
53/tcp    open  domain      ISC BIND 9.4.2
80/tcp    open  http        Apache httpd 2.2.8 ((Ubuntu) DAV/2)
111/tcp   open  rpcbind     2 (RPC #100000)
139/tcp   open  netbios-ssn Samba smbd 3.X (workgroup: WORKGROUP)
445/tcp   open  netbios-ssn Samba smbd 3.X (workgroup: WORKGROUP)
512/tcp   open  exec        netkit-rsh rexecd
513/tcp   open  login?
514/tcp   open  tcpwrapped
1099/tcp  open  rmiregistry GNU Classpath grmiregistry
1524/tcp  open  shell       Metasploitable root shell
2049/tcp  open  nfs         2-4 (RPC #100003)
2121/tcp  open  ftp         ProFTPD 1.3.1
3306/tcp  open  mysql       MySQL 5.0.51a-3ubuntu5
5432/tcp  open  postgresql  PostgreSQL DB 8.3.0 - 8.3.7
5900/tcp  open  vnc         VNC (protocol 3.3)
6000/tcp  open  X11         (access denied)
6667/tcp  open  irc         Unreal ircd
8009/tcp  open  ajp13       Apache Jserv (Protocol v1.3)
8180/tcp  open  http        Apache Tomcat/Coyote JSP engine 1.1
MAC Address: 08:00:27:92:5F:44 (Oracle VirtualBox virtual NIC)
Device type: general purpose
Running: Linux 2.6.X
OS CPE: cpe:/o:linux:linux_kernel:2.6
OS details: Linux 2.6.9 - 2.6.33
Network Distance: 1 hop
Service Info: Hosts:  metasploitable.localdomain, localhost, irc.Metasploitable.
LAN; OSs: Unix, Linux; CPE: cpe:/o:linux:linux_kernel

OS and Service detection performed. Please report any incorrect results at https
://nmap.org/submit/ .
Nmap done: 1 IP address (1 host up) scanned in 16.37 seconds
```

The basic nmap output remains the same as Figure 2.1, but we have added additional information in the version column, including the service name as well as the version and sometimes additional detail about the service protocol version or other details. This information can be used to check for patch levels or vulnerabilities and can also help to identify services that are running on nonstandard ports.

Common Tools

Nmap is the most commonly used command-line port scanner, and it is a free, open source tool. It provides a broad range of capabilities, including multiple scan modes intended to bypass firewalls and other network protection devices. In addition, it provides support for operating system fingerprinting, service identification, and many other capabilities.

Using nmap's basic functionality is quite simple. Port scanning a system merely requires that nmap be installed and that you provide the target system's hostname or IP address. Figure 2.4 shows an nmap of a Windows 10 system with its firewall turned off. The nmap scan provides quite a bit of information about the system—first, we see a series of common Microsoft ports, including 135, 139, and 445, running Microsoft

Remote Procedure Call (MSRPC), NetBIOS, and Microsoft's domain services, which are useful indicators that a remote system is a Windows host. The additional ports that are shown also reinforce that assessment, since ICSLAP (the local port opened by Internet Connection Sharing) is used for Microsoft internal proxying, Web Services on Devices API (WSDAPI) is a Microsoft devices API, and each of the other ports can be similarly easily identified by using a quick search for the port and service name nmap provides. This means that you can often correctly guess details about a system even without an OS identification scan.

FIGURE 2.4   Nmap of a Windows 10 system

```
root@demo:~# nmap 192.168.1.14

Starting Nmap 7.01 ( https://nmap.org ) at 2016-08-24 22:49 EDT
Nmap scan report for dynamo (192.168.1.14)
Host is up (1.0s latency).
Not shown: 992 closed ports
PORT      STATE SERVICE
135/tcp   open  msrpc
139/tcp   open  netbios-ssn
445/tcp   open  microsoft-ds
902/tcp   open  iss-realsecure
912/tcp   open  apex-mesh
2869/tcp  open  icslap
4242/tcp  open  vrml-multi-use
5357/tcp  open  wsdapi

Nmap done: 1 IP address (1 host up) scanned in 126.26 seconds
```

A more typical nmap scan is likely to include a number of nmap's command-line flags:

- A scan technique, like TCP SYN, which is the most popular scan method because it uses a TCP SYN packet to verify a service response, and quick and unobtrusive. Other connection methods are Connect, which completes a full connection; UDP scans for non-TCP services; ACK scans, which are used to map firewall rules; and a variety of other methods for specific uses.

- A port range, either specifying ports or including the full 1–65535 range. Scanning the full range of ports can be very slow, but it can be useful to identify hidden or unexpected services. Fortunately, nmap's default ports are likely to help find and identify most systems.

- Service version detection using the -sV flag, which as shown earlier can provide additional detail but may not be necessary if you intend to use a vulnerability scanner to follow up on your scans.

- OS detection using the -O flag, which can help provide additional information about systems on your network.

Nmap also has an official graphical user interface, Zenmap, which provides additional visualization capabilities, including a topology view mode that provides information about how hosts fit into a network.

Angry IP Scanner is a multiplatform (Windows, Linux, and macOS) port scanner with a graphical user interface. In Figure 2.5, you can see a sample scan run with Angry

IP Scanner with the details for a single scanned host displayed. Unlike nmap, Angry IP Scanner does not provide detailed identification for services and operating systems, but you can turn on different modules called "fetchers," including ports, time to live, filtered ports, and others. When running Angry IP Scanner, it is important to configure the ports scanned under the Preferences menu; otherwise, no port information will be returned! Unfortunately, Angry IP Scanner requires Java, which means that it may not run on systems where Java is not installed for security reasons.

FIGURE 2.5 Angry IP Scanner

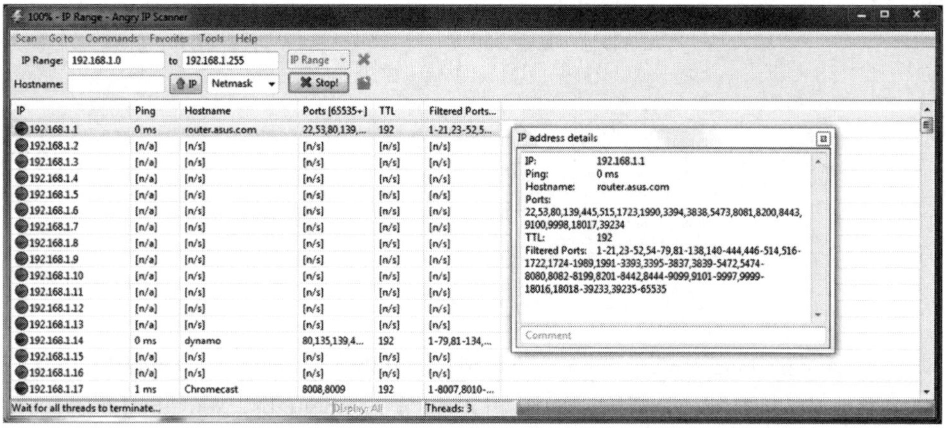

Angry IP Scanner is not as feature rich as nmap, but the same basic techniques can be used to gather information about hosts based on the port scan results. Figure 2.5 shows the information from a scan of a home router. Note that unlike nmap, Angry IP Scanner does not provide service names or service identification information.

In addition to these two popular scanners, security tools often build in a port scanning capability to support their primary functionality. Metasploit, the Qualys vulnerability management platform, and Tenable's Nessus vulnerability scanner are all examples of security tools that have built-in port scanning capabilities as part of their suite of tools.

Packet Capture for Pen Testers

Many penetration testers will use packet capture tools during their testing to capture additional data. Not only does this provide a potentially useful dataset for further analysis, but it can also be used to identify problems that result during the scan. Of course, port and vulnerability scanning can create a lot of data, so it pays to make sure you need the packet capture data before running a sniffer during scanning.

⊕ **Real World Scenario**

Determining an Internal Footprint

Gathering knowledge about the footprint of an organization from the inside is tremendously valuable. Organizations face both insider threats and very capable malicious actors who build malware and other tools designed to get them past external security layers to less protected internal networks and systems. A security professional must have a good understanding of how their organization's networks and defenses are laid out and what systems, devices, and services can be found in each part of the network.

Security practitioners who perform an internal footprinting exercise typically have the advantage of performing a crystal, or white-box, exercise where they have complete access to the knowledge that the organization has about itself. This means that rather than spending time trying to understand network topology, you can spend your time gathering information, scanning networks, and gathering system data. You may still be surprised! Often networks grow organically, and what is shown in your organization's documentation may not be an exact match for what your intelligence gathering shows.

The same cautions that apply to using the scanning tools we have discussed in this chapter still hold true for internal testing. Remember to use caution when scanning potentially delicate systems or those that control sensitive processes.

Passive Footprinting

Passive footprinting is far more challenging than active information gathering. Passive analysis relies on information that is available about the organization, systems, or network without performing your own probes. Passive fingerprinting typically relies on logs and other existing data, which may not provide all of the information needed to fully identify targets. Its reliance on stored data means that it may also be out of date!

Despite this, you can use a number of common techniques if you need to perform passive fingerprinting. Each relies on access to existing data, or to a place where data can be gathered in the course of normal business operations.

Log and Configuration Analysis

Log files can provide a treasure trove of information about systems and networks. If you have access to local system configuration data and logs, you can use the information they contain to build a thorough map of how systems work together, which users and systems exist, and how they are configured. Over the next few pages, we will look at how each of these types of log files can be used and some of the common locations where they can be found.

Network Devices

Network devices log their own activities, status, and events including traffic patterns and usage. Network device information includes network device logs, network device configuration files, and network flows.

Network Device Logs

By default, many network devices log messages to their console ports, which means that only a user logged in at the console will see them. Fortunately, most managed networks also send network logs to a central log server using the syslog utility. Many networks also leverage the Simple Network Management Protocol (SNMP) to send device information to a central control system.

Network device log files often have a log level associated with them. Although log level definitions vary, many are similar to Cisco's log levels, which are shown in Table 2.1.

TABLE 2.1   Cisco log levels

Level	Level name	Example
0	Emergencies	Device shutdown due to failure
1	Alerts	Temperature limit exceeded
2	Critical	Software failure
3	Errors	Interface down message
4	Warning	Configuration change
5	Notifications	Line protocol up/down
6	Information	ACL violation
7	Debugging	Debugging messages

Network device logs are often not as useful as the device configuration data is when you are focused on intelligence gathering, although they can provide some assistance with topology discovery based on the devices they communicate with. During penetration tests or when you are conducting security operations, network device logs can provide useful warning of attacks or can reveal configuration or system issues.

The Cisco router log shown in Figure 2.6 is accessed using the command show logging and can be filtered using an IP address, a list number, or a number of other variables. Since the Cybersecurity Analyst+ exam covers a broad range of devices, you should focus on techniques for reading logs like this. Here, we see a series of entries with a single packet denied from a remote host 10.0.2.50. The remote host is attempting to connect to its target system on a steadily increasing TCP port, likely indicating a port scan is in progress and being blocked by a rule in access list 210.

FIGURE 2.6   Cisco router log

```
002040: Oct 02 2016 13:01:20.450 EDT: %SEC-6-IPACCESSLOGP: list 210 denied tcp 10.0.2.50(15580) -> 192.168.2.1(22), 1 packet
002041: Oct 02 2016 13:01:21.455 EDT: %SEC-6-IPACCESSLOGP: list 210 denied tcp 10.0.2.50(16420) -> 192.168.2.1(23), 1 packet
002044: Oct 02 2016 13:01:21.458 EDT: %SEC-6-IPACCESSLOGP: list 210 denied tcp 10.0.2.50(41283) -> 192.168.2.1(25), 1 packet
002044: Oct 02 2016 13:01:21.462 EDT: %SEC-6-IPACCESSLOGP: list 210 denied tcp 10.0.2.50(7387) -> 192.168.2.1(25), 1 packet
002045: Oct 02 2016 13:01:21.470 EDT: %SEC-6-IPACCESSLOGP: list 210 denied tcp 10.0.2.50(60410) -> 192.168.2.1(26), 1 packet
002046: Oct 02 2016 13:01:22.350 EDT: %SEC-6-IPACCESSLOGP: list 210 denied tcp 10.0.2.50(35542) -> 192.168.2.1(27), 1 packet
002047: Oct 02 2016 13:02:22.375 EDT: %SEC-6-IPACCESSLOGP: list 210 denied tcp 10.0.2.50(32456) -> 192.168.2.1(28), 1 packet
002048: Oct 02 2016 13:02:22.450 EDT: %SEC-6-IPACCESSLOGP: list 210 denied tcp 10.0.2.50(18950) -> 192.168.2.1(29), 1 packet
002049: Oct 02 2016 13:02:24.150 EDT: %SEC-6-IPACCESSLOGP: list 210 denied tcp 10.0.2.50(14430) -> 192.168.2.1(30), 1 packet
002057: Oct 02 2016 13:02:26.250 EDT: %SEC-6-IPACCESSLOGP: list 210 denied tcp 10.0.2.50(11903) -> 192.168.2.1(31), 1 packet
```

Network Device Configuration

Configuration files from network devices can be invaluable when mapping network topology. Configuration files often include details of the network, routes, systems that the devices interact with, and other network details. In addition, they can provide details about syslog and SNMP servers, administrative and user account information, and other configuration items useful as part of information gathering.

Figure 2.7 shows a portion of the SNMP configuration from a typical Cisco router. Reading the entire file shows routing information, interface information, and details that will help you place the router in a network topology. The section shown provides in-depth detail of the SNMP community strings, the contact for the device, as well as what traps are enabled and where they are sent. In addition, you can see that the organization uses Terminal Access Controller Access Control System (TACACS) to control their servers and what the IP addresses of those servers are. As a security analyst, this is useful information— for an attacker, this could be the start of an effective social engineering attack!

FIGURE 2.7   SNMP configuration from a typical Cisco router

```
snmp-server community Example RO
snmp-server community Demo RW 2
snmp-server community Secure RW 51
snmp-server location Europe
snmp-server contact example@demo.org
snmp-server enable traps tty
snmp-server enable traps ike policy add
snmp-server enable traps ike policy delete
snmp-server enable traps ike tunnel start
snmp-server enable traps ike tunnel stop
snmp-server enable traps ipsec cryptomap add
snmp-server enable traps ipsec cryptomap delete
snmp-server enable traps ipsec cryptomap attach
snmp-server enable traps ipsec cryptomap detach
snmp-server enable traps ipsec tunnel start
snmp-server enable traps ipsec tunnel stop
snmp-server enable traps ipsec too-many-sas
snmp-server host 10.16.11.254 *****
snmp-server host 172.16.2.2 *****
snmp-server host 172.16.2.24 *****
!
tacacs-server host 172.16.3.126
tacacs-server host 172.16.65.33
tacacs-server directed-request
tacacs-server *****
```

Netflows

Netflow is a Cisco network protocol that collects IP traffic information, allowing network traffic monitoring. Flow data is used to provide a view of traffic flow and volume. A typical flow capture includes the IP and port source and destination for the traffic and the class of service. Netflows and a netflow analyzer (like PRTG and SolarWinds, which we discuss in Chapter 6, "Analyzing Symptoms for Incident Response") can help identify service problems and baseline typical network behavior and can also be useful in identifying unexpected behaviors.

 Vendors other than Cisco have created their own flow monitoring technology, and although "flows" or "netflow" is commonly used, they actually use their own names. Juniper's Jflow and cflowd, Citrix AppFlow, and HP's NetStream, as well as sFlow (an industry term for *sampled flow*), are all terms you may encounter.

Netstat

In addition to network log files, local host network information can also be gathered using *netstat* in Windows, Linux, and MacOS, as well as most Unix and Unix-like operating systems. Netstat provides a wealth of information, with its capabilities varying slightly between operating systems. It can provide such information as

- Active TCP and UDP connections, filtered by each of the major protocols: TCP, UDP, ICMP, IP, IPv6, and others—Figure 2.8 shows Linux netstat output for netstat -ta, showing active TCP connections. Here, an SSH session is open to a remote host. The -u flag would work the same way for UDP; -w shows RAW, and -X shows Unix socket connections.

FIGURE 2.8   Linux netstat -a output

```
root@demo:~# netstat -ta
Active Internet connections (servers and established)
Proto Recv-Q Send-Q Local Address        Foreign Address      State
tcp        0      0 demo:53042          10.0.2.4:ssh         ESTABLISHED
```

- Which executable file created the connection, or its process ID—Figure 2.9 shows a Windows netstat call using the -o flag to identify process numbers, which can then be referenced using the Windows Task Manager.

FIGURE 2.9   Windows netstat -o output

```
C:\WINDOWS\system32>netstat -o

Active Connections

  Proto  Local Address          Foreign Address        State           PID
  TCP    127.0.0.1:80           dynamo:52964           TIME_WAIT       0
  TCP    127.0.0.1:4243         dynamo:49741           ESTABLISHED     2792
  TCP    127.0.0.1:5354         dynamo:49669           ESTABLISHED     2768
  TCP    127.0.0.1:5354         dynamo:49671           ESTABLISHED     2768
  TCP    127.0.0.1:23560        dynamo:50122           ESTABLISHED     3112
  TCP    127.0.0.1:27015        dynamo:49744           ESTABLISHED     2784
  TCP    127.0.0.1:49669        dynamo:5354            ESTABLISHED     2784
  TCP    127.0.0.1:49671        dynamo:5354            ESTABLISHED     2784
  TCP    127.0.0.1:49692        dynamo:49693           ESTABLISHED     2792
  TCP    127.0.0.1:49693        dynamo:49692           ESTABLISHED     2792
```

- Ethernet statistics on how many bytes and packets have been sent and received—In Figure 2.10, netstat is run on a Windows system with the -e flag, providing interface statistics. This tracks the number of bytes sent and received, as well as errors, discards, and traffic sent via unknown protocols.

FIGURE 2.10   Windows netstat -e output

```
C:\WINDOWS\system32>netstat -e
Interface Statistics

                             Received          Sent

Bytes                       1802049200     116174058
Unicast packets                1542688        957264
Non-unicast packets              23014        395290
Discards                             0             0
Errors                               0             0
Unknown protocols                    0
```

- Route table information, including IPv4 and IPv6 information, as shown in Figure 2.11—This includes various information depending on the OS, with the Windows version showing the destination network, netmask, gateway, the interface the route is associated with, and a metric for the route that captures link speed and other details to establish preference for the route.

FIGURE 2.11   Windows netstat -nr output

```
===========================================================================
IPv4 Route Table
===========================================================================
Active Routes:
Network Destination        Netmask          Gateway       Interface  Metric
          0.0.0.0          0.0.0.0      192.168.1.1     192.168.1.14     25
        127.0.0.0        255.0.0.0         On-link         127.0.0.1    331
        127.0.0.1  255.255.255.255         On-link         127.0.0.1    331
  127.255.255.255  255.255.255.255         On-link         127.0.0.1    331
      169.254.0.0      255.255.0.0         On-link    169.254.71.244    281
      169.254.0.0      255.255.0.0         On-link     169.254.49.12    291
      169.254.0.0      255.255.0.0         On-link    169.254.129.13    291
      169.254.0.0      255.255.0.0         On-link     169.254.31.14    291
      169.254.0.0      255.255.0.0         On-link    169.254.245.26    291
      169.254.0.0      255.255.0.0         On-link    169.254.147.98    291
      169.254.0.0      255.255.0.0         On-link    169.254.107.29    291
      169.254.0.0      255.255.0.0         On-link   169.254.52.253    291
      169.254.0.0      255.255.0.0         On-link    169.254.34.58    291
```

This means that running netstat from a system can provide information about both the machine's network behavior and what the local network looks like. Knowing what machines a system has or is communicating with can help you understand local topology and services. Best of all, because netstat is available by default on so many operating systems, it makes sense to presume it will exist and that you can use it to gather information.

DHCP Logs and DHCP Server Configuration Files

DHCP, the Dynamic Host Configuration Protocol, is a client/server protocol that provides an IP address as well as information such as the default gateway and subnet mask for the network segment that the host will reside on. When you are conducting passive reconnaissance, DHCP logs from the DHCP server for a network can provide a quick way to identify many of the hosts on the network. If you combine DHCP logs with other logs like firewall logs, you can determine which hosts are provided with dynamic addresses and which hosts are using static addresses. As you can see in Figure 2.12, a Linux dhcp.conf file provides information about hosts and the network they are accessing.

FIGURE 2.12   Linux dhcp.conf file

```
#
# DHCP Server Configuration file.
#   see /usr/share/doc/dhcp-server/dhcpd.conf.example
#   see dhcpd.conf(5) man page
#

default-lease-time 600;
max-lease-time 7200;
option subnet-mask 255.255.255.0;
option broadcast-address 192.168.1.255;
option routers 192.168.1.1;
option domain-name-servers 192.168.1.1, 192.168.1.2;
option domain-search "example.com";
subnet 192.168.1.0 netmask 255.255.255.0{
        range 192.168.1.20 192.168.1.240;
}

host demo {
        option host-name "demo.example.com";
        hardware ethernet 08:00:27:fa:25:8e;
        fixed address 192.168.1.241;
}
```

The dhcp.conf and other configuration files can be easily accessed by using the more command to display the file. Most, but not all, configuration files are stored in the /etc directory for Linux systems, although some applications and services keep their configuration files elsewhere—if you can't find the configuration file in /etc, check the documentation!

In this example, the DHCP server provides IP addresses between 192.168.1.20 and 192.168.1.240; the router for the network is 192.168.1.1, and the DNS servers are 192.168.1.1 and 192.168.1.2. We also see a single system named "Demo" with a fixed DHCP address. Systems with fixed DHCP addresses are often servers or systems that need to have a known IP address for a specific function and are thus more interesting when gathering information.

DHCP logs for Linux are typically found in either /var/log/dhcpd.log or using the journalctl command to view logs depending on the distribution you are using. DHCP logs can provide information about systems, their MAC addresses, and their IP addresses, as seen in this sample log entry:

```
Oct  5 02:28:11 demo dhcpd[3957]: reuse_lease: lease age 80 (secs) under 25%
threshold, reply with unaltered, existing lease
Oct  5 02:28:11 demo dhcpd[3957]: DHCPREQUEST for 10.0.2.40 (10.0.2.32) from
08:00:27:fa:25:8e via enp0s3
Oct  5 02:28:11 demo dhcpd[3957]: DHCPACK on 10.0.2.40 to 08:00:27:fa:25:8e v
ia enp0s3
```

```
Oct  5 02:29:17 demo dhcpd[3957]: reuse_lease: lease age 146 (secs) under 25%
threshold, reply with unaltered, existing lease
Oct  5 02:29:17 demo dhcpd[3957]: DHCPREQUEST for 10.0.2.40 from 08:00:27:fa:
25:8e via enp0s3
Oct  5 02:29:17 demo dhcpd[3957]: DHCPACK on 10.0.2.40 to 08:00:27:fa:25:8e v
ia enp0s3
Oct  5 02:29:38 demo dhcpd[3957]: DHCPREQUEST for 10.0.2.40 from 08:00:27:fa:
25:8e via enp0s3
Oct  5 02:29:38 demo dhcpd[3957]: DHCPACK on 10.0.2.40 to 08:00:27:fa:25:8e
(demo) via enp0s3
```

This log shows a system with IP address 10.0.2.40 renewing its existing lease. The system has a hardware address of 08:00:27:fa:25:8e, and the server runs its DHCP server on the local interface enp0s3.

 Servers and network devices are often given either static addresses or permanently configured dynamic addresses set in the DHCP server configuration file. Workstations and other nonserver devices are more likely to receive DHCP addresses, making it easier to take a quick guess about what each device's may be.

Firewall Logs and Configuration Files

Router and firewall configurations files and logs often contain information about both successful and blocked connections. This means that analyzing router and firewall ACLs (access control lists) and logs can provide useful information about what traffic is allowed and can help with topological mapping by identifying where systems are based on traffic allowed through or blocked by rules. Configuration files make this even easier, since they can be directly read to understand how systems interact with the firewall.

Firewall logs can also allow penetration testers to reverse engineer firewall rules based the contents of the logs. Even without the actual configuration files, log files can provide a good view of how traffic flows. Like many other network devices, firewalls often use log levels to separate informational and debugging messages from more important messages. In addition, they typically have a vendor-specific firewall event log format that provides information based on the vendor's logging standards.

The Cybersecurity Analyst+ exam objectives include Cisco, Palo Alto, and Check Point firewalls, which means that you may encounter logs in multiple formats. Fortunately, all three have common features. Each provides a date/time stamp and details of the event in a format intended to be understandable. For example, Cisco ASA firewall logs can be accessed from the console using the show logging command (often typed as show log). Entries are reasonably readable, listing the date and time, the system, and the action taken. For example, a log might read:

```
Sep 13 10:05:11 10.0.0.1 %ASA-5-111008: User 'ASAadmin' executed the 'enable' command
```

This command indicates that the user ASAadmin ran the Cisco enable command, which is typically used to enter privileged mode on the device. If ASAadmin was not supposed to use administrative privileges, this would be an immediate red flag in your investigation.

> Cisco firewall logs use identifiers for messages; in the previous code snippet you can see the six-digit number after %ASA-5-. This identifier matches the command type, and common security mnemonic identifiers for ASAs include 4000xx, 106xxx, and 710003. Other commands may also be of interest depending on what data you are looking for. You can find a list, as well as tips on finding security incidents via ASA firewall logs, at www.cisco.com/c/en/us/about/security-center/identify-incidents-via-syslog.html.

A review of router/firewall ACLs can also be conducted manually. A portion of a sample Cisco router ACL is shown here:

```
ip access-list extended inb-lan
 permit tcp 10.0.0.0 0.255.255.255 any eq 22
 permit tcp 172.16.0.0 0.15.255.255 any eq 22
 permit tcp host 192.168.2.1 any eq 22
 deny tcp 8.16.0.0 0.15.255.255 any eq 22
```

This ACL segment names the access list and then sets a series of permitted actions along with the networks that are allowed to perform the actions. This set of rules specifically allows all addresses in the 10.0.0.0 network to use TCP 22 to send traffic, thus allowing SSH. The 172.16.0.0 network is allowed the same access, as is a host with IP address 192.168.2.1. The final deny rule will prevent the named network range from sending SSH traffic.

If you encounter firewall or router configuration files, log files, or rules on the exam, it may help to rewrite them into language you can read more easily. To do that, start with the action or command; then find the targets, users, or other things that are affected. Finally, find any modifiers that specify what will occur or what did occur. In the previous router configuration, you could write permit tcp 10.0.0.0 0.255.255.255 any eq 22 as: "Allow TCP traffic from the 10.0.0.0 network on any source port to destination port 22." Even if you're not familiar with the specific configuration or commands, this can help you understand many of the entries you will encounter.

System Log Files

System logs are collected by most systems to provide troubleshooting and other system information. Log information can vary greatly depending on the operating system, how it is configured, and what service and applications the system is running.

Linux systems typically log to the /var/log directory, although individual applications may have their own logging directory. Windows provides several types of event logs:

- Application logs, containing events logged by programs or applications. What is logged varies from program to program.

- Security logs, which can capture login events, resource and rights usage, and events like files being opened, created, or deleted. These options are set by administrators of the Windows system.

- Setup logs are captured when applications are set up.

- System logs contain events logged by Windows components. These are preset as part of Windows.

- ForwardedEvents logs are set up using event subscriptions and contain events collected from remote computers. These have to be specifically configured.

Log files can provide information about how systems are configured, what applications are running on them, which user accounts exist on the system, and other details, but they are not typically at the top of the list for reconnaissance. They are gathered if they are accessible, but most log files are kept in a secure location and are not accessible without system access.

Harvesting Data from DNS and Whois

The Domain Name System (DNS) is often one of the first stops when gathering information about an organization. Not only is *DNS* information publicly available, it is often easily connected to the organization by simply checking for Whois information about their website. With that information available, you can find other websites and hosts to add to your organizational footprint.

DNS and Traceroute Information

DNS converts domain names like google.com to IP addresses (as shown in Figure 2.13) or from IP addresses to human-understandable domain names. The command for this on Windows, Linux, and MacOS systems is *nslookup*.

FIGURE 2.13   Nslookup for google.com

```
root@demo:~# nslookup google.com
Server:         192.168.1.1
Address:        192.168.1.1#53

Non-authoritative answer:
Name:   google.com
Address: 172.217.4.238
```

Once you know the IP address that a system is using, you can look up information about the IP range it resides in. That can provide information about the company or about the hosting services that they use. Nslookup provides a number of additional flags and capabilities, including choosing the DNS server that you use by specifying it as the second parameter, as shown here with a sample query looking up Microsoft.com via Google's public DNS server 8.8.8.8:

```
nslookup microsoft.com 8.8.8.8
```

Other types of DNS records can be looked up using the -query flag, including MX, NS, SOA, and ANY as possible entries.

```
nslookup -query=mx microsoft.com
```

This results in a response like that shown in Figure 2.14.

FIGURE 2.14 nslookup using Google's DNS with MX query flag

```
C:\Users\dseidl>C:\Windows\System32\nslookup.exe bbc.co.uk
Server:  router.asus.com
Address:  192.168.1.1

Non-authoritative answer:
Name:    bbc.co.uk
Addresses:  212.58.244.22
            212.58.244.23
            212.58.246.79
            212.58.246.78
```

The IP address or hostname can also be used to gather information about the network topology around the system or device that has a given IP address. Using traceroute (or tracert on Windows systems), you can see the path packets take to the host. Since the Internet is designed to allow traffic to take the best path, you may see several different paths on the way to the system, but you will typically find that the last few responses stay the same. These are often the local routers and other network devices in an organization's network, and knowing how traffic gets to a system can give you insight into the company's internal network topology. In Figure 2.15, you can see that in a traceroute for bbc.co.uk some systems don't respond with hostname data, as shown by the asterisks and "request timed out" entries, and that the last two systems return only IP addresses. Traceroute can be helpful, but it often provides only part of the story, as you can see in Figure 2.15, which provides traceroute information to the BBC's website.

This traceroute starts by passing through the author's home router, then follows a path through Comcast's network with stops in the South Bend area, and then Chicago. The 4.68.63.125 address without a hostname resolution can be matched to Level 3 communications using a Whois website. The requests that timed out may be due to blocked ICMP responses or other network issues, but the rest of the path remains clear: another Level 3 communications host, then a BBC IP address, and two addresses that are under the control of RIPE, the European NIC. Here we can see details of upstream network providers and backbone networks and even start to get an idea of what might be some of the BBC's production network IP ranges.

FIGURE 2.15   Traceroute for bbc.co.uk

```
Tracing route to bbc.co.uk [212.58.244.22]
over a maximum of 30 hops:

  1   <1 ms    <1 ms    <1 ms   router.asus.com [192.168.1.1]
  2    9 ms     8 ms     9 ms   96.120.24.121
  3    9 ms     9 ms     9 ms   Te0-5-0-17-sur01.mishawaka.in.sbend.comcast.net [68.86.118.93]
  4   18 ms    17 ms    16 ms   te-1-7-0-2-ar01.area4.il.chicago.comcast.net [162.151.36.53]
  5    *       13 ms    12 ms   4.68.63.125
  6    *        *        *      Request timed out.
  7  107 ms   111 ms   106 ms   unknown.Level3.net [212.187.139.230]
  8    *        *        *      Request timed out.
  9  101 ms   101 ms   101 ms   ae0.er01.telhc.bbc.co.uk [132.185.254.109]
 10  106 ms   105 ms   108 ms   132.185.255.148
 11  105 ms   107 ms   107 ms   212.58.244.22

Trace complete.
```

> The routing information for an organization can provide insight into how their external network connectivity is set up. Fortunately for us, there are public Border Gateway Protocol (BGP) route information servers known as BGP looking glasses. You can find a list of them, including both global and regional servers, at www.bgp4.as/looking-glasses.

Domains and IP Ranges

Domain names are managed by domain name *registrars*. Domain registrars are accredited by generic top-level domain (gTLD) registries and/or country code top-level domain (ccTLD) registries. This means that registrars work with the domain name registries to provide registration services: the ability to acquire and use domain names. Registrars provide the interface between customers and the domain registries and handle purchase, billing, and day-to-day domain maintenance, including renewals for domain registrations.

> Domain transfer scams often target organizations whose domains are close to expiration. Make sure that the people responsible for domain registration for your organization know which registrar you work with and what to expect for your renewals.

Registrars also handle transfers of domains, either due to a sale or when a domain is transferred to another registrar. This requires authorization by the current domain owner, as well as a release of the domain to the new registrar.

We Forgot to Renew Our Domain!

If an organization doesn't renew their domain name, someone else can register it. This happens relatively frequently, and there are a number of examples of major companies that forgot to renew their domains. Google, Microsoft, Regions Bank, the Dallas Cowboys, and FourSquare all make the list for domain renewal issues. Google's recent story offers a good example of what can happen.

In 2015, Google's domain was not renewed—in fact, google.com was available via Google Domains, Google's own domain registry service. Sanmay Ved, a former Google employee, purchased google.com, and immediately received access to the messages that Google's own domain owners would have normally received. As you might imagine, he could have wreaked havoc if he had decided to abuse the power he suddenly had.

Google Domains quickly canceled the sale and refunded Sanmay's $12. Google later gave Sanmay a "bug bounty" for finding the problem, which Sanmay donated to charity.

If you'd like to read Sanmay's full story, you can find it at `https://www.linkedin.com/pulse/i-purchased-domain-googlecom-via-google-domains-sanmay-ved`.

The global IP address space is managed by IANA. In addition, IANA manages the DNS Root Zone, which handles the assignments of both gTLDs and ccTLDs. Regional authority over these resources are handled by five regional Internet registries (RIRs):

- African Network Information Center (AFRINIC) for Africa
- American Registry for Internet Numbers (ARIN) for the United States, Canada, parts of the Caribbean region, and Antarctica.
- Asia-Pacific Network Information Centre (APNIC) for Asia, Australia, New Zealand, and other countries in the region
- Latin America and Caribbean Network Information Centre (LACNIC) for Latin America and parts of the Caribbean not covered by ARIN
- Réseaux IP Européens Network Coordination Centre (RIPE NCC) for Central Asia, Europe, the Middle East, and Russia

Each of the RIRs provides Whois services to identify the assigned users of the IP space they are responsible for, as well as other services that help to ensure that the underlying IP and DNS foundations of the Internet function for their region.

You may encounter Autonomous System (AS) numbers when you're gathering information about an organization. AS numbers are assigned by RIRs to network operators as part of the routing infrastructure of the Internet. For our purposes, the AS number typically isn't a critical piece of information.

DNS Entries

In addition to the information provided using nslookup, DNS entries can provide useful information about systems simply through the hostname. A system named "AD4" is a more likely target for Active Directory–based exploits and Windows Server–specific scans, whereas hostnames that reflect a specific application or service can provide both target information and a clue for social engineering and human intelligence activities.

DNS Discovery

External DNS information for an organization is provided as part of its Whois information, providing a good starting place for DNS-based information gathering. Additional DNS servers may be identified either as part of active scanning or passive information gathering based on network traffic or logs, or even by reviewing an organization's documentation. This can be done using a port scan and searching for systems that provide DNS services on UDP or TCP port 53. Once you have found a DNS server, you can query it using dig or other DNS lookup commands, or you can test it to see if it supports zone transfers, which can make acquiring organizational DNS data easy.

Zone Transfers

One way to gather information about an organization is to perform a *zone transfer*. Zone transfers are intended to be used to replicate DNS databases between DNS servers, which makes them a powerful information gathering tool if a target's DNS servers allow a zone transfer. This means that most DNS servers are set to prohibit zone transfers to servers that aren't their trusted DNS peers, but security analysts, penetration testers, and attackers are likely to still check to see if a zone transfer is possible.

To check if your DNS server allows zone transfers from the command line, you can use either host or dig:

```
host -t axfr domain.name dns-server
dig axfr @dns-server domain.name
```

Running this against a DNS server that allows zone transfers will result in a large file with data like the following dump from digi.ninja, a site that allows practice zone transfers for security practitioners:

```
; <<>> DiG 9.9.5-12.1-Debian <<>> axfr @nsztm1.digi.ninja zonetransfer.me
; (1 server found)
;; global options: +cmd
zonetransfer.me.      7200    IN    SOA    nsztm1.digi.ninja.
robin.digi.ninja. 2014101603 172800 900 1209600 3600
zonetransfer.me.      7200    IN    RRSIG    SOA 8 2 7200 20160330133700
20160229123700 44244 zonetransfer.me. GzQojkYAP8zuTOB9UAx66mTDiEGJ26hVIIP2
ifk2DpbQLrEAPg4M77i4 M0yFWHpNfMJIuuJ8nMxQgFVCU3yTOeT/EMbN98FYC8lVYwEZeWHtb
MmS 88jVlF+cOz2WarjCdyV0+UJCTdGtBJriIczC52EXKkw2RCkv3gtdKKVa fBE=
```

```
zonetransfer.me.      7200    IN    NS      nsztm1.digi.ninja.
zonetransfer.me.      7200    IN    NS      nsztm2.digi.ninja.
zonetransfer.me.      7200    IN    RRSIG     NS 8 2 7200 20160330133700
20160229123700 44244 zonetransfer.me. TyFngBk2PMWxgJc6RtgCE/RhE0kqeWfwhYS
BxFxezupFLeiDjHeVXo+S WZxP54Xvwfk7jlFClNZ9lRNkL5qHyxRElhlH1JJI1hjvod0fycq
LqCnx XIqkOzUCkm2Mxr8OcGf2jVNDUcLPDO5XjHgOXCK9tRbVVKIpB92f4Qal ulw=
zonetransfer.me.      7200    IN    A       217.147.177.157
```

This transfer starts with a start of authority (SOA) record, which lists the primary name server; the contact for it, robin.digi.ninja (which should be read as robin@digi.ninja); and the current serial number for the domain, 2014101603. It also provides the time secondary name servers should wait between changes: 172,800 seconds, the time a primary name server should wait if it fails to refresh; 900 seconds, the time in seconds that a secondary name server can claim to have authoritative information; 1,209,600 seconds, the expiration of the record (two weeks); and 3,600 seconds, the minimum time to live for the domain. Both of the primary name servers for the domain are also listed—nsztm1 and nsztm2—and MX records and other details are contained in the file. These details, plus the full list of DNS entries for the domain, can be very useful when gathering information about an organization, and they are a major reason that zone transfers are turned off for most DNS servers.

> DigiNinja provides DNS servers that allow zone transfers to demonstrate how dangerous this can be. You try out domain zone transfers using the domain zonetransfer.me with name servers nsztm1.digi.ninja and nsztm2.digi.ninja. Full details of how to read the file are also available at https://digi.ninja/projects/zonetransferme.php.

DNS Brute Forcing

If a zone transfer isn't possible, DNS information can still be gathered from public DNS by brute force—simply sending a manual or scripted DNS query for each IP address that the organization uses can provide a useful list of systems. This can be partially prevented by using an IDS or IPS with a rule that will prevent DNS brute-force attacks or by sending queries at a slow rate or from a number of systems can bypass most prevention methods.

Whois

Whois allows you to search databases of registered users of domains and IP address blocks, and it can provide useful information about an organization or individual based on their registration information. In the sample Whois query for Google shown in Figure 2.16, you can see that information about Google, such as the company's headquarters location, contact information, and its primary name servers, is returned by the Whois query. This information can provide you with additional hints about the organization by looking for other domains registered with similar information, email addresses to contact, and details you can use during the information-gathering process.

FIGURE 2.16   Whois query data for google.com

```
Domain Name: google.com
Registry Domain ID: 2138514_DOMAIN_COM-VRSN
Registrar WHOIS Server: whois.markmonitor.com
Registrar URL: http://www.markmonitor.com
Updated Date: 2015-06-12T10:38:52-0700
Creation Date: 1997-09-15T00:00:00-0700
Registrar Registration Expiration Date: 2020-09-13T21:00:00-0700
Registrar: MarkMonitor, Inc.
Registrar IANA ID: 292
Registrar Abuse Contact Email: abusecomplaints@markmonitor.com
Registrar Abuse Contact Phone: +1.2083895740
Domain Status: clientUpdateProhibited (https://www.icann.org/epp#clientUpdateProhibited)
Domain Status: clientTransferProhibited (https://www.icann.org/epp#clientTransferProhibited)
Domain Status: clientDeleteProhibited (https://www.icann.org/epp#clientDeleteProhibited)
Domain Status: serverUpdateProhibited (https://www.icann.org/epp#serverUpdateProhibited)
Domain Status: serverTransferProhibited (https://www.icann.org/epp#serverTransferProhibited)
Domain Status: serverDeleteProhibited (https://www.icann.org/epp#serverDeleteProhibited)
Registry Registrant ID:
Registrant Name: Dns Admin
Registrant Organization: Google Inc.
Registrant Street: Please contact contact-admin@google.com, 1600 Amphitheatre Parkway
Registrant City: Mountain View
Registrant State/Province: CA
Registrant Postal Code: 94043
Registrant Country: US
Registrant Phone: +1.6502530000
Registrant Phone Ext:
Registrant Fax: +1.6506188571
Registrant Fax Ext:
Registrant Email: dns-admin@google.com
Registry Admin ID:
Admin Name: DNS Admin
Admin Organization: Google Inc.
Admin Street: 1600 Amphitheatre Parkway
Admin City: Mountain View
Admin State/Province: CA
Admin Postal Code: 94043
Admin Country: US
Admin Phone: +1.6506234000
Admin Phone Ext:
Admin Fax: +1.6506188571
Admin Fax Ext:
Admin Email: dns-admin@google.com
Registry Tech ID:
Tech Name: DNS Admin
Tech Organization: Google Inc.
Tech Street: 2400 E. Bayshore Pkwy
```

Other information can be gathered by using the host command in Linux. This command will provide information about a system's IPv4 and IPv6 addresses as well as its email servers, as shown in Figure 2.17.

FIGURE 2.17   host command response for google.com

```
root@demo:~# host google.com
google.com has address 216.58.216.238
google.com has IPv6 address 2607:f8b0:4009:809::200e
google.com mail is handled by 50 alt4.aspmx.l.google.com.
google.com mail is handled by 20 alt1.aspmx.l.google.com.
google.com mail is handled by 10 aspmx.l.google.com.
google.com mail is handled by 40 alt3.aspmx.l.google.com.
google.com mail is handled by 30 alt2.aspmx.l.google.com.
```

It can also be useful to know the history of domain ownership for a domain when conducting reconnaissance. Various services like domainhistory.net and whoismind.com provide a historical view of the domain registration information provided by Whois. Many domain owners reduce the amount of visible data after their domains have been registered for some time, meaning that historical domain registration information can be a treasure trove of useful details.

Information Aggregation and Analysis Tools

A variety of tools can help with aggregating and analyzing information gathering. Examples include theHarvester, a tool designed to gather emails, domain information, hostnames, employee names, and open ports and banners using search engines; Maltego, which builds relationship maps between people and their ties to other resources; and the Shodan search engine for Internet-connected devices and their vulnerabilities. Using a tool like theHarvester can help simplify searches of large datasets, but they're not a complete substitute for a human's creativity.

Information Gathering Using Packet Capture

A final method of passive information gathering requires access to the target network. This means that internal security teams can more easily rely on packet capture as a tool, whereas penetration testers (or attackers!) typically have to breach an organization's security to capture network traffic.

Packet capture utilities are also often called sniffers or packet analyzers.

Once you have access, however, packet capture can provide huge amounts of useful information. Capture from a single host can tell you what systems are on a given network by capturing broadcast packets, and OS fingerprinting can give you a good guess about a remote host's operating system. If you are able to capture data from a strategic location in a network using a network tap or span port, you'll have access to far more network traffic, and thus even more information about the network.

In Figure 2.18, you can see filtered packet capture data during an nmap scan. Using packet capture can allow you to dig into specific responses or to verify that you did test a specific host at a specific time. Thus, packet capture can be used both as an analysis tool and as proof that a task was accomplished.

FIGURE 2.18   Packet capture data from an nmap scan

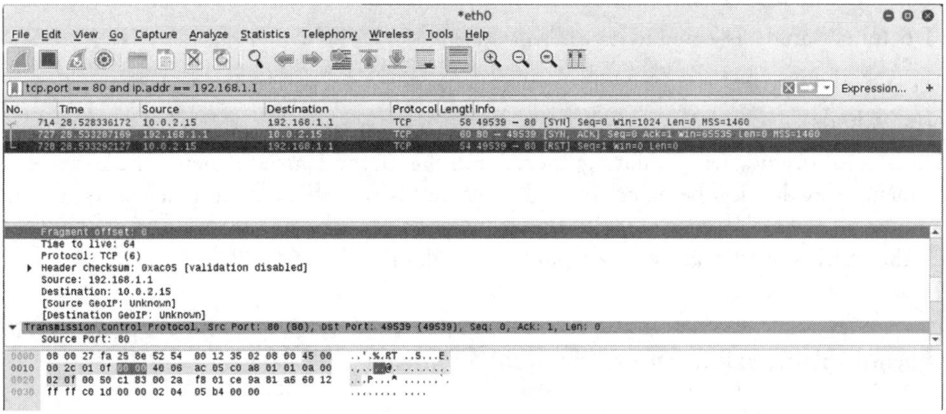

Additional details about how to read the output of tools like Wireshark and tcpdump can be found in Chapter 13, "Cybersecurity Toolkit."

Gathering Organizational Intelligence

The Cybersecurity Analyst+ exam objectives focus on technical capabilities, but an understanding of nontechnical information gathering can give you a real edge when conducting penetration testing or protecting your organization. Organizational data can provide clues to how systems and networks may be structured, useful information for social engineering, or details of specific platforms or applications that could be vulnerable.

Organizational Data

Gathering organizational data takes on many forms, from reviewing websites to searching through databases like the EDGAR financial database, gathering data from social networks, and even social engineering staff members to gather data.

Organizational data covers a broad range of information. Penetration testers often look for such information as

- Locations, including where buildings are, how they are secured, and even the business hours and workflow of the organization

- Relationships between departments, individuals, and even other organizations
- Organizational charts
- Document analysis—metadata and marketing
- Financial data
- Individuals

The type of organizational data gathered and the methods used depend on the type of assessment or evaluation being conducted. A no-holds-barred external penetration test may use almost all the techniques we will discuss, whereas an internal assessment may only verify that critical information is not publicly available.

Gathering Information About Physical Facilities

Reconnaissance isn't limited to only electronic means. Physical reconnaissance activities are also on the menu for penetration testers and attackers. Physical reconnaissance often starts with open data about the target, including satellite imagery, images of the exterior of buildings provided by tools like Google's Street View, public records, and information provided online about the organization's physical facilities, including data from social media and public photo-sharing sites. Common targets include location information; hours; and visible security precautions like fences, gates, and access control systems. Penetration testers typically focus on ways into the facility and blind spots for security cameras, guards, and other defenses.

Much like active network reconnaissance, physical testing will then move on to on-site information gathering through observation and actual nonintrusive testing. Once all of the needed information has been gathered, a plan is built, and a physical penetration test can be conducted.

Electronic Document Harvesting

Documents can provide a treasure trove of information about an organization. Document metadata often includes information like the author's name and information about the software used to create the document, and at times it can even include revisions, edits, and other data that you may not want to expose to others who access the files. Cell phone photos may have location data, allowing you to know when and where the photo was taken.

Tag data from photos, known as Exif data, is part of the Exchangeable Image File format and can easily be read using Exif data reading tools. One of the authors of this book demonstrates the power of tools like Exiftool, a metadata viewing tool, by asking students to email an innocuous photo during their spring break. A simple photo of a tasty lunch can result in identifying the restaurant that the student ate at—simply by plugging the photo's GPS metadata into an online mapping application.

Analytical data based on documents and email can also provide useful information about an organization. In Figure 2.19, an MIT Media Labs tool called Immersion provides information about the people who the demo email account emails regularly. This type of analysis can quickly help identify key contacts and topics, providing leads for further investigation.

FIGURE 2.19   Demonstration account from immersion.media.mit.edu

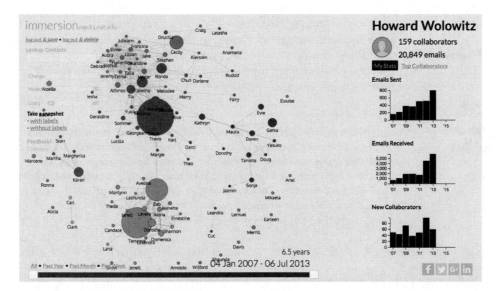

Fortunately, *metadata scrubbing* is easily handled by using a metadata scrubber utility or by using built-in tools like the Document Inspector built into Microsoft Word or the Examine Document tool in Adobe Acrobat. Many websites automatically strip sensitive metadata like location information.

> The advent of file sharing and collaboration cloud services means that organizational perimeters are even more porous than they were when employees tended to rely on internal file servers. If you can find an employee or a department that has publicly shared their Google Drive, Dropbox, or other working space, you (or an attacker!) may find yourself with internal information that the company has no way to monitor.

Websites

It might seem obvious to include an organization's website when gathering electronic documents, but simply gathering the current website's information doesn't provide a full view of the data that might be available. The Internet Archive (http://archive.org) and the Time Travel Service (http://timetravel.mementoweb.org/) both provide a way to search historic versions of websites. You can also directly search Google and other caches using a site like http://cachedview.com.

Historical and cached information can provide valuable data, including details that the organization believes are no longer accessible. Finding every instance of a cached copy and ensuring that they are removed can be quite challenging!

Social Media Analysis

Gathering information about an organization often includes gathering information about the organization's employees. Social media can provide a lot of information, from professional details about what employees do and what technologies and projects they work on to personal data that can be used for social engineering or password guessing. A social media and Internet presence profiling exercise may look at what social networks and profiles an individual has, who they are connected to, how much metadata their profiles contain, and what their tone and posting behaviors are.

Social media profiling may be paired with information from databases that provide paid access to information gathered about individuals from public records and other locations. These can provide home addresses, email and social media account information, phone numbers, details of relatives, and even arrest records. This type of in-depth information can help build a detailed profile about employees and can be helpful when conducting a penetration test or social engineering exercise.

In addition to their use as part of organizational information gathering, social media sites are often used as part of a social engineering attack. Knowing an individual's interests or details of their life can provide a much more effective way to ensure that they are caught by a social engineering attack.

Social Engineering

Social engineering, or exploiting the human element of security, targets individuals to gather information. This may be via phone, email, social media, or in person. Typically, social engineering targets specific access or accounts, but it may be more general in nature.

A number of toolkits are available to help with social engineering activities:

- The Social Engineering Toolkit (SET), which provides technical tools to enable social engineering attacks
- Creepy, a geolocation tool that uses social media and file metadata about individuals to provide better information about them
- Metasploit, which includes phishing and other tools to help with social engineering

Phishing, which targets account information or other sensitive information by pretending to be a reputable entity or organization via email or other channels, is commonly used as part of a social engineering process. Targeting an organization with a well-designed phishing attack is one of the most common ways to get credentials for an organization.

Detecting, Preventing, and Responding to Reconnaissance

Although reconnaissance doesn't always result in attacks, limiting the ability of potential attackers to gather information about your organization is a good idea. Unfortunately, organizations that are connected to the Internet are almost constantly being scanned, and that background noise can make it difficult to detect directed attacks. That means that detecting reconnaissance at your Internet border may be a process filled with a lot of background noise. Fortunately, the same techniques apply to limiting both casual and directed reconnaissance activities.

Capturing and Analyzing Data to Detect Reconnaissance

The first step in detecting reconnaissance is to capture data. In order to prioritize where data collection should occur, you first need to understand your own network topology. Monitoring at the connection points between network zones and where data sensitivity or privilege zones meet will provide the most benefit. Since most internal networks should be well protected, monitoring for internal scans is usually a lot easier than monitoring for external data gathering.

Data Sources

Typical data sources for analysis include the following:

- Network traffic analysis using intrusion detection systems (IDSs), intrusion prevention systems (IPSs), host intrusion detection systems (HIDSs), network intrusion detection systems (NIDSs), firewalls, or other network security devices. These devices often provide one or more of the following types of analysis capabilities:

  - Packet analysis, with inspection occurring at the individual packet level to detect issues with the content of the packets, behaviors related to the content of the packet, or signatures of attacks contained in them.

  - Protocol analysis, which examines traffic to ensure that protocol-level attacks and exploits are not being conducted.

  - Traffic and flow analysis intended to monitor behavior based on historic traffic patterns and behavior based models.

Wireless analysis uses the same types of tools and adds support for wireless specific protocols and features. Since wireless networks can be accessed from a distance, they are sometimes an easier target for local attackers.

- Device and system logs that can help identify reconnaissance and attacks when analyzed manually or using a tool.

- Port and vulnerability scans conducted internally to identify potential issues. This can help match known vulnerabilities to attempted exploits, alerting administrators to attacks that are likely to have succeeded.

- Security device logs that are designed to identify problems and that often have specific detection and/or response capabilities that can help limit the impact of reconnaissance.

- Security information and event management (SIEM) systems that centralize and analyze data, allowing reporting, notification, and response to security events based on correlation and analysis capabilities.

Hosted Services and Reconnaissance

Outsourced services can make detecting reconnaissance activities aimed at your organization's systems and data harder to detect. In some cases you will still be able to deploy security monitoring tools, but in most Software as a Service (SaaS) and Platform as a Service (PaaS) environments, you will have to rely on the outsourced provider. If that's the case, ensuring that they have a strong security program and regular external security audits is vital to a secure outsourced environment.

Data Analysis Methods

Collecting data isn't useful unless you can correlate and analyze it. Understanding the techniques available to analyze data can help you decide how to handle data and what tools you want to apply.

- *Anomaly analysis* looks for differences from established patterns or expected behaviors. Anomaly detection requires knowledge of what "normal" is to identify differences to build a base model. IDS and IP systems often use anomaly detection as part of their detection methods.

- *Trend analysis* focuses on predicting behaviors based on existing data. Trend analysis can help to identify future outcomes such as network congestion based on usage patterns and observed growth. It is not used as frequently as a security analysis method but can be useful to help ensure availability of services by ensuring they are capable of handling an organization's growth or increasing needs.

- *Signature analysis* uses a fingerprint or signature to detect threats or other events. This means that a signature has to exist before it can be detected, but if the signature is well designed, it can reliably detect the specific threat or event.

- *Heuristic*, or *behavioral analysis*, is used to detect threats based on their behavior. Unlike signature detection, heuristic detection can detect unknown threats since it focuses on what the threat does rather than attempting to match it to a known fingerprint.

- *Manual analysis* is also frequently performed. Human expertise and instinct can be useful when analyzing data and may detect something that would otherwise not be seen!

Your choice of analysis methods will be shaped by the tools you have available and the threats your organization faces. In many cases, you may deploy multiple detection and analysis methods in differing locations throughout your network and systems. Defense in depth remains a key concept when building a comprehensive security infrastructure.

Preventing Reconnaissance

Denying attackers information about your organization is a useful defensive strategy. Now that you have explored how to perform reconnaissance, you may want to review how to limit the effectiveness of the same strategies.

As you consider defenses against reconnaissance, remember that network defense in depth should implement many of the defenses needed to limit active reconnaissance. Passive reconnaissance and social engineering are less likely to be dealt with in a network security–centered defensive design.

Preventing Active Reconnaissance

Active reconnaissance can be limited by employing network defenses, but it cannot be completely stopped if you provide any services to the outside world. Active reconnaissance prevention typically relies on a few common defenses:

- Limiting external exposure of services and ensuring that you know your external footprint
- Using an IPS or similar defensive technology that can limit or stop probes to prevent scanning
- Using monitoring and alerting systems to notify you about events that continue despite these preventive measures

Detecting active reconnaissance on your internal network should be a priority, and policy related to the use of scanning tools should be a priority to ensure that attackers cannot probe your internal systems without being detected.

Preventing Passive Information Gathering

Preventing passive information gathering relies on controlling the information that you release. Reviewing passive information gathering techniques, then ensuring that your organization has intentionally decided what information should be available, is critical to ensuring that passive information gathering is not a significant risk.

Each passive information gathering technique has its own set of controls that can be applied. For example, DNS anti-harvesting techniques used by domain registrars can help prevent misuse. These include

- Blacklisting systems or networks that abuse the service
- Using CAPTCHAs to prevent bots

- Providing privacy services that use third-party registration information instead of the actual person or organization registering the domain
- Implementing rate limiting to ensure that lookups are not done at high speeds
- Not publishing zone files if possible, but gTLDs are required to publish their zone files, meaning this works for only some ccTLDs

Other types of passive information gathering each require a thorough review of exposed data and organization decisions about what should (or must) be exposed and what can be limited either by technical or administrative means.

Protecting social media information can be a challenge since most of the social media targets of an information gathering exercise will be individual accounts. If social media information gathering is a particular concern for your organization, an awareness campaign on social media security is typically the best option.

Summary

Reconnaissance is performed by both attackers and defenders. Both sides seek to gather information about potential targets using port scans, vulnerability scans, and information gathering, thus creating a view of an organization's networks and systems. Security professionals may use the information they gather to improve their defensive posture or to identify potential issues. Attackers may find the information they need to attack vulnerable infrastructure.

Organizational intelligence gathering is often performed in addition to the technical information that is often gathered during footprinting and active reconnaissance activities. Organizational intelligence focuses on information about an organization, such as its physical location and facilities security, internal hierarchy and structure, social media and web presence, and how policies and procedures work. This information can help attackers perform social engineering attacks or better leverage the information they gained during their technical reconnaissance activities.

Detecting reconnaissance typically involves instrumenting networks and systems using tools like IDS, IPS, and network traffic flow monitors. Scans and probes are common on public networks, but internal networks should experience scanning only from expected locations and times set by internal policies and procedures. Unexpected scans are often an indication of compromise or a flaw in the organization's perimeter security.

As a security practitioner, you need to understand how to gather information by port and vulnerability scanning, log review, passive information gathering, and organizational intelligence gathering. You should also be familiar with common tools like nmap;

vulnerability scanners; and local host utilities like dig, netstat, and traceroute. Together these skills will provide you with the abilities you need to understand the networks, systems, and other organizational assets that you must defend.

Exam Essentials

Active reconnaissance is critical to understanding system and network exposure.   Active reconnaissance involves probing systems and networks for information. Port scanning is a frequent first step during reconnaissance, and nmap is a commonly used tool for system, port, OS, and service discovery for part scanning. Active reconnaissance can also help determine network topology by capturing information and analyzing responses from network devices and systems. It is important to know common port and service pairings to help with analyzing and understanding discovered services.

Passive footprinting provides information without active probes.   Passive footprinting relies on data gathered without probing systems and networks. Log files, configuration files, and published data from DNS and Whois queries can all provide valuable data without sending any traffic to a system or network. Packet capture is useful when working to understand a network and can help document active reconnaissance activities as well as providing diagnostic and network data.

Gathering organizational intelligence is important to perform or prevent social engineering attacks.   Organizational intelligence includes information about the organization like its location, org charts, financial data, business relationships, and details about its staff. This data can be gathered through electronic data harvesting, social media analysis, and social engineering, or by gathering data in person.

Detecting reconnaissance can help identify security flaws and warn of potential attacks.   Detecting reconnaissance relies on capturing evidence of the intelligence gathering activities. This is typically done using tools like IDSs, IPSs, and log analysis, and by correlating information using a SIEM system. Automated data analysis methods used to detect reconnaissance look for anomalies, trends, signatures, and behaviors, but having a human expert in the process can help identify events that a program may miss.

Preventing, and responding to, reconnaissance relies on manual and automated analysis. Preventing information gathering typically requires limiting your organizational footprint, as well as detecting and preventing information gathering using automated means like an IPS or firewall. Proactive measures such as penetration testing and self-testing can help ensure that you know and understand your footprint and potential areas of exposure. Each technology and service that is in place requires a distinct plan to prevent or limit information gathering.

Lab Exercises

Activity 2.1: Port Scanning

In this exercise, you will use a Kali Linux virtual machine to

- Perform a port scan of a vulnerable system using nmap
- Identify the remote system's operating system and version
- Capture packets during the port scan

Part 1: Setting Up Virtual Machines

Information on downloading and setting up the Kali Linux and Metasploitable virtual machines can be found in the introduction of this book. You can also substitute your own system if you have one already set up to run nmap while capturing traffic using Wireshark.

1. Boot the Kali Linux and Metasploitable virtual machines and log into both. The username/password pair for Kali Linux is root/toor, and Metasploitable uses msfadmin/msfadmin.

2. Run ifconfig from the console of the Metasploitable virtual machine. Take note of the IP address assigned to the system.

Part 2: Scanning

Now we will perform a port scan of the Metasploitable virtual machine. Metasploitable is designed to be vulnerable, so we should anticipate seeing many services that might not otherwise be available on properly secured Linux system.

1. Open a Terminal window using the menu bar at the top of the screen.

2. To run nmap, simply type **nmap** and the IP address of the target system. Use the IP address of the Metasploitable system: **nmap** [*target IP*].

   What ports are open, and what services are identified? Do you believe that you have identified all of the open ports on the system?

3. Now we will identify the operating system of the Metasploitable virtual machine. This is enabled using the -O flag in nmap. Rerun your nmap, but this time type **nmap -O** [*target IP*] and add **-p 1-65535** to capture all possible ports.

   What operating system and version is the Metasploitable virtual machine running? What additional ports showed up?

Activity 2.2: Write an Intelligence Gathering Plan

For this activity, design a passive intelligence gathering plan for an organization of your choice. You may want to reference a resource like OSSTMM, NIST SP 800-115, or pentest-standard.org before you write the plan.

Your intelligence gathering plan should identify the following:

- The target
- How you would gather passive data, including what data you would look for
- What tools you would use

Once you are done, use one or more of the references listed earlier to review your plan. Identify what you missed and what additional data you could gather.

Repeat the activity, documenting how you would perform active intelligence gathering, including how you would determine network topology, what operating systems are in use, and what services are accessible. Remember to account for variables like wired and wireless networks, onsite and cloud hosting, and virtual versus physical hosts.

Activity 2.3: Intelligence Gathering Techniques

Match each of the information types in the following chart to the tool that can help gather it.

Route to a system	netstat
Open services via a network	Whois
IP traffic flow and volume	traceroute
Organizational contact information associated with domain registration	Creepy
Connections listed by protocol	nmap
Zone transfer	Wireshark
Packet capture	dig
Social media geotagging	netflow

Review Questions

1. What method is used to replicate DNS information for DNS servers but is also a tempting exploit target for attackers?

   A. DNSSEC

   B. AXR

   C. DNS registration

   D. Zone transfers

2. What flag does nmap use to enable operating system identification?

   A. -os

   B. -id

   C. -o

   D. -osscan

3. What command-line tool can be used to determine the path that traffic takes to a remote system?

   A. Whois

   B. traceroute

   C. nslookup

   D. routeview

4. What type of data can frequently be gathered from images taken on smartphones?

   A. Extended Graphics Format

   B. Exif

   C. JPIF

   D. PNGrams

5. Which Cisco log level is the most critical?

   A. 0

   B. 1

   C. 7

   D. 10

6. During passive intelligence gathering, you are able to run netstat on a workstation located at your target's headquarters. What information would you not be able to find using netstat on a Windows system?

   A. Active TCP connections

   B. A list of executables by connection

   C. Active IPX connections

   D. Route table information

7. Which of the following options is the most likely used for the host listed in the dhcpd.conf entry?

```
host db1 {
        option host-name "sqldb1.example.com";
        hardware ethernet 8a:00:83:aa:21:9f
        fixed address 10.1.240.10
```

   A. Active Directory server

   B. Apache web server

   C. Oracle database server

   D. Microsoft SQL server

8. Which type of Windows log is most likely to contain information about a file being deleted?

   A. httpd logs

   B. Security logs

   C. System logs

   D. Configuration logs

9. What organization manages the global IP address space?

   A. NASA

   B. ARIN

   C. WorldNIC

   D. IANA

10. Before Ben sends a Word document, he uses the built-in Document Inspector to verify that the file does not contain hidden content. What is this process called?

   A. Data purging

   B. Data remanence insurance

   C. Metadata scrubbing

   D. File cleansing

11. What type of analysis is best suited to identify a previously unknown malware package operating on a compromised system?

   A. Trend analysis

   B. Signature analysis

   C. Heuristic analysis

   D. Regression analysis

12. Which of the following is not a common DNS anti-harvesting technique?

   A. Blacklisting systems or networks

   B. Registering manually

   C. Rate limiting

   D. CAPTCHAs

13. What technique is being used in this command?

```
dig axfr @dns-server example.com
```

   A. DNS query

   B. nslookup

   C. dig scan

   D. Zone transfer

14. Which of the following is not a reason that penetration testers often perform packet capture while conducting port and vulnerability scanning?

   A. Work process documentation

   B. To capture additional data for analysis

   C. Plausible deniability

   D. To provide a timeline

15. What process uses information such as the way that a system's TCP stack responds to queries, what TCP options it supports, and the initial window size it uses?

   A. Service identification

   B. Fuzzing

   C. Application scanning

   D. OS detection

16. What tool would you use to capture IP traffic information to provide flow and volume information about a network?

   A. libpcap

   B. Netflow

   C. Netstat

   D. pflow

17. What method used to replicate DNS information between DNS servers can also be used to gather large amounts of information about an organization's systems?

   A. traceroute

   B. Zone transfer

   C. DNS sync

   D. dig

18. Selah believes that an organization she is penetration testing may have exposed information about their systems on their website in the past. What site might help her find an older copy of their website?

   A. The Internet Archive

   B. WikiLeaks

   C. The Internet Rewinder

   D. TimeTurner

19. During an information gathering exercise, Chris is asked to find out detailed personal information about his target's employees. What is frequently the best place to find this information?

   A. Forums

   B. Social media

   C. The company's website

   D. Creepy

20. Which lookup tool provides information about a domain's registrar and physical location?

   A. nslookup

   B. host

   C. Whois

   D. traceroute

Chapter
3

Designing a Vulnerability Management Program

THE COMPTIA CYBERSECURITY ANALYST+ EXAM OBJECTIVES COVERED IN THIS CHAPTER INCLUDE:

Domain 2: Vulnerability Management

✓ **2.1 Given a scenario, implement an information security vulnerability management process.**

Cybersecurity is a cat-and-mouse game where information technology professionals seek to combat the new vulnerabilities discovered by adversaries on an almost daily basis. Modern enterprises consist of hardware and software of almost unfathomable complexity, and buried within those systems are thousands of undiscovered security vulnerabilities waiting for an attacker to exploit them. *Vulnerability management programs* seek to identify, prioritize, and remediate these vulnerabilities before an attacker exploits them to undermine the confidentiality, integrity, or availability of enterprise information assets. Effective vulnerability management programs use an organized approach to scanning enterprise assets for vulnerabilities, using a defined workflow to remediate those vulnerabilities and performing continuous assessment to provide technologists and managers with insight into the current state of enterprise cybersecurity.

Identifying Vulnerability Management Requirements

As an organization begins developing a vulnerability management program, it should first undertake the identification of any internal or external requirements for vulnerability scanning. These requirements may come from the regulatory environment(s) in which the organization operates and/or internal policy-driven requirements.

Regulatory Environment

Many organizations find themselves bound by laws and regulations that govern the ways that they store, process, and transmit information. This is especially true when the organization handles sensitive personal information or information belonging to government agencies.

Many of these laws are not overly prescriptive and do not specifically address the implementation of a vulnerability management program. For example, the Health Insurance Portability and Accountability Act (HIPAA) regulates the ways that healthcare providers, insurance companies, and their business associates handle protected health information. Similarly, the Gramm-Leach-Bliley Act (GLBA) governs how financial institutions may handle customer financial records. Neither of these laws specifically requires that covered organizations conduct vulnerability scanning.

Two regulatory schemes, however, do specifically mandate the implementation of a vulnerability management program: the Payment Card Industry Data Security Standard (PCI DSS) and the Federal Information Security Management Act (FISMA).

Payment Card Industry Data Security Standard (PCI DSS)

PCI DSS prescribes specific security controls for merchants who handle credit card transactions and service providers who assist merchants with these transactions. This standard includes what are arguably the most specific requirements for vulnerability scanning of any standard.

 Contrary to what some believe, PCI DSS is *not* a law. The standard is maintained by an industry group known as the Payment Card Industry Security Standards Council (PCI SSC), which is funded by the industry to maintain the requirements. Organizations are subject to PCI DSS due to contractual requirements rather than a law.

PCI DSS prescribes many of the details of vulnerability scans. These include

- Organizations must run both internal and external vulnerability scans (PCI DSS requirement 11.2).

- Organizations must run scans on at least a quarterly basis and "after any significant change in the network (such as new system component installations, changes in network topology, firewall rule modifications, product upgrades)" (PCI DSS requirement 11.2).

- Internal scans must be conducted by qualified personnel (PCI DSS requirement 11.2.1).

- Organizations must remediate any high-risk vulnerabilities and repeat scans to confirm that they are resolved until they receive a "clean" scan report (PCI DSS requirement 11.2.1).

- External scans must be conducted by an Approved Scanning Vendor (ASV) authorized by PCI SSC (PCI DSS requirement 11.2.2).

Vulnerability scanning for PCI DSS compliance is a thriving and competitive industry, and many security consulting firms specialize in these scans. Many organizations choose to conduct their own scans first to assure themselves that they will achieve a passing result before requesting an official scan from an ASV.

 You should *never* conduct vulnerability scans unless you have explicit permission to do so. Running scans without permission can be a serious violation of an organization's security policy and may also be a crime.

Federal Information Security Management Act (FISMA)

The *Federal Information Security Management Act (FISMA)* requires that government agencies and other organizations operating systems on behalf of government agencies comply with a series of security standards. The specific controls required by these standards depend on whether the government designates the system as low impact, moderate impact, or high impact, according to the definitions shown in Figure 3.1. Further guidance on system classification is found in Federal Information Processing Standard (FIPS) 199: Standards for Security Categorization of Federal Information and Information Systems.

FIGURE 3.1   FIPS 199 Standards

Security Objective	POTENTIAL IMPACT		
	LOW	MODERATE	HIGH
Confidentiality Preserving authorized restrictions on information access and disclosure, including means for protecting personal privacy and proprietary information. [44 U.S.C., SEC. 3542]	The unauthorized disclosure of information could be expected to have a **limited** adverse effect on organizational operations, organizational assets, or individuals.	The unauthorized disclosure of information could be expected to have a **serious** adverse effect on organizational operations, organizational assets, or individuals.	The unauthorized disclosure of information could be expected to have a **severe or catastrophic** adverse effect on organizational operations, organizational assets, or individuals.
Integrity Guarding against improper information modification or destruction, and includes ensuring information non-repudiation and authenticity. [44 U.S.C., SEC. 3542]	The unauthorized modification or destruction of information could be expected to have a **limited** adverse effect on organizational operations, organizational assets, or individuals.	The unauthorized modification or destruction of information could be expected to have a **serious** adverse effect on organizational operations, organizational assets, or individuals.	The unauthorized modification or destruction of information could be expected to have a **severe or catastrophic** adverse effect on organizational operations, organizational assets, or individuals.
Availability Ensuring timely and reliable access to and use of information. [44 U.S.C., SEC. 3542]	The disruption of access to or use of information or an information system could be expected to have a **limited** adverse effect on organizational operations, organizational assets, or individuals.	The disruption of access to or use of information or an information system could be expected to have a **serious** adverse effect on organizational operations, organizational assets, or individuals.	The disruption of access to or use of information or an information system could be expected to have a **severe or catastrophic** adverse effect on organizational operations, organizational assets, or individuals.

(Source: FIPS 199)

All federal information systems, regardless of their impact categorization, must meet the basic requirements for vulnerability scanning found in NIST Special Publication 800-53: Security and Privacy Controls for Federal Information Systems and Organizations. These require that each organization subject to FISMA:

a. Scans for vulnerabilities in the information system and hosted applications and when new vulnerabilities potentially affecting the system/application are identified and reported;

b. Employs vulnerability scanning tools and techniques that facilitate interoperability among tools and automate parts of the vulnerability management process by using standards for:

    1. Enumerating platforms, software flaws, and improper configurations;

    2. Formatting checklists and test procedures; and

    3. Measuring vulnerability impact;

c. Analyzes vulnerability scan reports and results from security control assessments;

d. Remediates legitimate vulnerabilities in accordance with an organizational assessment of risk; and

e. Shares information obtained from the vulnerability scanning process and security control assessments to help eliminate similar vulnerabilities in other information systems (i.e. systemic weaknesses or deficiencies).

These requirements establish a baseline for all federal information systems. NIST 800-53 then describes eight control enhancements that may be required depending on the circumstances:

1. The organization employs vulnerability scanning tools that include the capability to readily update the information system vulnerabilities to be scanned.

2. The organization updates the information system vulnerabilities scanned prior to a new scan (and/or) when new vulnerabilities are identified and reported.

3. The organization employs vulnerability scanning procedures that can identify the breadth and depth of coverage (i.e., information system components scanned and vulnerabilities checked).

4. The organization determines what information about the information system is discoverable by adversaries and subsequently takes organization-defined corrective actions.

5. The information system implements privileged access authorization to information system components for selected vulnerability scanning activities.

6. The organization employs automated mechanisms to compare the results of vulnerability scans over time to determine trends in information system vulnerabilities.

8. The organization reviews historic audit logs to determine if a vulnerability identified in the information system has been previously exploited.

10. The organization correlates the output from vulnerability scanning tools to determine the presence of multi-vulnerability/multi-hop attack vectors.

Note that requirements 7 and 9 were control enhancements that were previously included in the standard but were later withdrawn.

In cases where a federal agency determines that an information system falls into the moderate impact category, it must implement control enhancements 1, 2, and 5, at a minimum. If the agency determines a system is high impact, it must implement at least control enhancements 1, 2, 4, and 5.

Corporate Policy

The prescriptive security requirements of PCI DSS and FISMA cover organizations involved in processing retail transactions and operating government systems, but those two groups constitute only a fraction of enterprises. Cybersecurity professionals widely agree that vulnerability management is a critical component of any information security program and, for this reason, many organizations mandate vulnerability scanning in corporate policy, even if this requirement is not imposed by regulatory requirements.

Identifying Scan Targets

Once an organization decides that it wishes to conduct vulnerability scanning and determines which, if any, regulatory requirements apply to their scans, they move on to the more
detailed phases of the planning process. The next step is to identify the systems that will be
covered by the vulnerability scans. Some organizations choose to cover all systems in their
scanning process whereas others scan systems differently (or not at all) depending on the
answers to many different questions, including

- What is the *data classification* of the information stored, processed, or transmitted by
  the system?

- Is the system exposed to the Internet or other public or semipublic networks?

- What services are offered by the system?

- Is the system a production, test, or development system?

Organizations also use automated techniques to identify the systems that may be
covered by a scan. Cybersecurity professionals use scanning tools to search the network for
connected systems, whether they were previously known or unknown, and build an *asset
inventory*. Figure 3.2 shows an example of an asset map developed using the QualysGuard
asset inventory functionality.

FIGURE 3.2   QualysGuard asset map

Administrators may then supplement this inventory with additional information about the type of system and the information it handles. This information then helps make determinations about which systems are critical and which are noncritical. Asset inventory and criticality information helps guide decisions about the types of scans that are performed, the frequency of those scans, and the priority administrators should place on remediating vulnerabilities detected by the scan.

Determining Scan Frequency

Cybersecurity professionals depend on automation to help them perform their duties in an efficient, effective manner. Vulnerability scanning tools allow the automated scheduling of scans to take the burden off administrators. Figure 3.3 shows an example of how these scans might be configured in Tenable's Nessus product. Administrators may designate a schedule that meets their security, compliance, and business requirements.

FIGURE 3.3   Configuring a Nessus scan

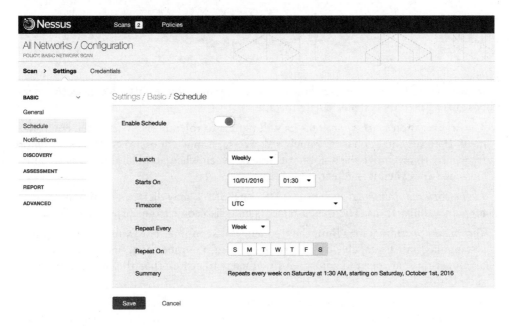

Administrators should configure these scans to provide automated alerting when they detect new vulnerabilities. Many security teams configure their scans to produce automated email reports of scan results, such as the report shown in Figure 3.4.

FIGURE 3.4   Sample Nessus scan report

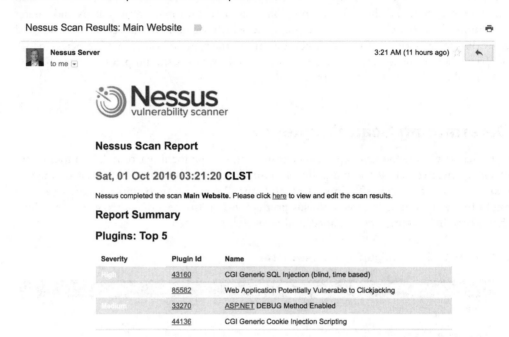

Many different factors influence how often an organization decides to conduct vulnerability scans against its systems. These include

- The organization's *risk appetite* is its willingness to tolerate risk within the environment. If an organization is extremely risk averse, it may choose to conduct scans more frequently to minimize the amount of time between when a vulnerability comes into existence and when it is detected by a scan.

- *Regulatory requirements,* such as PCI DSS or FISMA, may dictate a minimum frequency for vulnerability scans. These requirements may also come from corporate policies.

- *Technical constraints* may limit the frequency of scanning. For example, the scanning system may only be capable of performing a certain number of scans per day, and organizations may need to adjust scan frequency to ensure that all scans complete successfully.

- *Business constraints* may limit the organization from conducting resource-intensive vulnerability scans during periods of high business activity to avoid disruption of critical processes.

- *Licensing limitations* may curtail the bandwidth consumed by the scanner or the number of scans that may be conducted simultaneously.

Cybersecurity professionals must balance each of these considerations when planning a vulnerability scanning program. It is usually wise to begin small and slowly expand the scope and frequency of vulnerability scans over time to avoid overwhelming the scanning infrastructure or enterprise systems.

Selecting Vulnerability Scanning Tools

The examples in this chapter use two common network vulnerability scanning tools: Tenable's Nessus and Qualys's QualysGuard. The CompTIA Cybersecurity Analyst+ exam requires knowledge of both of these tools as well as Rapid7's Nexpose, the open source OpenVAS product, the Nikto web application vulnerability scanner, and Microsoft's Baseline Security Analyzer.

You'll find more information about all of these tools in Chapter 13, "Cybersecurity Toolkit."

Configuring and Executing Vulnerability Scans

Once security professionals have determined the basic requirements for their vulnerability management program, they must configure vulnerability management tools to perform scans according to the requirements-based scan specifications. These tasks include identifying the appropriate scope for each scan, configuring scans to meet the organization's requirements, and maintaining the currency of the vulnerability scanning tool.

Scoping Vulnerability Scans

The *scope* of a vulnerability scan describes the extent of the scan, including answers to the following questions:

- What systems and networks will be included in the vulnerability scan?
- What technical measures will be used to test whether systems are present on the network?
- What tests will be performed against systems discovered by a vulnerability scan?

Administrators should first answer these questions in a general sense and ensure that they have consensus from technical staff and management that the scans are appropriate and unlikely to cause disruption to the business. Once they've determined that the scans are well designed and unlikely to cause serious issues, they may then move on to configuring the scans within the vulnerability management tool.

Scoping for Compliance Purposes

Scoping is an important tool in the cybersecurity analyst's toolkit because it allows analysts to reduce problems to a manageable size. For example, an organization that processes credit cards may face the seemingly insurmountable task of achieving PCI DSS compliance across their entire network that consists of thousands of systems.

Through judicious use of network segmentation and other techniques, administrators may isolate the handful of systems actually involved in credit card processing, segregating them from the vast majority of systems on the organization's network. When done properly, this segmentation reduces the scope of PCI DSS compliance to the much smaller isolated network that is dedicated to payment card processing.

When the organization is able to reduce the scope of the PCI DSS network, it also reduces the scope of many of the required PCI DSS controls, including vulnerability scanning. Instead of contracting with an approved scanning vendor to conduct quarterly compliance scans of the organization's entire network, they may reduce the scope of that scan to those systems that actually engage in card processing. This will dramatically reduce the cost of the scanning engagement and the remediation workload facing cybersecurity professionals after the scan completes.

Configuring Vulnerability Scans

Vulnerability management solutions provide administrators with the ability to configure many different parameters related to scans. In addition to scheduling automated scans and producing reports, administrators may customize the types of checks performed by the scanner, provide credentials to access target servers, install scanning agents on target servers, and conduct scans from a variety of network perspectives.

Scan Sensitivity Levels

Cybersecurity professionals configuring vulnerability scans should pay careful attention to the configuration settings related to the scan sensitivity level. These settings determine the types of checks that the scanner will perform and should be customized to ensure that the scan meets its objectives while minimizing the possibility of disrupting the target environment.

Typically, administrators create a new scan by beginning with a template. This may be a template provided by the vulnerability management vendor and built into the product, such as the Nessus templates shown in Figure 3.5, or it may be a custom-developed template created for use within the organization. As administrators create their own scan configurations, they should consider saving common configuration settings in templates to allow efficient reuse of their work, saving time and reducing errors when configuring future scans.

FIGURE 3.5   Nessus scan templates

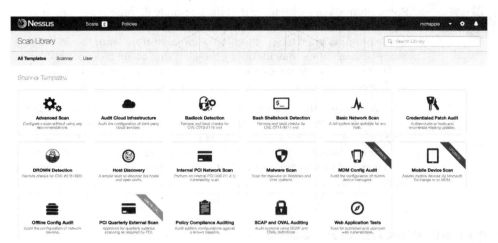

Administrators may also improve the efficiency of their scans by configuring the specific plug-ins that will run during each scan. Each plug-in performs a check for a specific vulnerability, and these plug-ins are often grouped into families based on the operating system, application, or device that they involve. Disabling unnecessary plug-ins improves the speed of the scan by bypassing unnecessary checks and also may reduce the number of false positive results detected by the scanner.

For example, an organization that does not use the Amazon Linux operating system may choose to disable all checks related to Amazon Linux in their scanning template. Figure 3.6 shows an example of disabling these plug-ins in Nessus.

FIGURE 3.6   Disabling unused plug-ins

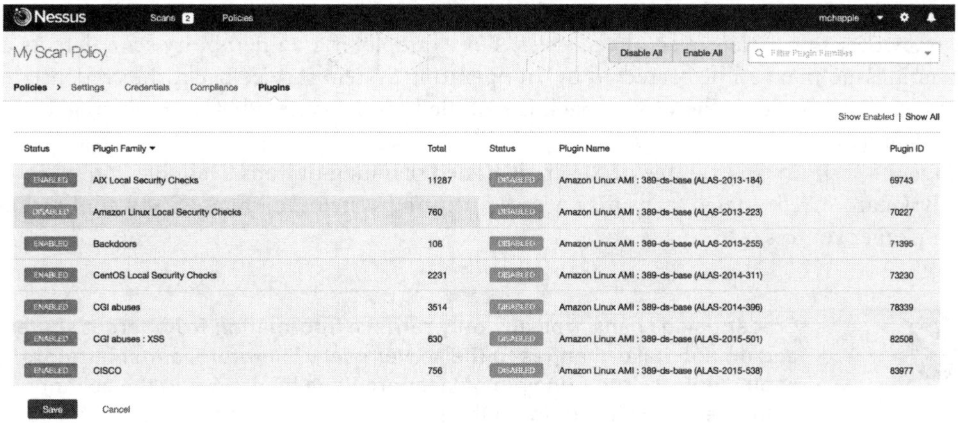

Some plug-ins perform tests that may actually disrupt activity on a production system or, in the worst case, damage content on those systems. These plug-ins are a tricky situation. Administrators want to run these scans because they may identify problems that could be exploited by a malicious source. At the same time, cybersecurity professionals clearly don't want to *cause* problems on the organization's network!

One way around this problem is to maintain a test environment containing copies of the same systems running on the production network and running scans against those test systems first. If the scans detect problems in the test environment, administrators may correct the underlying causes on both test and production networks before running scans on the production network.

Supplementing Network Scans

Basic vulnerability scans run over a network, probing a system from a distance. This provides a realistic view of the system's security by simulating what an attacker might see from another network vantage point. However, the firewalls, intrusion prevention systems, and other security controls that exist on the path between the scanner and the target server may affect the scan results, providing an inaccurate view of the server's security independent of those controls.

Additionally, many security vulnerabilities are difficult to confirm using only a remote scan. Vulnerability scans that run over the network may detect the possibility that a vulnerability exists but be unable to confirm it with confidence, causing a false positive result that requires time-consuming administrator investigation.

Modern vulnerability management solutions can supplement these remote scans with trusted information about server configurations. This information may be gathered in two ways. First, administrators can provide the scanner with credentials that allow the scanner to connect to the target server and retrieve configuration information. This information can then be used to determine whether a vulnerability exists, improving the scan's accuracy over noncredentialed alternatives. For example, if a vulnerability scan detects a potential issue that can be corrected by an operating system service pack, the credentialed scan can check whether the service pack is installed on the system before reporting a vulnerability.

Figure 3.7 shows an example of the credentialed scanning options available within QualysGuard. Credentialed scans may access operating systems, databases, and applications, among other sources.

Credentialed scans typically only retrieve information from target servers and do not make changes to the server itself. Therefore, administrators should enforce the principle of least privilege by providing the scanner with a read-only account on the server. This reduces the likelihood of a security incident related to the scanner's credentialed access.

FIGURE 3.7   Configuring authenticated scanning

Authentication

Authentication enables the scanner to log into hosts at scan time to extend detection capabilities. See the online help to learn how to configure this option.

☑ Windows
☑ Unix/Cisco IOS
☑ Oracle
☐ Oracle Listener
☐ SNMP
☐ VMware
☐ DB2
☐ HTTP
☐ MySQL

In addition to credentialed scanning, some scanners supplement the traditional server-based approach to vulnerability scanning with a complementary agent-based approach. In this approach, administrators install small software agents on each target server. These agents conduct scans of the server configuration, providing an "inside-out" vulnerability scan, and then report information back to the vulnerability management platform for analysis and reporting.

System administrators are typically wary of installing agents on the servers that they manage for fear that the agent will cause performance or stability issues. If you choose to use an agent-based approach to scanning, you should approach this concept conservatively, beginning with a small pilot deployment that builds confidence in the agent before proceeding with a more widespread deployment.

Scan Perspective

Comprehensive vulnerability management programs provide the ability to conduct scans from a variety of *scan perspectives*. Each scan perspective conducts the scan from a different location on the network, providing a different view into vulnerabilities. For example, an external scan is run from the Internet, giving administrators a view of what an attacker located outside the organization would see as potential vulnerabilities. Internal scans might run from a scanner on the general corporate network, providing the view that a malicious insider might encounter. Finally, scanners located inside the datacenter and agents located on the servers offer the most accurate view of the real state of the server by showing vulnerabilities that might be blocked by other security controls on the network.

The internal and external scans required by PCI DSS are a good example of scans performed from different perspectives. The organization may conduct its own internal scans but must supplement them with external scans conducted by an approved scanning vendor.

Vulnerability management platforms have the ability to manage different scanners and provide a consolidated view of scan results, compiling data from different sources. Figure 3.8 shows an example of how the administrator may select the scanner for a newly configured scan using QualysGuard.

FIGURE 3.8   Choosing a scan appliance

Launch Vulnerability Scan	Turn help tips: On I **Off** Launch Help

General Information

Give your scan a name, select a scan profile (a default is selected for you with recommended settings), and choose a scanner from the Scanner Appliance menu for internal scans, if visible.

Title:

Option Profile: *   Initial Options (default)   ⁺⋆ Select

Scanner Appliance: ✓ Default / External ... ⬦ 🗗 View
    All Scanners in Asset Group
    All Scanners in TagSet
    Build my list
    AWS_Internal

Choose Target Ho

Tell us which hosts (IP addresses) you want to scan.
◉ Assets   ○ Tags

Asset Groups   Select items...   ⟳ ▾   ⁺⋆ Select

IPs/Ranges   ⁺⋆ Select
    Example: 192.168.0.87-192.168.0.92, 192.168.0.200

Exclude IPs/Ranges   ⁺⋆ Select
    Example: 192.168.0.87-192.168.0.92, 192.168.0.200

Notification
☐ Send notification when this scan is finished.

Scanner Maintenance

As with any technology product, vulnerability management solutions require care and feeding. Administrators should conduct regular maintenance of their vulnerability scanner to ensure that the scanning software and vulnerability feeds remain up-to-date.

Scanning systems do provide automatic updating capabilities that keep the scanner and its vulnerability feeds up to date. Organizations can and should take advantage of these features, but it is always a good idea to check in once in a while and manually verify that the scanner is updating properly.

Scanner Software

Scanning systems themselves aren't immune from vulnerabilities. As shown in Figure 3.9, even vulnerability scanners can have security issues! Regular patching of scanner software protects an organization against scanner-specific vulnerabilities and also provides important bug fixes and feature enhancements to improve scan quality.

FIGURE 3.9   National Cyber Awareness System Vulnerability Summary

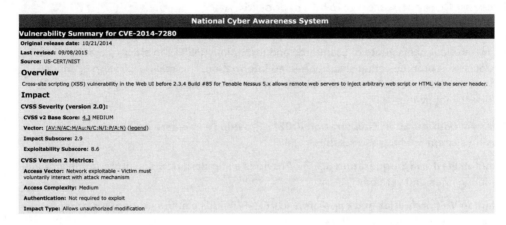

(Source: NIST)

Vulnerability Plug-in Feeds

Security researchers discover new vulnerabilities every week, and vulnerability scanners can only be effective against these vulnerabilities if they receive frequent updates to their plug-ins. Administrators should configure their scanners to retrieve new plug-ins on a regular basis, preferably daily. Fortunately, as shown in Figure 3.10, this process is easily automated.

FIGURE 3.10   Nessus Automatic Updates

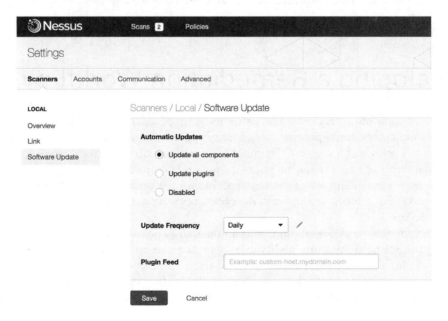

Security Content Automation Protocol (SCAP)

The Security Content Automation Protocol (SCAP) is an effort by the security community, led by the National Institute of Standards and Technology (NIST), to create a standardized approach for communicating security-related information. This standardization is important to the automation of interactions between security components. The SCAP standards include the following:

Common Configuration Enumeration (CCE)   Provides a standard nomenclature for discussing system configuration issues

Common Platform Enumeration (CPE)   Provides a standard nomenclature for describing product names and versions

Common Vulnerabilities and Exposures (CVE)   Provides a standard nomenclature for describing security-related software flaws

Common Vulnerability Scoring System (CVSS)   Provides a standardized approach for measuring and describing the severity of security-related software flaws

Extensible Configuration Checklist Description Format (XCCDF)   Is a language for specifying checklists and reporting checklist results

Open Vulnerability and Assessment Language (OVAL)   Is a language for specifying low-level testing procedures used by checklists

For more information on SCAP, see NIST SP 800-117: Guide to Adopting and Using the Security Content Automation Protocol (SCAP) Version 1.0 or the SCAP website (`http://scap.nist.gov`).

Developing a Remediation Workflow

Vulnerability scans often produce a fairly steady stream of security issues that require attention from cybersecurity professionals, system engineers, software developers, network engineers, and other technologists. The initial scans of an environment can produce an overwhelming number of issues requiring prioritization and eventual remediation. Organizations should develop a remediation workflow that allows for the prioritization of vulnerabilities and the tracking of remediation through the cycle of detection, remediation, and testing shown in Figure 3.11.

This remediation workflow should be as automated as possible, given the tools available to the organization. Many vulnerability management products include a built-in workflow mechanism that allows cybersecurity experts to track vulnerabilities through the remediation process and automatically close out vulnerabilities after testing confirms that the remediation was successful. Although these tools are helpful, other organizations often choose not to use them in favor of tracking vulnerabilities in the IT service management (ITSM) tool that the organization uses for other technology issues. This approach avoids asking technologists to use two different issue tracking systems and improves compliance with the remediation process. However, it also requires selecting vulnerability management tools that integrate natively with the organization's ITSM tool (or vice versa) or building an integration between the tools if one does not already exist.

FIGURE 3.11   Vulnerability management life cycle

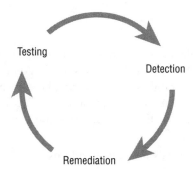

An important trend in vulnerability management is a shift toward *ongoing scanning* and *continuous monitoring*. Ongoing scanning moves away from the scheduled scanning approach that tested systems on a scheduled weekly or monthly basis and instead configures scanners to simply scan systems on a rotating basis, checking for vulnerabilities as often as scanning resources permit. This approach can be bandwidth and resource intensive, but it does provide earlier detection of vulnerabilities. Continuous monitoring incorporates data from agent-based approaches to vulnerability detection and reports security-related configuration changes to the vulnerability management platform as soon as they occur, providing the ability to analyze those changes for potential vulnerabilities.

Reporting and Communication

Communicating vulnerability scan results to technologists who have the ability to remediate them and managers responsible for the security of the environment is a critical component of vulnerability management. After all, if the team members who can correct the issue never see the results, vulnerability scanning is a waste of time!

Modern vulnerability management tools provide very strong reporting capabilities. These reports may be manually generated on-demand to answer specific questions, or administrators may set up automated reports that generate on a scheduled basis and are pushed out to those who need to see them. Additionally, administrators may set up alerting mechanisms to immediately notify key personnel of critical new vulnerabilities as soon as they are detected.

Management-level dashboards provide a very high-level summary of the cybersecurity health of the environment. This type of report is often used to provide leaders with a quick snapshot of the environment. An example of a dashboard from QualysGuard appears in Figure 3.12.

FIGURE 3.12 QualysGuard dashboard example

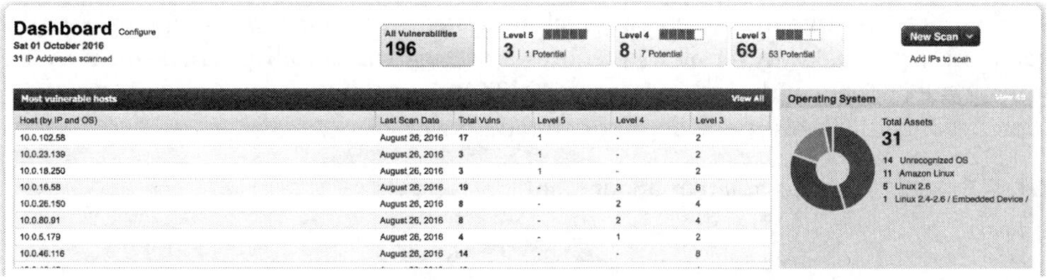

As cybersecurity analysts drill deeper into the vulnerability management system, they can see summary technical reports that show the specific vulnerabilities detected on the network and sort them by vulnerability type, severity, host group, and other issues. An example of this type of report from Nessus appears in Figure 3.13. These reports are useful in identifying the widespread issues that require attention from cybersecurity professionals.

FIGURE 3.13 Nessus report example by IP address

System engineers are typically more interested in detailed reports listing all of the vulnerabilities on the systems they administer. Figure 3.14 shows a Nessus report listing all of the vulnerabilities that exist on a single system scanned by the tool. The report provides a full listing of vulnerabilities, sorted by severity, and can serve as a checklist that system engineers can use to prioritize their remediation efforts for a system.

FIGURE 3.14   Nessus report example by criticality

Severity ▲	Plugin Name	Plugin Family	Count
CRITICAL	MS14-066: Vulnerability in Schannel Could Allow Remote Code Execution (2992611) (uncre...	Windows	1
CRITICAL	MS15-034: Vulnerability in HTTP.sys Could Allow Remote Code Execution (3042553) (uncre...	Windows	1
MEDIUM	Microsoft Exchange Client Access Server Information Disclosure	Windows	1
LOW	Web Server HTTP Header Internal IP Disclosure	Web Servers	2
LOW	SSL RC4 Cipher Suites Supported (Bar Mitzvah)	General	1
INFO	Service Detection	Service detection	3
INFO	HyperText Transfer Protocol (HTTP) Information	Web Servers	2
INFO	Nessus SYN scanner	Port scanners	2
INFO	Web Server No 404 Error Code Check	Web Servers	2
INFO	Additional DNS Hostnames	General	1
INFO	Common Platform Enumeration (CPE)	General	1
INFO	Device Type	General	1
INFO	Host Fully Qualified Domain Name (FQDN) Resolution	General	1

The final level of drill-down provides the nitty-gritty details required to fix an individual vulnerability on a system. Figure 3.15 shows an example of this type of reporting. The report identifies the vulnerability that was detected, explains the significance and cause of the vulnerability, and provides remediation instructions to help guide the administrator's efforts in correcting the underlying security issue.

FIGURE 3.15   Detailed vulnerability report

Prioritizing Remediation

As cybersecurity analysts work their way through vulnerability scanning reports, they must make important decisions about prioritizing remediation to use their limited resources to resolve the issues that pose the greatest danger to the organization. There is no cut-and-dry formula for prioritizing vulnerabilities. Rather, analysts must take several important factors into account when choosing where to turn their attention first.

Some of the most important factors in the remediation prioritization decision-making process include the following:

Criticality of the Systems and Information Affected by the Vulnerability   Criticality measures should take into account confidentiality, integrity, and availability requirements, depending on the nature of the vulnerability. For example, if the vulnerability allows a denial-of-service attack, cybersecurity analysts should consider the impact to the organization if the system became unusable due to an attack. If the vulnerability allows the theft of stored information from a database, cybersecurity analysts should consider the impact on the organization if that information were stolen.

Difficulty of Remediating the Vulnerability   If fixing a vulnerability will require an inordinate commitment of human or financial resources, that should be factored into the decision-making process. Cybersecurity analysts may find that they can fix five issues rated numbers 2 through 6 in priority order for the same investment that would be required to address the top issue. This doesn't mean that they should necessarily choose to make that decision based on cost and difficulty alone, but it is a consideration in the prioritization process.

Severity of the Vulnerability   The more severe an issue is, the more important it is to correct that issue. Analysts may turn to the Common Vulnerability Scoring System (CVSS) to provide relative severity rankings for different vulnerabilities. Remember from earlier in this chapter that CVSS is a component of SCAP.

Exposure of the Vulnerability   Cybersecurity analysts should also consider how exposed the vulnerability is to potential exploitation. For example, if an internal server has a serious SQL injection vulnerability but that server is accessible only from internal networks, remediating that issue may take a lower priority than remediating a less severe issue that is exposed to the Internet and, therefore, more vulnerable to external attack.

Identifying the optimal order of remediating vulnerabilities is more of an art than a science. Cybersecurity analysts must evaluate all of the information at their disposal and make informed decisions about the sequence of remediation that will deliver the most security value to their organization.

Testing and Implementing Fixes

Before deploying any remediation activity, cybersecurity professionals and other technologists should thoroughly test their planned fixes in a sandbox environment. This allows technologists to identify any unforeseen side effects of the fix and reduces the likelihood that remediation activities will disrupt business operations or cause damage to the organization's information assets.

Overcoming Barriers to Vulnerability Scanning

Vulnerability scanning is often a high priority for cybersecurity professionals, but other technologists in the organization may not see it as an important activity. Cybersecurity analysts should be aware of the barriers raised by others to vulnerability scanning and ways to address those concerns. Some common barriers to overcome include the following:

Service Degradations   The most common barrier to vulnerability scanning raised by technology professionals. Vulnerability scans consume network bandwidth and tie up the resources on systems that are the targets of scans. This may degrade system functionality and poses a risk of interrupting business processes. Cybersecurity professionals may address these concerns by tuning scans to consume less bandwidth and coordinating scan times with operational schedules. Figure 3.16 shows ways that administrators may adjust scan intensity in QualysGuard.

FIGURE 3.16   QualysGuard scan performance settings

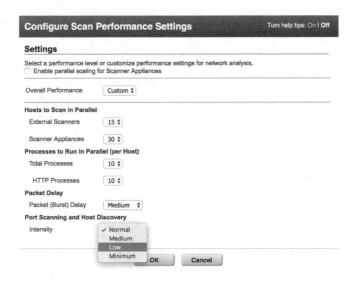

Customer Commitments   May create barriers to vulnerability scanning. *Memorandums of understanding (MOUs)* and *service-level agreements (SLAs)* with customers may create expectations related to uptime, performance, and security that the organization must fulfill. If scanning will negatively impact the organization's ability to meet customer commitments, customers may need to participate in the decision-making process.

Cybersecurity professionals can avoid issues with MOUs and SLAs by ensuring that they are involved in the creation of those agreements in the first place. Many concerns can be avoided if customer agreements include language that anticipates vulnerability scans and acknowledges that they may have an impact on performance. Most customers will understand the importance of conducting vulnerability scans as long as you provide them with advanced notice of the timing and potential impact of scans.

IT Governance and Change Management Processes   May create bureaucratic hurdles to making the configuration changes required to support scanning. Cybersecurity analysts should work within these organizational governance processes to obtain the resources and support required to support a vulnerability management program.

Summary

Vulnerability management programs allow cybersecurity professionals to identify and remediate gaps in the security of systems, applications, and devices under their control. Organizations that operate in highly regulated environments may be required to conduct vulnerability scanning by law or regulation, but many organizations outside those industries implement vulnerability management programs as a security best practice.

Cybersecurity analysts building a vulnerability management program should begin by identifying the scan requirements. This includes a review of possible scan targets and the selection of scan frequencies. Once these early decisions are made, analysts may configure and execute vulnerability scans on a regular basis, preferably through the use of automated scan scheduling systems.

Each vulnerability detected during a scan should be fed into a vulnerability remediation workflow that assigns tasks to the appropriate engineers, tracks completion of remediation effort, and follows up remediation work with a final vulnerability scan.

Working through the initial scan results may be an overwhelming task. Organizations should prioritize remediation work based on the criticality of the systems and information affected by the vulnerability, the difficulty of remediation, the severity of the vulnerability, and the exposure of the vulnerability to outside networks. As an organization cleans up its initial scan results, it may move on to an ongoing scanning approach that embraces continuous monitoring to quickly identify new vulnerabilities.

In Chapter 4, you'll learn how to analyze the results of vulnerability scans.

Exam Essentials

Requirements for vulnerability scanning may come from both internal and external sources.   In some cases, organizations may face legal and regulatory requirements to conduct vulnerability scanning. The Payment Card Industry Data Security Standard (PCI DSS) and Federal Information Security Management Act (FISMA) are two examples of these external requirements. In other cases, scanning may be driven by internal requirements, such as organizational policy.

Scan targets should be selected based on the results of discovery scans and organizational criteria.   Discovery scans provide organizations with an automated way to identify hosts that exist on the network and build an asset inventory. Cybersecurity professionals may then select scan targets based on data classification, system exposure, services offered, and the status of the system as a test, development, or production environment.

Scan frequency will vary based on the needs of the organization.   Administrators may choose to run scans on a daily, weekly, or monthly basis depending on the organization's risk appetite, regulatory requirements, licensing limitations, and business and technical constraints. Some organizations may choose to adopt continuous monitoring approaches to vulnerability detection.

Configuring scan settings allows customization to meet the organization's security requirements.   Cybersecurity professionals may customize scans by configuring the sensitivity level, including and excluding plug-ins, and supplementing basic network scans with information gathered from credentialed scans and server-based agents. Security teams may also conduct scans from more than one scan perspective, providing different views of the network.

Vulnerability scanners require maintenance like any other technology tool.   Administrators responsible for maintaining vulnerability scanning systems should perform two important administrative tasks. First, they should update the scanner software on a regular basis to correct security issues and add new functionality. Second, they should update plug-ins frequently to provide the most accurate and up-to-date vulnerability scans of their environment.

Organizations should use a consistent remediation workflow to identify, remediate, and test vulnerabilities.   Remediation workflows should be as automated as possible and integrate with other workflow technology used by the IT organization. As technologists correct vulnerabilities, they should validate that the remediation was effective through security testing and close out the vulnerability in the tracking system. The vulnerability management system should provide a range of reporting and alerting tools to supplement these efforts.

Cybersecurity professionals should prioritize remediation activities to make effective use of limited resources.   It simply isn't possible to correct every vulnerability immediately. Security teams should prioritize their work based on the criticality of the systems and information affected by the vulnerability, the difficulty of remediating the vulnerability, the severity of the vulnerability, and the exposure of the affected system.

Cybersecurity professionals must be prepared to overcome objections to scanning from other members of the IT team. Common objections to vulnerability scanning include the effect that service degradation caused by scanning will have on IT services, commitments to customers in MOUs and SLAs, and the use of IT governance and change management processes.

Lab Exercises

Activity 3.1: Installing a Vulnerability Scanner

In this lab, you will install the Nessus vulnerability management package on a system.

This lab requires access to a Linux system that you can use to install Nessus (preferably Ubuntu, Debian, Red Hat, SUSE, or Fedora.

Part 1: Obtain a Nessus Home Activation Code

- Visit the Nessus website (`https://www.tenable.com/products/nessus-home`) and fill out the form to obtain an activation code.

  Save the email containing the code for use during the installation and activation process.

Part 2: Download Nessus and Install It on Your System

1. Visit the Nessus download page (`https://www.tenable.com/products/nessus/select-your-operating-system#download`) and download the appropriate version of Nessus for your system.

2. Install Nessus following the documentation available at `https://docs.tenable.com/nessus/6_8/Content/UnixInstall.htm`.

3. Verify that your installation was successful by logging into your Nessus server.

Activity 3.2: Running a Vulnerability Scan

In this lab, you will run a vulnerability scan against a server of your choice. It is important to note that you should *never* run a vulnerability scan without permission.

You will need access to both your vulnerability scanning server that you built in Activity 3.1 and a target server for your scan. If you do not have a server to scan that you currently have permission to scan, you may build one using a cloud service provider, such as Amazon Web Services, Microsoft Azure, or Google Compute Platform.

Conduct a vulnerability scan against your server and save the resulting report. If you need assistance, consult the Nessus documentation. You will need the report from this vulnerability scan to complete the activities in the next chapter.

Review Questions

1. What federal law requires the use of vulnerability scanning on information systems operated by federal government agencies?

   A. HIPAA

   B. GLBA

   C. FISMA

   D. FERPA

2. Gary is the system administrator for a federal agency and is responsible for a variety of information systems. Which systems must be covered by vulnerability scanning programs?

   A. Only high-impact systems

   B. Only systems containing classified information

   C. High- or moderate-impact systems

   D. High-, moderate-, or low-impact systems

3. What tool can administrators use to help identify the systems present on a network prior to conducting vulnerability scans?

   A. Asset inventory

   B. Web application assessment

   C. Router

   D. DLP

4. Tonya is configuring vulnerability scans for a system that is subject to the PCI DSS compliance standard. What is the minimum frequency with which she must conduct scans?

   A. Daily

   B. Weekly

   C. Monthly

   D. Quarterly

5. Which one of the following is not an example of a vulnerability scanning tool?

   A. QualysGuard

   B. Snort

   C. Nessus

   D. OpenVAS

6. Bethany is the vulnerability management specialist for a large retail organization. She completed her last PCI DSS compliance scan in March. In April, the organization upgraded their point-of-sale system, and Bethany is preparing to conduct new scans. When must she complete the new scan?

    A. Immediately

    B. June

    C. December

    D. No scans are required

7. Renee is configuring her vulnerability management solution to perform credentialed scans of servers on her network. What type of account should she provide to the scanner?

    A. Domain administrator

    B. Local administrator

    C. Root

    D. Read-only

8. Jason is writing a report about a potential security vulnerability in a software product and wishes to use standardized product names to ensure that other security analysts understand the report. Which SCAP component can Jason turn to for assistance?

    A. CVSS

    B. CVE

    C. CPE

    D. OVAL

9. Bill would like to run an internal vulnerability scan on a system for PCI DSS compliance purposes. Who is authorized to complete one of these scans?

    A. Any employee of the organization

    B. An approved scanning vendor

    C. A PCI DSS service provider

    D. Any qualified individual

10. Which type of organization is the most likely to face a regulatory requirement to conduct vulnerability scans?

    A. Bank

    B. Hospital

    C. Government agency

    D. Doctor's office

11. What minimum level of impact must a system have under FISMA before the organization is required to determine what information about the system is discoverable by adversaries?

   A. Low

   B. Moderate

   C. High

   D. Severe

12. What term describes an organization's willingness to tolerate risk in their computing environment?

   A. Risk landscape

   B. Risk appetite

   C. Risk level

   D. Risk adaptation

13. Which one of the following factors is least likely to impact vulnerability scanning schedules?

   A. Regulatory requirements

   B. Technical constraints

   C. Business constraints

   D. Staff availability

14. Barry placed all of his organization's credit card processing systems on an isolated network dedicated to card processing. He has implemented appropriate segmentation controls to limit the scope of PCI DSS to those systems through the use of VLANs and firewalls. When Barry goes to conduct vulnerability scans for PCI DSS compliance purposes, what systems must he scan?

   A. Customer systems

   B. Systems on the isolated network

   C. Systems on the general enterprise network

   D. Both B and C

15. Ryan is planning to conduct a vulnerability scan of a business critical system using dangerous plug-ins. What would be the best approach for the initial scan?

   A. Run the scan against production systems to achieve the most realistic results possible.

   B. Run the scan during business hours.

   C. Run the scan in a test environment.

   D. Do not run the scan to avoid disrupting the business.

16. Which one of the following activities is not part of the vulnerability management life cycle?

A. Detection

B. Remediation

C. Reporting

D. Testing

17. What approach to vulnerability scanning incorporates information from agents running on the target servers?

A. Continuous monitoring

B. Ongoing scanning

C. On-demand scanning

D. Alerting

18. Brian is seeking to determine the appropriate impact categorization for a federal information system as he plans the vulnerability scanning controls for that system. After consulting management, he discovers that the system contains information that, if disclosed improperly, would have a serious adverse impact on the organization. How should this system be categorized?

A. Low impact

B. Moderate impact

C. High impact

D. Severe impact

19. Jessica is reading reports from vulnerability scans run by different part of her organization using different products. She is responsible for assigning remediation resources and is having difficulty prioritizing issues from different sources. What SCAP component can help Jessica with this task?

A. CVSS

B. CVE

C. CPE

D. XCCDF

20. Sarah would like to run an external vulnerability scan on a system for PCI DSS compliance purposes. Who is authorized to complete one of these scans?

A. Any employee of the organization

B. An approved scanning vendor

C. A PCI DSS service provider

D. Any qualified individual

Chapter

4

Analyzing Vulnerability Scans

THE COMPTIA CYBERSECURITY ANALYST+ EXAM OBJECTIVES COVERED IN THIS CHAPTER INCLUDE:

Domain 2: Vulnerability Management

✓ **2.2** Given a scenario, analyze the output resulting from a vulnerability scan.

✓ **2.3** Compare and contrast common vulnerabilities found in common targets within an organization.

Cybersecurity analysts spend a significant amount of time analyzing and interpreting the reports generated by vulnerability scanners. Although scanners are extremely effective at automating the manual work of vulnerability identification, the results that they generate require interpretation by a trained analyst to eliminate false positive reports, prioritize remediation activities, and delve into the root causes of vulnerability reports. In this chapter, you will learn how cybersecurity analysts apply their knowledge and experience to the review of vulnerability scan reports.

Reviewing and Interpreting Scan Reports

Vulnerability scan reports provide analysts with a significant amount of information that assists with the interpretation of the report. In addition to the high-level report examples shown in Chapter 3, "Designing a Vulnerability Management Program," vulnerability scanners provide detailed information about each vulnerability that they identify. Figure 4.1 shows an example of a single vulnerability reported by the Nessus vulnerability scanner.

FIGURE 4.1 Nessus vulnerability scan report

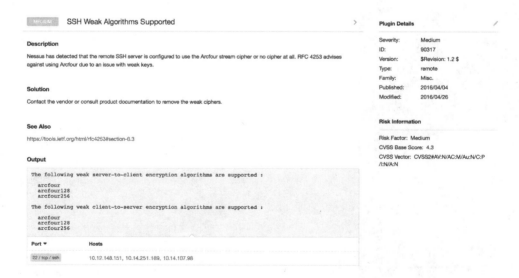

Let's take a look at this report, section by section, beginning in the top left and proceeding in a counterclockwise fashion.

At the very top of the report, we see two critical details: the *name of the vulnerability*, which offers a descriptive title, and the *overall severity* of the vulnerability, expressed as a general category, such as low, medium, high, or critical. In this example report, the scanner is reporting that a server's secure shell (SSH) service supports weak encryption algorithms. It is assigned to the medium severity category.

Next, the report provides a *detailed description* of the vulnerability. In this case, the vulnerability has a fairly short, two-sentence description, but these descriptions can be several paragraphs long depending on the complexity of the vulnerability. In this case, the description informs us that the server's SSH service only supports the insecure Arcfour stream cipher and explains that this service has an issue with weak encryption keys.

The next section of the report provides a *solution* to the vulnerability. When possible, the scanner offers detailed information about how system administrators, security professionals, network engineers, and/or application developers may correct the vulnerability. In this case, no detailed solution is available and administrators are advised to contact the vendor for instructions on removing the weak cipher support.

In the section of the report titled "See Also," the scanner provides *references* where administrators can find more details on the vulnerability described in the report. In this case, the scanner refers the reader to Internet Engineering Task Force (IETF) Request for Comments (RFC) document number 4253. RFC 4253 describes the SSH protocol in great detail. It includes the following advice regarding the Arcfour cipher: "The Arcfour cipher is believed to be compatible with the RC4 cipher Arcfour (and RC4) has problems with weak keys, and should be used with caution."

The *output* section of the report shows the detailed information returned by the remote system when probed for the vulnerability. This information can be extremely valuable to an analyst because it often provides the verbatim output returned by a command. Analysts can use this to better understand why the scanner is reporting a vulnerability, identify the location of a vulnerability, and potentially identify false positive reports. In this case, the output section shows the specific weak ciphers supported by the SSH server.

The *port/hosts* section provides details on the server(s) that contain the vulnerability as well as the specific services on that server that have the vulnerability. In this case, the same vulnerability exists on three different servers: those at IP addresses 10.12.148.151, 10.14.251.189 and 10.14.107.98. These three servers are all running an SSH service on TCP port 22 that supports the Arcfour cipher.

The *risk information* section includes useful information for assessing the severity of the vulnerability. In this case, the scanner reports that the vulnerability has an overall risk of Medium (consistent with the tag next to the vulnerability title). It also provides details on how the vulnerability rates when using the Common Vulnerability Scoring System (CVSS). In this case, the vulnerability has a CVSS base score of 4.3 and has the CVSS vector:

```
CVSS2#AV:N/AC:M/Au:N/C:P/I:N/A:N
```

We'll discuss the details of CVSS scoring in the next section of this chapter.

The final section of the vulnerability report provides details on the vulnerability scanner plug-in that detected the issue. This vulnerability was reported by Nessus plug-in ID 90317, which was published in April 2016.

> Although this chapter focuses on interpreting the details of a Nessus vulnerability scan, the process is extremely similar for other vulnerability scanners. The format of the reports generated by different products may vary, but they generally contain the same information. For example, Figure 4.2 shows the output of a Qualys vulnerability report.

FIGURE 4.2   Qualys vulnerability scan report

Understanding CVSS

The *Common Vulnerability Scoring System (CVSS)* is an industry standard for assessing the severity of security vulnerabilities. It provides a technique for scoring each vulnerability on a variety of measures. Cybersecurity analysts often use CVSS ratings to prioritize response actions.

Analysts scoring a new vulnerability begin by rating the vulnerability on six different measures. Each measure is given both a descriptive rating and a numeric score. The first three measures evaluate the exploitability of the vulnerability, whereas the last three evaluate the impact of the vulnerability.

Access Vector Metric

The *access vector metric* describes how an attacker would exploit the vulnerability and is assigned according to the criteria shown in Table 4.1.

TABLE 4.1   CVSS access vector metric

Value	Description	Score
Local (L)	The attacker must have physical or logical access to the affected system.	0.395
Adjacent Network (A)	The attacker must have access to the local network that the affected system is connected to.	0.646
Network (N)	The attacker can exploit the vulnerability remotely over a network.	1.000

Access Complexity Metric

The *access complexity metric* describes the difficulty of exploiting the vulnerability and is assigned according to the criteria shown in Table 4.2.

TABLE 4.2   CVSS access complexity metric

Value	Description	Score
High (H)	Exploiting the vulnerability requires "specialized" conditions that would be difficult to find.	0.350
Medium (M)	Exploiting the vulnerability requires "somewhat specialized" conditions.	0.610
Low (L)	Exploiting the vulnerability does not require any specialized conditions.	0.710

Authentication Metric

The *authentication metric* describes the authentication hurdles that an attacker would need to clear to exploit a vulnerability and is assigned according to the criteria in Table 4.3.

TABLE 4.3   CVSS authentication metric

Value	Description	Score
Multiple (M)	Attackers would need to authenticate two or more times to exploit the vulnerability.	0.450
Single (S)	Attackers would need to authenticate once to exploit the vulnerability.	0.560
None (N)	Attackers do not need to authenticate to exploit the vulnerability.	0.704

Confidentiality Metric

The *confidentiality metric* describes the type of information disclosure that might occur if an attacker successfully exploits the vulnerability. The confidentiality metric is assigned according the criteria in Table 4.4.

TABLE 4.4   CVSS confidentiality metric

Value	Description	Score
None (N)	There is no confidentiality impact.	0.000
Partial (P)	Access to some information is possible, but the attacker does not have control over what information is compromised.	0.275
Complete (C)	All information on the system is compromised.	0.660

Integrity Metric

The *integrity metric* describes the type of information alteration that might occur if an attacker successfully exploits the vulnerability. The integrity metric is assigned according to the criteria in Table 4.5.

TABLE 4.5   CVSS integrity metric

Value	Description	Score
None (N)	There is no integrity impact.	0.000
Partial (P)	Modification of some information is possible, but the attacker does not have control over what information is modified.	0.275
Complete (C)	The integrity of the system is totally compromised, and the attacker may change any information at will.	0.660

Availability Metric

The *availability metric* describes the type of disruption that might occur if an attacker successfully exploits the vulnerability. The availability metric is assigned according to the criteria in Table 4.6.

TABLE 4.6   CVSS authentication metric

Value	Description	Score
None (N)	There is no availability impact.	0.000
Partial (P)	The performance of the system is degraded.	0.275
Complete (C)	The system is completely shut down.	0.660

The Forum of Incident Response and Security Teams (FIRST) released CVSS version 3 in June 2015, but the new version of the standard has not yet been widely adopted. As of this writing, major vulnerability scanners still use CVSS version 2.

Interpreting the CVSS Vector

The *CVSS vector* uses a single-line format to convey the ratings of a vulnerability on all six of the metrics described in the preceding sections. For example, recall the CVSS vector presented in Figure 4.1:

```
CVSS2#AV:N/AC:M/Au:N/C:P/I:N/A:N
```

This vector contains seven components. The first section, "CVSS2#," simply informs the reader (human or system) that the vector was composed using CVSS version 2. The next six sections correspond to each of the six CVSS metrics. In this case, the SSH cipher vulnerability in Figure 4.1 received the following ratings:

- Access Vector: Network (score: 1.000)
- Access Complexity: Medium (score: 0.610)
- Authentication: None (score: 0.704)
- Confidentiality: Partial (score: 0.275)
- Integrity: None (score: 0.000)
- Availability: None (score: 0.000)

Summarizing CVSS Scores

The CVSS vector provides good detailed information on the nature of the risk posed by a vulnerability, but the complexity of the vector makes it difficult to use in prioritization exercises. For this reason, analysts can calculate the *CVSS base score*, which is a single number representing the overall risk posed by the vulnerability. Arriving at the base score requires first calculating the *exploitability score*, *impact score*, and *impact function*.

Calculating the Exploitability Score

Analysts may calculate the exploitability score for a vulnerability using this formula:

$$Exploitability = 20 \times AccessVector \times AccessComplexity \times Authentication$$

Plugging in values for our SSH vulnerability, we get

$$Exploitability = 20 \times 1.000 \times 0.610 \times 0.704$$

$$Exploitability = 8.589$$

Calculating the Impact Score

Analysts may calculate the impact score for a vulnerability using this formula:

$$Impact = 10.41 \times (1 - (1 - Confidentiality) \times (1 - Integrity) \times (1 - Availability))$$

Plugging in values for our SSH vulnerability, we get

$$Impact = 10.41 \times (1 - (1 - 0.275) \times (1 - 0) \times (1 - 0))$$

$$Impact = 10.41 \times (1 - (0.725) \times (1) \times (1))$$

$$Impact = 10.41 \times (1 - 0.725)$$

$$Impact = 10.41 \times 0.275$$

$$Impact = 2.863$$

Determining the Impact Function Value

The impact function is a simple check. If the impact score is 0, the impact function value is also 0. Otherwise, the impact function value is 1.176. So, in our example case:

$$ImpactFunction = 1.176$$

Calculating the Base Score

With all of this information at hand, we can now calculate the CVSS base score using this formula:

BaseScore = ((0.6 × Impact) + (0.4 × Exploitability) − 1.5) × ImpactFunction

Plugging in values for our SSH vulnerability, we get

BaseScore = ((0.6 × 2.863) + (0.4 × 8.589) − 1.5) × 1.176

BaseScore = (1.718 + 3.436 − 1.5) × 1.176

BaseScore = 3.654 × 1.176

BaseScore = 4.297

Rounding this result, we get a CVSS base score of 4.3, which is the same value found in Figure 4.1.

Categorizing CVSS Base Scores

Many vulnerability scanning systems further summarize CVSS results by using risk categories, rather than numeric risk ratings. For example, Nessus uses the risk rating scale shown in Table 4.7 to assign vulnerabilities to categories based on their CVSS base score.

TABLE 4.7   Nessus risk categories and CVSS scores

CVSS score	Risk category
Under 4.0	Low
4.0 or higher, but less than 6.0	Medium
6.0 or higher, but less than 10.0	High
10.0	Critical

Continuing with the SSH vulnerability example from Figure 4.1, we calculated the CVSS score for this vulnerability as 4.3. This places it into the Medium risk category, as shown in the header of Figure 4.1.

Validating Scan Results

Cybersecurity analysts interpreting reports often perform their own investigations to confirm the presence and severity of vulnerabilities. These investigations may include the use of external data sources that supply additional information valuable to the analysis.

False Positives

Vulnerability scanners are useful tools, but they aren't foolproof. Scanners do sometimes make mistakes for a variety of reasons. The scanner might not have sufficient access to the target system to confirm a vulnerability, or it might simply have an error in a plug-in that generates an erroneous vulnerability report. When a scanner reports a vulnerability that does not exist, this is known as a *false positive error.*

Cybersecurity analysts should confirm each vulnerability reported by a scanner. In some cases, this may be as simple as verifying that a patch is missing or an operating system is outdated. In other cases, verifying a vulnerability requires a complex manual process that simulates an exploit. For example, verifying a SQL injection vulnerability may require actually attempting an attack against a web application and verifying the result in the backend database.

When verifying a vulnerability, analysts should draw on their own expertise as well as the subject matter expertise of others throughout the organization. Database administrators, system engineers, network technicians, software developers, and other experts have domain knowledge that is essential to the evaluation of a potential false positive report.

Documented Exceptions

In some cases, an organization may decide not to remediate a vulnerability for one reason or another. For example, the organization may decide that business requirements dictate the use of an operating system that is no longer supported. Similarly, development managers may decide that the cost of remediating a vulnerability in a web application that is exposed only to the internal network outweighs the security benefit.

Unless analysts take some action to record these exceptions, vulnerability scans will continue to report them each time a scan runs. It's good practice to document exceptions in the vulnerability management system so that the scanner knows to ignore them in future reports. This reduces the level of noise in scan reports and increases their usefulness to analysts.

Be careful when deciding to allow an exception. As discussed in Chapter 3, many organizations are subject to compliance requirements for vulnerability scanning. Creating an exception may violate those compliance obligations or go against best practices for security.

Understanding Informational Results

Vulnerability scanners often supply very detailed information when run using default configurations. Not everything reported by a vulnerability scanner actually represents a significant security issue. Nevertheless, scanners provide as much information as they are able to determine to show the types of information that an attacker might be able to gather when conducting a reconnaissance scan.

Figure 4.3 provides an example of a high-level report generated from a vulnerability scan run against a web server. Note that about two-thirds of the vulnerabilities in this report fit into the "Info" risk category. This indicates that the plug-ins providing results are not even categorized according to the CVSS. Instead, they are simply informational results. Most organizations do not go to the extent of removing all possible sources of information about a system because it can be difficult, if not impossible, to do so.

FIGURE 4.3 Scan report showing vulnerabilities and best practices

	Severity ▲	Plugin Name	Plugin Family	Count
☐	HIGH	CGI Generic SQL Injection (blind, time based)	CGI abuses	1
☐	MEDIUM	Web Application Potentially Vulnerable to Clickjacking	Web Servers	2
☐	MEDIUM	ASP.NET DEBUG Method Enabled	CGI abuses	1
☐	MEDIUM	CGI Generic Cookie Injection Scripting	CGI abuses	1
☐	MEDIUM	CGI Generic HTML Injections (quick test)	CGI abuses : XSS	1
☐	MEDIUM	CGI Generic XSS (comprehensive test)	CGI abuses : XSS	1
☐	MEDIUM	CGI Generic XSS (extended patterns)	CGI abuses : XSS	1
☐	MEDIUM	CGI Generic XSS (quick test)	CGI abuses : XSS	1
☐	INFO	CGI Generic Tests Load Estimation (all tests)	CGI abuses	2
☐	INFO	CGI Generic Tests Timeout	CGI abuses	2
☐	INFO	External URLs	Web Servers	2
☐	INFO	HTTP Methods Allowed (per directory)	Web Servers	2
☐	INFO	HTTP Server Type and Version	Web Servers	2
☐	INFO	HyperText Transfer Protocol (HTTP) Information	Web Servers	2
☐	INFO	Missing or Permissive Content-Security-Policy HTTP Res...	CGI abuses	2
☐	INFO	Missing or Permissive X-Frame-Options HTTP Response ...	CGI abuses	2

Scan Details

Name:	Main Website
Status:	Completed
Policy:	Web Application Tests
Scanner:	Local Scanner
Folder:	My Scans
Start:	Today at 1:30 AM
End:	Today at 3:20 AM
Elapsed:	2 hours
Targets:	

Vulnerabilities

- High
- Medium
- Info

A cybersecurity analyst encountering the scan report in Figure 4.3 should first turn his or her attention to the high-severity SQL injection vulnerability that exists. Once that is remediated, seven medium-severity vulnerabilities require attention. The remaining informational vulnerabilities can likely be left alone. Many organizations will adopt a formal policy regarding how they handle these informational messages. For example, some organizations may decide that once a message appears in two or three consecutive scans, they will create a journal entry documenting the actions they took in response to the message or the reasons they chose not to take actions. This approach is particularly important for highly audited organizations that have stringent compliance requirements. Creating a formal record of the decision-making process satisfies auditors that the organization conducted due diligence.

Reconciling Scan Results with Other Data Sources

Vulnerability scans should never take place in a vacuum. Cybersecurity analysts interpreting these reports should also turn to other sources of security information as they perform their analysis. Valuable information sources for this process include the following:

▪ *Logs* from servers, applications, network devices, and other sources that might contain information about possible attempts to exploit detected vulnerabilities

▪ *Security information and event management (SIEM)* systems that correlate log entries from multiple sources and provide actionable intelligence

▪ *Configuration management systems* that provide information on the operating system and applications installed on a system

Each of these information sources can prove invaluable when an analyst attempts to reconcile a scan report with the reality of the organization's computing environment.

Trend Analysis

Trend analysis is also an important part of a vulnerability scanning program. Managers should watch for overall trends in vulnerabilities, including the number of new vulnerabilities arising over time, the age of existing vulnerabilities, and the time required to remediate vulnerabilities. Figure 4.4 shows an example of the trend analysis reports available in Nessus SecurityCenter.

FIGURE 4.4   Vulnerability trend analysis

Source: Tenable Network Security, Inc.

Common Vulnerabilities

Each vulnerability scanning system contains plug-ins able to detect thousands of possible vulnerabilities, ranging from major SQL injection flaws in web applications to more mundane information disclosure issues with network devices. Though it's impossible to discuss each of these vulnerabilities in a book of any length, cybersecurity analysts should be familiar with the most commonly detected vulnerabilities and some of the general categories that cover many different vulnerability variants.

Chapter 3 discussed the importance of regularly updating vulnerability scanners to make them effective against newly discovered threats. Although this is true, it is also important to note that even old vulnerabilities can present significant issues to the security of organizations. Each year Verizon conducts a widely respected analysis of all the data breaches they investigated over the course of the prior year. Figure 4.5 shows some of the results from the 2016 Data Breach Investigations Report.

FIGURE 4.5   Vulnerabilities exploited in 2015 by year of initial discovery

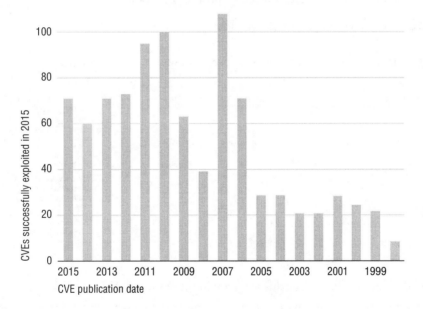

Figure 4.5 underscores the importance of addressing old vulnerabilities and the stark reality that many organizations fail to do so. Many of the vulnerabilities exploited during data breaches in 2015 exploited vulnerabilities discovered more than a *decade* earlier. That's an astounding statistic.

Server and Endpoint Vulnerabilities

Computer systems are quite complex. The operating systems run on both servers and end-points comprising millions of lines of code, and the differing combinations of applications they run make each system fairly unique. It's no surprise, therefore, that many of the vulnerabilities detected by scans exist on server and endpoint systems, and these vulnerabilities are often among the most complex to remediate.

Missing Patches

Applying security patches to systems should be one of the core practices of any information security program, but this routine task is often neglected due to a lack of resources for preventive maintenance. One of the most common alerts from a vulnerability scan is that one or more systems on the network are running an outdated version of an operating system or application and require security patch(es).

Figure 4.6 shows an example of one of these scan results. The server located at 10.64.142.211 has a remote code execution vulnerability. Though the scan result is fairly brief, it does contain quite a bit of helpful information:

FIGURE 4.6   Missing patch vulnerability

- The description tells us that this is a flaw in the Windows HTTP stack.

- The service information in the Output section of the report confirms that the server is running an HTTPS service on TCP port 443.

- We see in the header that this is a critical vulnerability, and this is confirmed in the Risk Information section, where we see that it has a CVSS base score of 10.

- We can parse the CVSS vector to learn a little more about this vulnerability:

  - *AV:N* tells us that the vulnerability can be exploited remotely by a hacker over the network.

- *AC:L* tells us that the access complexity is low, meaning that a relatively unskilled attacker can exploit it.
- *Au:N* tells us that no authentication is required to exploit the vulnerability.
- *C:C*, *I:C*, and *A:C* tell us that someone exploiting this vulnerability is likely to completely compromise the confidentiality, integrity, and availability of the system.

 I won't continue to parse the CVSS vectors for each of the vulnerabilities discussed in this chapter. However, you may wish to do so on your own as an exercise in assessing the severity of a vulnerability.

Fortunately, there is an easy way to fix this problem. The Solution section tells us that Microsoft released patches for the affected operating systems, and the See Also section provides a direct link to the Microsoft security bulletin (MS15-034) that describes the issue and solution in greater detail.

Mobile Device Security

This section refers to the vulnerabilities typically found on traditional servers and endpoints, but it's important to note that mobile devices have a host of security issues of their own and must be carefully managed and patched to remain secure.

The administrators of mobile devices can use a mobile device management (MDM) solution to manage the configuration of those devices, automatically installing patches, requiring the use of encryption, and providing remote wiping functionality. MDM solutions may also restrict the applications that can be run on a mobile device to those that appear on an approved list.

That said, mobile devices do not typically show up on vulnerability scans because they are not often sitting on the network when those scans run. Therefore, administrators should pay careful attention to the security of those devices even when they do not show up as requiring attention after a vulnerability scan.

Unsupported Operating Systems and Applications

Software vendors eventually discontinue support for every product they make. This is true for operating systems as well as applications. Once they announce the final end of support for a product, organizations that continue running the outdated software put themselves at a significant risk of attack. The vendor simply will not investigate or correct security flaws that arise in the product after that date. Organizations continuing to run the unsupported product are on their own from a security perspective, and unless you happen to maintain a team of operating system developers, that's not a good situation to find yourself in.

Perhaps the most famous end of support for a major operating system occurred in July 2015 when Microsoft discontinued support for the more-than-a-decade-old Windows Server 2003. Figure 4.7 shows an example of the report generated by Nessus when it identifies a server running this outdated operating system.

FIGURE 4.7   Unsupported operating system vulnerability

We can see from this report that the scan detected two servers on the network running Windows Server 2003. The description of the vulnerability provides a stark assessment of what lies in store for organizations continuing to run any unsupported operating system:

> Lack of support implies that no new security patches for the product will be released by the vendor. As a result, it is likely to contain security vulnerabilities. Furthermore, Microsoft is unlikely to investigate or acknowledge reports of vulnerabilities.

The solution for organizations running unsupported operating systems is simple in its phrasing but complex in implementation. "Upgrade to a version of Windows that is currently supported" is a pretty straightforward instruction, but it may pose a significant challenge for organizations running applications that simply can't be upgraded to newer versions of Windows. In cases where the organization simply must continue using an unsupported operating system, best practice dictates isolating the system as much as possible, preferably not connecting it to any network, and applying as many compensating security controls as possible, such as increased monitoring and implementing strict network firewall rules.

Buffer Overflows

Buffer overflow attacks occur when an attacker manipulates a program into placing more data into an area of memory than is allocated for that program's use. The goal is to overwrite other information in memory with instructions that may be executed by a different process running on the system.

Buffer overflow attacks are quite commonplace and tend to persist for many years after they are initially discovered. For example, the 2016 Verizon Data Breach Investigation report identified ten vulnerabilities that were responsible for 85 percent of the compromises in their study. Among the top ten were four overflow issues:

- CVE 1999-1058: Buffer overflow in Vermillion FTP Daemon

- CVE 2001-0876: Buffer overflow in Universal Plug and Play (UPnP) on Windows 98, 98SE, ME, and XP

- CVE 2002-0126: Buffer overflow in BlackMoon FTP Server 1.0 through 1.5

- CVE 2003-0818: Multiple integer overflows in Microsoft ASN.1 library

> One of the listed vulnerabilities is an "integer overflow." This is simply a variant of a buffer overflow where the result of an arithmetic operation attempts to store an integer that is too large to fit in the specified buffer.

The four-digit number following the letters CVE in each vulnerability title indicates the year that the vulnerability was discovered. In a study of breaches that took place in 2015, four of the top ten issues causing breaches were exploits of overflow vulnerabilities that were between 12 and 16 years old!

Cybersecurity analysts discovering a buffer overflow vulnerability during a vulnerability scan should seek out a patch that corrects the issue. In most cases, the scan report will directly identify an available patch.

Privilege Escalation

Privilege escalation attacks seek to increase the level of access that an attacker has to a target system. They exploit vulnerabilities that allow the transformation of a normal user account into a more privileged account, such as the root superuser account.

In October 2016, security researchers announced the discovery of a Linux kernel vulnerability dubbed Dirty COW. This vulnerability, present in the Linux kernel for nine years, was extremely easy to exploit and provided successful attackers with administrative control of affected systems.

In an attempt to spread the word about this vulnerability and encourage prompt patching of Linux kernels, security researchers set up the dirtycow.ninja website, shown in Figure 4.8. This site provides details on the flaw and corrective measures.

FIGURE 4.8   Dirty COW website

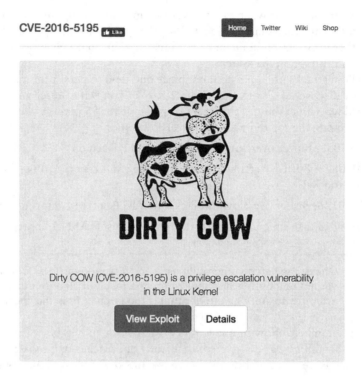

Arbitrary Code Execution

Arbitrary code execution vulnerabilities allow an attacker to run software of his or her choice on the targeted system. This can be a catastrophic event, particularly if the vulnerability allows the attacker to run the code with administrative privileges. *Remote code execution* vulnerabilities are an even more dangerous subset of code execution vulnerabilities because the attacker can exploit the vulnerability over a network connection without having physical or logical access to the target system.

Figure 4.9 shows an example of a remote code execution vulnerability detected by Nessus.

Notice that the CVSS access vector in Figure 4.9 shows that the access vector for this vulnerability is network based. This is consistent with the description of a remote code execution vulnerability. The impact metrics in the vector show that the attacker can exploit this vulnerability to completely compromise the system.

Fortunately, as with most vulnerabilities detected by scans, there is an easy fix for the problem. Microsoft issued patches for the versions of Windows affected by the issue and describes them in Microsoft Security Bulletin MS14-066.

FIGURE 4.9 Code execution vulnerability

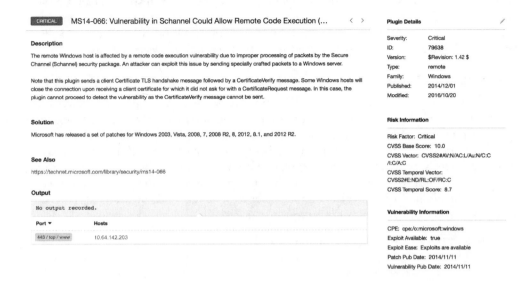

Insecure Protocol Use

Many of the older protocols used on networks in the early days of the Internet were designed without security in mind. They often failed to use encryption to protect usernames, passwords, and the content sent over an open network, exposing the users of the protocol to eavesdropping attacks. Telnet is one example of an insecure protocol used to gain command-line access to a remote server. The File Transfer Protocol (FTP) provides the ability to transfer files between systems but does not incorporate security features. Figure 4.10 shows an example of a scan report that detected a system that supports the insecure FTP protocol.

FIGURE 4.10 FTP cleartext authentication vulnerability

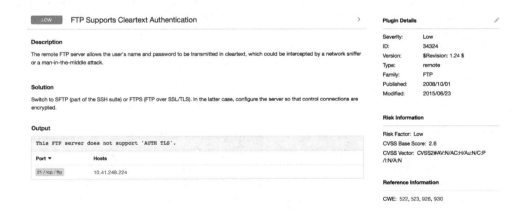

The solution for this issue is to simply switch to a more secure protocol. Fortunately, encrypted alternatives exist for both Telnet and FTP. System administrators can use the Secure Shell (SSH) as a secure replacement for Telnet when seeking to gain command-line access to a remote system. Similarly, the Secure File Transfer Protocol (SFTP) and FTP-Secure (FTPS) both provide a secure method to transfer files between systems.

Debugging Modes

Many application development platforms support *debug modes* that give developers crucial information needed to troubleshoot applications in the development process. Debug mode typically provides detailed information on the inner workings of an application and server, as well as supporting databases. Although this information can be useful to developers, it can inadvertently assist an attacker seeking to gain information about the structure of a database, authentication mechanisms used by an application, or other details. For this reason, vulnerability scans do alert on the presence of debug mode on scanned servers. Figure 4.11 shows an example of this type of scan result.

FIGURE 4.11   Debug mode vulnerability

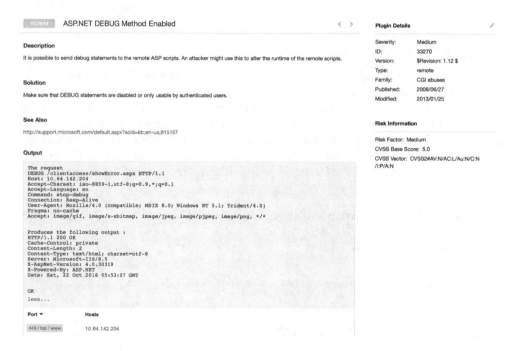

In this particular example, the target system appears to be a Windows Server supporting the ASP.NET development environment. The Output section of the report demonstrates that the server responds when sent a DEBUG request by a client.

Solving this issue requires the cooperation of developers and disabling debug modes on systems with public exposure. In mature organizations, software development should always take place in a dedicated development environment that is only accessible from private networks. Developers should be encouraged (or ordered!) to conduct their testing only on systems dedicated to that purpose, and it would be entirely appropriate to enable debug mode on those servers. There should be no need for supporting this capability on public-facing systems.

Network Vulnerabilities

Modern interconnected networks use a complex combination of infrastructure components and network appliances to provide widespread access to secure communications capabilities. These networks and their component parts are also susceptible to security vulnerabilities that may be detected during a vulnerability scan.

Missing Firmware Updates

Operating systems and applications aren't the only devices that require regular security updates. Vulnerability scans may also detect security problems in network devices that require firmware updates from the manufacturer to correct. These vulnerabilities result in reports similar to the operating system missing patch report in Figure 4.6 and typically direct administrators to the location on the vendor's site where the firmware update is available for download.

SSL and TLS Issues

The *Secure Sockets Layer (SSL)* protocol and its successor, *Transport Layer Security (TLS)*, offer a secure means to exchange information over the Internet and private networks. Although these protocols can be used to encrypt almost any type of network communication, they are most commonly used to secure connections to web servers and are familiar to end users as the "S" in HTTPS.

Many cybersecurity analysts incorrectly use the acronym SSL to refer to both the SSL and TLS protocols. It's important to understand that SSL is no longer secure and should not be used. TLS is a replacement for SSL that offers similar functionality but does not have the security flaws contained in SSL. Be careful to use this terminology precisely and question those who use the term SSL about whether they are really referring to TLS to avoid ambiguity.

Outdated SSL/TLS Versions

SSL is no longer considered secure and should not be used on production systems. The same is true for early versions of TLS. Vulnerability scanners may report that web servers are using these protocols, and cybersecurity analysts should understand that any connections making use of these outdated versions of SSL and TLS may be subject to eavesdropping attacks. Figure 4.12 shows an example of a scan report from a network containing multiple systems that support the outdated SSL version 3.

FIGURE 4.12   Outdated SSL version vulnerability

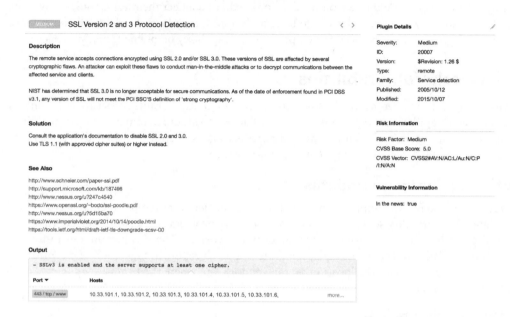

The administrators of servers supporting outdated versions of SSL and TLS should disable support for these older protocols on their servers and support only newer protocols, such as TLS version 1.2.

Insecure Cipher Use

SSL and TLS are commonly described as cryptographic algorithms, but in fact, this is not the case. The SSL and TLS protocols describe how cryptographic ciphers may be used to secure network communications, but they are not cryptographic ciphers themselves. Instead, they allow administrators to designate the cryptographic ciphers that can be used with those protocols on a server-by-server basis. When a client and server wish to communicate using SSL/TLS, they exchange a list of ciphers that each system supports and agree on a mutually acceptable cipher.

Some ciphers contain vulnerabilities that render them insecure because of their susceptibility to eavesdropping attacks. For example, Figure 4.13 shows a scan report from a system that supports the insecure RC4 cipher.

Solving this common problem requires altering the set of supported ciphers on the affected server and ensuring that only secure ciphers may be used.

FIGURE 4.13   Insecure SSL cipher vulnerability

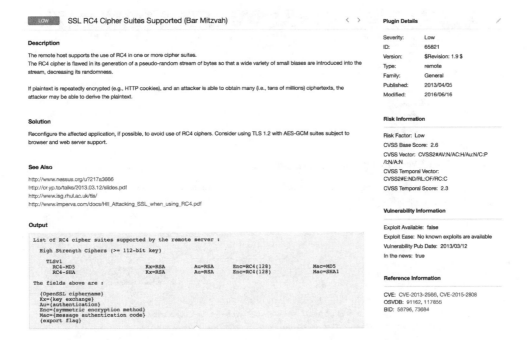

Certificate Problems

SSL and TLS rely on the use of digital certificates to validate the identity of servers and exchange cryptographic keys. Website users are familiar with the error messages displayed in web browsers, such as that shown in Figure 4.14. These errors often contain extremely important information about the security of the site being accessed but, unfortunately, are all too often ignored.

Vulnerability scans may also detect issues with the certificates presented by servers that support SSL and/or TLS. Common errors include the following:

Mismatch between the Name on the Certificate and the Name of the Server   This is a very serious error because it may indicate the use of a certificate taken from another site. It's the digital equivalent of someone using a fake ID "borrowed" from a friend.

Expiration of the Digital Certificate   Digital certificates have validity periods and expiration dates. When you see an expired certificate, it most likely means that the server administrator failed to renew the certificate in a timely manner.

FIGURE 4.14 Invalid certificate warning

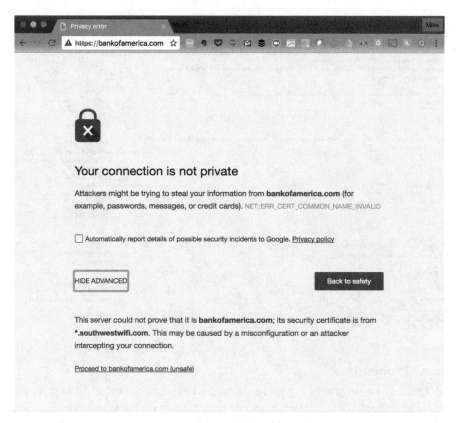

Unknown Certificate Authority (CA) Anyone can create a digital certificate, but digital certificates are useful only if the recipient of a certificate trusts the entity that issued it. Operating systems and browsers contain instructions to trust well-known CAs but will show an error if they encounter a certificate issued by an unknown or untrusted CA.

The error shown in Figure 4.14 indicates that the user is attempting to access a website that is presenting an invalid certificate. From the URL bar, we see that the user is attempting to access bankofamerica.com. However, looking in the details section, we see that the certificate being presented was issued to southwestwifi.com. This is a typical occurrence on networks that use a captive portal to authenticate users joining a public wireless network. This example is from the in-flight Wi-Fi service offered by Southwest Airlines. The error points out to the user that he or she is not communicating with the intended website owned by Bank of America and should not provide sensitive information.

Domain Name Service (DNS)

The *Domain Name System (DNS)* provides a translation service between domain names and IP addresses. DNS allows end users to remember user-friendly domain names, such as apple.com, and not worry about the mind-numbing IP addresses actually used by those servers.

DNS servers are a common source of vulnerabilities on enterprise networks. Despite the seemingly simple nature of the service, DNS has a track record of many serious security vulnerabilities and requires careful configuration and patching. Many of the issues with DNS services are those already discussed in this chapter, such as buffer overflows, missing patches, and code execution vulnerabilities, but others are specific to the DNS service.

Figure 4.15 shows an example of a vulnerability scan that detected a *DNS amplification* vulnerability on two servers on an organization's network. In this type of attack, the attacker sends spoofed DNS requests to a DNS server that are carefully designed to elicit responses that are much larger in size than the original requests. These large response packets then go to the spoofed address where the DNS server believes the query originated. The IP address used in the spoofed request is actually the target of a denial-of-service attack and is bombarded by very large responses from DNS servers all over the world to queries that it never sent. When conducted in sufficient volume, DNS amplification attacks can completely overwhelm the targeted systems, rendering them inoperable.

FIGURE 4.15   DNS amplification vulnerability

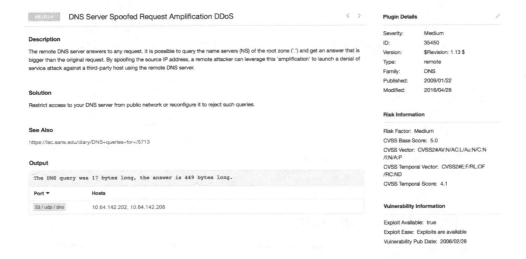

Internal IP Disclosure

IP addresses come in two different variants: public IP addresses, which can be routed over the Internet, and private IP addresses, which can be used only on local networks. Any server that is accessible over the Internet must have a public IP address to allow that access, but that address is typically managed by a firewall that uses the *Network Address Translation (NAT)* protocol to map that public address to the server's true, private IP address. Systems on the local network can use the server's private address to access it directly, but remote systems should never be aware of that address.

Servers that are not properly configured may leak their private IP addresses to remote systems. This can occur when the system includes its own IP address in the header information returned in the response to an HTTP request. The server is not aware that NAT is in use, so it uses the private address in its response. Attackers can use this information to learn more about the internal configuration of a firewalled network. Figure 4.16 shows an example of this type of information disclosure vulnerability.

FIGURE 4.16   Internal IP disclosure vulnerability

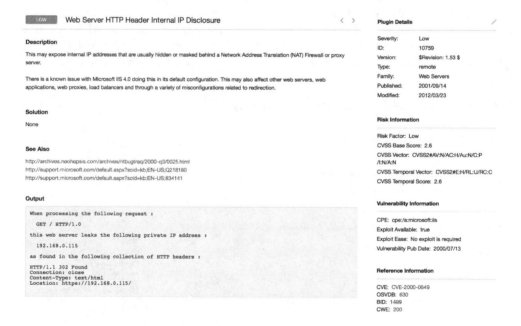

Virtual Private Network Issues

Many organizations use *virtual private networks (VPNs)* to provide employees with secure remote access to the organization's network. As with any application protocol, administrators must ensure that the VPN services offered by the organization are fully patched to current levels. In addition, VPNs require the use of cryptographic ciphers and suffer from similar issues as SSL and TLS when they support the use of insecure ciphers.

Virtualization Vulnerabilities

Most modern datacenters make extensive use of *virtualization* technology to allow multiple guest systems to share the same underlying hardware. In a virtualized datacenter, the virtual host hardware runs a special operating system known as a *hypervisor* that mediates access to the underlying hardware resources. Virtual machines then run on top of this virtual infrastructure provided by the hypervisor, running standard operating systems such as Windows and Linux variants. The virtual machines may not be aware that they are running in a virtualized environment because the hypervisor tricks them into thinking that they have normal access to the underlying hardware when, in reality, that hardware is shared with other systems.

Figure 4.17 provides an illustration of how a hypervisor mediates access to the underlying hardware resources in a virtual host to support multiple virtual guest machines.

FIGURE 4.17   Inside a virtual host

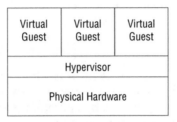

The example described in this chapter, where the hypervisor runs directly on top of physical hardware, is known as bare-metal virtualization. This is the approach commonly used in datacenter environments. There is another type of virtualization, known as hosted virtualization, where a host operating system sits between the hardware and the hypervisor. This is commonly used in cases where the user of an endpoint system wants to simultaneously run multiple operating systems on that device. Parallels is a popular hosted virtualization platform for the Mac.

VM Escape

Virtual machine escape vulnerabilities are the most serious issue that may exist in a virtualized environment, particularly when a virtual host runs systems of differing security levels. In an escape attack, the attacker has access to a single virtual host and then manages to leverage that access to intrude on the resources assigned to a different virtual machine. The hypervisor is supposed to prevent this type of access by restricting a virtual machine's access to only those resources assigned to that machine. Escape attacks allow a process running on the virtual machine to "escape" those hypervisor restrictions.

Management Interface Access

Virtualization engineers use the management interface for a virtual infrastructure to configure the virtualization environment, set up new guest machines, and regulate access to resources. This management interface is extremely sensitive from a security perspective, and access should be tightly controlled to prevent unauthorized individuals from gaining access. In addition to using strong multifactor authentication on the management interface, cybersecurity professionals should ensure that the interface is never directly accessible from a public network. Vulnerability scans that detect the presence of an accessible management interface will report this as a security concern.

Virtual Host Patching

This chapter already discussed the importance of promptly applying security updates to operating systems, applications, and network devices. It is equally important to ensure that virtualization platforms receive security updates that may affect the security of virtual guests or the entire platform. Patches may correct vulnerabilities that allow virtual machine escape attacks or other serious security flaws.

Virtual Guest Issues

Cybersecurity analysts should think of each guest machine running in a virtualized environment as a separate server that requires the same security attention as any other device on the network. Guest operating systems and applications running on the guest OS must be promptly patched to correct security vulnerabilities and be otherwise well maintained. There's no difference from a security perspective between a physical server and a virtualized server.

Virtual Network Issues

As data centers become increasingly virtualized, a significant amount of network traffic never actually touches a network! Communications between virtual machines that reside on the same physical hardware can occur in memory without ever touching a physical network. For this reason, virtual networks must be maintained with the same attention to security that administrators would apply to physical networks. This includes the use of virtual firewalls to control the flow of information between systems and the isolation of systems of differing security levels on different virtual network segments.

Internet of Things (IoT)

In some environments, cybersecurity analysts may encounter the use of *supervisory control and data acquisition (SCADA)* systems, *industrial control systems (ICS)*, and other examples of the *Internet of Things (IoT)*. These systems allow the connection of physical devices and processes to networks and provide tremendous sources of data for organizations seeking to make their business processes more efficient and effective. However, they also introduce new security concerns that may arise on vulnerability scans.

As with any other device on a network, IoT devices may have security vulnerabilities and are subject to network-based attacks. However, it is often more difficult to patch IoT devices than their traditional server counterparts because it is difficult to obtain patches. IoT device manufacturers may not use automatic update mechanisms, and the only way that cybersecurity analysts may become aware of an update is through a vulnerability scan or by proactively subscribing to the security bulletins issued by IoT device manufacturers.

IoT Uprising

On October 21, 2016, a widespread distributed denial-of-service (DDoS) attack shut down large portions of the Internet, affecting services run by Amazon, The New York Times, Twitter, Box, and other providers. The attack came in waves over the course of the day and initially mystified technologists seeking to bring systems back online.

Investigation later revealed that the outages occurred when Dyn, a global provider of DNS services, suffered a debilitating attack that prevented it from answering DNS queries. Dyn received massive amounts of traffic that overwhelmed its servers.

The source of all of that traffic? Attackers used an IoT botnet named Mirai to leverage the bandwidth available to baby monitors, DVRs, security cameras, and other IoT devices in the homes of normal people. Those botnetted devices received instructions from a yet-unknown attacker to simultaneously bombard Dyn with requests, knocking it (and a good part of the Internet!) offline.

Web Application Vulnerabilities

Web applications are complex environments that often rely not only on web servers but also on backend databases, authentication servers, and other components to provide services to end users. These web applications may also contain security holes that allow attackers to gain a foothold on a network and modern vulnerability scanners are able to probe web applications for these vulnerabilities.

 Network vulnerability scanners typically have a limited ability to scan for web application vulnerabilities. Many organizations choose to supplement these scanners with dedicated web application vulnerability scanners. You'll learn more about these packages in Chapter 13, "Cybersecurity Toolkit."

Injection Attacks

Injection attacks occur when an attacker is able to send commands through a web server to a backend system, bypassing normal security controls and fooling the backend system into believing that the request came from the web server. The most common form of this attack is the *SQL injection attack*, which exploits web applications to send unauthorized commands to a backend database server.

Web applications often receive input from users and use it to compose a database query that provides results that are sent back to a user. For example, consider the search function on an e-commerce site. If a user enters **orange tiger pillows** into the search box, the web server needs to know what products in the catalog might match this search term. It might send a request to the backend database server that looks something like this:

```
SELECT ItemName, ItemDescription, ItemPrice
FROM Products
WHERE ItemName LIKE '%orange%' AND
ItemName LIKE '%tiger%' AND
ItemName LIKE '%pillow%'
```

This command retrieves a list of items that can be included in the results returned to the end user. In a SQL injection attack, the attacker might send a very unusual-looking request to the web server, perhaps searching for

```
orange tiger pillow'; SELECT CustomerName, CreditCardNumber FROM Orders; --
```

If the web server simply passes this request along to the database server, it would do this (with a little reformatting for ease of viewing):

```
SELECT ItemName, ItemDescription, ItemPrice
FROM Products
WHERE ItemName LIKE '%orange%' AND
ItemName LIKE '%tiger%' AND
ItemName LIKE '%pillow';
SELECT CustomerName, CreditCardNumber
FROM Orders;
--%'
```

This command, if successful, would run two different SQL queries (separated by the semicolon). The first would retrieve the product information, and the second would retrieve a listing of customer names and credit card numbers.

The two best ways to protect against SQL injection attacks are input validation and the enforcement of least privilege restrictions on database access. Input validation ensures that users don't provide unexpected text to the web server. It would block the use of the apostrophe that is needed to "break out" of the original SQL query. Least privilege restricts the tables that may be accessed by a web server and can prevent the retrieval of credit card information by a process designed to handle catalog information requests.

Vulnerability scanners can detect injection vulnerabilities, such as the one shown in Figure 4.18. When cybersecurity analysts notice a potential injection vulnerability, they should work closely with developers to validate that the vulnerability exists and fix the affected code.

FIGURE 4.18   SQL injection vulnerability

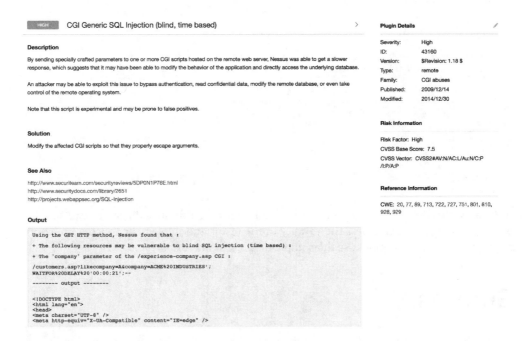

Cross-Site Scripting

In a *cross-site scripting (XSS)* attack, an attacker embeds scripting commands on a website that will later be executed by an unsuspecting visitor accessing the site. The idea is to trick a user visiting a trusted site into executing malicious code placed there by an untrusted third party.

Figure 4.19 shows an example of an XSS vulnerability detected during a Nessus vulnerability scan.

FIGURE 4.19   Cross-site scripting vulnerability

Cybersecurity analysts discovering potential XSS vulnerabilities during a scan should work with developers to assess the validity of the result and implement appropriate controls to prevent this type of attack, such as implementing input validation.

Summary

Vulnerability management programs produce a significant amount of information that requires analysis by trained cybersecurity professionals. Cybersecurity analysts must be familiar with the interpretation of vulnerability scan results and the prioritization of remediation efforts to provide value to their organizations.

Vulnerability scanners usually rank detected issues using the Common Vulnerability Scoring System (CVSS). CVS provides six different measures of each vulnerability: the access vector metric, the access complexity metric, the authentication metric, the confidentiality metric, the integrity metric, and the availability metric. Together, these metrics provide a look at the potential that a vulnerability will be successfully exploited and the impact it could have on the organization.

As analysts interpret scan results, they should be careful to watch for common issues. False positive reports occur when the scanner erroneously reports a vulnerability that does not actually exist. If an analyst is suspicious about the accuracy of a result, they should verify it manually. When verifying a vulnerability, analysts should draw on their own expertise as well as the subject matter expertise of others throughout the organization.

To successfully interpret vulnerability reports, analysts must be familiar with the vulnerabilities that commonly occur. Common server and endpoint vulnerabilities include missing patches, unsupported operating systems and applications, buffer overflows, privilege escalation, arbitrary code execution, insecure protocol usage, and the presence of debugging modes. Common network vulnerabilities include missing firmware updates, SSL/TLS issues, DNS misconfigurations, internal IP disclosures, and VPN issues. Virtualization vulnerabilities include virtual machine escape vulnerabilities, management interface access, missing patches on virtual hosts, and security misconfigurations on virtual guests and virtual networks.

Exam Essentials

Vulnerability scan reports provide critical information to cybersecurity analysts. In addition to providing details about the vulnerabilities present on a system, vulnerability scan reports also offer crucial severity and troubleshooting information. The report typically includes the request and response that triggered a vulnerability report as well as a suggested solution to the problem.

The Common Vulnerability Scoring System (CVSS) provides a consistent standard for scoring vulnerability severity. The CVSS base score computes a standard measure on a 10-point scale that incorporates information about the access vector required to exploit a vulnerability, the complexity of the exploit, and the authentication required to execute an attack. The base score also considers the impact of the vulnerability on the confidentiality, integrity, and availability of the affected system.

Servers and endpoint devices are a common source of vulnerability. Missing patches and outdated operating systems are two of the most common vulnerability sources and are easily corrected by proactive device maintenance. Buffer overflow, privilege escalation, and arbitrary code execution attacks typically exploit application flaws. Devices supporting insecure protocols are also a common source of vulnerabilities.

Network devices also suffer from frequent vulnerabilities. Network administrators should ensure that network devices receive regular firmware updates to patch security issues. Improper implementations of SSL and TLS encryption also cause vulnerabilities when they use outdated protocols, insecure ciphers, or invalid certificates.

Virtualized infrastructures add another layer of potential vulnerability. Administrators responsible for virtualized infrastructure must take extra care to ensure that the hypervisor is patched and protected against virtual machine escape attacks. Additionally, administrators should carefully restrict access to the virtual infrastructure's management interface to prevent unauthorized access attempts.

Lab Exercises

Activity 4.1: Interpreting a Vulnerability Scan

In Activity 3.2, you ran a vulnerability scan of a network under your control. In this lab, you will interpret the results of that vulnerability scan.

Review the scan results carefully and develop a remediation plan for your network. This plan should carefully consider the severity of each vulnerability, the potential that each may be a false positive result, and the time required to complete the remediation.

Activity 4.2: Analyzing a CVSS Vector

In this lab, you will interpret the CVSS vectors found in a vulnerability scan report to assess the severity and impact of two vulnerabilities.

Review the vulnerability reports in Figures 4.20 and 4.21.

FIGURE 4.20   First vulnerability report

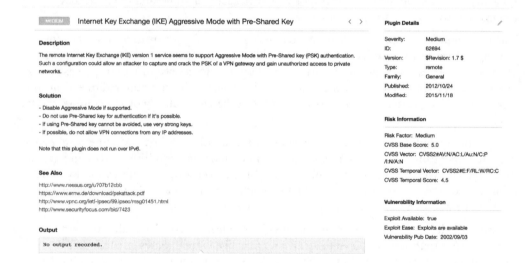

FIGURE 4.21   Second vulnerability report

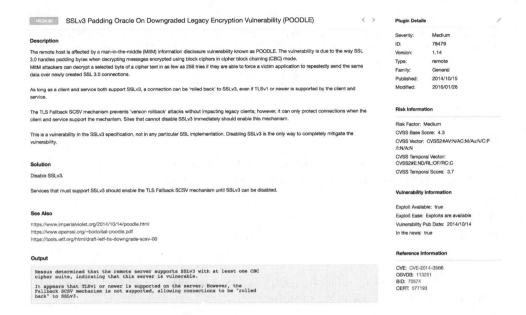

Explain the components of the CVSS vector for each of these vulnerabilities. Which vulnerability is more serious? Why?

Activity 4.3: Remediating a Vulnerability

In this lab, you will remediate one of the vulnerabilities that you identified in Activity 4.1.

1. Review the scan report from Activity 4.1 and select a vulnerability that is a high remediation priority where you have the ability to correct the issue yourself.

2. Perform the remediation.

3. Run a new vulnerability scan to confirm that the vulnerability was successfully remediated.

Review Questions

1. Tom is reviewing a vulnerability scan report and finds that one of the servers on his network suffers from an internal IP address disclosure vulnerability. What protocol is likely in use on this network that resulted in this vulnerability?

   A. TLS

   B. NAT

   C. SSH

   D. VPN

2. Which one of the CVSS metrics would contain information about the number of times that an attacker must successfully authenticate to execute an attack?

   A. AV

   B. C

   C. Au

   D. AC

3. Which one of the following values for the CVSS access complexity metric would indicate that the specified attack is simplest to exploit?

   A. High

   B. Medium

   C. Low

   D. Severe

4. Which one of the following values for the confidentiality, integrity, or availability CVSS metric would indicate the potential for total compromise of a system?

   A. N

   B. A

   C. P

   D. C

5. What is the most recent version of CVSS that is currently available?

   A. 1.0

   B. 2.0

   C. 2.5

   D. 3.0

6. Which one of the following metrics is not included in the calculation of the CVSS exploitability score?

   A. Access vector

   B. Vulnerability age

   C. Access complexity

   D. Authentication

7. Kevin recently identified a new security vulnerability and computed its CVSS base score as
   6.5. Which risk category would this vulnerability fall into?

   A. Low

   B. Medium

   C. High

   D. Critical

8. Tara recently analyzed the results of a vulnerability scan report and found that a vulnerability reported by the scanner did not exist because the system was actually patched as
   specified. What type of error occurred?

   A. False positive

   B. False negative

   C. True positive

   D. True negative

9. Which one of the following is not a common source of information that may be correlated
   with vulnerability scan results?

   A. Logs

   B. Database tables

   C. SIEM

   D. Configuration management system

10. Which one of the following operating systems should be avoided on production networks?

    A. Windows Server 2003

    B. Red Hat Enterprise Linux 7

    C. CentOS 7

    D. Ubuntu 16

11. In what type of attack does the attacker place more information in a memory location than
    is allocated for that use?

    A. SQL injection

    B. LDAP injection

    C. Cross-site scripting

    D. Buffer overflow

12. The Dirty COW attack is an example of what type of vulnerability?

    A. Malicious code

    B. Privilege escalation

    C. Buffer overflow

    D. LDAP injection

13. Which one of the following protocols should never be used on a public network?

    A. SSH

    B. HTTPS

    C. SFTP

    D. Telnet

14. Betty is selecting a transport encryption protocol for use in a new public website she is creating. Which protocol would be the best choice?

    A. SSL 2.0

    B. SSL 3.0

    C. TLS 1.0

    D. TLS 1.1

15. Which one of the following conditions would not result in a certificate warning during a vulnerability scan of a web server?

    A. Use of an untrusted CA

    B. Inclusion of a public encryption key

    C. Expiration of the certificate

    D. Mismatch in certificate name

16. What software component is responsible for enforcing the separation of guest systems in a virtualized infrastructure?

    A. Guest operating system

    B. Host operating system

    C. Memory controller

    D. Hypervisor

17. In what type of attack does the attacker seek to gain access to resources assigned to a different virtual machine?

    A. VM escape

    B. Management interface brute force

    C. LDAP injection

    D. DNS amplification

18. Which one of the following terms is not typically used to describe the connection of physical devices to a network?

A. IoT

B. IDS

C. ICS

D. SCADA

19. Monica discovers that an attacker posted a message in a web forum that she manages that is attacking users who visit the site. Which one of the following attack types is most likely to have occurred?

A. SQL injection

B. Malware injection

C. LDAP injection

D. Cross-site scripting

20. Alan is reviewing web server logs after an attack and finds many records that contain semicolons and apostrophes in queries from end users. What type of attack should he suspect?

A. SQL injection

B. LDAP injection

C. Cross-site scripting

D. Buffer overflow

Chapter
5

Building an Incident Response Program

THE COMPTIA CYBERSECURITY ANALYST+ EXAM OBJECTIVES COVERED IN THIS CHAPTER INCLUDE:

Domain 3: Cyber Incident Response

✓ **3.1 Given a scenario, distinguish threat data or behavior to determine the impact of an incident.**

✓ **3.3 Explain the importance of communication during the incident response process.**

No matter how well an organization prepares its cybersecurity defenses, the time will come that it suffers a computer security incident that compromises the confidentiality, integrity, and availability of information or systems under its control. This incident may be a minor virus infection that is quickly remediated or a serious breach of personal information that comes into the national media spotlight. In either event, the organization must be prepared to conduct a coordinated, methodical response effort. By planning in advance, business leaders, technology leaders, cybersecurity experts, and technologists can decide how they will handle these situations and prepare a well-thought-out response.

Security Incidents

Many IT professionals use the terms *security event* and *security incident* casually and interchangeably, but this is not correct. Members of a cybersecurity incident response team should use these terms carefully and according to their precise definitions within the organization. The National Institute for Standards and Technology (NIST) offers the following standard definitions for use throughout the U.S. government, and many private organizations choose to adopt them as well:

- An event is any observable occurrence in a system or network. A security event includes any observable occurrence that relates to a security function. For example, a user accessing a file stored on a server, an administrator changing permissions on a shared folder, and an attacker conducting a port scan are all examples of security events.

- An adverse event is any event that has negative consequences. Examples of adverse events include a malware infection on a system, a server crash, and a user accessing a file that he or she is not authorized to view.

- A security incident is a violation or imminent threat of violation of computer security policies, acceptable use policies, or standard security practices. Examples of security incidents include the accidental loss of sensitive information, an intrusion into a computer system by an attacker, the use of a keylogger on an executive's system to steal passwords, and the launch of a denial-of-service attack against a website.

Every security incident includes one or more security events, but not every security event is a security incident.

Computer security incident response teams (CSIRTs) are responsible for responding to computer security incidents that occur within an organization by following standardized response procedures and incorporating their subject matter expertise and professional judgment.

For brevity's sake, we will use the term "incident" as shorthand for "computer security incident" in the remainder of this book.

Phases of Incident Response

Organizations depend on members of the CSIRT to respond calmly and consistently in the event of a security incident. The crisis-like atmosphere that surrounds many security incidents may lead to poor decision making unless the organization has a clearly thought-out and refined process that describes how it will handle cybersecurity incident response. Figure 5.1 shows the simple incident response process advocated by NIST.

FIGURE 5.1   Incident response process

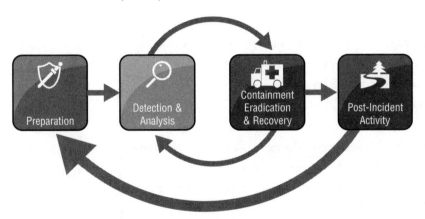

Source: NIST SP 800-61: Computer Security Incident Handling Guide

Notice that this process is not a simple progression of steps from start to finish. Instead, it includes loops that allow responders to return to prior phases as needed during the response. These loops reflect the reality of responses to actual cybersecurity incidents. Only in the simplest of incidents would an organization detect an incident, analyze data, conduct a recovery, and close out the incident in a straightforward sequence of steps. Instead, the containment process often includes several loops back through the detection and analysis phase to identify whether the incident has been successfully resolved. These loops are a normal part of the cybersecurity incident response process and should be expected.

Preparation

CSIRTs do not spring up out of thin air. As much as managers may wish it were so, they cannot simply will a CSIRT into existence by creating a policy document and assigning staff members to the CSIRT. Instead, the CSIRT requires careful preparation to ensure that the CSIRT has the proper policy foundation, has operating procedures that will be effective in the organization's computing environment, receives appropriate training, and is prepared to respond to an incident.

The next two sections of this chapter, "Building the Foundation for Incident Response" and "Creating an Incident Response Team," describe the preparation phase in greater detail.

The preparation phase also includes building strong cybersecurity defenses to reduce the likelihood and impact of future incidents. This process of building a defense-in-depth approach to cybersecurity often includes many personnel who might not be part of the CSIRT.

During the preparation phase, the organization should also assemble the hardware, software, and information required to conduct an incident investigation. NIST recommends that every organization's incident response toolkit should include, at a minimum, the following:

- Digital forensic workstations
- Backup devices
- Laptops for data collection, analysis, and reporting
- Spare server and networking equipment
- Blank removable media
- Portable printer
- Forensic and packet capture software
- Bootable USB media containing trusted copies of forensic tools
- Office supplies and evidence collection materials

You'll learn more about the tools used to conduct the incident response process in Chapters 6, 7, 8, and 13.

The preparation phase of the incident response plan is not a "one and done" planning process. Notice in Figure 5.1 that there is a loop from the post-incident activity phase back to the preparation phase. Whenever the organization is not actively involved in an incident response effort, it should be planning for the next incident.

Detection and Analysis

The detection and analysis phase of incident response is one of the trickiest to commit to a routine process. Although cybersecurity analysts have many tools at their disposal that may assist in identifying that a security incident is taking place, many incidents are only detected because of the trained eye of an experienced analyst.

NIST 800-61 describes four major categories of security event indicators:

- *Alerts* that originate from intrusion detection and prevention systems, security information and event management systems, antivirus software, file integrity checking software, and/or third-party monitoring services

- *Logs* generated by operating systems, services, applications, network devices, and network flows

- *Publicly available information* about new vulnerabilities and exploits detected "in the wild" or in a controlled laboratory environment

- *People* from inside the organization or external sources who report suspicious activity that may indicate a security incident is in progress

When any of these information sources indicate that a security incident may be occurring, cybersecurity analysts should shift into the initial validation mode, where they attempt to determine whether an incident is taking place that merits further activation of the incident response process. This analysis is often more art than science and is very difficult work. NIST recommends the following actions to improve the effectiveness of incident analysis:

Profile networks and systems to measure the characteristics of expected activity. This will improve the organization's ability to identify abnormal activity during the detection and analysis process.

Understand normal behavior of users, systems, networks, and applications. This behavior will vary between organizations, at different times of the day, week, and year and with changes in the business cycle. A solid understanding of normal behavior is critical to recognizing deviations from those patterns.

Create a logging policy that specifies the information that must be logged by systems, applications, and network devices. The policy should also specify where those log records should be stored (preferably in a centralized log management system) and the retention period for logs.

Perform event correlation to combine information from multiple sources. This function is typically performed by a *security information and event management (SIEM) system*.

Synchronize clocks across servers, workstations, and network devices. This is done to facilitate the correlation of log entries from different systems. Organizations may easily achieve this objective by operating a *Network Time Protocol (NTP)* server.

Maintain an organization-wide knowledge base that contains critical information about systems and applications. This knowledge base should include information about system profiles, usage patterns, and other information that may be useful to responders who are not familiar with the inner workings of a system.

Capture network traffic as soon as an incident is suspected. If the organization does not routinely capture network traffic, responders should immediately begin packet captures during the detection and analysis phase. This information may provide critical details about an attacker's intentions and activity.

Filter information to reduce clutter.   Incident investigations generate massive amounts of information, and it is basically impossible to interpret it all without both inclusion and exclusion filters. Incident response teams may wish to create some predefined filters during the preparation phase to assist with future analysis efforts.

Seek assistance from external resources.   Responders should know the parameters for involving outside sources in their response efforts. This may be as simple as conducting a Google search for a strange error message, or it may involve full-fledged coordination with other response teams.

You'll learn more about the process of detecting and analyzing a security incident in Chapter 6, "Analyzing Symptoms for Incident Response."

Containment, Eradication, and Recovery

During the incident detection and analysis phase, the CSIRT engages in primarily passive activities designed to uncover and analyze information about the incident. After completing this assessment, the team moves on to take active measures designed to contain the effects of the incident, eradicate the incident from the network, and recover normal operations.

At a high level, the containment, eradication, and recovery phase of the process is designed to achieve these objectives:

1. Select a containment strategy appropriate to the incident circumstances.
2. Implement the selected containment strategy to limit the damage caused by the incident.
3. Gather additional evidence, as needed to support the response effort and potential legal action.
4. Identify the attacker(s) and attacking system(s).
5. Eradicate the effects of the incident and recover normal business operations.

You'll learn more about the techniques used during the containment, eradication, and recovery phase of incident response in Chapter 8, "Containment, Eradication, and Recovery."

Post-Incident Activity

Security incidents don't end after security professionals remove attackers from the network or complete the recovery effort to restore normal business operations. Once the immediate danger passes and normal operations resume, the CSIRT enters the post-incident activity phase of incident response. During this phase, team members conduct a lessons-learned review and ensure that they meet internal and external evidence retention requirements.

Lessons-Learned Review

During the lessons-learned review, responders conduct a thorough review of the incident and their response, with an eye toward improving procedures and tools for the next incident. This review is most effective if conducted during a meeting where everyone is present for the discussion (physically or virtually!). Although some organizations try to conduct lessons-learned reviews in an offline manner, this approach does not lead to the back-and-forth discussion that often yields the greatest insight.

The lessons-learned review should be facilitated by an independent facilitator who was not involved in the incident response and is perceived by everyone involved as an objective outsider. This allows the facilitator to guide the discussion in a productive manner without participants feeling that he or she is advancing a hidden agenda. NIST recommends that lessons learned processes answer the following questions:

- Exactly what happened and at what times?

- How well did staff and management perform in responding to the incident?

- Were the documented procedures followed? Were they adequate?

- What information was needed sooner?

- Were any steps or actions taken that might have inhibited the recovery?

- What would the staff and management do differently the next time a similar incident occurs?

- How could information sharing with other organizations have been improved?

- What corrective actions can prevent similar incidents in the future?

- What precursors or indicators should be watched for in the future to detect similar incidents?

- What additional tools or resources are needed to detect, analyze, and mitigate future incidents?

Once the group answers these questions, management must ensure that the organization takes follow-up actions, as appropriate. Lessons-learned reviews are only effective if they surface needed changes and those changes then occur to improve future incident response efforts.

Evidence Retention

At the conclusion of an incident, the CSIRT has often gathered large quantities of evidence. The team leader should work with staff to identify both internal and external evidence retention requirements. If the incident may result in civil litigation or criminal prosecution, the team should consult attorneys prior to discarding any evidence. If there is no likelihood that the evidence will be used in court, the team should follow any retention policies that the organization has in place.

If the organization does not have an existing evidence retention policy for cybersecurity incidents, now would be a good time to create one. Many organizations choose to implement a two-year retention period for evidence not covered by other requirements. This allows incident handlers time to review the evidence at a later date during incident handling program reviews or while handling future similar incidents.

At the conclusion of the post-incident activity phase, the CSIRT deactivates, and the incident-handling cycle returns to the preparation and detect and analyze phases.

 U.S. federal government agencies must retain all incident handling records for at least three years. This requirement appears in the National Archives General Records Schedule 24, Item 7. See https://www.archives.gov/records-mgmt/grs/grs24.html for more information.

You'll read more about the activities undertaken during the post-incident activity phase in Chapter 8.

Building the Foundation for Incident Response

One of the major responsibilities that organizations have during the preparation phase of incident response is building a solid policy and procedure foundation for the program. This creates the documentation required to support the program's ongoing efforts.

Policy

The incident response policy serves as the cornerstone of an organization's incident response program. This policy should be written to guide efforts at a high level and provide the authority for incident response. The policy should be approved at the highest level possible within the organization, preferably by the chief executive officer. For this reason, policy authors should attempt to write the policy in a manner that makes it relatively timeless. This means that the policy should contain statements that provide authority for incident response, assign responsibility to the CSIRT, and describe the role of individual users and state organizational priorities. The policy is *not* the place to describe specific technologies, response procedures, or evidence-gathering techniques. Those details may change frequently and should be covered in more easily changed procedure documents.

NIST recommends that incident response policies contain these key elements:

- Statement of management commitment
- Purpose and objectives of the policy
- Scope of the policy (to whom it applies and under what circumstances)
- Definition of cybersecurity incidents and related terms
- Organizational structure and definition of roles, responsibilities, and level of authority
- Prioritization or severity rating scheme for incidents
- Performance measures for the CSIRT
- Reporting and contact forms

Including these elements in the policy provides a solid foundation for the CSIRT's routine and crisis activities.

Procedures and Playbooks

Procedures provide the detailed, tactical information that CSIRT members need when responding to an incident. They represent the collective wisdom of team members and subject matter experts collected during periods of calm and ready to be applied in the event of an actual incident. CSIRT teams often develop *playbooks* that describe the specific procedures that they will follow in the event of a specific type of cybersecurity incident. For example, a financial institution CSIRT might develop playbooks that cover

- Breach of personal financial information
- Web server defacement
- Phishing attack targeted at customers
- Loss of a laptop
- General security incident not covered by another playbook

This is clearly not an exhaustive list, and each organization will develop playbooks that describe their response to both high severity and frequently occurring incident categories. The idea behind the playbook is that the team should be able to pick it up and find an operational plan for responding to the security incident that they may follow. Playbooks are especially important in the early hours of incident response to ensure that the team has a planned, measured response to the first reports of a potential incident.

For good examples of real-world cybersecurity incident playbooks, see the Ransomware Playbook published by Demisto (https://www.demisto.com/playbook-for-handling-ransomware-infections/) or the Windows incident response playbook from the University of Central Florida (www.cst .ucf.edu/wp-content/uploads/infosec/Procedure_for_Windows_ Incident_Response.pdf).

Playbooks are designed to be step-by-step recipe-style responses to cybersecurity incidents. They should guide the team's response, but they are not a substitute for professional judgment. The responders handling an incident should have appropriate professional expertise and the authority to deviate from the playbook when circumstances require a different approach.

Documenting the Incident Response Plan

When developing the incident response plan documentation, organizations should pay particular attention to creating tools that may be useful during an incident response. These tools should provide clear guidance to response teams that may be quickly read and interpreted during a crisis situation. For example, the incident response checklist shown in Figure 5.2 provides a high-level overview of the incident response process in checklist form. The CSIRT leader may use this checklist to ensure that the team doesn't miss an important step in the heat of the crisis environment.

FIGURE 5.2   Incident response checklist

	Action	Completed
	Detection and Analysis	
1.	Determine whether an incident has occurred	
1.1	Analyze the precursors and indicators	
1.2	Look for correlating information	
1.3	Perform research (e.g., search engines, knowledge base)	
1.4	As soon as the handler believes an incident has occurred, begin documenting the investigation and gathering evidence	
2.	Prioritize handling the incident based on the relevant factors (functional impact, information impact, recoverability effort, etc.)	
3.	Report the incident to the appropriate internal personnel and external organizations	
	Containment, Eradication, and Recovery	
4.	Acquire, preserve, secure, and document evidence	
5.	Contain the incident	
6.	Eradicate the incident	
6.1	Identify and mitigate all vulnerabilities that were exploited	
6.2	Remove malware, inappropriate materials, and other components	
6.3	If more affected hosts are discovered (e.g., new malware infections), repeat the Detection and Analysis steps (1.1, 1.2) to identify all other affected hosts, then contain (5) and eradicate (6) the incident for them	
7.	Recover from the incident	
7.1	Return affected systems to an operationally ready state	
7.2	Confirm that the affected systems are functioning normally	
7.3	If necessary, implement additional monitoring to look for future related activity	
	Post-Incident Activity	
8.	Create a follow-up report	
9.	Hold a lessons learned meeting (mandatory for major incidents, optional otherwise)	

Source: NIST SP 800-61: Computer Security Incident Handling Guide

The National Institute of Standards and Technology publishes a Computer Security Incident Handling Guide (SP 800-61) that contains a wealth of information that is useful to both government agencies and private organizations developing incident response plans. The current version of the guide, NIST SP 800-61 revision 2, is available online at http://nvlpubs .nist.gov/nistpubs/SpecialPublications/NIST.SP.800-61r2.pdf.

Creating an Incident Response Team

There are many different roles that should be represented on a CSIRT. Depending on the organization and its technical needs, some of these roles may be core team members who are always activated, whereas others may be called in as needed on an incident-by-incident basis. For example, a database administrator might be crucial when investigating the aftermath of a SQL injection attack but would probably not be very helpful when responding to a stolen laptop.

The core incident response team normally consists of cybersecurity professionals with specific expertise in incident response. In larger organizations, these may be full-time employees dedicated to incident response, whereas smaller organizations may call on cybersecurity experts who fill other roles for their "day jobs" to step into CSIRT roles in the aftermath of an incident.

The Role of Management

Management should have an active role in incident response efforts. The primary responsibility of IT managers and business leaders is to provide the authority, resources, and time required to respond appropriately to a security incident. This includes ensuring that the CSIRT has the budget and staff required to plan for security incidents and access to subject matter experts during a response.

Management may also be called on during an incident response to make critical business decisions about the need to shut down critical servers, communicate with law enforcement or the general public, and assess the impact of an incident on key stakeholders.

In addition to the core team members, the CSIRT may include representation from the following:

- Technical subject matter experts whose knowledge may be required during a response. This includes system engineers, network administrators, database administrators, desktop experts, and application experts.

- IT support staff who may be needed to carry out actions directed by the CSIRT.

- Legal counsel responsible for ensuring that the team's actions comply with legal, policy, and regulatory requirements and can advise team leaders on compliance issues.

- Human resources staff responsible for investigating potential employee malfeasance.

- Public relations and marketing staff who can coordinate communications with the media and general public.

The CSIRT should be run by a designated leader with the clear authority to direct incident response efforts and serve as a liaison to management. This leader should be a skilled incident responder who is either assigned to lead the CSIRT as a full-time responsibility or serves in a cybersecurity leadership position.

Incident Response Providers

In addition to including internal team members on the CSIRT, the organization may decide to outsource some or all of their actions to an incident response provider. Retaining an incident response provider gives the organization access to expertise that might not otherwise exist inside the firm. This may come at significant expense, so the organizations should decide what types of incidents may be handled internally and which justify the use of an outside provider. Additionally, the organization should understand the provider's guaranteed response time and ensure that it has a plan in place to respond to the early stages of an incident before the provider assumes control.

CSIRT Scope of Control

The organization's incident response policy should clearly outline the scope of the CSIRT. This includes answers to the following questions:

- What triggers the activation of the CSIRT? Who is authorized to activate the CSIRT?

- Does the CSIRT cover the entire organization or is it responsible only for certain business units, information categories, or other divisions of responsibility?

- Is the CSIRT authorized to communicate with law enforcement or other external parties and, if so, which ones?

- Does the CSIRT have internal communication and/or escalation responsibilities? If so, what triggers those requirements?

Testing the Incident Response Plan

Testing cybersecurity incident response plans is a critical component of any organization's incident response strategy. Testing reassures the organization that the plan will function properly in the event of an actual incident and provides a critical training exercise for the team members who would respond to a real-world cybersecurity crisis.

The Cybersecurity Analyst+ exam does not include coverage of incident response tests as one of its exam objectives, so we do not cover testing in this book. That said, if you are responsible for your organization's incident response plan, you should conduct regular simulation tests to walk team members through the processes they would follow when responding to a real cybersecurity incident.

Coordination and Information Sharing

During an incident response effort, CSIRT team members often need to communicate and share information with both internal and external partners. Smooth information sharing is essential to an effective and efficient incident response, but it must be done within clearly established parameters. The organization's incident response policies should limit communication to trusted parties and put controls in place to prevent the inadvertent release of sensitive information outside of those trusted partners.

Internal Communications

Internal communications among the CSIRT and with other employees within the organization should take place over secure communications channels that are designated in advance and tested for security. This may include email, instant messaging, message boards, and other collaboration tools that pass security muster. The key is to evaluate and standardize those communications tools in advance so that responders are not left to their own devices to identify tools in the heat of an incident.

External Communications

CSIRT team members, business leaders, public relations teams, and legal counsel may all bring to the table requirements that may justify sharing limited or detailed information with external entities. The incident response plan should guide these efforts. Types of external communications may include the following:

- Law enforcement may wish to be involved when a cybersecurity incident appears to be criminal in nature. The organization may choose to cooperate or decline participation in an investigation but should always make this decision with the advice of legal counsel.

- Information sharing partners, such as the Information Sharing and Analysis Center (ISAC), provide community-based warnings of cybersecurity risks. The organization may choose to participate in one of these consortiums and, in some cases, share information about ongoing and past security incidents to partners in that consortium.

- Vendors may be able to provide information crucial to the response. The manufacturers of hardware and software used within the organization may be able to provide patches, troubleshooting advice, or other guidance crucial to the response effort.

- Other organizations may be actual or potential victims of the same attack. CSIRT members may wish to coordinate their incident response with other organizations.

- Communications with the media and the general public may be mandatory under regulatory or legislative requirements, voluntary, or forced by media coverage of a security incident.

It is incumbent upon the CSIRT leader to control and coordinate external communications in a manner that meets regulatory requirements and best serves the response effort.

Classifying Incidents

Each time an incident occurs, the CSIRT should classify the incident by both the type of threat and the severity of the incident according to a standardized incident severity rating system. This classification aids other personnel in understanding the nature and severity of the incident and allows the comparison of the current incident to past and future incidents.

Threat Classification

In many cases, the incident will come from a known threat source that facilitates the rapid identification of the threat. NIST provides the following attack vectors that are useful for classifying threats:

External/Removable Media   An attack executed from removable media or a peripheral device—for example, malicious code spreading onto a system from an infected USB flash drive.

Attrition   An attack that employs brute-force methods to compromise, degrade, or destroy systems, networks, or services—for example, a DDoS attack intended to impair or deny access to a service or application or a brute-force attack against an authentication mechanism.

Web   An attack executed from a website or web-based application—for example, a cross-site scripting attack used to steal credentials or redirect to a site that exploits a browser vulnerability and installs malware.

Email   An attack executed via an email message or attachment—for example, exploit code disguised as an attached document or a link to a malicious website in the body of an email message.

Impersonation   An attack involving replacement of something benign with something malicious—for example, spoofing, man-in-the-middle attacks, rogue wireless access points, and SQL injection attacks all involve impersonation.

Improper Usage   Any incident resulting from violation of an organization's acceptable usage policies by an authorized user, excluding the previous categories; for example, a user installs file sharing software, leading to the loss of sensitive data, or a user performs illegal activities on a system.

Loss or Theft of Equipment   The loss or theft of a computing device or media used by the organization, such as a laptop, smartphone, or authentication token.

Unknown   An attack of unknown origin.

Other   An attack of known origin that does not fit into any of the previous categories.

In addition to understanding these attack vectors, cybersecurity analysts should be familiar with the concept of an *advanced persistent threat (APT)*. APT attackers are highly skilled and talented attackers focused on a specific objective. These attackers are often funded by nation-states, organized crime, and other sources with tremendous resources. APT attackers are known for taking advantage of *zero-day vulnerabilities*: vulnerabilities that are unknown to the security community and, as a result, are not included in security tests performed by vulnerability scanners and other tools and have no patches available to correct them.

Severity Classification

CSIRT members may investigate dozens, hundreds, or even thousands of security incidents each year, depending on the scope of their responsibilities and the size of the organization. Therefore, it is important to use a standardized process to communicate the severity of each incident to management and other stakeholders. Incident severity information assists in the prioritization and scope of incident response efforts.

Two key measures used to determine the incident severity are the scope of the impact and the types of data involved in the incident.

Scope of Impact

The scope of an incident's impact depends on the degree of impairment that it causes the organization as well as the effort required to recover from the incident.

Functional Impact

The functional impact of an incident is the degree of impairment that it causes to the organization. This may vary based on the criticality of the system(s) or process(es) affected by the incident as well as the organization's ability to continue providing services to users as an incident unfolds and in the aftermath of the incident. NIST recommends using four categories to describe the functional impact of an incident, as shown in Table 5.1.

TABLE 5.1   NIST functional impact categories

Category	Definition
None	No effect to the organization's ability to provide all services to all users.
Low	Minimal effect; the organization can still provide all critical services to all users but has lost efficiency.
Medium	Organization has lost the ability to provide a critical service to a subset of system users.
High	Organization is no longer able to provide some critical services to any users.

Source: NIST SP 800-61

There is one major gap in the functional impact assessment criteria provided by NIST: it does not include any assessment of the economic impact of a security incident on the organization. This may be because the NIST guidelines are primarily intended to serve a government audience. Organizations may wish to modify the categories in Table 5.1 to incorporate economic impact or measure financial impact using a separate scale, such as the one shown in Table 5.2.

TABLE 5.2   Economic impact categories

Category	Definition
None	The organization does not expect to experience any financial impact or the financial impact is negligible.
Low	The organization expects to experience a financial impact of $10,000 or less.
Medium	The organization expects to experience a financial impact of more than $10,000 but less than $500,000.
High	The organization expects to experience a financial impact of $500,000 or more.

The financial thresholds included in Table 5.2 are intended as examples only and should be adjusted according to the size of the organization. For example, a security incident causing a $500,000 loss may be crippling for a small business, whereas a Fortune 500 company may easily absorb this loss.

Recoverability Effort

In addition to measuring the functional and economic impact of a security incident, organizations should measure the time that services will be unavailable. This may be expressed as a function of the amount of downtime experienced by the service or the time required to recover from the incident. Table 5.3 shows the NIST suggested recommendations for assessing the recoverability impact of a security incident.

TABLE 5.3   NIST recoverability effort categories

Category	Definition
Regular	Time to recovery is predictable with existing resources.
Supplemented	Time to recovery is predictable with additional resources.
Extended	Time to recovery is unpredictable; additional resources and outside help are needed.
Not Recoverable	Recovery from the incident is not possible (e.g., sensitive data exfiltrated and posted publicly); launch investigation.

Source: NIST SP 800-61

Data Types

The nature of the data involved in a security incident also contributes to the incident severity. When a security incident affects the confidentiality or integrity of sensitive information, cybersecurity analysts should assign a data impact rating. The data impact rating scale recommended by NIST appears in Table 5.4.

TABLE 5.4   NIST information impact categories

Category	Definition
None	No information was exfiltrated, changed, deleted, or otherwise compromised.
Privacy breach	Sensitive personally identifiable information (PII) of taxpayers, employees, beneficiaries, and so on was accessed or exfiltrated.
Proprietary breach	Unclassified proprietary information, such as protected critical infrastructure information (PCII) was accessed or exfiltrated.
Integrity loss	Sensitive or proprietary information was changed or deleted.

Source: NIST SP 800-61

Although the impact scale presented in Table 5.4 is NIST's recommendation, it does have some significant shortcomings. Most notably, the definitions included in the table are skewed toward the types of information that might be possessed by a government agency and might not map well to information in the possession of a private organization. Some analysts might also object to the inclusion of "integrity loss" as a single category separate from the three classification-dependent breach categories.

Table 5.5 presents an alternative classification scheme that private organizations might use as the basis for their own information impact categorization schemes.

TABLE 5.5   Private organization information impact categories

Category	Definition
None	No information was exfiltrated, changed, deleted, or otherwise compromised.
Regulated information breach	Information regulated by an external compliance obligation was accessed or exfiltrated. This may include personally identifiable information (PII) that triggers a data breach notification law, protected health information (PHI) under HIPAA, and/or payment card information protected under PCI DSS.

TABLE 5.5   Private organization information impact categories *(continued)*

Category	Definition
Intellectual property breach	Sensitive intellectual property was accessed or exfiltrated. This may include product development plans, formulas, or other sensitive trade secrets.
Confidential information breach	Corporate confidential information was accessed or exfiltrated. This includes information that is sensitive but does not fit under the categories of regulated information or intellectual property. Examples might include corporate accounting information or information about mergers and acquisitions.
Integrity loss	Sensitive or proprietary information was changed or deleted.

As with the financial impact scale, organizations will need to customize the information impact categories in Table 5.5 to meet the unique requirements of their business processes.

Summary

Incident response programs provide organizations with the ability to respond to security issues in a calm, repeatable manner. Security incidents occur when there is a known or suspected violation or imminent violation of an organization's security policies. When a security incident occurs, the organization should activate its computer security incident response team (CSIRT).

The CSIRT guides the organization through the four stages of incident response: preparation; detection and analysis; containment, eradication, and recovery; and post-incident activities. During the preparation phase, the organization ensures that the CSIRT has the proper policy foundation, has operating procedures that will be effective in the organization's computing environment, receives appropriate training, and is prepared to respond to an incident.

During the detection and analysis phase, the organization watches for signs of security incidents. This includes monitoring alerts, logs, publicly available information, and reports from internal and external staff about security anomalies. When the organization suspects a security incident, it moves into the containment, eradication, and recovery phase, which is designed to limit the damage and restore normal operations as quickly as possible.

Restoration of normal activity doesn't signal the end of incident response efforts. At the conclusion of an incident, the post-incident activities phase provides the organization with the opportunity to reflect upon the incident by conducting a lessons-learned review. During this phase, the organization should also ensure that evidence is retained for future use according to policy.

Exam Essentials

Security events are occurrences that may escalate into a security incident.   An event is any observable occurrence in a system or network. A security event includes any observable occurrence that relates to a security function. A security incident is a violation or imminent threat of violation of computer security policies, acceptable use policies, or standard security practices. Every incident consists of one or more event, but every event is not an incident.

The cybersecurity incident response process has four phases.   The four phases of incident response are preparation; detection and analysis; containment, eradication, and recovery; and post-incident activities. The process is not a simple progression of steps from start to finish. Instead, it includes loops that allow responders to return to prior phases as needed during the response.

Security event indicators include alerts, logs, publicly available information and people. Alerts originate from intrusion detection and prevention systems, security information and event management systems, antivirus software, file integrity checking software, and third-party monitoring services. Logs are generated by operating systems, services, applications, network devices, and network flows. Publicly available information exists about new vulnerabilities and exploits detected "in the wild" or in a controlled laboratory environment. People from inside the organization or external sources report suspicious activity that may indicate that a security incident is in progress.

Policies, procedures, and playbooks guide incident response efforts.   The incident response policy serves as the cornerstone of an organization's incident response program. This policy should be written to guide efforts at a high level and provide the authority for incident response. Procedures provide the detailed, tactical information that CSIRT members need when responding to an incident. CSIRT teams often develop playbooks that describe the specific procedures that they will follow in the event of a specific type of cybersecurity incident.

Incident response teams should represent diverse stakeholders.   The core incident response team normally consists of cybersecurity professionals with specific expertise in incident response. In addition to the core team members, the CSIRT may include representation from technical subject matter experts, IT support staff, legal counsel, human resources staff, and public relations and marketing teams.

Incidents may be classified according to the attack vector where they originate.   Common attack vectors for security incidents include external/removable media, attrition, the web, email, impersonation, improper usage, loss or theft of equipment, and other/unknown sources.

Response teams classify the severity of an incident.   The functional impact of an incident is the degree of impairment that it causes to the organization. The economic impact is the amount of financial loss that the organization incurs. In addition to measuring the functional and economic impact of a security incident, organizations should measure the time that services will be unavailable and the recoverability effort. Finally, the nature of the data involved in an incident also contributes to the severity as the information impact.

Lab Exercises

Activity 5.1: Incident Severity Classification

You are the leader of cybersecurity incident response team for a large company that is experiencing a denial-of-service attack on its website. This attack is preventing the organization from selling products to its customers and is likely to cause lost revenue of at least $2 million per day until the incident is resolved.

The attack is coming from many different sources and you have exhausted all of the response techniques at your disposal. You are currently looking to identify an external partner that can help with the response.

Classify this incident using the criteria described in this chapter. Assign categorical ratings for functional impact, economic impact, recoverability effort, and information impact. Justify each of your assignments.

Activity 5.2: Incident Response Phases

Identify the correct phase of the incident response process that corresponds to each of the following activities:

Activity	Phase
Conducting a lessons-learned review session.	
Receiving a report from a staff member about a malware infection.	
Upgrading the organization's firewall to block a new type of attack.	
Recovering normal operations after eradicating an incident.	
Identifying the attacker(s) and attacking system(s).	
Interpreting log entries using a SIEM to identify a potential incident.	
Assembling the hardware and software required to conduct an incident investigation.	

Activity 5.3: Developing an Incident Communications Plan

You are the CSIRT leader for a major ecommerce website, and you are currently responding to a security incident where you believe attackers used a SQL injection attack to steal transaction records from your backend database.

Currently, only the core CSIRT members are responding. Develop a communication plan that describes the nature, timing, and audiences for communications to the internal and external stakeholders that you believe need to be notified.

Review Questions

1. Which one of the following is an example of a computer security incident?

   A. User accesses a secure file

   B. Administrator changes a file's permission settings

   C. Intruder breaks into a building

   D. Former employee crashes a server

2. During what phase of the incident response process would an organization implement defenses designed to reduce the likelihood of a security incident?

   A. Preparation

   B. Detection and analysis

   C. Containment, eradication, and recovery

   D. Post-incident activity

3. Alan is responsible for developing his organization's detection and analysis capabilities. He would like to purchase a system that can combine log records from multiple sources to detect potential security incidents. What type of system is best suited to meet Alan's security objective?

   A. IPS

   B. IDS

   C. SIEM

   D. Firewall

4. Ben is working to classify the functional impact of an incident. The incident has disabled email service for approximately 30 percent of his organization's staff. How should Ben classify the functional impact of this incident according to the NIST scale?

   A. None

   B. Low

   C. Medium

   D. High

5. What phase of the incident response process would include measures designed to limit the damage caused by an ongoing breach?

   A. Preparation

   B. Detection and analysis

   C. Containment, eradication, and recovery

   D. Post-incident activity

6. Grace is the CSIRT team leader for a business unit within NASA, a federal agency. What is the minimum amount of time that Grace must retain incident handling records?

    A. Six months

    B. One year

    C. Two years

    D. Three years

7. Karen is responding to a security incident that resulted from an intruder stealing files from a government agency. Those files contained unencrypted information about protected critical infrastructure. How should Karen rate the information impact of this loss?

    A. None

    B. Privacy breach

    C. Proprietary breach

    D. Integrity loss

8. Matt is concerned about the fact that log records from his organization contain conflicting timestamps due to unsynchronized clocks. What protocol can he use to synchronize clocks throughout the enterprise?

    A. NTP

    B. FTP

    C. ARP

    D. SSH

9. Which one of the following document types would outline the authority of a CSIRT responding to a security incident?

    A. Policy

    B. Procedure

    C. Playbook

    D. Baseline

10. A cross-site scripting attack is an example of what type of threat vector?

    A. Impersonation

    B. Email

    C. Attrition

    D. Web

11. Which one of the following parties is not commonly the target of external communications during an incident?

    A. The perpetrator

    B. Law enforcement

    C. Vendors

    D. Information sharing partners

12. Robert is finishing a draft of a proposed incident response policy for his organization. Who would be the most appropriate person to sign the policy?

    A. CEO

    B. Director of security

    C. CIO

    D. CSIRT leader

13. Which one of the following is not an objective of the containment, eradication, and recovery phase of incident response?

    A. Detect an incident in progress

    B. Implement a containment strategy

    C. Identify the attackers

    D. Eradicate the effects of the incident

14. Renee is responding to a security incident that resulted in the unavailability of a website critical to her company's operations. She is unsure of the amount of time and effort that it will take to recover the website. How should Renee classify the recoverability effort?

    A. Regular

    B. Supplemented

    C. Extended

    D. Not recoverable

15. Which one of the following is an example of an attrition attack?

    A. SQL injection

    B. Theft of a laptop

    C. User installs file sharing software

    D. Brute-force password attack

16. Who is the best facilitator for a post-incident lessons-learned session?

    A. CEO

    B. CSIRT leader

    C. Independent facilitator

    D. First responder

17. Which one of the following elements is not normally found in an incident response policy?

    A. Performance measures for the CSIRT

    B. Definition of cybersecurity incidents

    C. Definition of roles, responsibilities, and levels of authority

    D. Procedures for rebuilding systems

18. A man-in-the-middle attack is an example of what type of threat vector?

    A. Attrition

    B. Impersonation

    C. Web

    D. Email

19. Tommy is the CSIRT team leader for his organization and is responding to a newly discovered security incident. What document is most likely to contain step-by-step instructions that he might follow in the early hours of the response effort?

    A. Policy

    B. Baseline

    C. Playbook

    D. Textbook

20. Hank is responding to a security event where the CEO of his company had her laptop stolen. The laptop was encrypted but contained sensitive information about the company's employees. How should Hank classify the information impact of this security event?

    A. None

    B. Privacy breach

    C. Proprietary breach

    D. Integrity loss

Chapter

6

Analyzing Symptoms for Incident Response

THE COMPTIA CYBERSECURITY ANALYST+ EXAM OBJECTIVES COVERED IN THIS CHAPTER INCLUDE:

Domain 3: Cyber Incident Response

✓ **3.4 Given a scenario, analyze common symptoms to select the best course of action to support incident response**

Responding to security incidents and network events is a common task for cybersecurity analysts. Network problems such as excessive or suspicious bandwidth consumption, probes and scans, and rogue devices are all likely to be encountered by security professionals. Host and application issues are also frequently part of response processes, including host performance problems, malware, and more focused attacks. That makes knowing what to look for, how to find it, and what your response options are an important part of cybersecurity operations.

In the first section of this chapter, you will learn about common network events ranging from bandwidth use and data exfiltration to scans, probes, and denial-of-service attacks, as well as some of the tools that are frequently used detect them and to perform that analysis. In the sections that follow, you will learn about host and application problems, detection and analysis techniques to address them, and examples of handling methods for common issues related to these symptoms.

Analyzing Network Events

Many incidents start with the discovery of suspicious or unexpected network traffic. These events may take the form of bandwidth consumption, attack traffic, or unexpected devices showing up on the network. As a cybersecurity analyst, you need to be able to gather, correlate, and analyze the data from a multitude of systems and network devices to detect, or better, to prevent these incidents from becoming serious issues.

Many organizations differentiate between events and incidents. Events are typically defined as observable events like an email or a file download. Incidents are often classified as a violation of a security policy, unauthorized use or access, denial of service, or other malicious actions that may cause harm. Alerts are sent when events cause notification to occur. Make sure you know how your organization describes events, incidents, and alerts to help prevent confusion.

Capturing Network Events

One of the first steps in gaining a high-level understanding of a network is getting visibility into how the available bandwidth for the network is being used. This is typically done through one of three common methods: router-based monitoring, active monitoring, or passive monitoring.

Router-Based Monitoring

Router-based monitoring relies on routers or switches with routing capabilities to provide information about the flow of traffic on the network and the status of the network device itself. Since routers are normally placed at network borders or other internal boundaries, router-based monitoring can provide a useful view of traffic at those points.

Most router-based monitoring relies on capturing data about the traffic that is passing through the device. This information about traffic flow is often referred to as *network flows*. A number of technologies exist to capture flows and other router information, including

- *Netflow*, or similar technologies like *sFlow*, *J-Flow*, and others, are standards for monitoring *traffic flows*. They count information about traffic at network device interfaces and then send that information to flow collectors. Flows are often sampled due to the sheer quantity of data, meaning that one in a thousand, or one in a hundred packets, are sampled rather than every packet.

- *RMON* was developed to monitor local area networks and operates at layers 1–4 of the network stack. RMON typically operates in a client/server model and uses monitoring devices (probes) to gather data. It is implemented as a *management information base (MIB)*, which provides monitoring groups to get information about networks and focuses on flow-based information, including statistics, history, alarms, and events.

- In addition to flow based reporting, the *Simple Network Management Protocol (SNMP)* is commonly used to collect information from routers and other network devices and provides more information about the devices themselves instead of the network traffic flow information provided by RMON or Netflow or related flow-capture protocols.

SNMPv3 added encryption, authentication, and users to help keep SNMP traffic secure. If you encounter SNMPv1 or v2, you should find out why it is in use—SNMPv3 has been available for years, and properly securing SNMP traffic is important!

In Figure 6.1, a simple example of a typical network shows how the central placement of routers can provide visibility into the overall traffic flow of a network. Traffic sent from the distribution switches to the other division's network, or to the Internet, will be sent through the division routers and possibly through the border router, allowing network flow information to be captured on a central flow collection system.

FIGURE 6.1 Routers provide a central view of network traffic flow by sending data to flow collectors.

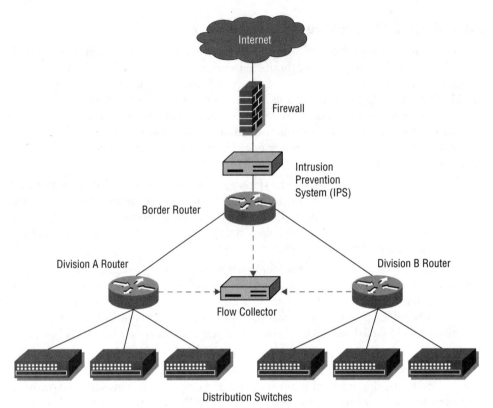

Flow information can look a lot like information from a typical phone bill—you can see who you called, what number they were at, and how long you talked. With flows, you can see the source, its IP address, the destination, its IP address, how many packets were sent, how much data was sent, and the port and protocol that was used, allowing a good guess about what application was in use. Figure 6.2 shows an example of PRTG's NetFlow tool, with this data listed in a way that allows data to be sorted and searched.

This information can be very useful for both day-to-day monitoring and for investigations. In addition, feeding flow data to a security monitoring tool that uses behavior-based detection capabilities can identify issues like unexpected communications to remote command and control (C&C) systems. In Figure 6.2, you can see that local hosts are browsing remote sites—192.168.1.14 visits 157.240.2.35—a Facebook content delivery network host. If you saw traffic that was not expected when you reviewed traffic or if you were investigating suspicious traffic, flows can provide a useful way to quickly review what a given host is doing. Network flow data can be used both proactively, to monitor overall network

FIGURE 6.2   Netflow data example

Pos	Source IP	Source Port	Destination IP	Destination Port	Protocol	Bytes ▲	
1.	216.58.216.235	443	192.168.1.227	63287	6	197 Byte	14 %
2.	192.168.1.227	63287	216.58.216.235	443	6	196 Byte	14 %
3.	192.168.1.14	53250	198.41.215.68	443	6	190 Byte	13 %
4.	192.168.1.14	53273	157.240.2.35	443	6	190 Byte	13 %
5.	192.168.1.14	53276	157.240.2.25	443	6	190 Byte	13 %
6.	NP-13A185131948 (192.168.1.215)	38970	ec2-54-186-29-214.us-west-2.compute.amazonaws.com (54.186.29.214)	443	6	135 Byte	10 %
7.	198.41.215.68	443	192.168.1.14	53250	6	92 Byte	6 %
8.	android-cbf9ddc66a19c6ef (192.168.1.212)	42671	ord30s26-in-f228.1e100.net (216.58.192.228)	443	6	83 Byte	6 %
9.	157.240.2.25	443	192.168.1.14	53276	6	52 Byte	4 %
10.	157.240.2.35	443	192.168.1.14	53273	6	52 Byte	4 %
11.	ord30s26-in-f228.1e100.net (216.58.192.228)	443	android-cbf9ddc66a19c6ef (192.168.1.212)	42671	6	40 Byte	3 %
Other						0 Byte	< 1 %

health and traffic levels, and reactively, to monitor for unexpected traffic or for sudden changes in network bandwidth usage. This data is often combined with other network and system log and event data using a security information and event management (SIEM) device or log analysis tool to provide deeper analysis and response capabilities.

Active Monitoring

Active monitoring techniques reach out to remote systems and devices to gather data. Unlike flows and SNMP monitoring, where data is gathered by sending information to collectors, active monitors are typically the data gathering location (although they may then forward that information to a collector). Active monitoring typically gathers data about availability, routes, packet delay or loss, and bandwidth.

Two examples of active monitoring are:

- *Pings*—Network data can also be acquired actively by using ICMP to ping remote systems. This only provides basic up/down information, but for basic use, ICMP can provide a simple solution.

- *iPerf*—A tool that measures the maximum bandwidth that an IP network can handle. Public iPerf servers allow remote testing of link bandwidth in addition to internal bandwidth testing. iPerf testing data can help establish a baseline for performance to help identify when a network will reach its useful limits.

Both active and router-based monitoring add traffic to the network, which means that the network monitoring systems may be competing with the traffic they are monitoring. When there are significant network bandwidth utilization issues, this type of network monitoring data may be lost or delayed as higher-priority traffic is likely to be prioritized over monitoring data.

Although it is possible to implement your own ping script for monitoring, tools like Nagios have available ping plug-ins that can use both ICMP and TCP pings with a variety of additional capabilities. Using a full-featured monitoring tool can allow active ping monitoring to be combined with other data easily, providing far more useful analysis capabilities than a ping script.

Passive Monitoring

Passive monitoring relies on capturing information about the network as traffic passes a location on a network link. In Figure 6.3, a network monitor uses a network tap to send a copy of all of the traffic sent between endpoints A and B. This allows the monitoring system to capture the traffic that is sent, providing a detailed view of the traffic's rate, protocol, and content, as well as details of the performance of sending and receiving packets.

FIGURE 6.3   Passive monitoring between two systems

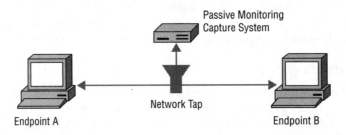

Unlike active and router-based monitoring, passive monitoring does not add additional traffic to the network. It also performs after-the-fact analysis, as packets must be captured and analyzed, rather than being recorded in real time as they are sent. This means that the trade-offs between each monitoring method should be considered when choosing a technique.

Network Monitoring Tools

Network monitoring involves much more than a view of just the routers or the traffic passing through interfaces. Gathering information from multiple network devices and combining that data into useful views for analysis and reporting is critical to ensuring that you have a good view of what is occurring on your network. Fortunately, tools are available that are specifically designed to provide this visibility.

PRTG

One common choice for monitoring bandwidth usage is PRTG (the Paessler Router Traffic Grapher). PRTG provides a variety of network monitoring capabilities, including server monitoring, network monitoring, and bandwidth monitoring. PRTG combines four types of monitoring to provide a more accurate picture of bandwidth utilization:

- Packet sniffing, which only monitors the headers of packets to determine what type of traffic is being sent. This can identify information from packets that the sensor can read, but an encrypted session may not reveal much.

- Flows, which can send either information about all connections, or a sampled dataset.

- SNMP (Simple Network Management Protocol), a protocol that allows network devices to send information about important events as *SNMP traps.*

- *WMI* (Windows Management Instrumentation), which provides an interface that allows script and application access for automation of administrative tasks, as well as a means of accessing management data for the operating system, and can provide reports to tools like System Center Operations Manager for Windows systems. A hybrid mode allows access to Windows performance counters using the remote registry service, with WMI as a fallback. This approach can make a Windows system's native monitoring capability useful for a central view

Figure 6.4 shows PRTG's overview window. Traffic over time as well as flow information are shown in near real time. To investigate a problem, you can simply drill down by clicking the appropriate view.

FIGURE 6.4   PRTG network overview

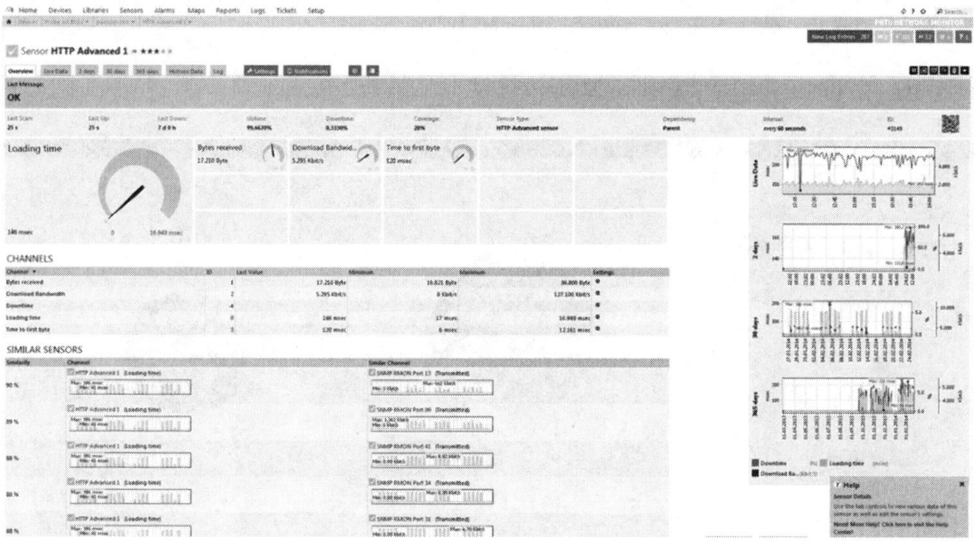

Overview and dashboard screens in tools like PRTG are often used to provide a high-level overview of network performance. A sudden drop-off or increase in network usage can be quickly seen on the overview chart, and drilling down by clicking the chart can help to isolate or identify a system or interface that is affected or that may be causing the issue. More detailed searches and filters can also be accessed in tools like this to answer specific questions if you are working from existing knowledge like an IP address or interface that needs to be investigated.

Capturing data from large networks or networks with a lot of bandwidth usage can result in so much traffic that network analysis tools can't handle the load. That's where sampling comes in handy. Often, traffic analysis is done using trend and anomaly analysis rather than looking for specific individual behaviors. With this in mind, a sample rate of 1 in 10, or even 1 in 1000, can still provide useful aggregate data. If your flow collector or analysis system is having problems keeping up, consider using sampling instead of complete capture.

SolarWinds

SolarWinds sells a variety of network monitoring tools that address multiple types of data gathering. Their products aimed at network troubleshooting and bandwidth management include the following:

- Netflow Traffic Analyzer, which is specifically designed to handle network bandwidth analysis using flows, as shown in Figure 6.5. Flow sources, utilization, and endpoints are all easily seen in the interface, allowing for quick analysis. Additional detail can be accessed by drilling down on any of the linked data.

- Network Performance Monitor, which is built around network fault detection and availability management. Figure 6.6 shows the SolarWinds Performance Monitor view for a single router. Detailed statistics and performance information are available, as well as drill-down visibility into device logs and other information. Overall network health and performance can also be viewed from the tool.

FIGURE 6.5   Netflow Traffic Analyzer

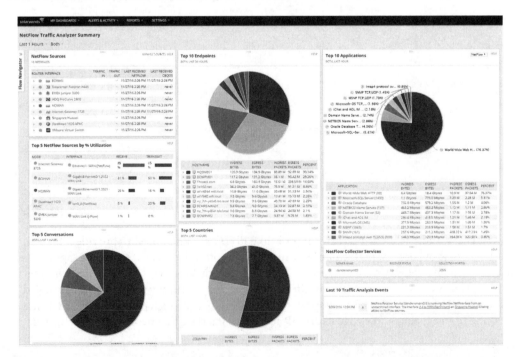

FIGURE 6.6 SolarWinds Performance Monitor

Combining the ability to identify network issues and intelligence about network bandwidth and flows can provide a better view of what is occurring on a network, making a pairing of tools like this a good solution when trying to understand complex network issues.

 SolarWinds provides a demo of their tools at `http://oriondemo` `.solarwinds.com/Orion/`. You can watch videos of each of the tools at `http://demo.solarwinds.com/sedemo/` for more detail on how to use them.

Nagios

Nagios is a popular network and system log monitoring tool. Nagios supports a broad range of plug-ins, including the ability to build and integrate your own plug-ins using Perl or executable applications. Nagios provides a broad range of monitoring capabilities beyond network monitoring, making it a useful tool if you want to have a central view of system and network data in one place.

Nagios Core provides a GUI view of systems, services, and monitoring capabilities, as shown in Figure 6.7. This tactical overview allows you to quickly review issues based on their severity.

FIGURE 6.7   Nagios Core tactical view

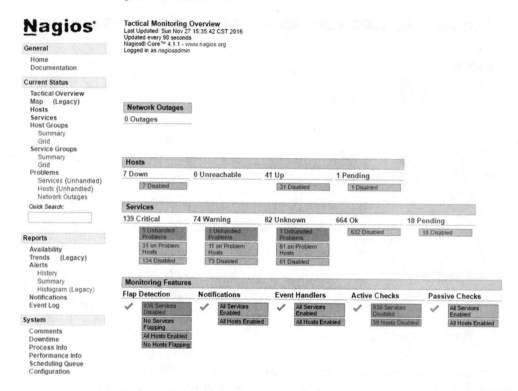

Navigating in the web interface for Nagios Core provides deeper review capabilities, as shown in Figure 6.8. Critical items, which are set based on log levels and alerting thresholds, allow you to modify which items will show in this view. Here, Nagios can't read the output from a host, resulting in a critical error. This could be an indicator of a security event, but is likely a failed host, an incorrectly configured syslog service, or an unexpected output from the logging service that Nagios cannot interpret.

FIGURE 6.8   Nagios Core notifications view

Host	Service	Type	Time	Contact	Notification Command	Information
linux-snmp2.nagios.local	Youtube Usage	OK	11-27-2016 15:37:58	nagiosadmin	notify-service-by-email	OK: 3 MB/s reported
windows-switch.nagios.local	Youtube Usage	WARNING	11-27-2016 15:37:58	nagiosadmin	notify-service-by-email	WARNING: 6 MB/s reported
rhel1.nagios.local	Port 80 Bandwidth	WARNING	11-27-2016 15:37:48	nagiosadmin	notify-service-by-email	WARNING: 57 MB/s reported
centos2.nagios.local	Apache 404 Errors	OK	11-27-2016 15:37:48	nagiosadmin	notify-service-by-email	OK: 67 matching entries found
fedora-switch.nagios.local	Youtube Usage	WARNING	11-27-2016 15:37:48	nagiosadmin	notify-service-by-email	WARNING: 10 MB/s reported
Network-Analyzer2.nagios.local	Failed SSH Logins	OK	11-27-2016 15:37:48	nagiosadmin	notify-service-by-email	OK: 7 matching entries found
centos4.nagios.local	Failed SSH Logins	OK	11-27-2016 15:37:28	nagiosadmin	notify-service-by-email	OK: 1 matching entries found
mysql1.nagios.local	Failed SSH Logins	OK	11-27-2016 15:37:09	nagiosadmin	notify-service-by-email	OK: 3 matching entries found
Log-Server.nagios.local	Linux Failed Logins	OK	11-27-2016 15:37:09	nagiosadmin	notify-service-by-email	OK: 3 matching entries found
localhost	MySQL Crashed Tables	OK	11-27-2016 15:37:09	nagiosadmin	notify-service-by-email	OK: 1 matching entries found
rhel-switch.nagios.local	Youtube Usage	OK	11-27-2016 15:37:09	nagiosadmin	notify-service-by-email	OK: 5 MB/s reported
rhel2.nagios.local	System Logging Daemon	CRITICAL	11-27-2016 15:37:09	nagiosadmin	notify-service-by-email	NRPE: Unable to read output
Network-Analyzer2.nagios.local	Bandwidth Spike	OK	11-27-2016 15:37:09	nagiosadmin	notify-service-by-email	OK: 56 MB/s reported
Network-Analyzer2.nagios.local	Failed SSH Logins	WARNING	11-27-2016 15:36:49	nagiosadmin	notify-service-by-email	WARNING: 9 matching entries found
centos2.nagios.local	Apache 404 Errors	CRITICAL	11-27-2016 15:36:49	nagiosadmin	notify-service-by-email	CRITICAL: 93 matching entries found
centos4.nagios.local	Failed SSH Logins	WARNING	11-27-2016 15:36:28	nagiosadmin	notify-service-by-email	WARNING: 9 matching entries found

There are two major versions of Nagios: Nagios Core, which is open source and free, and Nagios XI, which is a commercial tool. If you want to give Nagios Core a try, you can at https://exchange.nagios.org/directory/ Demos/Nagios-Core-Online-Demo/visit.

Cacti

Cacti is an open source tool that uses SNMP polling to poll network devices for status information and provides graphical views of network and device status. Additional data can be included by using scripts with data stored in a database, allowing Cacti to provide visibility into a range of devices and data types. Cacti leverages RRDTool, a graphing and analysis package to provide detailed graphical views of the data it gathers.

Detecting Common Network Issues

Once you have visibility into your network's bandwidth and device status, you can use that knowledge to track common network problems. These common problems include bandwidth consumption, link and connection failures, beaconing, and unexpected traffic. Although each of these problems is common, the causes of each type of issue can be quite varied!

Bandwidth Consumption

Bandwidth consumption can cause service outages and disruptions of business functions, making it a serious concern for both security analysts and network managers. In a well-designed network, the network will be configured to use logging and monitoring methods that fit its design, security, and monitoring requirements, and that data will be sent to a central system that can provide bandwidth usage alarms. Techniques we have already discussed in this chapter can provide the information needed to detect bandwidth consumption issues:

- Tools like PRTG that use flow data can show trend and status information indicating that network bandwidth utilization has peaked.

- Monitoring tools can be used to check for high usage levels and can send alarms based on thresholds.

- Real-time or near-real-time graphs can be used to monitor bandwidth as usage occurs.

- SNMP data can be used to monitor for high load and other signs of bandwidth utilization at the router or network device level.

Real World Scenario

The Importance of Detecting Data Exfiltration

In 2015, Penn State University disclosed a breach of systems in their College of Engineering. The breach was reported to potentially include research that was being conducted for the U.S. Department of Defense—a critical concern for both the U.S. military and the university.

When attackers specifically target an organization, they're often looking for data. That means that once they find a way in and get to the data that they're interested in, they'll need to get the data out. Data exfiltration is a major worry for organizations that rely on the security of their data.

Monitoring for data exfiltration can be incredibly challenging. At a university like Penn State, massive amounts of data of all types move between systems on a daily basis, and the prevalence of encrypted communications can make it hard to determine whether the traffic sent to an external site is legitimate traffic or your sensitive data heading out the door.

Network monitoring can help to prevent exfiltration if a network is well controlled and well understood. Servers shouldn't reach out to external systems, and large data transfers to outside systems from sensitive file stores should be expected. That means that a combination of anomaly detection and behavior analysis as well as technologies like data loss prevention systems or software can help.

Unfortunately, determined attackers are likely to figure out a way to steal data, and proving that data didn't leave can be nearly impossible. That means that protecting data from being accessed is a much better solution than trying to stop bad guys as they take the data out of your network.

Link Failure

Link failure can be caused by physical failures like a bad connector or a cable being unplugged, or can occur at the network device level, due to bad hardware, firmware, or software. Detecting link failures is important because it can allow faster repair and restoration of service. Troubleshooting specific types of link failure is beyond the scope of this book, but the general troubleshooting process is typically to replace the most common failure items (like cables and interface modules) one at a time, testing after each is replaced first, and then proceed through each of the possible items that may have failed until the interface is restored.

Link failures can be detected directly by using SNMP monitoring or syslog events. Bandwidth monitoring tools like network flows can also provide insight into link failures by monitoring for complete drops in traffic levels. Figure 6.9 shows an example of a disconnected link resulting in an immediate drop-off of traffic levels to a flat line at 0 kilobits per second. At the same time, SNMP monitoring tools for the same network would reveal that the interface dropped offline.

FIGURE 6.9   Network bandwidth monitoring showing a dropped link

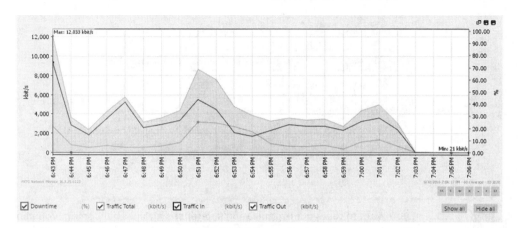

When a failed link is redundant, it may go unnoticed unless appropriate monitoring is in place. Once a part of a redundant link fails, your network is likely running with a single point of failure—and you may not even know!

Beaconing

Beaconing activity (sometimes a heartbeat) is activity sent to a C&C system as part of a botnet or malware remote control system and is typically sent as either HTTP or HTTPS traffic. Beaconing can request commands, provide status, download additional malware, or perform other actions. Since beaconing is often encrypted and blends in with other web traffic, it can be difficult to identify, but detecting beaconing behavior is a critical part of detecting malware infections.

Detection of beaconing behavior is often handled by using an IDS or IPS system with detection rules that identify known botnet controllers or botnet-specific behavior. In addition, using flow analysis or other traffic monitoring tools to ensure that systems are not sending unexpected traffic that could be beaconing is also possible. This means that inspecting outbound traffic to ensure that infected systems are not resident in your network is as important as controls that handle inbound traffic.

Figure 6.10 shows simulated beaconing behavior, with a host reaching out to a remote site via HTTP every 10 seconds. This type of repeated behavior can be difficult to find when it is slow, but automated analysis can help to identify it. Using a tool like Wireshark to directly capture the traffic, as shown in the figure, can be useful for detailed analysis, but flows and IDS and IPS systems are more useful for a broader view of network traffic.

FIGURE 6.10   Beaconing in Wireshark

No.	Time	Source	Destination	Protoc▾
66	31.538876037	10.0.2.15	192.168.1.1	DNS
67	31.540080521	192.168.1.1	10.0.2.15	DNS
68	31.672776791	192.168.1.1	10.0.2.15	DNS
8	0.369157221	10.0.2.15	104.155.5.19	HTTP
15	0.483471214	104.155.5.19	10.0.2.15	HTTP
28	10.754906620	10.0.2.15	104.155.5.19	HTTP
35	10.886511298	104.155.5.19	10.0.2.15	HTTP
48	21.303051037	10.0.2.15	104.155.5.19	HTTP
59	21.531966939	104.155.5.19	10.0.2.15	HTTP
72	31.789818761	10.0.2.15	104.155.5.19	HTTP
83	32.017497173	104.155.5.19	10.0.2.15	HTTP
5	0.252749594	10.0.2.15	104.155.5.19	TCP
6	0.368868964	104.155.5.19	10.0.2.15	TCP
7	0.368930078	10.0.2.15	104.155.5.19	TCP
9	0.482285602	104.155.5.19	10.0.2.15	TCP

If you want to test your organization's defenses against beaconing, you can simulate a beacon with techniques discussed at http://blog.opensecurity-research.com/2012/12/testing-your-defenses-beaconing.html.

Unexpected Traffic

Unexpected traffic on a network can take many forms: scans and probes, peer-to-peer traffic between systems that aren't expected to communicate directly, or more direct attack traffic. Unexpected traffic can be detected by behavior-based detection capabilities built into IDS and IPS systems, by traffic monitoring systems, or manually by observing traffic between systems. Understanding what traffic is expected and what traffic is unexpected relies on three major techniques:

- *Baselines*, or *anomaly-based detection*, which requires knowledge of what normal traffic is. Baselines are typically gathered during normal network operations. Once baseline data is gathered, monitoring systems can be set to alarm when the baselines are exceeded by a given threshold or when network behavior deviates from the baseline behaviors that were documented.

- *Heuristics*, or *behavior-based detection,* using network security devices and defined rules for attack traffic and other network issues.

- *Protocol analysis*, which uses a protocol analyzer to capture packets and check for problems. Protocol analyzers can help find unexpected traffic, like VPN traffic in a network where no VPN traffic is expected, or IPv6 tunnels running from a production IPv4 network.

Not all unexpected traffic is malicious, but it is important to ensure that you have appropriate systems and methods in place to detect anomalies and unexpected behaviors and that you can identify when unexpected traffic is occurring so that you can respond appropriately.

Figure 6.11 shows an IDS detection based on unexpected traffic between a local host (Iodine) and a system in Russia. This detection was flagged as a potential malware download based on its behavior.

FIGURE 6.11   Unexpected network traffic shown in flows

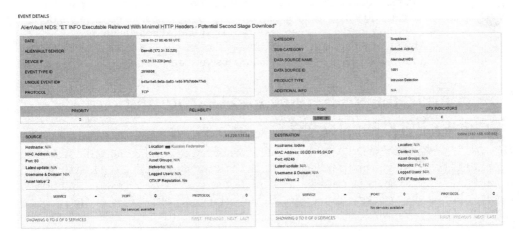

Handling Network Probes and Attacks

Many of the events detected by intrusion detection systems, firewalls, and other network security devices will be probes, scans, or potential attack traffic. Handling the volume of traffic that could be an attack or information gathering can drive you to distraction if you don't have a good system in place for detecting them and then taking appropriate action.

Detecting Scans and Probes

Scans and probes are typically not significant threats to infrastructure by themselves, but they are often a precursor to more focused attacks. Detecting scans and probes is often quite simple: network scans are often easily detectable due to the behaviors they include, such as sequential testing of service ports, connecting to many IP addresses in a network, and repeated requests to services that may not be active. More stealthy scans and probes can be harder to detect among the general noise of a network, and detecting stealthy scans from multiple remote systems on a system connected to the Internet can be quite challenging.

Fortunately, most IDS and IPS systems, as well as other network security devices like firewalls and network security appliances, have built-in scan detection capabilities. Enabling these can result in a lot of noise, and in many cases there is little you can do about a scan. Many organizations choose to feed their scan detection data to a security information management tool to combine with data from attacks and other events, rather than responding to the scans and probes directly.

To test your ability to detect scans and probes, use a scanning tool like nmap and verify that you can detect your own scans. Increase the difficulty by using more advanced features like stealth scans (using the **nmap -sS** flag) and nmap's timing flag, where **-T0** is the slowest scan, and **-T5** is a full-speed aggressive scan.

Detecting Denial-of-Service and Distributed Denial-of-Service Attacks

Denial-of-service attacks (DoS) can take many forms, but the goal remains the same: preventing access to a system or service. They can be conducted from a single system, or from many systems as part of a distributed denial-of-service attack. Detecting and preventing denial-of-service attacks is an increasingly important part of a cybersecurity analyst's skillset.

DoS Attacks

DoS attacks typically include one or more of the following patterns of attack:

- Attempts to overwhelm a network or service through the sheer volume of requests or traffic
- Attacks on a specific service or system vulnerability to cause the system or service to fail
- Attacks on an intermediary system or network to prevent traffic from making it between two locations

Each of these types of attacks requires slightly different methods of detection. This means that your network, system, and service monitoring capabilities need to be set up to monitor for multiple types of attacks depending on which might target your infrastructure.

A DoS attack from a single system or network can typically be stopped by blocking that system or network using a firewall or other network security device. IPS systems can also block known attack traffic, preventing a DoS attack from occurring. Single-system DoS attacks are not as likely as distributed denial-of-service attacks unless the target suffers from a specific service or application vulnerability, or the target can be easily overwhelmed by a single remote system due to limited bandwidth or other resources.

Distributed Denial-of-Service Attacks

Distributed denial-of-service (DDoS) attacks come from many systems or networks at the same time. They can be harder to detect due to the traffic coming from many places, and that also makes them much harder to stop. Many DDoS attacks are composed of compromised systems in botnets, allowing attackers to send traffic from hundreds or thousands of systems.

Tools like the Low Orbit Ion Cannon (LOIC) have also made participation in DDoS attacks a voluntary effort as part of hacktivist efforts from groups like Anonymous. Understanding why your organization might be targeted, and by whom, is an important part of planning for and responding to DoS and DDOS attacks.

Detecting DoS and DDoS Attacks

Since there are many flavors of DoS and DDoS attacks, building an effective DoS and DDoS detection capability usually involves multiple types of tools and monitoring systems. These often include the following:

- Performance monitoring using service performance monitoring tools
- Connection monitoring using local system or application logs
- Network bandwidth or system bandwidth monitoring
- Dedicated tools like IDS or IPS systems with DoS and DDoS detection rules enabled

During incident response, the same command-line tools that you can use to analyze network traffic (like netstat) can help with troubleshooting on local servers, but a view from the network or service perspective will typically provide a broader view of the issue.

 Real World Scenario

Surviving a Denial-of-Service Attack

If your organization has a public Internet presence, you're likely to have to deal with a DoS attack at some point, whether it's on purpose or accidental. Fortunately, services and tools now exist to help organizations weather these attacks.

Here are two common ways to survive a DDoS attack:

- Using a dedicated service designed to handle these attacks that uses a large distributed network of endpoints combined with DDoS mitigation tools to ensure that your service (typically a website) can be accessed even if one or more distribution locations is offline. In Figure 6.12, a DDoS mitigation system distributes copies of a website's content to globally distributed content distribution network (CDN) servers while blocking DDoS attacks using a centrally managed defense mechanism. This ensures that legitimate users receive a response from a CDN node that is close to them, avoiding potential issues with the main website or networks that serve it during a DDoS.

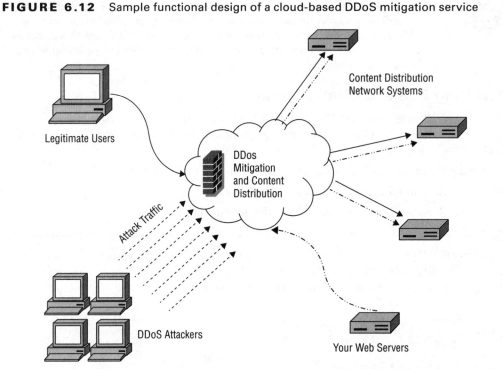

FIGURE 6.12   Sample functional design of a cloud-based DDoS mitigation service

- Deploying a DDoS mitigation device or technology. These often analyze flows or sit in-line between the protected systems and the public Internet. They then gather data to provide a view of traffic to a network or service, and redirect or drop bad traffic based on signatures or behavior analysis.

Detecting Other Network Attacks

Other network-based attacks can be detected using the same techniques outlined earlier:

- Use an IDS or IPS
- Monitor flows, SNMP, and other network information for suspect behaviors
- Feed logs from firewalls, routers, switches, and other network devices to a central log analysis and monitoring system
- Use a SIEM device to review and automatically alarm on problem traffic

    A subscription to a frequently updated and well-managed feed of IDS/ IPS rules and subscribing to groups that monitor for trending attacks can help make sure that you stay ahead of the attacks you may find aimed at your network.

Detecting and Finding Rogue Devices

Rogue devices are devices that are connected to a network that should not be, either by policy or because they have been added by an attacker. Finding rogue devices can be challenging—many networks have hundreds or thousands of devices, and device management may not be consistent across the network.

There are a number of common methods of identifying rogue devices:

Valid MAC Address Checking   Uses MAC address information provided to network devices to validate the hardware address presented by the device to a list of known devices.

MAC Address Vendor Information Checking   Vendors of network equipment use a vendor prefix for their devices. This means that many devices can be identified based on their manufacturer.

Network Scanning   Performed using a tool like nmap to identify new devices.

Site Surveys   Involve physically reviewing the devices at a site either by manual verification or by checking wireless networks on-site.

Traffic Analysis   Used to identify irregular or unexpected behavior.

You can look up hardware vendors from a MAC address at sites like www.macvendors.com or www.macvendorlookup.com. Remember that it is possible to change MAC addresses, so the address presented by a device isn't guaranteed to be correct!

Wired and wireless networks face slightly different threats from rogue devices, and you need to be aware of those differences when responding to potential incidents.

Wired Rogues

Most wired rogues rely on open or unauthenticated networks to connect. Open networks without access controls like *port security*, which checks for trusted MAC address, or *network access control* (NAC) technology are easy targets for wired rogue devices. A wired rogue device typically means that one of two likely scenarios has occurred:

- An employee or other trusted member of the organization has connected a device, either without permission or without following the process required to connect a device.
- An attacker has connected a device to the network.

The first scenario may be a simple mistake, but the second implies that an attacker has had physical access to your network! In either case, rogue devices connected to a wired network should be responded to quickly so that they can be removed or otherwise handled appropriately.

Preventing wired rogue devices can be accomplished by either restricting which devices can connect (via port security or a similar MAC address limiting technology) or via NAC and requiring authentication to the network. Unfortunately, MAC address filtering won't stop determined attackers—they only need to replace a legitimate device with their own with the MAC address set to match the trusted device—but it will stop casual attempts to connect.

Wireless Rogues

Wireless rogues can create additional challenges because they can't always easily be tracked to a specific physical location. That means that tracking down a rogue may involve using signal strength measures and mapping the area where the rogue is to attempt to locate it. Fortunately, if the wireless rogue is plugged into your network, using a port scan with operating system identification turned on can often help locate the device. In Figure 6.13, a common consumer router was scanned after it was connected to a network. In this example, nmap cannot immediately identify the device, but it is obvious that it is not a typical desktop system since it shows the router as potentially being a VoIP phone, firewall, or other embedded device.

FIGURE 6.13 nmap scan of a potential rogue system

```
Starting Nmap 7.01 ( https://nmap.org ) at 2016-09-04 11:55 EDT
Nmap scan report for demo.localnet.com (192.168.1.1)
Host is up (0.11s latency).
Not shown: 997 closed ports
PORT     STATE SERVICE
53/tcp   open  domain
80/tcp   open  http
1723/tcp open  pptp
Device type: VoIP phone|firewall|specialized
Running (JUST GUESSING): Grandstream embedded (90%), FireBrick embedded (87%), 2N embedded (87%)
OS CPE: cpe:/h:grandstream:gxp1105 cpe:/h:firebrick:fb2700 cpe:/h:2n:helios
Aggressive OS guesses: Grandstream GXP1105 VoIP phone (90%), FireBrick FB2700 firewall (87%), 2N Helios
IP VoIP doorbell (87%)
No exact OS matches for host (test conditions non-ideal).

OS detection performed. Please report any incorrect results at https://nmap.org/submit/ .
Nmap done: 1 IP address (1 host up) scanned in 130.45 seconds
```

Wireless rogues can also create issues by spoofing legitimate networks, persuading legitimate users that they're part of your organization's network. This normally involves overpowering legitimate access points, so using enterprise wireless controllers that can detect interference and report on it (or even automatically overpower it!) can help prevent the problem.

Investigating Host Issues

Security issues for servers and workstations can be challenging to identify. Modern malware is extremely good at remaining hidden. Fortunately, system monitoring tools can help identify unexpected behaviors by checking for host-related issues. That means system monitoring is useful for both security and day-to-day system health purposes.

System Resources

The most basic monitoring for most servers and workstations is resource monitoring. Utilization information for system resources like CPU, memory, disk, and network can provide valuable details about the state of the system, its workloads, and whether a problem exists.

Processor Monitoring

Understanding what processes are consuming CPU time, how much CPU utilization is occurring, and when the processes are running can be useful for incident detection and response. Sudden spikes in CPU usage on a system with otherwise consistent usage levels may indicate new software or a process that was not previously active. Consistently high levels of CPU usage can also point to a DoS condition. Used alone, CPU load information typically will not tell the whole story, but it should be part of your monitoring efforts.

Memory Monitoring

Most operating system level memory monitoring is focused on memory utilization, rather than what is being stored in memory. That means your visibility into memory usage is likely to focus on consumption and process identification. Most protective measures for memory-based attacks occur as part of an operating system's built-in memory management or when code is compiled.

Most organizations set memory monitoring levels for alarms and notification based on typical system memory usage and an "emergency" level when a system or application is approaching an out-of-memory condition. This can be identified by tracking memory usage during normal and peak usage and then setting *monitoring thresholds*, or levels where alarms or alerts will occur, based on that data.

WARNING   If you're troubleshooting memory issues in Windows, you may encounter a result code titled `Buffer Overflow`—this doesn't mean you're under attack. Instead, it indicates that an application requested data but did not have sufficient memory space allocated. The Windows `Buffer Overflow` result tag simply indicates insufficient memory allocation.

Memory Leaks

Memory leaks are a frequent culprit in system crashes and outages. A memory leak occurs when a program doesn't release memory after it is no longer needed. Over time, an application with a memory leak will consume more and more memory until the application fails or the operating system runs out of available memory. This can cause an application or system crash.

Memory monitoring can help prevent memory leaks from resulting in a crash by sounding the alarm when memory utilization increases, but it can't stop a memory leak. If there is no patch for the issue, the only recourse for an application or service with a memory leak is to periodically restart the service or the system it runs on.

Drive Capacity Monitoring

Drive capacity monitoring typically focuses on specific capacity levels and is intended to prevent the drive or volume from filling up, causing an outage. Tools to monitor this are available for all major operating systems, as well as centralized monitoring and management systems like *System Center Operations Manager (SCOM)* for Windows or Nagios for Linux. System Center Configuration Manager (SCCM) can also provide information about disk usage, but it is not a real-time reporting mechanism. Disk monitoring in real time can help prevent outages and issues more easily than a daily report since disks can fill up quickly.

System Resource Monitoring Tools

Windows provides built-in resource and performance monitoring tools. *Resource Monitor*, or *resmon*, is the Windows resource monitor and provides easy visibility into the CPU, memory, disk, and network utilization for a system. In addition to utilization, its network monitoring capability shows processes with network activity, which TCP connections are open, and what services are associated with open ports on the system. Figure 6.14 shows the Resource Monitor overview screen for sample Windows 10 system.

FIGURE 6.14   The Windows Resource Monitor view of system resources

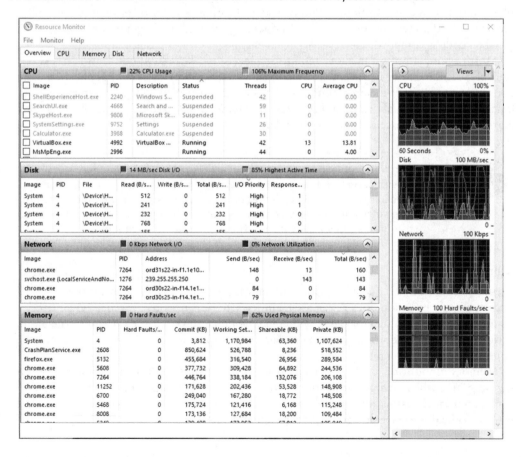

Performance Monitor, or *perfmon*, provides much more detailed data, with counters ranging from energy usage to disk and network activity. It also supports collection from remote systems, allowing a broader view of system activity. For detailed data collection, perfmon is a better solution, whereas resmon is useful for checking the basic usage measures for a machine quickly. Figure 6.15 shows perfmon configured with a disk and processor monitor. This data can be combined into user- or system-defined reports.

FIGURE 6.15   The Windows Performance Monitor view of system usage

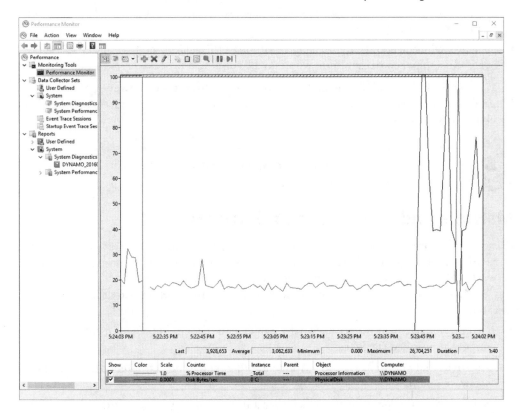

The Sysinternals suite for Windows provides extensive monitoring capabilities beyond the built-in set of tools. You can download the Sysinternals tools at `https://technet` `.microsoft.com/en-us/sysinternals/`, or you can run them live at the Windows command prompt or from File Explorer by entering `https://live.sysinternals` `.com/toolname`, replacing ***toolname*** with the name of the tool you want to use.

To start resmon or perfmon (as well as other Windows Control Panel plug-ins), simply type their names into the Windows search or run menu.

Linux has a number of built-in tools that can be used to check CPU, disk, and memory usage. They include the following:

- ps provides information about CPU and memory utilization, the time that a process was started, and how long it has run, as well as the command that started each process.

- top provides CPU utilization under CPU stats and also shows memory usage as well as other details about running processes. top also provides interaction via hotkeys, including allowing quick identification of top consumers by entering **A**.

- df displays a report of the system's disk usage, with various flags providing additional detail or formatting.

- w shows which accounts are logged in. Although this isn't directly resource related, it can be useful when determining who may be running a process.

Many other Linux tools are available, including graphical tools; however, almost all Linux distributions will include ps, top, and df, making them a good starting point when checking the state of a system.

 Use the -h flag for df to show filesystem usage in a human-readable format.

Malware and Unauthorized Software

Unauthorized software and malware is a major cause of system issues. Software issues can range from application and driver incompatibilities to unauthorized software that sends network traffic, resulting in issues for other systems on the network.

Detecting malware and unauthorized software typically relies on one of four major methods:

- Central management tools like SCCM, which can manage software installation and report on installed software.

- Antivirus and antimalware tools, which are designed to detect potentially harmful software and files.

- Software and file *blacklisting*, which uses a list of disallowed software and files and prohibits its installation. This differs from antivirus and antimalware by potentially providing a broader list of prohibited files than only malicious or similar files.

- *Application whitelisting*, which allows only permitted files and applications on a system. In a fully whitelisted environment, no files that are not previously permitted are allowed on a system.

Most managed environments will use more than one of these techniques to manage the software and applications that are present on workstations, servers, and mobile devices.

Real World Scenario

When Innocuous Tools Aren't

A common Linux command-line utility known as netcat, or its Windows equivalent nc.exe is often associated with penetration testing and compromises. Netcat allows you to create UDP or TCP connections using simple commands like nc -l -p 37337 -e cmd.exe (which opens a remote shell on port 37337 which connects to cmd.exe). Due to this, it is often baked into exploits to provide easy connectivity. If you find netcat (or nc.exe) on a system where it shouldn't be, your system may have been owned!

Unauthorized Access, Changes, and Privileges

Unauthorized access to systems and devices, as well as use of privileges that result in unexpected changes, are a major cause for alarm. Unfortunately, the number and variety of systems, as well as the complexity of the user and permissions models in use in many organizations, can make monitoring for unauthorized activity challenging.

The good news is that monitoring for unauthorized access, changes, and privileges uses many of the same set of techniques and technologies we have already discussed. Table 6.1 lists some of the possible methods for detection for each of these types of unauthorized use.

TABLE 6.1   Unauthorized use and detection mechanisms

Unauthorized use type	Data logged	Location of data	Analysis tools
Unauthorized access	Authentication User creation	Authentication logs User creation logs	Central management suite SIM/SIEM
Unauthorized changes	File creation Settings changes	System logs Application logs Monitoring tools	Central management suite SIM/SIEM File and directory integrity checking tools (Tripwire)
Unauthorized privilege use	Privilege use attempts Privilege escalation	Security event logs Application logs	SIM/SIEM Log analysis tools

Each of these techniques requires a strong understanding of what access is expected on each system or devices so that exceptions can be detected. Change management, permission management, and identity management are all important administrative processes to apply in addition to the technical controls listed earlier.

Unauthorized privileges can be harder to track, particularly if they are not centrally managed and audited. Fortunately, tools like Sysinternals' AccessChk can help by validating the access that a specific user or group has to objects like files, registry keys, and services. On the other hand, while the audit system in Linux can help detect uses of privileges, checking for specific permissions will typically require you to write a script to check the specific privileges you are concerned about.

Investigating Service and Application Issues

Investigating application and service issues requires information about what services and applications are running and how they are expected to behave as well as self-reported and system-reported information about the services. In many organizations, active service monitoring will also be used to determine if the service is working properly.

Application- and service-related events like incorrect behavior, unexpected log messages or errors, new users or processes, and file changes are all common signs of a possibly compromised service. Fortunately, many of the tools you need to investigate these problems are already built into Windows and Linux systems.

Application and Service Monitoring

Monitoring applications and services is critical to an organization's operations and can also provide important security insight by showing where unexpected behavior is occurring or where applications and services are being abused.

> In this section, we will use the terms *application* and *service* interchangeably. Some organizations will separate them, with services characterized as specialized and often accessed by other programs, and applications more generalized and often accessed by humans. This distinction can get a bit fuzzy!

Application and service monitoring can be categorized into a few common monitoring areas:

- Up/down—is the service running?
- Performance—does it respond quickly and as expected?
- Transactional logging—information about the function of the service is captured, such as what actions users take or what actions are performed.
- Application or service logging—logs about the function or status of the service.

Each of these areas provides part of the puzzle for visibility into an application's or service's status, performance, and behavior. During an investigation, you will often need to identify behavior that does not match what the service typically logs.

Service Anomaly Detection

Anomalous behavior from services is relatively common. A variety of non-security-related problems can result in service issues, such as

- Service-specific errors, including authentication errors, service dependency issues, and permissions issues
- Services that don't start on boot, either because of a service-specific error or because the service is disabled
- Service failures, which are often caused by updates, patches, or other changes

Service failure troubleshooting typically starts with an attempt to start, or restart, the service. If that is not successful, a review of the service's log message or error messages can provide the information needed to resolve the problem.

Anomalies in services due to security issues may be able to be detected using the same monitoring techniques; however, additional tools can be useful to ensure that the service and its constituent files and applications are not compromised. In addition to common service and log monitoring tools. you might choose to deploy additional protection such as the following:

- Antimalware and antivirus
- File integrity checking tools
- Whitelisting tools

 Windows provides WinDbg for debugging of issues. Crash dump debugging is outside the scope of this book, but you can find details at https://msdn.microsoft.com/en-us/library/windows/hardware/mt219729(v=vs.85).aspx.

Windows Service Status

Windows service status can be checked either via the Services administrative tool (services.msc) or by using command-line tools like sc, the Service Controller application, which accepts command-line flags set the start type for service, the error level it should set if it fails during boot, and details of the service. PowerShell also provides service interaction scriptlets like Start-Service to interact with services on local and remote Windows hosts.

Linux Service Status

Linux services can be checked on most systems by using the service command. service [servicename] status will return the status of many, but not all, Linux services. You can try the command to list the state of all services by running

```
service --status-all
```

Linux systems that use init.d can be checked by running a command like

```
/etc/init.d/servicename status
```

Linux service restart processes vary depending on the distribution. Check your distribution to verify how it expects services to be restarted.

Application Error Monitoring

Most Windows applications log to the Windows Application log (although some maintain their own dedicated log files as well). To check for application errors, you can view the Application log via the Windows Event Viewer. You can also centralize these logs using SCOM.

Many Linux applications provide useful details in the /var/log directory or in a specific application log location. Using the tail command, these logs can be monitored while the application is tested. Much like Windows, some Linux applications store their files in an application-specific location, so you may have to check the application's documentation to track down all the data the application provides.

Application Behavior Analysis

Applications that have been compromised or that have been successfully attacked can suddenly start to behave in ways that aren't typical: outbound communications may occur, the application may make database or other resource requests that are not typically part of its behavior, or new files or user accounts may be created. Understanding typical application behavior requires a combination of

- Documentation of the application's normal behavior, such as what systems it should connect to and how those connections should be made

- Logging, to provide a view of normal operations

- Heuristic (behavioral) analysis using antimalware tools and other security-monitoring systems to flag when behaviors deviate from the norm

Application and Service Issue Response and Restoration

There are many reasons that applications and services encounter issues, ranging from incorrect credentials or rights, bad patches, and component versions to software flaws and actual attacks. Detecting issues with applications relies on many of the same techniques used for network and system issues, with the addition of application-specific monitoring tools and service-monitoring software.

When an application or service encounters an issue, it will often report an error. That means it is possible to handle errors and exceptions automatically by creating scripts or automated service restarts when the error is thrown.

Application monitoring services can also be scripted to take action when a service or server is offline. This requires that the monitoring system have rights to restart the appropriate system or service, and if the monitoring system is not correct about the outage, it can disrupt service. Automated responses should be carefully tested to ensure that they do not cause disruption rather than fix it.

Detecting Attacks on Applications

Attacks on applications can take a number of forms, ranging from web application attacks to malware that targets executable files. Focusing on the behaviors that indicate attacks can be one of the most important tools in your arsenal. Detecting the behaviors listed here as they happen, or before they result from an attack, is preferable, but being able to perform an analysis of *why* they have happened is often necessary too.

- *Anomalous activity*, or activity that does not match the application's typical behavior, is often the first indicator of an attack or compromise. Log analysis, behavior baselines, and filesystem integrity checking can all help detect unexpected behavior. User and administrator awareness training can also help make sure you hear about applications that are behaving in abnormal ways.

- *New accounts*, particularly those with administrative rights, are often a sign of compromise. Application account creation is not always logged in a central location, making it important to find ways to track both account creation and privileges granted to accounts. Administrative controls that match a change management workflow and approvals to administrative account creation, paired with technical controls, can provide a stronger line of defense.

- *Unexpected output* can take many forms, from improper output or garbled data to errors and other signs of an underlying application issue. Unexpected output can also be challenging to detect using centralized methods for user-level applications. Server-based applications that provide file- or API-level output are often easier to check for errors based on validity checkers (if they exist!). This is another type of application error where user and administrator training can help identify problems.

- *Unexpected outbound communication* like beaconing, outbound file transfers, or attacks are all common types of application exploit indicators. Using network monitoring software as well as a capable and well-tuned intrusion detection or prevention system monitoring outbound traffic is critical to detecting these problems.

- *Service interruption* can indicate a simple application problem that requires a service or server restart but can also indicate a security issue like a DoS attack or a compromised application. Monitoring tools should monitor application or service status as well as user experience to capture both views of how a service is working.

- *Memory overflows* may result in operating system errors and crashes, making crash dump reporting important. Monitoring for memory overflow errors can be a challenge due to limitations in memory handling for operating systems and applications, so your first warning may be an application crash or system reboot. Logging reboots and service restarts can help but may not detect a properly executed attack.

Summary

Incident response requires visibility into networks, systems, services, and applications. Gathering and centralizing information from each component of your organization's infrastructure and systems can allow you to more easily detect, respond to, or even prevent incidents.

Network monitoring is often done via router-based monitoring, which relies on network flows, SNMP, and RMON, all common means of gathering information. Flows provide summary data about traffic, protocols, and endpoints; SNMP is used to gather device information; and RMON uses probes to gather statistical, historical, and event-based data. In addition, organizations employ active monitoring using ping and performance monitoring tools like iPerf to gather data by sending traffic. Passive monitoring relies on capturing information about the network and its performance as traffic travels through network devices. Passive monitoring doesn't add traffic to the network and acts after the fact, rather than providing real-time information, making it more useful for analysis than prevention of issues.

Network monitoring tools like PRTG, SolarWinds, and Cacti centralize multiple types of network data and provide both central visibility and detailed drill-down analysis capabilities. They are important to incident response and event management because they allow both easy visibility and the ability to look at data from multiple data sources in a single place, potentially allowing you to detect problems like link failure, beaconing, and unexpected traffic identified more easily. Attacks and probes can be detected using monitoring tools and sometimes may be identified and then prevented by network security devices.

Monitoring hosts requires visibility into resources, applications, and logs. Host resource monitoring typically focuses on processor, memory, and disk utilization, whereas applications are often managed using central management tools like SCCM. Log monitoring relies on an understanding of what is logged and which issues are important to review.

Service and application issues are often detected by monitoring for service anomalies like errors, failures, or changes in service behavior. Security professionals look for anomalous activity, new and unexpected account creation, unexpected outputs or outbound communication, service interruptions, and memory overflow issues.

Exam Essentials

Network incidents start with the detection of a problem, suspicious, or unexpected network traffic. Understanding how network bandwidth is consumed is an important part of detecting and analyzing events. Flows, SNMP, active, and passive monitoring all provide a view of network health and usage. Network monitoring tools like PRTG, Nagios, Cacti, and SolarWinds help to make large volumes of data from diverse devices accessible and centrally visible. Common network issues include bandwidth consumption, link failure, beaconing, and unexpected traffic.

Network attacks and probes require specific responses.   Scans and probes can be difficult to detect but can indicate interest by attackers or security issues that allow them to succeed. Denial-of-service attacks can be detected and techniques exist to limit their impact, including network security devices and DDoS mitigation services. Rogue devices, or devices that are not expected to be on a network, can be either wired or wireless. Wired rogues can be limited by using network admission technology, whereas wireless rogues require a monitoring and detection plan.

Host issues include resource exhaustion, unwelcome software, and abuse of accounts, access, and privileges.   Monitoring system resource usage, including CPU, memory, and disk space, can help to identify host issues. Monitoring tools like resmon and perfmon for Windows and ps, top, df, and w for Linux provide insight into the current state of a system's resources. Unauthorized software and malware can be detected by purpose-designed tools or can be controlled using whitelists, blacklists, and central management tools like SCCM. Unauthorized access, changes, and privilege use can indicate a compromise, intentional, or inadvertent misuse. System and application logs as well as file integrity monitoring applications can help to catch issues as they occur or with investigation after the fact.

Service and application issues may be due to flaws, configuration issues, or attacks. Monitoring applications relies on active monitoring of the application or service status, logging, and behavior analysis. Service anomalies can be detected by checking for errors or active monitoring but may not provide a direct indication of security issues. Successful attacks on applications are often indicated by new accounts, unexpected communications or output, service interruptions, or other anomalous activity.

Lab Exercises

Activity 6.1: Identify a Network Scan

In this lab you will use Wireshark to identify a network scan of a Linux system.

Part 1: Boot a Kali Linux system and a target system and set up the exercise

1. Start your Kali Linux virtual machine and the Metasploitable virtual machine; log in to both.

2. Open a terminal window and Wireshark on the Kali Linux system (Wireshark can be found in the Applications menu under option 09 Sniffing & Spoofing).

3. Determine the IP address of the target system. From the command prompt on the Metasploitable system, enter `ifconfig -a` and record its IP address.

4. Start the Wireshark capture. Select the eth0 interface and then choose Capture ➢ Start.

Part 2: Perform a network scan and visit the web server

1. From the terminal, execute the following command: **nmap -p 1-65535**
   [*ip address of the Metasploitable machine*].

2. Record one of the ports listed as open.

3. Start the IceWeasel browser in Kali and navigate to the IP address of the Metasploitable system.

Part 3: Identify scan traffic

1. Stop the Wireshark capture. Click the red square stop button at the top left of the
   Wireshark screen.

2. Review the traffic you captured. Search for the port you found by entering
   tcp.port==[*port you identified*] into the Filter box.

3. What traffic was sent? If you rerun this scan with other TCP connection options like
   -sS or **-ST**, does this change?

4. Review traffic for port 80. You should see both the scan and a visit from the Kali
   Linux web browser. How do these differ?

Activity 6.2: Write a Service Issue Response Plan

Write an identification and response plan for services that an organization you are familiar
with relies on. Your response plan should presume that a service issue or outage has been
reported, but the cause is not known. Ensure that you cover key elements discussed in this
chapter, including

- How you would identify potential issues using the application and system logs

- How you would monitor the service for problems

- What types of issues you would look for

- What the organization's response should be

   Once you have completed your plan, walk through it using an example issue. Ensure
that your plan would address the issue and that you would be able to provide a complete
report to your organization's management about the issue.

Activity 6.3: Security Tools

Match each of the following tools to the correct description:

Flows	A Linux command that displays processes, memory utilization, and other details about running programs
Resmon	Traffic sent to a command and control system by a PC that is part of a botnet
iPerf	A Windows tool that monitors memory, CPU, and disk usage
PRTG	A protocol for collecting information like status and performance about devices on a network
Beaconing	A set of packets passing from a source system to a destination in a given time interval
SNMP	A network management and monitoring tool that provides central visibility into flows and SNMP data for an entire network
top	A Windows tool that monitors a wide range of devices and services, including energy, USB, and disk usage
Perfmon	A tool for testing the maximum available bandwidth for a network

Review Questions

1. Which of the following Linux commands will show you how much disk space is in use?

   A. top

   B. df

   C. lsof

   D. ps

2. What Windows tool provides detailed information including information about USB host controllers, memory usage, and disk transfers?

   A. statmon

   B. resmon

   C. perfmon

   D. winmon

3. What type of network information should you capture to be able to provide a report about how much traffic systems in your network sent to remote systems?

   A. Syslog data

   B. WMI data

   C. Resmon data

   D. Flow data

4. Which of the following technologies is best suited to prevent wired rogue devices from connecting to a network?

   A. NAC

   B. PRTG

   C. Port security

   D. NTP

5. As part of her job, Danielle sets an alarm to notify her team via email if her Windows server uses 80 percent of its memory and to send a text message if it reaches 90 percent utilization. What is this setting called?

   A. A monitoring threshold

   B. A preset notification level

   C. Page monitoring

   D. Perfmon calibration

6. Chris wants to use an active monitoring approach to test his network. Which of the following techniques is appropriate?

   A. Collecting NetFlow data

   B. Using a protocol analyzer

   C. Pinging remote systems

   D. Enabling SNMP

7. What term describes a system sending heartbeat traffic to a botnet command and control server?

   A. Beaconing

   B. Zombie ping

   C. CNCstatus

   D. CNClog

8. Lauren wants to be able to detect a denial-of-service attack against her web server. Which of the following tools should she avoid?

   A. Log analysis

   B. Flow monitoring

   C. iPerf

   D. IPS

9. What can the MAC address of a rogue device tell you?

   A. Its operating system version

   B. The TTL of the device

   C. What type of rogue it is

   D. The manufacturer of the device

10. How can Jim most effectively locate a wireless rogue access point that is causing complaints from employees in his building?

   A. Nmap

   B. Signal strength and triangulation

   C. Connecting to the rogue AP

   D. NAC

11. Which of the following tools does not provide real-time drive capacity monitoring for Windows?

   A. SCCM

   B. Resmon

   C. SCOM

   D. Perfmon

12. What three options are most likely to be used to handle a memory leak?

   A. Memory management, patching, and buffer overflow prevention

   B. Patching, service restarts, and system reboots

   C. Service restarts, memory monitoring, and stack smashing prevention

   D. System reboots, memory management, and logging

13. Jack is planning to prohibit a variety of files, including games, from being installed on the Windows workstations he manages. What technology is his best option to prevent known, unwanted files from being installed or copied to machines?

    A.   Blacklisting

    B.   SCCM

    C.   SCOM

    D.   Whitelisting

14. While Susan is monitoring a router via network flows, she sees a sudden drop in network traffic levels to zero, and the traffic chart shows a flat line. What has likely happened?

    A.   The sampling rate is set incorrectly.

    B.   The router is using SNMP.

    C.   The monitored link failed.

    D.   A DDoS attack is occurring.

15. What features make SNMPv3 more secure than SNMPv2?

    A.   Encryption, administration, and user accounts

    B.   Encryption, authentication, and user accounts

    C.   Support for flow monitoring, TLS, and ACLs

    D.   Encryption, flow monitoring, and MIB support

16. Which of the following options is not a valid way to check the status of a service in Windows?

    A.   Use `sc` at the command line

    B.   Use `service --status` at the command line

    C.   Use `services.msc`

    D.   Query service status via PowerShell

17. Susan has been asked to identify unexpected traffic on her organization's network. Which of the following is not a technique she should use?

    A.   Protocol analysis

    B.   Heuristics

    C.   Baselining

    D.   Beaconing

18. Olivia suspects that a system in her datacenter may be sending beaconing traffic to a remote system. Which of the following is not a useful tool to help verify her suspicions?

    A.   Flows

    B.   A protocol analyzer

    C.   SNMP

    D.   An IDS or IPS

19. Alex wants to prohibit software that is not expressly allowed by his organization's desktop management team from being installed on workstations. What type of tool should he use?

   A. Whitelisting

   B. Heuristic

   C. Blacklisting

   D. Signature comparison

20. Ben wants to see a list of processes along with their CPU utilization in an interactive format. What built-in Linux tool should he use?

   A. df

   B. top

   C. tail

   D. cpugrep

Chapter

7

Performing Forensic Analysis

THE COMPTIA CYBERSECURITY ANALYST+ EXAM OBJECTIVES COVERED IN THIS CHAPTER INCLUDE:

Domain 3: Cyber Incident Response

✓ **3.2 Given a scenario, prepare a toolkit and use appropriate forensics tools during an investigation.**

Computer forensic investigations are used to determine what activities, changes, and other actions have occurred on a system, who or what performed them, and what data is stored there. This means that computer forensic techniques are used in a variety of scenarios, including police investigations, inquiries into system administrator misuse, compromise and malware analysis, and investigations related to internal policy violations.

In this chapter you will learn how to be prepared to conduct forensic investigations. You will learn about forensics kits, their contents, and the use of the devices and tools they contain. Then, you will explore forensic suites and tools that provide the capabilities needed to capture and preserve forensics data and to perform forensic investigations. Finally, we will use those tools to perform elements of a sample investigation.

Building a Forensics Capability

One of the first steps to being able to conduct a forensic investigation is to gather the right set of tools. Forensic tools come with a broad variety of capabilities, costs, and purposes. You should determine what types of investigations you are likely to conduct, what types of systems and devices you will need to analyze, and what evidentiary standards you will need to comply with before you build your toolkit.

The Cybersecurity Analyst+ body of knowledge specifically calls out the contents of a forensic kit, including technological components like write blockers and administrative tools such as chain-of-custody forms. Make sure you are familiar with what role each of these components has in a forensic investigation.

Building a Forensic Toolkit

A complete forensic toolkit is an important part of any forensic investigation. Not only can having the right tools and materials make the process easier, but it can also help ensure that your investigation has the right documentation and support materials in case you need to provide proof of your process—either in court, to management, or to auditors.

Over the next few pages you will learn about the major components of a forensic toolkit, including a forensic workstation, data capture tools and devices, and the administrative tools that help provide proper chain-of-custody tracking. Keep in mind how your organization is likely to conduct forensic investigations—not all of these components may be needed for your use cases.

Key Toolkit Components

The following components are common to most forensic toolkits. Forensic workstations may be a desktop, a laptop, or even a server, and the specific components should be tailored to your organization. But this basic set of items will allow you to perform forensic investigations under most circumstances.

- A *digital forensics workstation*. A good forensic workstation is designed to allow for data capture and analysis, and those tasks can benefit from a powerful, multicore CPU and plenty of RAM. Having lots of fast, reliable storage is also important, since large investigations can deal with terabytes of data.

- A *forensic investigation suite* or *forensic software* like FTK, EnCase, the SANS Investigate Forensic Kit (SIFT), or the Sleuth Kit (TSK) that provides the ability to capture and analyze forensic images as well as track forensic investigations.

- *Write blockers*, which ensure that drives connected to a forensic system or device cannot be written to. This helps to ensure the integrity of the forensic investigation; having file access times changed—or worse, having the system that is analyzing the data modify the content of the files on the drive—can prevent forensic evidence from being useful.

- *Forensic drive duplicators*, which are designed to copy drives for forensic investigation and then provide validation that the original drive and the content of the new drive match. Many forensic tools and suites also offer this capability, but a dedicated cloning device can be useful (and can sometimes make it easier to prove that the duplication process was completed in a forensically sound manner).

- *Wiped drives* and *wiped removable media* of sufficient capacity to handle any drive or system that you are likely to encounter. Fortunately, large SATA hard drives, portable NAS devices, and large SSDs make it a lot easier to capture and transport multiple forensic images. Removable media, in the form of large USB thumb drives, writable Blu-ray or DVD media, or flash media, can also be valuable for transporting forensic data or for sending it to other organizations when necessary.

Properly wiping the media to ensure that you don't have any remnant data is crucial—remnant data can call your entire forensic process into question! It is particularly important to understand how wear leveling on flash media and SSDs can impact data remanence.

- *Cables* and *drive adapters* of various types to ensure that you can connect to most types of devices you are likely to encounter. In a corporate environment, you are likely to know what types of machines and drives your organization deploys, allowing you to select the right adapters and cables to match what you have. In a law enforcement, consulting, or other environment where you may not know what you will encounter, having a broad selection of cables and adapters can be incredibly helpful.

- A *camera* to document system configurations, drive labels, and other information. Cameras are a surprisingly important part of forensic capture because they can speed up data recording and can provide a visual record of the state of a system or device.

- Labeling and documentation tools, including a label maker or labels, indelible pens, and other tools to help with *chain of custody* and forensic process documentation.
- Notebooks and pre-prepared documentation forms and checklists to record forensic investigation processes and notes. Common types of forms include *chain-of-custody forms* that track who was in possession of evidence at any time, *incident response forms* for tracking a response process, *incident response plans* and *incident forms*, and *escalation lists* or *call lists* of people to contact during a response process. These are sometimes replaced by a forensic recording software package or another software tool that provides ways to validate log entries and that tracks changes. Figure 7.1 shows an example of a chain-of-custody form.

FIGURE 7.1 Sample chain-of-custody form

Affix Case Number Tag Here

Example Organization

COMPUTER EVIDENCE CHAIN OF CUSTODY TRACKING FORM

Case Number: ____________________ Item Number: ____________________

Evidence Description: ______________________________________

____

____

Collection method: ______________________________________

____

Evidence storage method: ______________________________________

How is evidence secured? ______________________________________

Collected by: (Name/ID#) ______________________________________

Signature of collector: ______________________________________

Copy History		
Date	Copied method	Disposition of original and all copies

Chain of Custody				
Item #	Date/Time	Released by (Signature & ID#)	Received by (Signature & ID#)	Comments/Location

APD_Form_#PE003_v.1 (12/2012) Page 1 of 2 pages (See back)

- Law enforcement investigations often also use specialized tools like *crime scene tape* (referenced as *crime tape* by the exam objectives) to help control the physical area as well as *tamper-proof seals* to aid in the preservation of physical evidence.

Forensic Workstations

If you are using commercial forensic software, the vendor is likely to provide minimum specifications for the software package. Both EnCase and FTK have system recommendation guidelines:

Guidance Software, makers of EnCase provides theirs at `https://www.guidancesoftware.com/document/whitepaper/encase-processor-hardware-and-configuration-recommendations`.

FTK's can be found at `http://accessdata.com/solutions/digital-forensics/forensic-toolkit-ftk/technical`.

Both EnCase and FTK provide distributed processing capabilities that can help by spreading the load between multiple systems—a useful capability if you frequently do large-scale forensic data analysis.

Make sure that you have an ongoing budget to upgrade or refresh your forensic workstation and equipment on a periodic basis. Technology changes and increases in the volume of data acquired can make an older forensic workstation out of date surprisingly quickly.

Mobile Device Forensic Toolkit Components

Handling *mobile device forensics* can create additional challenges. The diversity of mobile device operating systems, connection types, security options, and software versions can make capturing data from devices difficult. Having the right tools plays a big role in successfully connecting to and capturing data from mobile devices. If you need to build a mobile forensic toolkit, you may need to add some or all of the following to your existing forensic kit:

- Tools for accessing *SIM cards* and flash memory cards. For some phones, this is simply a pin-style push device, whereas others may require small screwdrivers or other tools.

- A mobile device connection cable kit that includes the most common connector types for current and recent phones. This has become simpler in recent years, and having USB mini, micro, and USB C cables, as well as Apple 30 pin dock and Lightning connectors, will cover many if not most smartphones. Connecting to older phones and non-smartphones can still require additional proprietary cables. Fortunately, many vendors provide mobile device forensic cable kits, allowing you to buy many of the most common cables at once.

- Mobile device–specific forensic software and tools designed to target mobile device operating systems.

It might seem as if it is nearly impossible to break into a phone that has a passcode set but that doesn't have a known exploit or other method available to access the data stored on the phone. Fortunately, companies like Susteen Inc. have built robotic tools that can use a camera to identify the keypad on a phone and try thousands of passcodes in an automated fashion until the phone unlocks. This type of mobile device brute-force attack only works if the phone isn't set to wipe after a set number of attempts to access it, but it's a cleverly engineered way to break into "burner" phones that may not otherwise allow access to the data they contain. You can see it in action at http://secureview.us/burner-breaker.html.

Training and Certification

Full-time forensic professionals or professionals who may need to present forensic findings for legal cases often obtain specialized certifications in computer forensics. The most common forensic certifications are

- CCE, or Certified Computer Examiner
- CFCE, Certified Forensic Computer Examiner
- CHFI, Computer Hacking Forensic Investigator
- GCFA, GIAC Certified Forensic Analyst
- GCFE, GIAC Certified Forensic Examiner
- CSFA, Cybersecurity Forensic Analyst

Vendor-specific certifications are also common, particularly the ACE, or AccessData Certified Examiner (for FTK and other AccessData products), and EnCE, or EnCase Certified Examiner.

Understanding Forensic Software

There are many types of forensic software, ranging from purpose-built forensic suites and tools like FTK, EnCase, Caine, Autopsy, and SIFT to forensic utilities like DumpIt and Memoryze. Many common Linux and Windows utilities also have forensic applications, including utilities like dd and WinDbg.

Capabilities and Application

Forensic investigations can take many forms, which means that you'll need a broad software toolkit to handle situations, systems, and specific requirements you encounter. Key forensic tool capabilities to include in your forensic software toolkit are imaging, analysis, hashing and validation, process and memory dump analysis, password cracking, and log viewers.

Imaging Media and Drives

The first step in many forensic investigations is to create copies of the media or disks that may contain data useful for the investigation. This is done using an *imaging utility*, which can create a forensic image of a complete disk, a disk partition, or a logical volume.

Forensic images exactly match the original source drive, volume, partition, or device, including slack space and unallocated space. Slack space is the space left when a file is written. This unused space can contain fragments of files previously written to the space or even files that have been intentionally hidden. Unallocated space is space that has not been partitioned. When used properly, imaging utilities ensure that you have captured all of this data.

Forensic copies and drive wiping programs may not properly handle spare sectors and bad sectors on traditional spinning disks or reserved space retained to help with wear leveling for SSDs. This means it is possible to miss potentially useful forensic data, and it's something you should be particularly aware of when wiping disks.

Analysis Utilities

Forensic analysis utilities provide a number of useful capabilities that can help offer insight into what occurred on a system. Examples include the following:

- Timelines of system changes
- Validation tools that check known-good versions of files against those found on a system
- Filesystem analysis capabilities that can look at filesystem metadata (like the Windows Master File Table for NTFS) to identify file changes, access, and deletions
- Windows Registry analysis
- Log file parsing and review

These analysis tools can help identify information that is useful for a forensic investigation, but using them well requires detailed forensic knowledge to avoid missing important data.

Many forensic investigators use open source utilities like SIFT, CAINE, and Autopsy since they are freely available. Although commercial forensic tools can be costly, they may be easier to defend in court, which means you'll sometimes see professional forensic investigators using commercial tools like FTK or EnCase rather than freely available open source tools. Make sure your organization is comfortable with the pros and cons of any tool that you choose to use.

Chain-of-Custody Tracking

Support for properly maintaining chain-of-custody documentation in an automated and logged manner is an important part of a forensic suite. This ensures that drive images and other data, as well as the actions taken using the suite, are properly validated and available for review, thus reducing the potential for legal challenges based on poor custodial practices.

Hashing and Validation

Verification of the forensic integrity of an image is an important part of forensic imaging. Fortunately, this can be done using *hashing utilities* built into a forensics suite or run independently to get a hash of the drive to validate the contents of the copy. The goal of this process is to ensure that the copy exactly matches the source drive or device.

Forensic image formats like EnCase's EO1 format provide built-in hashing as part of the file. In cases where formats like these are not used, both MD5 and SHA1 hashes are frequently used for this purpose. Hashing large drives can take quite a bit of time even using a fast algorithm like MD5, but the process itself is quite simple as shown here. The following provides the MD5 hash of a volume mounted on a Linux system:

```
user@demo:~# md5sum /dev/sda1
9b98b637a132974e41e3c6ae1fc9fc96  /dev/sda1
```

To validate an image, a hash is generated for both the original and the copy. If the hashes match, the images are identical. Both hashes should be recorded as part of the forensic log for the investigation.

You may be wondering why MD5 is used for forensic imaging when most security practitioners recommend against using it. MD5 remains in use because it is fast and widely available, and the attacks against MD5 are primarily threats for reasons that don't apply to forensic images. As a practitioner, you are unlikely to encounter someone who can or would intentionally make two drives with different contents hash to the same value.

Operating System, Process, and Memory Dump Analysis

Information about the state of the operating system (OS), including the data that is stored in memory by processes, can be important to both forensic investigations as well as investigations of malware infections or compromise. Often data that is otherwise kept encrypted is accessible in memory to processes, or the encryption keys that those processes use to access encrypted data are available. The ability to capture memory, process information and data, as well as operate specific analysis capabilities is a useful forensic capability. OS analysis can provide key data about what was occurring on a system during the timeframe targeted by an investigation.

In addition to live memory capture and analysis, memory dump analysis can be particularly valuable when recovering decryption keys for full disk encryption products like

BitLocker. Hibernation files and crash dumps can both contain the data needed to decrypt the drive, which makes accessing an unlocked machine critically important for a forensic practitioner.

Mobile Device and Cell Phone Forensics

Mobile device forensic capabilities exist in many commercial forensic suites, as well as in the form of stand-alone tools. Due to the security features that many phone operating systems provide, they often have specialized decryption or brute-forcing capabilities to allow them to capture data from a locked and encrypted phone or phone volume.

Phone backup forensic capabilities are also a useful tool for mobile forensics. Backups may not have all current data, but they can contain older data that was deleted and may not have the same level of security that the phone itself does, thus making them an attractive target for forensic acquisition and review.

Password Crackers and Password Recovery

An increasing number of drives and devices are encrypted or use a password to protect the system or files. This makes *password recovery tools* (also called *password crackers*) very useful to a forensic examiner. Common places to discover password protection beyond the operating system or account level include Microsoft Office files, PDFs, as well as ZIP and RAR compressed files.

Recovering passwords for forensic investigations can be challenging, but tools like ElcomSoft's Advanced Office Password Breaker (AOPB), shown in Figure 7.2, provide brute-force password breaking for a range of file types. In this case, AOPB took just over two days to break encryption on a Microsoft Word document using a brute-force process and a single CPU core.

FIGURE 7.2   Advanced Office Password Breaker cracking a Word DOC file

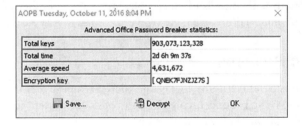

 Some forensic workstations include powerful graphics cards. This is partially due to the ability of many password cracking tools to use the graphics card or GPU to perform password cracking operations. Using a GPU can result in massive speed increases over traditional CPU-based cracking, making a powerful CPU a worthwhile investment if you ever need to perform a brute-force password cracking attack and your forensic tools support it.

Cryptography Tools

Cryptographic tools are common both to protect forensic data and to protect data and applications from forensics. Forensic tools often have encryption capabilities to ensure that sensitive data under forensic investigation is not breached as part of the investigation when drives or files are transferred, or if the forensic environment is compromised.

Encryption tools are also needed to handle encrypted drives and network protocols. These capabilities vary from tool to tool, but handling BitLocker, Microsoft Office, and other common encryption mechanisms are common tasks during forensic investigations.

When forensic techniques are used to investigate malware, encryption and other protection schemes are frequently encountered as a means of preventing code analysis of malware. Many malware packages use tools called "packers," intended to protect them from reverse engineering. Packers are intended to make direct analysis of the code difficult or impossible. Some forensic tools provide support for unpacking and decoding from packing techniques like base-64 encoding.

Log Viewers

Log files can provide information about the system state, actions taken on the system, and errors or problems, as well as a wide variety of other information. This makes log entries particularly useful when you are attempting to understand what occurred on a system or device. Forensic suites typically build in *log viewers* that can match log entries to other forensic information, but specialized logs may require additional tools.

Conducting a Forensic Investigation

Forensic investigations rely on more than just a forensic toolkit and a forensic suite. The process of conducting an investigation is often complex due to the number of systems, devices, individuals, and other material involved. Next, we will look at a typical forensic process.

The Forensic Process

Forensic investigations can take many forms and there are many formal models for forensic investigations, but the basic process involved when conducting them remains the same. In almost all investigations you will take these steps:

1. Determine what you are trying to find out. You may be asked to investigate a compromised system, to analyze the actions taken by malware, or to find out if a system administrator made an unauthorized change to a system. This forms the problem statement that helps to define what forensic activities you will take.

2. Outline the locations and types of data that would help you answer the questions you are answering from step 1. Data may exist in many forms, and applications and systems can determine the format and accessibility of the data. Knowing where and how you need to collect data will also influence what your forensic process looks like. At this

stage, you may not know the specific hardware or log locations, but you should be able to come up with the types of data and systems you will need to capture data from.

3. Document and review your plan.

4. Acquire and preserve evidence. The acquisition process may require cloning media, seizing systems or devices, or making live memory images to ensure that information is not lost when a system is powered off.

5. Perform initial analysis, carefully tracking your actions, the systems and data you work with, and your findings, as well as any questions you need to answer.

6. Use the initial analysis to guide further work, including deeper investigation and review where the initial analysis pointed to additional data, or where information is missing that is needed to answer the questions you originally asked.

7. Report on the findings of the investigation.

Acquisition processes need to take into account the *order of volatility*, which measures how easily data is to lose. This means that data stored in memory or caches is considered highly volatile, since it will be lost if the system is turned off, whereas data stored in printed form or as a backup is considered much less volatile. Figure 7.3 shows a view of the order of volatility of common storage locations that data is likely to be acquired from during a forensic investigation.

FIGURE 7.3 Order of volatility of common storage locations

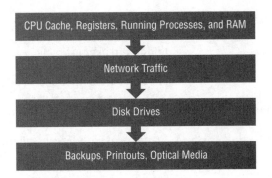

Unexpected Forensic Discoveries

Forensic investigations can result in finding data that you did not intend to uncover as part of the investigation. Knowing what you will do if you find signs of issues or problems outside of the scope of the investigation you are conducting is helpful to avoid problems. This can be as simple as finding evidence of an employee violating company policies while investigating a compromise, or as potentially complex as discovering evidence of illegal activities during an investigation. Make sure you know if you have a duty to report certain types of finding, either under local, state, or federal law, or due to your own organization's policies.

Target Locations

Target locations differ based on operating system or device type, but Windows, macOS, and Linux systems are the most common targets of forensic acquisition. Table 7.1 lists some of the most common locations and examples of how they might be used for Windows forensics.

TABLE 7.1   Forensic application of Windows system artifacts

Windows	Use
Windows Registry	Information about files and services, locations of deleted files, evidence of applications being run
Autorun keys	Programs set to run at startup (often associated with malware or compromise)
Master File Table (MFT)	Details of inactive/removed records
Event logs	Logins, service start/stop, evidence of applications being run
INDX files and change logs	Evidence of deleted files, MAC timestamps
Volume shadow copies	Point-in-time information from prior actions
User directories and files	Logged-in user artifacts
Recycle Bin contents	Files that were intended to be deleted but forgotten
Hibernation files and memory dumps	Memory artifacts of commands run
Temporary directories	Artifacts of software installation, user temporary file storage, or other limited lifespan data
Application logs	Application-specific data
Removable drives (including flash drives)	System logs may indicate drives were plugged in; data may be relevant to investigations

This isn't an exhaustive list, and the needs of each forensic investigation will vary, but knowing where to look and what files you may need can help guide your decisions when determining which systems and volumes to image. Unfortunately, each Linux distribution and macOS version tends to have slightly different locations, making it harder to provide a simple list of common locations. You can find a useful macOS 10.9 listing at http://forensicswiki.org/wiki/Mac_OS_X_10.9_-_Artifacts_Location. Linux forensics analysts will often target the contents of /var, /home, and /etc as excellent starting locations for system logs, user data, and configuration information.

Acquiring and Validating Drive Images

Drive and media images must be captured in a forensically sound manner. They also require hashing and validation, and with the exception of live system forensics where it cannot be completely avoided, forensic duplication should not change the source drive or device. To do this, an exact bit-for-bit copy is made using an imaging utility, write blockers are employed to prevent the possibility of modifying the source drive, and multiple copies are made so that the original drive can be retained for evidence.

 You may discover that your investigation touches systems, networks, or data that you or your organization do not own. Company bring-your-own-device practices, cloud services, and employee use of third-party services for their private use on institutional systems can all complicate forensic examinations. Make sure you know your organization's policies about each of those areas, as well as privacy policies and related standards, before you begin a forensic investigation.

Forensic Copies

Forensic copies of media don't work the same way that simply copying the files from one drive to another would. Forensic copies retain the exact same layout and content for the entire device or drive, including the contents of "empty" space, unallocated space, and the slack space that remains when a file does not fill all the space in a cluster.

The need for a verifiable, forensically sound image means that you need to use an imaging tool to create forensic images rather than using the copy command or dragging and dropping files in a file manager. Fortunately, there are a number of commonly available tools like dd or FTK's Imager Lite built into major forensic suites that can create forensic images.

The Importance of Bit-by-Bit Copies

One reason that copies are not done using a copy command is to ensure that slack space and unallocated space are both copied as part of the image. This captures deleted files that have not yet been overwritten, fragments of older files in the space that was not written to by new files, and data that was stored on a drive before it was partitioned. Slack and unallocated space can provide rich detail about the history of a system, and simply copying files will not provide that visibility.

Imaging with dd

The Linux *dd* utility is often used to clone drives in RAW format, a bit-by-bit format. dd provides a number of useful operators that you should set to make sure your imaging is done quickly and correctly.

- Block size is set using the bs flag and is defined in bytes. By default, dd uses a 512-byte block size, but this is far smaller than the block size of most modern disks. Using a larger block size will typically be much faster, and if you know the block size for the device you are copying, using its native block size can provide huge speed increases. This is set using a flag like bs = 64k.
- The operator if sets the input file; for example, if = /dev/disk/sda1.
- The operator of sets the output file; for example, of = /mnt/usb/.

Avoiding Mistakes: DD Input and Output Locations

It is critical that you verify the input and output locations for a dd command. To list drives, you can use commands like fdisk -l or lsblk. You can ask lsblk for more detail by using additional flags: lsblk --output NAME,FSTYPE,LABEL,UUID,MODE will show the device name, filesystem type, the disk label, the UUID, and the mode it is mounted in, giving you a much better view. Take careful note of which drive is which, and review your command before pressing Enter. This is where a write blocker can save the day!

Figure 7.4 shows a sample dd copy of a mounted drive image to a USB device. The speed of copies can vary greatly based on block size, the relative speeds of the source and destination drive, and other variables like whether the system is virtual or physical.

FIGURE 7.4   dd of a volume

```
root@demo:/dev/disk/by-label# dd bs=64k if=/dev/disk/by-label/IR3_SSS_X64FREE_EN
-US_DV9 of=/dev/disk/by-label/Blank
59309+1 records in
59309+1 records out
4542291968 bytes (4.5 GB) copied, 949.99 s, 4.8 MB/s
```

 While it isn't included in the CSA+ body of knowledge, dc3dd is a useful alternative to dd that adds on-the-fly hashing, a progress meter, and other forensic capabilities. Unlike DCFLdd, another open source competitor, dc3dd continues to be updated. If you're able to bring your own dd derivative, you may want to consider dc3dd.

Imaging with FTK Imager Lite

FTK is a full forensic suite and provides imaging capabilities for many types of devices. Figure 7.5 shows FTK's free Imager Lite in use for a filesystem copy for a sample Windows workstation with a 1 TB system drive. As you can see, forensic imaging is not a fast process, with images of large drives taking hours to complete and hours to verify.

FIGURE 7.5 FTK imaging of a system

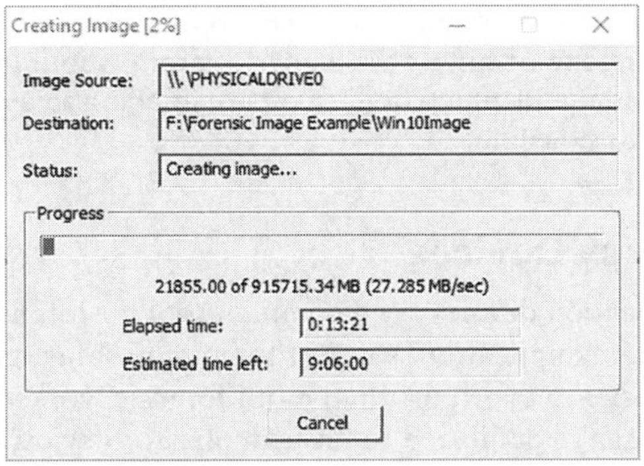

A Complete Chain of Custody

Maintaining a fully documented chain of custody is critical for investigations performed by law enforcement or that may need to survive scrutiny in court. That means you need to document what is collected; who collected or analyzed the data; when each action occurred; and when devices and other evidence were transferred, handled, accessed, and securely stored. That means you have to track this information for each drive, device, machine, or other item you handle during an investigation. You may need a third party in the room to validate your statements for the entire process.

FTK includes a number of features designed to help forensic analysts with their documentation and chain-of-custody process. Evidence item meta tags are created when the imaging process is started, ensuring that each image has appropriate data captured, as shown in Figure 7.6.

FIGURE 7.6 FTK image metadata

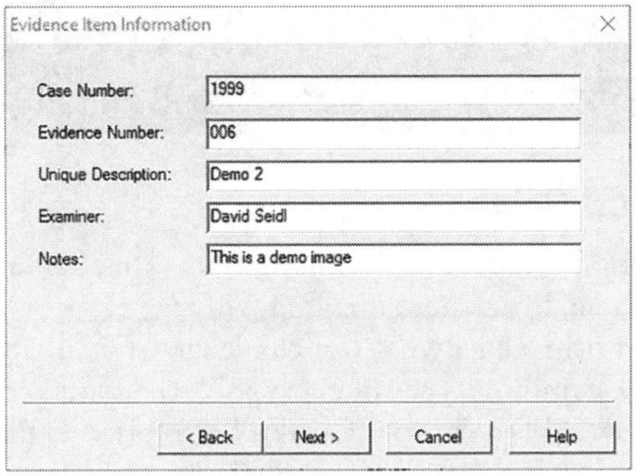

Imaging live systems can be tricky because the system is in use, which means you have to balance the need to acquire data against the potential for change to occur. Be particularly careful about the changes you make to the system and which drives you are imaging to avoid as many potential issues as possible.

Using Forensic Copy Devices

Dedicated forensic duplication devices are a common tool for forensic investigators. They generally allow direct drive duplication, support forensic hashing, generate chain-of-custody data, and are easier to transport than a full forensic workstation. Figure 7.7 shows Logicube's Forensic Dossier, a dedicated forensic duplicator device.

FIGURE 7.7 Logicube's Forensic Dossier duplicator device

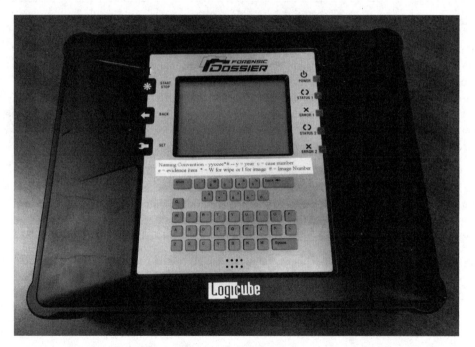

Handling Encrypted Drives

Drive and device encryption is increasingly common, making dealing with drive images more challenging. Of course, live system imaging will avoid many of the issues found with encrypted volumes, but it brings its own set of challenges. Fortunately, commercial forensic suites handle many of the common types of encryption that you are likely to encounter, as long as you have the password for the volume. They also provide distributed cracking methods that use multiple computers to attack encrypted files and volumes.

Avoiding Brute Force

Brute-force cracking of encryption keys can be very slow. Getting the encryption key from the user or an administrator, or by retrieving it from the memory of a live system, is preferable if at all possible.

In 2013, the FBI located Ross Ulbricht, the operator of the Silk Road, a darknet trading site. Ulbricht, also known as the Dread Pirate Roberts, was captured in a public library where he was logged into the Silk Road site and other accounts. Since he was known to use disk encryption, the FBI waited until his computer was open and logged in and then arrested him and got access to his laptop before he could lock or turn off the system. This gave the FBI the opportunity to image the system without defeating the strong encryption that Ulbricht was likely to use to secure it.

Using Write Blockers

Write blockers are an important tool for both forensic investigation and forensic drive image acquisition. During drive acquisition, using a write blocker can ensure that attaching the drive to a forensic copy device or workstation does not result in modifications being made to drive, thus destroying the forensic integrity of the process. The same capability to prevent writes is useful during forensic analysis of drives and other media because it ensures that no modifications are made to the drive accidentally.

Hardware Write Blockers

Hardware write blockers like the model shown in Figure 7.8 physically prevent writes from occurring while a drive is connected through them. Hardware write blockers can be certified to a NIST standard, and testing information is available via the NIST Computer Forensics Tool Testing program at www.cftt.nist.gov/hardware_write_block.htm.

FIGURE 7.8   A Tableau SATA- and IDE-capable hardware write blocker

Software Write Blockers

Software write blockers are typically less popular than hardware write blockers, making them less common. Due to the possibility of problems, hardware write blockers are more frequently used when preventing writes from occurring is important.

Verifying Images

Image verification is critical to ensuring that your data is forensically sound. Commercial tools use built-in verification capabilities to make sure the entire image matches the original. When investigators use dd or other manual imaging tools, md5sum or sha1sum hashing utilities are frequently used to validate images. Each time you generate an image, you should record the hash or verification information for both the original and the cloned copy, and that information should be recorded in your forensic logbook or chain-of-custody form. FTK's Imager Lite will display the hash values in a report at the end of the process, as shown in Figure 7.9.

FIGURE 7.9   FTK image hashing and bad sector checking

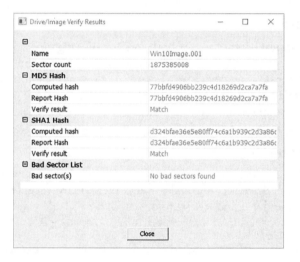

Imaging Live Systems

When systems are using full disk encryption, or when applications, malware, or other software may be memory resident without a copy on the disk, an image may need to be collected while the system is running.

Live imaging may not obtain some desirable data:

- Live imaging can leave remnants due to the imaging utility being mounted from a removable drive or installed.
- The contents of a drive or memory may change during the imaging process.

- Malware or other software may be able to detect the imaging tool and could take action to avoid it or disable it.

- Live images typically do not include unallocated space.

Both commercial and open source tools provide portable versions that can be loaded on a live system to provide live imaging capabilities.

Acquiring Other Data

There are many other types of specialized data beyond drive images that you may want to specifically target during acquisition. Fortunately, in most cases, forensic images of the host drives will also provide access to that data if it is resident on the systems. A few of the other areas you may want to specifically target include log data, USB device histories, application data, browser cache and history, email, and user-generated files.

Acquiring and Reviewing Log Data

Log data is often stored remotely and may not be accurate in the case of a compromised machine or if an administrator was taking actions they wanted to conceal. At other times an investigation may involve actions that are logged centrally or on network devices, but not on a single local system or device that you are likely to create a forensic image of. In those cases, preserving logs is important and will require additional work.

To preserve and analyze logs:

1. Determine where the logs reside and what format they are stored in.

2. Determine the time period that you need to preserve. Remember that you may want to obtain logs from a longer period in case you find out that an issue or compromise started before you initially suspected.

3. Work with system or device administrators to obtain a copy of the logs and document how the logs were obtained. Checksums or other validation are often appropriate.

4. Identify items of interest. This might include actions, user IDs, event IDs, timeframes, or other elements identified in your scope.

5. Use log analysis tools like Splunk, Sawmill, Event Log Analyzer, or even a text editor to search and review the logs.

Viewing USB Device History

Windows tracks the history of USB devices connected to a system, providing a useful forensic record of thumb drives and other devices. USB Historian can be used to review this based on a mounted drive image. During a forensic examination, the information provided by USB Historian or similar tools can be used to match an inventory of drives to those used on a computer, or to verify whether specific devices were in use at a given time. USB Historian, shown in Figure 7.10, provides such data as the system name, the device name, its serial number, the time it was in use, the vendor ID of the device, what type of device it is, and various other potentially useful information.

FIGURE 7.10 USB Historian drive image

Computer Name	Friendly Name	Serial No	Setup Api Install Date...	Mount Point 2	Drive Letter	Volume Name
DELLMINI	SAMSUNG HD103SJ ...	27E1C3019658				
DELLMINI	SanDisk Ultra II 960G...	161401800004				
DELLMINI	SanDisk Ultra II 960G...	DDSHU3B000000001				
DELLMINI	ST310005 28AS USB ...	95A888888888				
DELLMINI	ST310005 28AS USB ...	DDSHU3B000000001				

USB Historian v1.3

5 USB Devices Found.

Capturing Memory-Resident Data

Shutting down a system typically results in the loss of the data stored in memory. That means that forensic data like information in a browser memory cache or program states will be lost. While capture information in memory isn't always important in a forensic investigation, it is critical to be able to capture memory when needed.

There are a number of popular tools for memory captures, with a variety of capabilities, including the following:

- fmem and LiME, both Linux kernel modules that allow access to physical memory. fmem is designed to be used with dd or similar tools; LiME directly copies data to a designated path and file.

- DumpIt, a Windows memory capture tool that simply copies a system's physical memory to the folder where the DumpIt program is. This allows easy capture to a USB thumb drive and makes it a useful part of a forensic capture kit.

- The Volatility Framework supports a broad range of operating systems, including Windows, Linux, and macOS, and has a range of capabilities, including tools to extract encryption keys and passphrases, user activity analysis, and rootkit analysis.

- Both EnCase and FTK have built-in memory capture and analysis capabilities as well.

Using Core Dumps and Hibernation Files

In addition to memory images, core dumps and crash dump files can provide useful forensic information, both for criminal and malware investigations. Since they contain the contents of live memory, they can include data that might not otherwise be accessible on the drive of a system, such as memory-resident encryption keys, malware that runs only in memory, and other items not typically stored to the disk.

The Windows crash dump file can be found by checking the setting found under Control Panel ➢ System And Security ➢ System ➢ Advanced System Settings ➢ Startup And Recovery ➢ Settings. Typically, crash dump files will be located in the system root directory: %SystemRoot%\MEMORY.DMP. Windows memory dump files can be analyzed using WinDbg; however, you shouldn't need to analyze a Windows kernel dump for the Cybersecurity Analyst+ exam.

 Many of the techniques involved in a forensic investigation are useful for incident response and internal investigations that may not have the same evidentiary requirements that a forensic investigation may require. This means it is often reasonable to bypass some of the strictest parts of chain-of-custody documentation and other procedural requirements—but only if you are absolutely certain that the investigation will not become a legal or police matter. When in doubt, it is safer to err on the side of over-documentation to avoid problems in court.

Acquisitions from Mobile Devices

Mobile device forensic acquisition typically starts with disabling the device's network connectivity and then ensuring that access to the device is possible by disabling passcodes and screen lock functionality. Once this is done, physical acquisition of the SIM card, media cards, and device backups occurs. Finally, the device is imaged, although many devices may be resistant to imaging if the passcode is not known or the device is locked.

There are four primary modes of data acquisition from mobile devices:

- Physical, by acquisition of the SIM card, memory cards, or backups
- Logical, which usually requires a forensic tool to create an image of the logical storage volumes
- Manual access, which involves reviewing the contents of the live, unlocked phone and taking pictures and notes about what is found
- Filesystem, which can provide details of deleted files as well as existing files and directories

Much like desktop and server operating system forensics, a key part of mobile forensics is knowing the key file locations for useful forensic data. Table 7.2 lists some of the key locations for iOS devices.

TABLE 7.2   Key iOS file locations

Location	Content
com.apple.commcenter.plist	Device identification data
com.apple.Maps.plist	Map search history and latitude/longitude data
SystemConfiguration/com.apple.wifi.plist	Wi-Fi network data

TABLE 7.2   Key iOS file locations *(continued)*

Location	Content
`Library/CallHistory/call_history.db`	Phone call logs
`Library/SMS/sms.db`	SMS messages
`Library/SMS/Attachments`	MMS files
`Library/Safari`	Safari web browser data
`Library/Caches/com.apple.WebAppCache/ApplicationCache.db`	Web browser cache
`Library/Accounts/Accounts3.sqlite`	Account information
`/private/var/mobile/Library/Caches/com.apple.routined/`	Frequent location data (binary plist)

Similar information exists on Android, Windows, and other devices, although different carriers and OS versions may place data in slightly different locations. As you can see from the partial list of important files in Table 7.2, mobile phones can provide a very detailed history of an individual's location, communications, and other data if all of their data can be acquired.

 SANS provides a detailed smartphone acquisition guide in poster form at `https://digital-forensics.sans.org/media/DFIR-Smartphone-Forensics-Poster.pdf`, which breaks out iOS, Android, and other mobile operating system procedures.

Performing Cloud Service Forensics

Performing forensic investigations on cloud services can be challenging, if not impossible. Shared tenant models mean that forensic data can be hard to get and often require the cloud service provider to participate in the investigation. Maintaining a proper chain of custody, preserving data, and many other parts of the forensic process are more difficult in many cloud environments.

If a cloud service is likely to be part of your forensic investigation, you may want to do the following:

1. Determine what your contract says about investigations.
2. Determine what legal recourse you have with the vendor.
3. Identify the data that you need and whether it is available via methods you or your organization controls.
4. Work with the vendor to identify a course of action if you do not control the data.

More detail about cloud computing forensic challenges can be found in NIST draft NISTIR 8006, NIST Cloud Computing Forensic Challenges, at http://csrc.nist.gov/publications/drafts/nistir-8006/ draft_nistir_8006.pdf.

Forensic Investigation: An Example

In the following section, you will learn the basics of a forensic analysis using FTK. Since we have already discussed imaging, we will start from a previously acquired forensic image and will perform analysis, including:

- Import of the data into FTK, including indexing and case management
- Evidence of the data leakage
- Email communication with third parties about the files
- Web browser information pointing to anti-forensic activities
- Evidence of application installs
- Evidence of filesystem changes, including renaming files

Remember that a full forensic examination of a system can involve more tasks than those listed here and that the scope and direction of the investigation will help to determine what those tasks are. You are also likely to encounter additional clues that will point you in new directions for forensic examination as you explore a system image.

Examples in this section were prepared using the Data Leakage Case found at http://www.cfreds.nist.gov/data_leakage_case/data-leakage-case.html, part of the NIST Computer Forensic Reference Data Sets (CFReDS). The case includes 60 different forensic tasks, including those listed in this chapter. If you want to practice forensic techniques in more depth, you can download the forensic dataset and a forensic toolkit like SIFT or CAINE to test your skills. The dd image file for just the Windows 7 workstation used in this case is 20 GB when extracted, so make sure you have plenty of available hard drive space. It is important to note that some companies may not want you to download tools like this and may have policies or even technology in place that will prevent it. Our technical editor had to get special permission to do so at her company!

Importing a Forensic Image

Once you have a forensic image in hand and have made a copy to use in your investigation, you will typically import it into your forensic tool. Figure 7.11 shows how information about the case is captured as an image is imported.

FIGURE 7.11   Initial case information and tracking

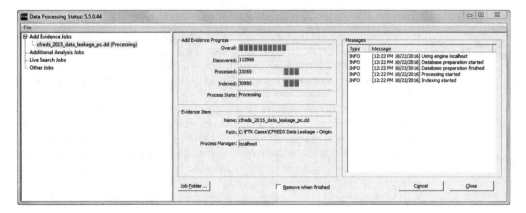

Once your image has been imported into a case and properly logged, the image is then indexed and analyzed. This includes identifying file types, searching slack and unallocated space, building an index of file timestamps, and other analysis items. This can take some time, especially with large drives. Figure 7.12 shows the forensic image used for this case partially through the indexing process.

FIGURE 7.12   Initial case information and tracking

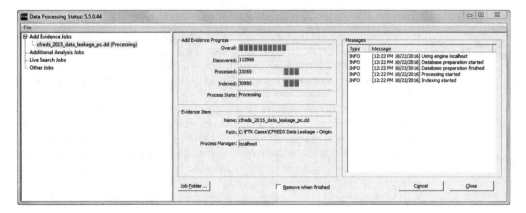

With indexing done, you can now begin to explore the forensic image. FTK provides a series of tabs with common evidence categories, including email, graphics, video, Internet/ chat, bookmarks, and others. Most investigators will take some time to ensure that the operating system, time zone, and other computer information (like which users have accounts on the system) are recorded at this stage.

Analyzing the Image

Since this is a data leakage case, Internet browser history and email are likely to be of particular interest. Figure 7.13 shows how email can be read via FTK's browser capability. We can see an email that was sent reading "successfully secured." Other emails also mention a USB device, and that spy would like it if the informant can deliver the storage devices directly. This provides another clue for further investigation.

FIGURE 7.13   Email extraction

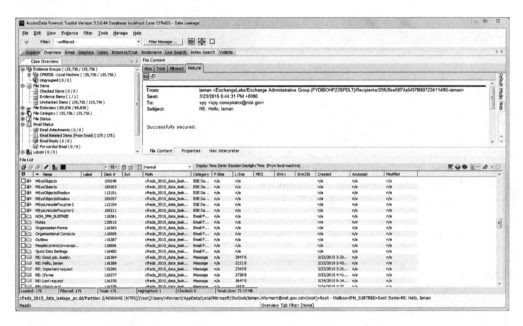

Searching the web browser history provides more information about the informant's likely behavior. The history file for Chrome includes searches for anti-forensics techniques and a visit to the anti-forensics techniques page of forensicswiki.org, as shown in Figure 7.14.

FIGURE 7.14 Web search history

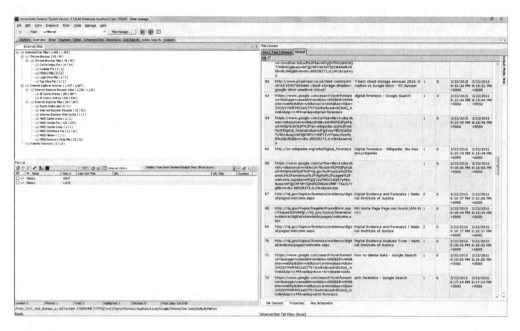

Since the informant searched for anti-forensic techniques, it is likely that they applied them with some degree of success. A visit to the anti-forensics techniques page, as well as searches for data that was deleted or otherwise hidden, is needed.

Some of this additional information can be gathered by reviewing data cached by Windows, including install information from the local user directories. Since the sample image is a Windows 7 machine, install information resides in C:\Users\<*username*>\AppData\Local\Temp. Checking there shows that iCloud was installed in the middle of the timeframe that email communications were occurring, as shown in Figure 7.15.

FIGURE 7.15 iCloud setup log with timestamp

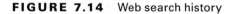

FTK also indexes and displays deleted files, allowing you to see that CCleaner, a system cleanup program that removes browser history and cache and wipes other information useful for forensic investigations, was removed from the system in Figure 7.16, and that Eraser, a file wiping utility, appears to have been partially deleted but left a remnant directory in the Program Files folder. Both of these utilities are likely to be found as part of an anti-forensics attempt, providing further evidence of the user's intention to delete evidence.

FIGURE 7.16   CCleaner remnant data via the Index Search function

At the end of the timeline for the informant in our case, a resignation letter is created and printed. This can be found easily using a timeline of events on the system, or as part of a manual file review using the indexed list of files and searching for Microsoft Office documents, as shown in Figure 7.17.

FIGURE 7.17   Resignation letter found based on document type

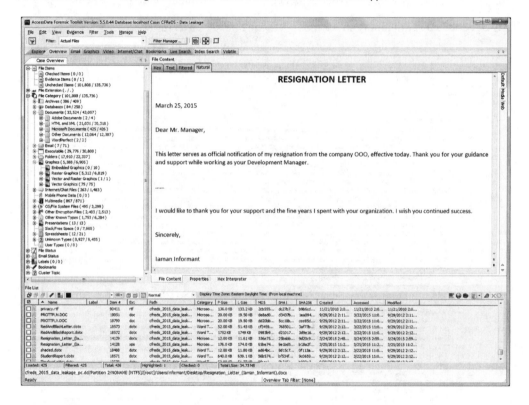

Reporting

The final stage of forensic investigation is preparing and presenting a report. Reports should include three major components: the goals and scope of the investigation; the target or targets of the forensic activities, including all systems, devices, and media; and a complete listing of the findings and results.

Goals of the Investigation

This section of your report should include the goals of the investigation, including the initial scope statement for the forensic activities. This section will also typically include information about the person or organization that asked for the investigation. An example of a statement of the goals of an investigation is "John Smith, the Director of Human

Resources, requested that we review Alice Potter's workstation, email, and the systems she administrates to ensure that the data that was recently leaked to a competitor was not sent from her email account or workstation."

Targets

The report you create should include a list of all of the devices, systems, and media that was captured and analyzed. Targets should all be listed in your tracking notes and chain-of-custody forms if you are using them. The same level of detail used to record the system or device should be used in this listing. A sample entry might read:

> Alice Potter's workstation, internal inventory number 6108, Lenovo W540 laptop, with Samsung SSD serial number S12KMFBD644850, item number 344

If large numbers of devices or systems were inspected, the full listing of targets is often moved to an appendix, and the listing of what was reviewed will list a high-level overview of systems, applications, devices, and other media, with a reference to the appendix for full detail.

Findings and Analysis

Findings are the most critical part of the document and should list what was discovered, how it was discovered, and why it is important. The Stroz Friedberg forensic investigation conducted as part of a contract dispute about the ownership of Facebook provides an example of the detail needed in forensic findings, as shown in Figure 7.18.

FIGURE 7.18   Sample forensic finding from Stroz Friedberg's Facebook contract investigation

Stroz Friedberg found seven entries related to this file on a floppy disk produced in Chicago, Illinois. One of the seven entries relates to an active file and the remaining six relate to deleted versions of the file. The active file purports to have been created, last modified, and last accessed on July 23, 2004. However, two of the records related to deleted copies indicate that the file was created, last modified, and last accessed on the earlier date of October 21, 2003, as follows:

File Name	State	File Created	Last Written	Last Accessed
Mark harvard emails up to Dec.doc	Active	07/23/2004 09:47:01 AM	07/23/2004 06:15:54 PM	7/23/2004
Mark harvard emails up to Dec.doc	Deleted	10/21/2003 11:54:12 AM	10/21/2003 11:54:14 AM	10/21/2003
Mark harvard emails up to Dec.doc	Deleted	10/21/2003 11:54:49 AM	10/21/2003 11:54:50 AM	10/21/2003

Again, a document that was last modified in October 2003 could not contain authentic emails from December 2003. It also is highly unlikely that this file would be named "Mark harvard emails up to Dec.doc" if it actually had been created and last modified in October 2003. This discrepancy likely resulted from the files having been saved with a computer whose system clock had been backdated to October 21, 2003, which is the same date as the deleted version of "Mark emails july04.doc" was saved.

Wired provided the full Stroz Friedberg forensic report from the public record for the case, and it can be found at www.wired.com/images_blogs/threatlevel/2012/03/celiginvestigation.pdf.

Summary

Cybersecurity analysts need to understand the tools, techniques, and processes required to conduct forensics. Forensics toolkits are typically built around powerful forensic workstations that may run a purpose-built forensic investigation suite or may provide individual forensic utilities and tools. Toolkits also often include write blockers, forensic duplicators, media, and documentation equipment and supplies. Specialized tools exist for mobile device forensics, law enforcement, and other types of specific forensic investigations.

Forensic software provides the ability to image and analyze systems, drives, and devices. It also often supports important forensic functions, allowing analysts to maintain chain-of-custody documentation to provide who had access to an image and what was done with it. Hashing and validation are also critical to prove that forensic images match the original.

The forensic process includes identifying targets, conducting acquisition and validating that the images match, analysis, and reporting. A host of specific tools, techniques, file locations, and other elements come together as part of an investigation to create a complete forensic case. In the end, a forensic report must include the goals of the investigation, the targets, a listing of what was found, and careful analysis of what that data means.

Exam Essentials

Forensic investigations require a complete forensic toolkit.   Forensic toolkits include digital forensics workstations, forensic software, write blockers, wiped drives, cables and drive adapters, cameras, chain-of-custody forms, incident response forms and plans, and escalation lists. Law enforcement investigations may include specialized items like tamper-proof seals and crime scene tape to restrict access to the scene or devices.

Forensic software provides specialized capabilities for investigations.   Forensic tools include analysis utilities that can provide timelines; file validation; filesystem analysis for changes, deletions, and other details; log file viewing; and other analysis. Key data acquisition capabilities include dead, or offline system, cloning and validation via hashing, chain-of-custody and activity logging, and live system imaging. Password cracking and recovery, as well as the ability to decrypt common types of encrypted files, are necessary for many systems. Mobile forensic tools provide the ability to perform the same types of activities for iOS, Android, and other mobile platforms and their unique types of data.

Conducting a forensic investigation follows the forensic process.   This stage includes scoping, identifying locations of relevant data, planning, acquisition, analysis, and reporting. Targets include system information; file modification, access, and change detail; lots; user artifacts; and stored data like memory dumps, shadow copies, and Recycle Bin contents. Acquisition requires forensic validation and care to not modify the source data, typically including the use of write blockers.

Forensic investigations use specialized tools to review what occurred on a targeted system or device. Chain of custody and tracking of actions taken are critical to conducting a sound forensic investigation. Tools to read email, web history, deleted files, installed files, and other events make analysis simpler. Forensic discoveries will often result in further work to fully understand the timeline of events on a system.

Lab Exercises

Activity 7.1: Create a Disk Image

In this exercise you will use dd to create a disk image and then verify the checksum of the image.

Part 1: Boot a Kali Linux system and mount a drive

1. Start your Kali Linux virtual machine.

2. Select a USB thumb drive that is formatted as FAT32 to make an image of for this practice session. A smaller drive will be faster to image, and you should make sure you image a drive smaller than the space you have available for your Kali Linux system.

3. In the Devices menu for the running Kali virtual machine, select USB and then the drive you have inserted. The device should now show up on your Kali Linux desktop.

4. Verify that you can navigate to the drive from the command line. Open a terminal window, then navigate to /dev/disk/by-label, and make sure you see the name of the thumb drive you have mounted.

Part 2: Clone the drive

1. Create a temporary working directory for your volume by running

   `mkdir ~/tmp`

   in your terminal window. This will create a directory called tmp in your home directory.

2. Create an MD5 checksum of the volume you intend to clone in your home directory:

   `md5sum /dev/disk/by-label/[label of your drive] > ~/exercise7_1_original.md5`

3. Clone the volume or disk:

   `dd if=/dev/disk/by-label/[label of your drive] of=~/tmp/exercise7_1_disk.img bs=64k`

4. Once this completes, verify the integrity of the image using MD5:

   `md5sum ~/tmp/exercise7_1_disk.img > ~/exercise7_1_clone.md5`

5. Now compare the MD5 files. You can do that by using the more command to view the files, or you can record the values here:

_____

_____

The values should be the same if your clone was successful.

Activity 7.2: Conduct the NIST Rhino Hunt

The National Institute of Standards and Technology provides a set of practice forensic images that can be freely downloaded and used to hone your forensic skills. You can find the full set at www.cfreds.nist.gov/. For this exercise we will use the Rhino hunt scenario as well as the SANS SIFT image available from https://digital-forensics.sans.org/community/downloads.

1. Run SIFT. If you prefer VMWare, you can run it directly; otherwise use the import tool to import it into VirtualBox. (If you import the VM into VirtualBox, you will need to run sudo apt-get install virtualbox-guest-dkms and then reboot to get a useful screen resolution.)

2. Log in using the default username with the password forensics.

3. Download the SANS Rhino hunt:

wget http://www.cfreds.nist.gov/dfrws/DFRWS2005-RODEO.zip

4. Unzip the Rhino hunt:

unzip DFRWS2005-RODEO.zip

5. Use SIFT to find the rhino pictures.

   ▪ Mount the file:

   sudo mount -o loop, ro RHINOUSB.dd /mnt/usb

   ▪ Review the contents of the mount:

   ls /mnt/usb

   Note that you will only see two recipes for gumbo. Something was done to this drive that overwrote the original contents, and they need to be recovered!

   Next we will recover deleted files using foremost, a utility that automatically recovers files based on file headers and other information.

6. Create a directory for the output:

mkdir output

7. Run foremost against the RHINOUSB image.

foremost -o output/ RHINOUSB.dd

8. Review the output.

To open the file you have recovered, click the filing cabinet icon at the top left of the screen, navigate to Home ➤ Output ➤ Doc, and then double-click on the DOC file you recovered. Read to the end of the file to determine what happened to the hard drive.

Once you know where the hard drive went, you are done with this exercise. The Rhino hunt has a lot more to it, so feel free to continue based on the NIST page's instructions.

Activity 7.3: Security Tools

Match each of the following tools to the correct description:

dd	A memory forensics and analysis suite
md5sum	A drive and file wiping utility sometimes used for anti-forensic purposes
Volatility Framework	A device used to prevent forensic software from modifying a drive while accessing it
FTK	Used to validate whether a drive copy if forensically sound
Eraser	A Linux tool used to create disk images
Write blocker	A device designed to create a complete forensic image and validate it without a PC
WinDBG	A full-featured forensic suite
Forensic drive duplicator	A tool used to review Windows memory dumps

Review Questions

1. Which format does dd produce files in?

    A. ddf

    B. RAW

    C. EN01

    D. OVF

2. Files remnants found in clusters that have been only partially rewritten by new files found are in what type of space?

    A. Outer

    B. Slack

    C. Unallocated space

    D. Non-Euclidean

3. Mike is looking for information about files that were changed on a Windows system. Which of the following is least likely to contain useful information for his investigation?

    A. The MFT

    B. INDX files

    C. Event logs

    D. Volume shadow copies

4. Alice wants to copy a drive without any chance of it being modified by the copying process. What type of device should she use to ensure that this does not happen?

    A. A read blocker

    B. A drive cloner

    C. A write blocker

    D. A hash validator

5. Frederick wants to determine if a thumb drive was ever plugged into a Windows system. How can he test for this?

    A. Review the MFT

    B. Check the system's live memory

    C. Use USB Historian

    D. Create a forensic image of the drive

6. What two files may contain encryption keys normally stored only in memory on a Window system?

    A. The MFT and the hash file

    B. The Registry and hibernation files

    C. Core dumps and encryption logs

    D. Core dumps and hibernation files

7. Jeff is investigating a system compromise and knows that the first event was reported on October 5th. What forensic tool capability should he use to map other events found in logs and files to this date?

   A. A timeline

   B. A log viewer

   C. Registry analysis

   D. Timestamp validator

8. During her forensic copy validation process Danielle received the following MD5 sums from her original drive and the cloned image after using dd. What is likely wrong?

   ```
   b49794e007e909c00a51ae208cacb169  original.img
   d9ff8a0cf6bc0ab066b6416e7e7abf35  clone.img
   ```

   A. The original was modified.

   B. The clone was modified.

   C. dd failed.

   D. An unknown change or problem occurred.

9. Jennifer wants to perform memory analysis and forensics for Windows, macOS, and Linux systems. Which of the following is best suited to her needs?

   A. LiME

   B. DumpIt

   C. fmem

   D. The Volatility Framework

10. Alex is conducting a forensic examination of a Windows system and wants to determine if an application was installed. Where can he find the Windows installer log files for a user named Jim?

    A. `C:\Windows\System 32\Installers`

    B. `C:\Windows\Install.log`

    C. `C:\Windows\Jim\Install.log`

    D. `C:\Windows\Jim\AppData\Local\Temp`

11. Kathleen needs to find data contained in memory but only has an image of an offline Windows system. Where does she have the best chance of recovering the information she needs?

    A. The Registry

    B. `%SystemRoot%\MEMORY.DMP`

    C. A system restore point file

    D. `%SystemRoot%/WinDBG`

12. Carl does not have the ability to capture data from a cell phone using forensic or imaging software, and the phone does not have removable storage. Fortunately, the phone was not set up with a PIN or screen lock. What is his best option to ensure he can see email and other data stored there?

   A. Physical acquisition

   B. Logical access

   C. File system access

   D. Manual access

13. What forensic issue might the presence of a program like CCleaner indicate?

   A. Anti-forensic activities

   B. Full disk encryption

   C. Malware packing

   D. MAC time modifications

14. Which of the following is not a potential issue with live imaging of a system?

   A. Remnant data from the imaging tool

   B. Unallocated space will be captured

   C. Memory or drive contents may change during the imaging process

   D. Malware may detect the imaging tool and work to avoid it

15. During his investigation, Jeff, a certified forensic examiner, is provided with a drive image created by an IT staff member and is asked to add it to his forensic case. What is the most important issue could Jeff encounter if the case goes to court?

   A. Bad checksums

   B. Hash mismatch

   C. Anti-forensic activities

   D. Inability to certify chain of custody

16. Jeff is investigating a system that is running malware that he believes encrypts its data on the drive. What process should he use to have the best chance of viewing that data in an unencrypted form?

   A. Live imaging

   B. Offline imaging

   C. Brute-force encryption cracking

   D. Cause a system crash and analyze the memory dump

17. Susan has been asked to identify the applications that start when a Windows system does. Where should she look first?

   A. INDX files

   B. Volume shadow copies

   C. The Registry

   D. The MFT

18. During a forensic investigation Ben asks Chris to sit with him and to sign off on the actions he has taken. What is he doing?

   A. Maintaining chain of custody

   B. Over-the-shoulder validation

   C. Pair forensics

   D. Separation of duties

19. Which tool is not commonly used to generate the hash of a forensic copy?

   A. MD5

   B. FTK

   C. SHA1

   D. AES

20. Which of the following Linux command-line tools will show you how much disk space is in use?

   A. top

   B. df

   C. lsof

   D. ps

Chapter

8

Recovery and Post-Incident Response

THE COMPTIA CYBERSECURITY ANALYST+ EXAM OBJECTIVES COVERED IN THIS CHAPTER INCLUDE:

Domain 3: Cyber Incident Response

✓ **3.5 Summarize the incident recovery and post-incident response process.**

Chapter 5, "Building an Incident Response Program," provided an overview of the steps required to build and implement a cybersecurity incident response program according to the process advocated by the National Institute of Standards and Technology (NIST). In their *Computer Security Incident Handling Guide*, NIST outlines the four-phase incident response process shown in Figure 8.1.

FIGURE 8.1 Incident response process

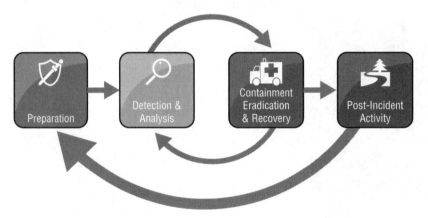

Source: NIST SP 800-61: *Computer Security Incident Handling Guide*

The remainder of Chapter 5 provided an overview of the Preparation phase of incident response. Chapter 6, "Analyzing Symptoms for Incident Response," and Chapter 7, "Performing Forensic Analysis," covered the details behind the Detection and Analysis phase, including sources of cybersecurity information and forensic analysis. This chapter concludes the coverage of CSA+ Domain 3: Cyber Incident Response with a detailed look at the final two phases of incident response: Containment, Eradication, and Recovery, and Post-Incident Activity.

Containing the Damage

The Containment, Eradication, and Recovery phase of incident response moves the organization from the primarily passive incident response activities that take place during the Detection and Analysis phase to more active undertakings. Once the organization understands that a cybersecurity incident is underway, it takes actions designed to minimize the damage caused by the incident and restore normal operations as quickly as possible.

Containment is the first activity that takes place during this phase, and it should begin as quickly as possible after analysts determine that an incident is underway. Containment activities are designed to isolate the incident and prevent it from spreading further. If that phrase sounds somewhat vague, that's because containment means very different things in the context of different types of security incidents. For example, if the organization is experiencing active exfiltration of data from a credit card processing system, incident responders might contain the damage by disconnecting that system from the network, preventing the attackers from continuing to exfiltrate information. On the other hand, if the organization is experiencing a denial-of-service attack against its website, disconnecting the network connection would simply help the attacker achieve its objective. In that case, containment might include placing filters on an upstream Internet connection that blocks all inbound traffic from networks involved in the attack or blocking web requests that bear a certain signature.

Containment activities typically aren't perfect and often cause some collateral damage that disrupts normal business activity. Consider the two examples described in the previous paragraph. Disconnecting a credit card processing system from the network may bring transactions to a halt, causing potentially significant losses of business. Similarly, blocking large swaths of inbound web traffic may render the site inaccessible to some legitimate users. Incident responders undertaking containment strategies must understand the potential side effects of their actions while weighing them against the greater benefit to the organization.

Containment Strategy Criteria

Selecting appropriate containment strategies is one of the most difficult tasks facing incident responders. Containment approaches that are too drastic may have unacceptable impact on business operations. On the other hand, responders who select weak containment approaches may find that the incident escalates to cause even more damage.

In the *Computer Security Incident Handling Guide*, NIST recommends using the following criteria to develop an appropriate containment strategy and weigh it against business interests:

- Potential damage to and theft of resources

- Need for evidence preservation

- Service availability (e.g., network connectivity, services provided to external parties)

- Time and resources needed to implement the strategy

- Effectiveness of the strategy (e.g., partial containment, full containment)

- Duration of the solution (e.g., emergency workaround to be removed in four hours, temporary workaround to be removed in two weeks, permanent solution)

Unfortunately, there's no formula or decision tree that guarantees responders will make the "right" decision while responding to an incident. Incident responders should understand these criteria, the intent of management, and their technical and business operating environment. Armed with this information, responders will be well positioned to follow their best judgment and select an appropriate containment strategy.

Segmentation

Cybersecurity analysts often use *network segmentation* as a proactive strategy to prevent the spread of future security incidents. For example, the network shown in Figure 8.2 is designed to segment different types of users from each other and from critical systems. An attacker who is able to gain access to the guest network would not be able to interact with systems belonging to employees or in the datacenter without traversing the network firewall.

FIGURE 8.2   Proactive network segmentation

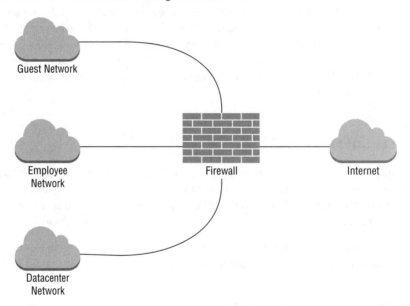

You'll learn more about how network segmentation is used as a proactive control in a defense-in-depth approach to information security in Chapter 10, "Defense-in-Depth Security Architectures."

In addition to being used as a proactive control, network segmentation may play a crucial role in incident response. During the early stages of an incident, responders may realize that a portion of systems are compromised but wish to continue to observe the activity on those systems while they determine other appropriate responses. However, they certainly want to protect other systems on the network from those potentially compromised systems.

Figure 8.3 shows an example of how an organization might apply network segmentation during an incident response effort. Cybersecurity analysts suspect that several systems in the datacenter were compromised and built a separate virtual LAN (VLAN) to contain those systems. That VLAN, called the quarantine network, is segmented from the rest of the datacenter network and controlled by very strict firewall rules. Putting the systems on this network segment provides some degree of isolation, preventing them from damaging systems on other segments but allowing continued live analysis efforts.

FIGURE 8.3 Network segmentation for incident response

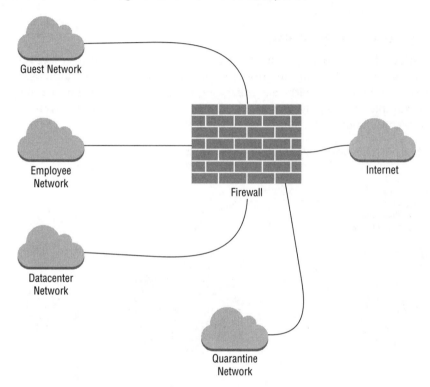

Isolation

Although segmentation does limit the access that attackers have to the remainder of the network, it sometimes doesn't go far enough to meet containment objectives. Cybersecurity analysts may instead decide that it is necessary to use stronger *isolation* practices to cut off an attack. Two primary isolation techniques may be used during a cybersecurity incident response effort: isolating affected systems and isolating the attacker.

WARNING   Segmentation and isolation strategies carry with them significant risks to the organization. First, the attacker retains access to the compromised system, creating the potential for further expansion of the security incident. Second, the compromised system may be used to attack other systems on the Internet. In the best case, an attack launched from the organization's network against a third party may lead to some difficult conversations with cybersecurity colleagues at other firms. In the worst case, the courts may hold the organization liable for knowingly allowing the use of their network in an attack. Cybersecurity analysts considering a segmentation or isolation approach to containment should consult with both management and legal counsel.

Isolating Affected Systems

Isolating affected systems is, quite simply, taking segmentation to the next level. Affected systems are completely disconnected from the remainder of the network although they may still be able to communicate with each other and the attacker over the Internet. Figure 8.4 shows an example of taking the quarantine VLAN from the segmentation strategy and converting it to an isolation approach.

FIGURE 8.4 Network isolation for incident response

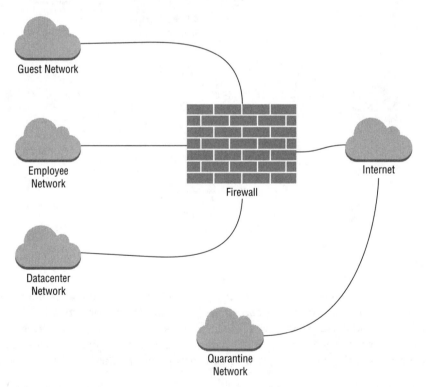

Notice that the only difference between Figures 8.3 and 8.4 is where the quarantine network is connected. In the segmentation approach, the network is connected to the firewall and may have some limited access to other networked systems. In the isolation approach, the quarantine network connects directly to the Internet and has no access to other systems. In reality, this approach may be implemented by simply altering firewall rules rather than bypassing the firewall entirely. The objective is to continue to allow the attacker to access the isolated systems but restrict their ability to access other systems and cause further damage.

Isolating the Attacker

Isolating the attacker is an interesting variation on the isolation strategy and depends on the use of *sandbox* systems that are set up purely to monitor attacker activity and do not contain any information or resources of value to the attacker. Placing attackers in a sandboxed environment allows continued observation in a fairly safe, contained environment. Some organizations use honeypot systems for this purpose. For more information on honeypots, see Chapter 1, "Defending Against Cybersecurity Threats."

Removal

Removal of compromised systems from the network is the strongest containment technique in the cybersecurity analyst's incident response toolkit. As shown in Figure 8.5, removal differs from segmentation and isolation in that the affected systems are completely disconnected from other networks, although they may still be allowed to communicate with other compromised systems within the quarantine VLAN. In some cases, each suspect system may be physically disconnected from the network so that they are prevented from communicating even with each other. The exact details of removal will depend on the circumstances of the incident and the professional judgment of incident responders.

FIGURE 8.5   Network removal for incident response

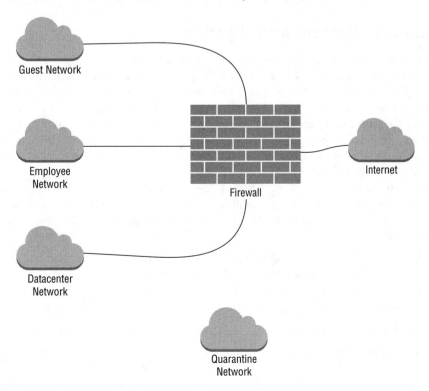

🌐 Real World Scenario

Removal Isn't Foolproof

Removing a system from the network is a common containment step designed to prevent further damage from taking place, but NIST points out in their *Computer Security Incident Handling Guide* that it isn't foolproof. They present a hypothetical example of an attacker using a simple ping as a sort of "dead man's switch" for a compromised system, designed to identify when the adversary detects the attack and removes the system from the network.

In this scenario, the attacker simply sets up a periodic ping request to a known external host, such as the Google public DNS server located at 8.8.8.8. This server is almost always accessible from any network and the attacker can verify this connectivity after initially compromising a system.

The attacker can then write a simple script that monitors the results of those ping requests and, after detecting several consecutive failures, assumes that the attack was detected and the system was removed from the network. The script can then wipe out evidence of the attack or encrypt important information stored on the server.

The moral of the story is that while removal is a strong weapon in the containment toolkit, it isn't foolproof!

Evidence Gathering and Handling

The primary objective during the containment phase of incident response is to limit the damage to the organization and its resources. While that objective may take precedence over other goals, responders may still be interested in gathering evidence during the containment process. This evidence may be crucial in the continuing analysis of the incident for internal purposes, or it may be used during legal proceedings against the attacker.

Chapter 7 provided a thorough review of the forensic strategies that might be used during an incident investigation. Chapter 1 also included information on reverse engineering practices that may be helpful during an incident investigation.

If incident handlers suspect that evidence gathered during an investigation may be used in court, they should take special care to preserve and document evidence during the course of their investigation. NIST recommends that investigators maintain a detailed evidence log that includes the following:

- Identifying information (for example, the location, serial number, model number, hostname, MAC addresses, and IP addresses of a computer)
- Name, title, and phone number of each individual who collected or handled the evidence during the investigation
- Time and date (including time zone) of each occurrence of evidence handling
- Locations where the evidence was stored

Failure to maintain accurate logs will bring the evidence chain-of-custody into question and may cause the evidence to be inadmissible in court.

Identifying Attackers

Identifying the perpetrators of a cybersecurity incident is a complex task that often leads investigators down a winding path of redirected hosts that crosses international borders. Although you might find IP address records stored in your logs, it is incredibly unlikely that they correspond to the actual IP address of the attacker. Any attacker other than the most rank of amateurs will relay his or her communications through a series of compromised systems, making it very difficult to trace their actual origin.

Before heading down this path of investigating an attack's origin, it's very important to ask yourself why you are pursuing it. Is there really business value in uncovering *who* attacked you, or would your time be better spent on containment, eradication, and recovery activities? The NIST *Computer Security Incident Handling Guide* addresses this issue head-on, giving the opinion that "Identifying an attacking host can be a time-consuming and futile process that can prevent a team from achieving its primary goal—minimizing the business impact."

Law enforcement officials may approach this situation with objectives that differ from those of the attacked organization's cybersecurity analysts. After all, one of the core responsibilities of law enforcement organizations is to identify criminals, arrest them, and bring them to trial. That responsibility may conflict with the core cybersecurity objectives of containment, eradication, and recovery. Cybersecurity and business leaders should take this conflict into consideration when deciding whether to involve law enforcement agencies in an incident investigation and the degree of cooperation they will provide to an investigation that is already underway.

Law enforcement officers have tools at their disposal that aren't available to private cybersecurity analysts. If you do have a pressing need to identify an attacker, it may be wise to involve law enforcement. They have the ability to obtain search warrants that may prove invaluable during an investigation. Officers can serve search warrants on Internet service providers and other companies that may have log records that assist in untangling the winding trail of an attack. Additionally, law enforcement agencies may have access to sensitive government databases that contain information on known attackers and their methodologies.

Incident Eradication and Recovery

Once the cybersecurity team successfully contains an incident, it is time to move on to the *eradication* phase of the response. The primary purpose of eradication is to remove any of the artifacts of the incident that may remain on the organization's network. This could include the removal of any malicious code from the network, the sanitization of compromised media, and the securing of compromised user accounts.

The *recovery* phase of incident response focuses on restoring normal operations and correcting security control deficiencies that may have led to the attack. This could include rebuilding and patching systems, reconfiguring firewalls, updating malware signatures, and similar activities. The goal of recovery is not just to rebuild the organization's network but to do so in a manner that reduces the likelihood of a successful future attack.

CompTIA vs. NIST

The CSA+ curriculum deviates from the NIST standard process. Instead of grouping activities into the eradication and recovery phases, CompTIA classifies them into two groups: eradication activities and validation activities. This can be somewhat confusing for students studying for the exam who have real-world incident response experience and are more familiar with the standard NIST approach.

The division becomes even more confusing because some of the activities do not fit into the official bucket that would be most logical. For example, most cybersecurity analysts would consider patching systems to be a recovery activity (or arguably an eradication activity). CompTIA, however, classifies it as a validation activity.

Don't lose too much sleep trying to figure out the logic behind this classification scheme. Go about your real-world life operating as you normally do! You should, however, understand how CompTIA classifies these activities as you may see related questions on the exam.

CompTIA considers the following activities part of the security incident eradication effort:

- Sanitization

- Reconstruction/reimaging

- Secure disposal

CompTIA then classifies these remaining activities as components of the validation effort:

- Patching

- Permissions

- Scanning

- Verify logging/communication to security monitoring

And now back to our regularly scheduled programming.

During the eradication and recovery effort, cybersecurity analysts should develop a clear understanding of the incident's root cause. This is critical to implementing a secure recovery that corrects control deficiencies that led to the original attack. After all, if you don't understand how an attacker breached your security controls in the first place, it will be hard to correct those controls so the attack doesn't reoccur! Understanding the root cause of an attack is a completely different activity than identifying the attacker. Root cause assessment is a critical component of incident recovery while, as mentioned earlier, identifying the attacker can be a costly distraction.

Root cause analysis also helps an organization identify other systems they operate that might share the same vulnerability. For example, if an attacker compromises a Cisco router and root cause analysis reveals an error in that device's configuration, administrators may correct the error on other routers they control to prevent a similar attack from compromising those devices.

Reconstruction and Reimaging

During an incident, attackers may compromise one or more systems through the use of malware, web application attacks, or other exploits. Once an attacker gains control of a system, security professionals should consider it completely compromised and untrustworthy. It is not safe to simply correct the security issue and move on because the attacker may still have an undetected foothold on the compromised system. Instead, the system should be rebuilt, either from scratch or by using an image or backup of the system from a known secure state.

Rebuilding and/or restoring systems should always be done with the incident root cause analysis in mind. If the system was compromised because it contained a security vulnerability, as opposed to through the use of a compromised user account, backups and images of that system likely have that same vulnerability. Even rebuilding the system from scratch may reintroduce the earlier vulnerability, rendering the system susceptible to the same attack. During the recovery phase, administrators should ensure that rebuilt or restored systems are remediated to address known security issues.

Patching Systems and Applications

During the incident recovery effort, cybersecurity analysts will patch operating systems and applications involved in the attack. This is also a good time to review the security patch status of all systems in the enterprise, addressing other security issues that may lurk behind the scenes.

Cybersecurity analysts should first focus their efforts on systems that were directly involved in the compromise and then work their way outward, addressing systems that were indirectly related to the compromise before touching systems that were not involved at all. Figure 8.6 shows the phased approach that cybersecurity analysts should take to patching systems and applications during the recovery phase.

FIGURE 8.6 Patching priorities

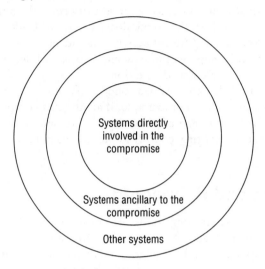

Systems directly
involved in the
compromise

Systems ancillary to the
compromise

Other systems

Sanitization and Secure Disposal

During the recovery effort, cybersecurity analysts may need to dispose of or repurpose media from systems that were compromised during the incident. In those cases, special care should be taken to ensure that sensitive information that was stored on that media is not compromised. Responders don't want the recovery effort from one incident to lead to a second incident!

Generally speaking, there are three options available for the secure disposition of media containing sensitive information: clear, purge, and destroy. NIST defines these three activities clearing in NIST SP 800-88: *Guidelines for Media Sanitization*:

- *Clear* applies logical techniques to sanitize data in all user-addressable storage locations for protection against simple non-invasive data recovery techniques; this is typically applied through the standard Read and Write commands to the storage device, such as by rewriting with a new value or using a menu option to reset the device to the factory state (where rewriting is not supported).

- *Purge* applies physical or logical techniques that render target data recovery infeasible using state-of-the-art laboratory techniques. Examples of purging activities include overwriting, block erase, and cryptographic erase activities when performed through the use of dedicated, standardized device commands. *Degaussing* is another form of purging that uses extremely strong magnetic fields to disrupt the data stored on a device.

- *Destroy* renders target data recovery infeasible using state-of-the-art laboratory techniques and results in the subsequent inability to use the media for storage of data. Destruction techniques include disintegration, pulverization, melting, and incinerating.

These three levels of data disposal are listed in increasing order of effectiveness as well as difficulty and cost. Physically incinerating a hard drive, for example, removes any possibility that data will be recovered but requires the use of an incinerator and renders the drive unusable for future purposes.

Figure 8.7 shows a flowchart designed to help security decision makers choose appropriate techniques for destroying information and can be used to guide incident recovery efforts. Notice that the flowchart includes a Validation phase after efforts to clear, purge, or destroy data. Validation ensures that the media sanitization was successful and that remnant data does not exist on the sanitized media.

FIGURE 8.7   Sanitization and disposition decision flow

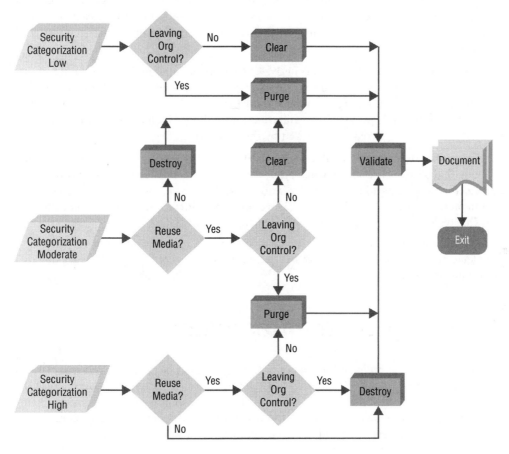

Source: NIST SP 800-88: Guidelines for Media Sanitization

Validating the Recovery Effort

Before concluding the recovery effort, incident responders should take time to verify that the recovery measures put in place were successful. The exact nature of this verification will depend on the technical circumstances of the incident and the organization's infrastructure. Four activities that should always be included in these validation efforts follow:

Validate that only authorized user accounts exist on every system and application in the organization.   In many cases, organizations already undertake periodic account reviews that verify the authorization for every account. This process should be used during the recovery validation effort.

Verify the permissions assigned to each account.   During the account review, responders should also verify that accounts do not have extraneous permissions that violate the principle of least privilege. This is true for normal user accounts, administrator accounts, and service accounts.

Verify that all systems are logging properly.   Every system and application should be configured to log security-related information to a level that is consistent with the organization's logging policy. Those log records should be sent to a centralized log repository that preserves them for archival use. The validation phase should include verification that these logs are properly configured and received by the repository.

Conduct vulnerability scans on all systems.   Vulnerability scans play an important role in verifying that systems are safeguarded against future attacks. Analysts should run thorough scans against systems and initiate remediation workflows where necessary. For more information on this process, see Chapter 3, "Developing a Vulnerability Management Program," and Chapter 4, "Analyzing Vulnerability Scans."

These actions form the core of an incident recovery validation effort and should be complemented with other activities that validate the specific controls put in place during the Containment, Eradication, and Recovery phase of incident response.

Wrapping Up the Response

After the immediate, urgent actions of containment, eradication, and recovery are complete, it is very tempting for the CSIRT to take a deep breath and consider their work done. While the team should take a well-deserved break, the incident response process is not complete until the team completes post-incident activities that include managing change control processes, conducting a lessons-learned session, and creating a formal written incident report.

Managing Change Control Processes

During the containment, eradication, and recovery process, responders may have bypassed the organization's normal change control and configuration management processes in an effort to respond to the incident in an expedient manner. These processes provide important management controls and documentation of the organization's technical infrastructure. Once the urgency of response efforts pass, the responders should turn back to these processes and use them to document any emergency changes made during the incident response effort.

Conducting a Lessons-Learned Session

At the conclusion of every cybersecurity incident, everyone involved in the response should participate in a formal lessons learned session that is designed to uncover critical information about the response. This session also highlights potential deficiencies in the incident response plan and procedures. For more information on conducting the post-incident lessons learned session, see "Lessons-Learned Review" in Chapter 5, "Building an Incident Response Program."

During the lessons-learned session, the organization may uncover potential changes to the incident response plan. In those cases, the leader should propose those changes and move them through the organization's formal change process to improve future incident response efforts.

Developing a Final Report

Every incident that activates the CSIRT should conclude with a formal written report that documents the incident for posterity. This serves several important purposes. First, it creates an institutional memory of the incident that is useful when developing new security controls and training new security team members. Second, it may serve as an important record of the incident if there is ever legal action that results from the incident. Finally, the act of creating the written report can help identify previously undetected deficiencies in the incident response process that may feed back through the lessons-learned process.

Important elements that the CSIRT should cover in a post-incident report include the following:

- Chronology of events for the incident and response efforts
- Root cause of the incident
- Location and description of evidence collected during the incident response process
- Specific actions taken by responders to contain, eradicate, and recover from the incident, including the rationale for those decisions
- Estimates of the impact of the incident on the organization and its stakeholders
- Results of post-recovery validation efforts
- Documentation of issues identified during the lessons-learned review

Incident summary reports should be classified in accordance with the organization's classification policy and stored in an appropriately secured manner. The organization should also have a defined retention period for incident reports and destroy old reports when they exceed that period.

Summary

After identifying a security incident in progress, CSIRT members should move immediately into the containment, eradication, and recovery phase of incident response. The first priority of this phase is to contain the damage caused by a security incident to lower the impact on the organization. Once an incident is contained, responders should take actions to eradicate the effects of the incident and recovery normal operations. Once the immediate response efforts are complete, the CSIRT should move into the post-incident phase, conduct a lessons-learned session, and create a written report summarizing the incident response process.

Exam Essentials

Containment activities seek to limit the impact of an incident.   After identifying a potential incident in progress, responders should take immediate action to contain the damage. They should select appropriate containment strategies based on the nature of the incident and impact on the organization. Potential containment activities include network segmentation, isolation, and removal of affected systems.

Evidence not collected during a response may disappear.   Much of the evidence of a cybersecurity incident is volatile in nature and may not be available later if not collected during the response. CSIRT members must determine the priority that evidence collection will take during the containment, eradication, and recovery phase and then ensure that they properly handle any collected evidence that can later be used in legal proceedings.

Identifying attackers can be a waste of valuable resources.   Most efforts to identify the perpetrators of security incidents are futile, consuming significant resources before winding up at a dead end. The primary focus of incident responders should be on protecting the business interests of the organization. Law enforcement officials have different priorities, and responders should be aware of potentially conflicting objectives.

Eradication and recovery is a time-consuming but important process.   After containing the damage, responders should move on to eradication and recovery activities that seek to remove all traces of an incident from the organization's network and restore normal operations as quickly as possible. This should include validation efforts that verify security controls are properly implemented before closing the incident.

Post-incident activities provide a time for process improvement and documentation.   At the conclusion of a cybersecurity incident response effort, CSIRT members should conduct a formal lessons-learned session that reviews the entire incident response process and recommends changes to the organization's incident response plan, as needed. The team should also complete a formal written report that serves to document the incident for posterity.

Lab Exercises

Activity 8.1: Incident Containment Options

Label each one of the following figures with the type of incident containment activity pictured.

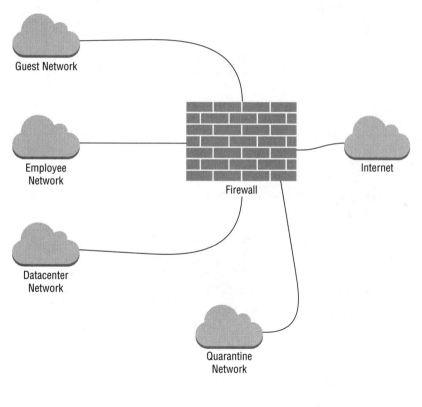

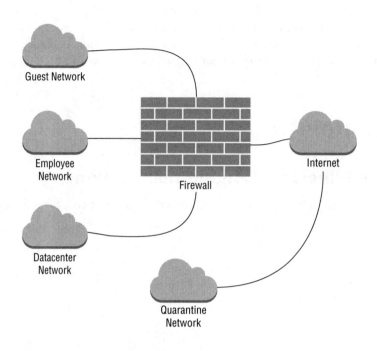

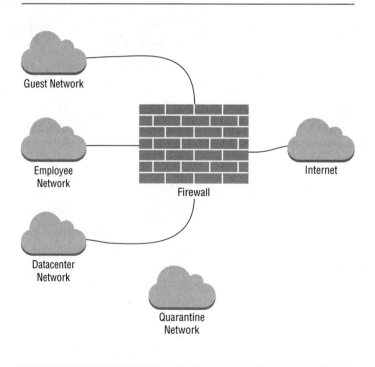

Activity 8.2: Incident Response Activities

For each of the following incident response activities, assign it to one of the following CompTIA categories:

- Containment
- Eradication
- Validation
- Post-Incident Activities

Remember that the categories assigned by CompTIA differ from those used by NIST and other incident handling standards.

Patching	_____
Sanitization	_____
Lessons learned	_____
Reimaging	_____
Secure disposal	_____
Isolation	_____
Scanning	_____
Removal	_____
Reconstruction	_____
Permission verification	_____
User account review	_____
Segmentation	_____

Activity 8.3: Sanitization and Disposal Techniques

Fill in the flowchart below with the appropriate dispositions for information being destroyed following a security incident.

Each box should be completed using one of the following three words:

Clear

Purge

Destroy

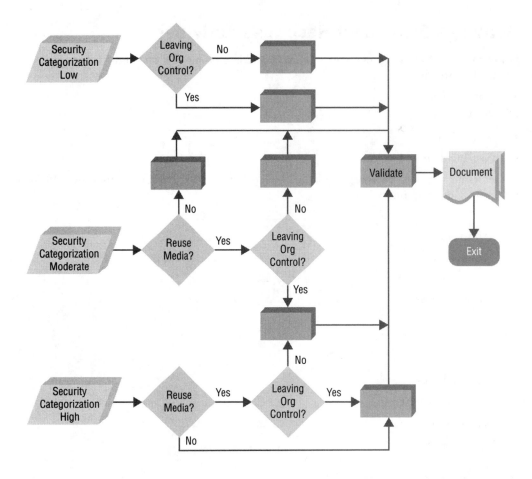

Review Questions

1. Which one of the phases of incident response involves primarily active undertakings designed to limit the damage that an attacker might cause?

    A.   Containment, Eradication, and Recovery

    B.   Preparation

    C.   Post-Incident Activity

    D.   Detection and Analysis

2. Which one of the following criteria is *not* normally used when evaluating the appropriateness of a cybersecurity incident containment strategy?

    A.   Effectiveness of the strategy

    B.   Evidence preservation requirements

    C.   Log records generated by the strategy

    D.   Cost of the strategy

3. Alice is responding to a cybersecurity incident and notices a system that she suspects is compromised. She places this system on a quarantine VLAN with limited access to other networked systems. What containment strategy is Alice pursuing?

    A.   Eradication

    B.   Isolation

    C.   Segmentation

    D.   Removal

4. Alice confers with other team members and decides that even allowing limited access to other systems is an unacceptable risk and decides instead to prevent the quarantine VLAN from accessing any other systems by putting firewall rules in place that limit access to other enterprise systems. The attacker can still control the system to allow Alice to continue monitoring the incident. What strategy is she now pursuing?

    A.   Eradication

    B.   Isolation

    C.   Segmentation

    D.   Removal

5. After observing the attacker, Alice decides to remove the Internet connection entirely, leaving the systems running but inaccessible from outside the quarantine VLAN. What strategy is she now pursuing?

    A.   Eradication

    B.   Isolation

    C.   Segmentation

    D.   Removal

6. Which one of the following tools may be used to isolate an attacker so that he or she may not cause damage to production systems but may still be observed by cybersecurity analysts?

   A. Sandbox

   B. Playpen

   C. IDS

   D. DLP

7. Tamara is a cybersecurity analyst for a private business that is suffering a security breach. She believes the attackers have compromised a database containing sensitive information. Which one of the following activities should be Tamara's first priority?

   A. Identifying the source of the attack

   B. Eradication

   C. Containment

   D. Recovery

8. Which one of the following activities does CompTIA classify as part of the recovery validation effort?

   A. Rebuilding systems

   B. Sanitization

   C. Secure disposal

   D. Scanning

9. Which one of the following pieces of information is most critical to conducting a solid incident recovery effort?

   A. Identity of the attacker

   B. Time of the attack

   C. Root cause of the attack

   D. Attacks on other organizations

10. Lynda is disposing of a drive containing sensitive information that was collected during the response to a cybersecurity incident. The information is categorized as a high security risk and she wishes to reuse the media during a future incident. What is the appropriate disposition for this information?

   A. Clear

   B. Erase

   C. Purge

   D. Destroy

11. Which one of the following activities is not normally conducted during the recovery validation phase?

   A. Verify the permissions assigned to each account

   B. Implement new firewall rules

   C. Conduct vulnerability scans

   D. Verify logging is functioning properly

12. What incident response activity focuses on removing any artifacts of the incident that may remain on the organization's network?

    A. Containment

    B. Recovery

    C. Post-Incident Activities

    D. Eradication

13. Which one of the following is not a common use of formal incident reports?

    A. Training new team members

    B. Sharing with other organizations

    C. Developing new security controls

    D. Assisting with legal action

14. Which one of the following data elements would not normally be included in an evidence log?

    A. Serial number

    B. Record of handling

    C. Storage location

    D. Malware signatures

15. Sondra determines that an attacker has gained access to a server containing critical business files and wishes to ensure that the attacker cannot delete those files. Which one of the following strategies would meet Sondra's goal?

    A. Isolation

    B. Segmentation

    C. Removal

    D. None of the above

16. Joe would like to determine the appropriate disposition of a flash drive used to gather highly sensitive evidence during an incident response effort. He does not need to reuse the drive but wants to return it to its owner, an outside contractor. What is the appropriate disposition?

    A. Destroy

    B. Clear

    C. Erase

    D. Purge

17. Which one of the following is not typically found in a cybersecurity incident report?

    A. Chronology of events

    B. Identity of the attacker

    C. Estimates of impact

    D. Documentation of lessons learned

18. What NIST publication contains guidance on cybersecurity incident handling?

    A. SP 800-53

    B. SP 800-88

    C. SP 800-18

    D. SP 800-61

19. Which one of the following is not a purging activity?

    A. Resetting to factory state

    B. Overwriting

    C. Block erase

    D. Cryptographic erase

20. Ben is responding to a security incident and determines that the attacker is using systems on Ben's network to attack a third party. Which one of the following containment approaches will prevent Ben's systems from being used in this manner?

    A. Removal

    B. Isolation

    C. Detection

    D. Segmentation

Chapter

9

Policy and Compliance

THE COMPTIA CYBERSECURITY ANALYST+ EXAM OBJECTIVES COVERED IN THIS CHAPTER INCLUDE:

Domain 4: Security Architecture and Tool Sets

✓ **4.1 Explain the relationship between frameworks, common policies, controls, and procedures.**

Policy serves as the foundation for any cybersecurity program, setting out the principles and rules that guide the execution of security efforts throughout the enterprise. Often, organizations base these policies on best practice frameworks developed by industry groups, such as the National Institute of Standards and Technology (NIST) or the International Organization for Standardization (ISO). In many cases, organizational policies are also influenced and directed by external compliance obligations that regulators impose on the organization. In this chapter, you will learn about the important elements of the cybersecurity policy framework.

Understanding Policy Documents

An organization's *information security policy framework* contains a series of documents designed to describe the organization's cybersecurity program. The scope and complexity of these documents vary widely, depending on the nature of the organization and its information resources. These frameworks generally include four different types of document:

- Policies
- Standards
- Procedures
- Guidelines

In the remainder of this section, you'll learn the differences between each of these document types. However, keep in mind that the definitions of these categories vary significantly from organization to organization and it is very common to find the lines between them blurred. While at first glance that may seem "incorrect," it's a natural occurrence as security theory meets the real world. As long as the documents are achieving their desired purpose, there's no harm and no foul.

Policies

Policies are high-level statements of management intent. Compliance with policies is mandatory. An information security policy will generally contain broad statements about cybersecurity objectives, including

- A statement of the importance of cybersecurity to the organization

- Requirements that all staff and contracts take measures to protect the confidentiality, integrity, and availability of information and information systems
- Statement on the ownership of information created and/or possessed by the organization
- Designation of the chief information security officer (CISO) or other individual as the executive responsible for cybersecurity issues
- Delegation of authority granting the CISO the ability to create standards, procedures, and guidelines that implement the policy

In many organizations, the process to create a policy is laborious and requires very high-level approval, often from the chief executive officer (CEO). Keeping policy statements at a high level provides the CISO with the flexibility to adapt and change specific security requirements with changes in the business and technology environments. For example, the five-page information security policy at the University of Notre Dame simply states

> The Information Governance Committee will create handling standards for each Highly Sensitive data element. Data stewards may create standards for other data elements under their stewardship. These information handling standards will specify controls to manage risks to University information and related assets based on their classification. All individuals at the University are responsible for complying with these controls.

By way of contrast, the federal government's Centers for Medicare & Medicaid Services (CMS) has an 87-page information security policy. This mammoth document contains incredibly detailed requirements, such as

> A record of all requests for monitoring must be maintained by the CMS CIO along with any other summary results or documentation produced during the period of monitoring. The record must also reflect the scope of the monitoring by documenting search terms and techniques. All information collected from monitoring must be controlled and protected with distribution limited to the individuals identified in the request for monitoring and other individuals specifically designated by the CMS Administrator or CMS CIO as having a specific need to know such information.

The CMS document even goes so far as to include a three-page chart describing exactly what type of security training the department will provide to every category of employee and the number of hours that training should consume. An excerpt from that chart appears in Figure 9.1.

This approach may meet the needs of CMS, but it is hard to imagine the long-term maintenance of that document. Lengthy security policies often quickly become outdated as necessary changes to individual requirements accumulate and become neglected because staff are weary of continually publishing new versions of the policy.

FIGURE 9.1   Excerpt from CMS training matrix

Table 1. CMS Minimum Role-Based Training Requirements

Specialized Roles	Populations	Role Definitions	Minimum Annual Training Requirement
General Population		• Federal Employees and Contractors (All Users) • Supervisors	Awareness training
Federal Executives	Mandatory Population: • All members of the Senior Executive Service (SES)	• Administrator • CFO • Personnel and Physical Security Officer • Operations Executive • CRO • CDO	1 hour targeted training
Chief Information and Technology Officers	Mandatory Population: • CIO, direct managerial reports and component organizations, and CTO Optional Population: None specified	• CIO • CTO • Direct Managerial Reports • Component Organizations[22]	4 hours targeted training
Chief Information Security Officer and Senior Official for Privacy	Mandatory Population: • CISO, SOP • All information security employees or contractors working for or contracted by the CMS CISO Optional Population: None specified	• CISO • SOP • CISO and SOP Staff • CISO and SOP Support Contractors	8 hours targeted training
Other Information Officers	Mandatory Population: • All personnel identified as Privacy Act Officer, Configuration Management Executive, CRA, Director for Marketplace Security	• Privacy Act Officer • Configuration Management Executive • CRA • Director for Marketplace Security	8 hours targeted training

Source: Centers for Medicare and Medicaid Services Information Systems Security and Privacy Policy, April 26, 2016. (https://www.cms.gov/Research-Statistics-Data-and-Systems/CMS-Information-Technology/InformationSecurity/Downloads/IS2P2.pdf)

Organizations commonly include the following documents in their information security policy library:

- *Information security policy* that provides high-level authority and guidance for the security program
- *Acceptable use policy (AUP)* that provides network and system users with clear direction on permissible uses of information resources
- *Data ownership policy* that clearly states the ownership of information created or used by the organization
- *Data classification policy* that describes the classification structure used by the organization and the process used to properly assign classifications to data
- *Data retention policy* that outlines what information the organization will maintain and the length of time different categories of information will be retained prior to destruction
- *Account management policy* that describes the account life cycle from provisioning through active use and decommissioning
- *Password policy* that sets forth requirements for password length, complexity, reuse, and similar issues

As you read through the list, you may notice that some of the documents listed tend to conflict with our description of policies as high-level documents and seem to better fit the definition of a standard in the next section. That's a reasonable conclusion to draw.

CompTIA specifically includes these items as elements of information security policy while many organizations would move some of them, such as password requirements, into standards documents.

Standards

Standards provide mandatory requirements describing how an organization will carry out its information security policies. These may include the specific configuration settings used for a common operating system, the controls that must be put in place for highly sensitive information, or any other security objective. Standards are typically approved at a lower organizational level than policies and, therefore, may change more regularly.

For example, the University of California at Berkeley maintains a detailed document titled the *Minimum Security Standards for Electronic Information*, available online at https://security.berkeley.edu/minimum-security-standards-electronic-information. This document divides information into four different data protection levels (DPLs) and then describes what controls are required, optional, and not required for data at different levels, using a detailed matrix. An excerpt from this matrix appears in Figure 9.2.

FIGURE 9.2 Excerpt from UC Berkeley *Minimum Security Standards for Electronic Information*

MSSEI Controls	DPL 0 (TBD)	DPL 1 Individual	DPL 1 Privileged	DPL 1 Institutional	DPL 2 Individual	DPL 2 Privileged	DPL 2 Institutional	DPL 3 (TBD)	Guidelines
1.1 Removal of non-required covered data	o	√	√	√	√	√			see secure deletion guideline and UCOP disposition schedules database
1.2 Covered system inventory			√	√		√	√		1.2 guideline
1.3 Covered system registration			+	√		√	√		1.3 guideline
1.4 Annual registration renewal			√	√		√	√		1.4 guideline
2.1 Managed software inventory			+	√	o	√	√		2.1 guideline
3.1 Secure configurations	o		+	√	√	√	√		3.1 guideline
4.1 Continuous vulnerability assessment & remediation			+	√		√	√		4.1 guideline

Source: University of California at Berkeley Minimum Security Standards for Electronic Information

The standard then provides detailed descriptions for each of these requirements with definitions of the terms used in the requirements. For example, requirement 3.1 in Figure 9.2 simply reads "Secure device configurations." Later in the document, UC Berkeley expands this to read "Resource Custodians must utilize well-managed security configurations for hardware, software, and operating systems based upon industry standards." It goes on to defined "well-managed" as

- Devices must have secure configurations in place prior to deployment.

- Any deviations from defined security configurations must be approved through a change management process and documented. A process must exist to annually review deviations from the defined security configurations for continued relevance.

- A process must exist to regularly check configurations of devices and alert the Resource Custodian of any changes.

This approach provides a document hierarchy that is easy to navigate for the reader and provides access to increasing levels of detail as needed. Notice also that many of the requirement lines in Figure 9.2 provide links to guidelines. Clicking on those links leads to advice to organizations subject to this policy that begins with this text:

> UC Berkeley security policy mandates compliance with Minimum Security Standard for Electronic Information for devices handling covered data. The recommendations below are provided as optional guidance.

This is a perfect example of three elements of the information security policy framework working together. Policy sets out the high-level objectives of the security program and requires compliance with standards, which includes details of required security controls. Guidelines provide advice to organizations seeking to comply with the policy and standards.

In some cases, organizations may operate in industries that have commonly accepted standards that the organization either must follow or chooses to follow as a best practice. Failure to follow industry best practices may be seen as negligence and can cause legal liability for the organization. Many of these industry standards are expressed in the standard frameworks discussed later in this chapter.

Procedures

Procedures are detailed, step-by-step processes that individuals and organizations must follow in specific circumstances. Similar to checklists, procedures ensure a consistent process for achieving a security objective. Organizations may create procedures for building new systems, releasing code to production environments, responding to security incidents, and many other tasks. Compliance with procedures is mandatory.

For example, Visa publishes a document titled *What to Do if Compromised* (`https://usa.visa.com/dam/VCOM/download/merchants/cisp-what-to-do-if-compromised.pdf`) that lays out a mandatory process that merchants suspecting a credit card compromise must follow. Although the document doesn't contain the word *procedure* in the title, the introduction clearly states, "This document contains required procedures and timelines for reporting and responding to a suspected or confirmed account data compromise." The document provides requirements covering the following areas of incident response:

- Preserve evidence

- Provide Visa with an initial investigation report

- Perform a forensic investigation

- Provide all exposed accounts

Each of these sections provides detailed information on how Visa expects merchants to handle incident response activities. For example, the forensic investigation section describes the use of Payment Card Industry Forensic Investigators (PFI) and reads as follows:

> Upon discovery of an account data compromise, or receipt of an independent forensic investigation notification, an entity must:
>
> - Engage a PFI (or sign a contract) within five (5) business days.
>
> - Provide Visa with the initial forensic (i.e. preliminary) report within ten (10) business days from when the PFI is engaged (or the contract is signed).
>
> - Provide Visa with a final forensic report within ten (10) business days of the completion of the review.

There's not much room for interpretation in this type of language. Visa is laying out a clear and mandatory procedure describing what actions the merchant must take, the type of investigator they should hire, and the timeline for completing different milestones.

Organizations commonly include the following procedures in their policy frameworks:

- *Monitoring procedures* that describe how the organization will perform security monitoring activities, including the possible use of continuous monitoring technology

- *Evidence production procedures* that describe how the organization will respond to subpoenas, court orders, and other legitimate requests to produce digital evidence

- *Patching procedures* that describe the frequency and process of applying patches to applications and systems under the organization's care

Of course, cybersecurity teams may decide to include many other types of procedures in their frameworks, as dictated by the organization's operational needs.

Guidelines

Guidelines provide best practices and recommendations related to a given concept, technology, or task. Compliance with guidelines is not mandatory, and guidelines are offered in the spirit of providing helpful advice. That said, the "optionality" of guidelines may vary significantly depending on the organization's culture.

In April 2016, the chief information officer (CIO) of the state of Washington published a 25-page document providing guidelines on the use of electronic signatures by state agencies. The document is not designed to be obligatory but, rather, offers advice to agencies seeking to adopt electronic signature technology. The document begins with a purpose section that outlines three goals of guideline:

1. Help agencies determine if, and to what extent, their agency will implement and rely upon electronic records and electronic signatures.

2. Provide agencies with information they can use to establish policy or rule governing their use and acceptance of digital signatures.

3. Provide direction to agencies for sharing of their policies with the Office of the Chief Information Officer (OCIO) pursuant to state law.

The first two stated objectives line up completely with the function of a guideline. Phrases like "help agencies determine" and "provide agencies with information" are common in guideline documents. There is nothing mandatory about them and, in fact, the guidelines explicitly state that Washington state law "does not mandate that any state agency accept or require electronic signatures or records."

The third objective might seem a little strange to include in a guideline. Phrases like "provide direction" are more commonly found in policies and procedures. Browsing through the document, the text relating to this objective is only a single paragraph within a 25-page document, reading

> The Office of the Chief Information Officer maintains a page on the OCIO.wa.gov website listing links to individual agency electronic signature and record submission policies. As agencies publish their policies, the link and agency contact information should be emailed to the OCIO Policy Mailbox. The information will be added to the page within 5 working days. Agencies are responsible for notifying the OCIO if the information changes.

Reading this paragraph, the text does appear to clearly outline a mandatory procedure and would not be appropriate in a guideline document that fits within the strict definition of the term. However, it is likely that the committee drafting this document thought it would be much more convenient to the reader to include this explanatory text in the related guideline rather than drafting a separate procedure document for a fairly mundane and simple task.

    The full Washington state document, *Electronic Signature Guidelines*, is available for download from the Washington State CIO's website at https://ocio.wa.gov/policy/electronic-signature-guidelines.

Exceptions and Compensating Controls

When adopting new security policies, standards, and procedures, organizations should also provide a mechanism for exceptions to those rules. Inevitably, unforeseen circumstances will arise that require a deviation from the requirements. The policy framework should lay out the specific requirements for receiving an exception and the individual or committee with the authority to approve exceptions.

The state of Washington uses an exception process that requires the requestor document the following information:

- Standard/requirement that requires an exception
- Reason for noncompliance with the requirement
- Business and/or technical justification for the exception
- Scope and duration of the exception

- Risks associated with the exception
- Description of any supplemental controls that mitigate the risks associated with the exception
- Plan for achieving compliance
- Identification of any unmitigated risks

Many exception processes require the use of *compensating controls* to mitigate the risk associated with exceptions to security standards. The Payment Card Industry Data Security Standard (PCI DSS) includes one of the most formal compensating control processes in use today. It sets out three criteria that must be met for a compensating control to be satisfactory:

1. The control must meet the intent and rigor of the original requirement.

2. The control must provide a similar level of defense as the original requirement, such that the compensating control sufficiently offsets the risk that the original PCI DSS requirement was designed to defend against.

3. The control must be "above and beyond" other PCI DSS requirements.

For example, an organization might find that it needs to run an outdated version of an operating system on a specific machine because software necessary to run the business will only function on that operating system version. Most security policies would prohibit using the outdated operating system because it might be susceptible to security vulnerabilities. The organization could choose to run this system on an isolated network with either very little or no access to other systems as a compensating control.

The general idea is that a compensating control finds alternative means to achieve an objective when the organization cannot meet the original control requirement. While PCI DSS offers a very formal process for compensating controls, the use of compensating controls is a common strategy in many different organizations, even those not subject to PCI DSS. Compensating controls balance the fact that it simply isn't possible to implement every required security control in every circumstance with the desire to manage risk to the greatest feasible degree.

In many cases, organizations adopt compensating controls to address a temporary exception to a security requirement. In those cases, the organization should also develop remediation plans designed to bring the organization back into compliance with the letter and intent of the original control.

Complying with Laws and Regulations

Legislators and regulators around the world take an interest in cybersecurity due to the potential impact of cybersecurity shortcomings on individuals, government and society. While the European Union has a broad-ranging data protection regulation, cybersecurity analysts in the United States are forced to deal with a patchwork of security regulations covering different industries and information categories.

Some of the major information security regulations facing U.S. organizations include the following:

- The *Health Insurance Portability and Accountability Act (HIPAA)* includes security and privacy rules that affect healthcare providers, health insurers, and health information clearinghouses.

- The *Payment Card Industry Data Security Standard (PCI DSS)* provides detailed rules about the storage, processing, and transmission of credit and debit card information. PCI DSS is not a law but rather a contractual obligation that applies to credit card merchants and service providers.

- The *Gramm-Leach-Bliley Act (GLBA)* covers financial institutions, broadly defined. It requires that those institutions have a formal security program and designate an individual as having overall responsibility for that program.

- The *Sarbanes-Oxley (SOX) Act* applies to the financial records of publicly traded companies and requires that those companies have a strong degree of assurance around the IT systems that store and process those records.

- The *Family Educational Rights and Privacy Act (FERPA)* requires that educational institutions implement security and privacy controls for student educational records.

- Various *data breach notification laws* describe the requirements that individual states place on organizations that suffer data breaches regarding notification of individuals affected by the breach.

Remember that this is only a brief listing of security regulations. There are many other laws and obligations that apply to specific industries and data types. You should always consult your organization's legal counsel and subject matter experts when designing a compliance strategy for your organization. The advice of a well-versed attorney is crucial when interpreting and applying cybersecurity regulations to your specific business and technical environment.

The CSA+ exam objectives only mention compliance in a generic sense, with a single bullet reading "regulatory compliance" as one of the topics that cybersecurity analysts should be able to explain. Rather than diving into the details of specific regulations, you should have a good working knowledge of what regulations might apply to a specific industry and how to integrate an understanding of compliance issues into a cybersecurity program.

Adopting a Standard Framework

Developing a cybersecurity program from scratch is a formidable undertaking. Organizations will have a wide variety of control objectives and tools at their disposal to meet those objectives. Teams facing the task of developing a new security program or evaluating an existing program may find it challenging to cover a large amount of ground without a roadmap. Fortunately, there are several standard security frameworks available to assist with this task and provide a standardized approach to developing cybersecurity programs.

NIST Cybersecurity Framework

The National Institute for Standards and Technology (NIST) is responsible for developing cybersecurity standards across the U.S. federal government. The guidance and standard documents they produce in this process often have wide applicability across the private sector and are commonly referred to by nongovernmental security analysts due to the fact that they are available in the public domain and are typically of very high quality.

In 2014, NIST released a Cybersecurity Framework designed to assist organizations attempting to meet one or more of the following five objectives:

1. Describe their current cybersecurity posture.

2. Describe their target state for cybersecurity.

3. Identify and prioritize opportunities for improvement within the context of a continuous and repeatable process.

4. Assess progress toward the target state.

5. Communicate among internal and external stakeholders about cybersecurity risk.

The NIST framework includes three components:

- The Framework Core, shown in Figure 9.3, is a set of five security functions that apply across all industries and sectors: identify, protect, detect, respond, and recover. The framework then divides these functions into categories, subcategories, and informative references. Figure 9.4 shows a small excerpt of this matrix in completed form, looking specifically at the Identify (ID) function and the Asset Management category. If you would like to view a fully completed matrix, see NIST's document *Framework for Improving Critical Infrastructure Cybersecurity.*

- The Framework Implementation Tiers assess how an organization is positioned to meet cybersecurity objectives. Table 9.1 shows the framework implementation tiers and their criteria. This approach is an example of a *maturity model* that describes the current and desired positioning of an organization along a continuum of progress. In the case of the NIST maturity model, organizations are assigned to one of four maturity model tiers.

- Framework Profiles describe how a specific organization might approach the security functions covered by the Framework Core. An organization might use a framework profile to describe its current state and then a separate profile to describe its desired future state.

FIGURE 9.3   NIST Cybersecurity Framework Core Structure

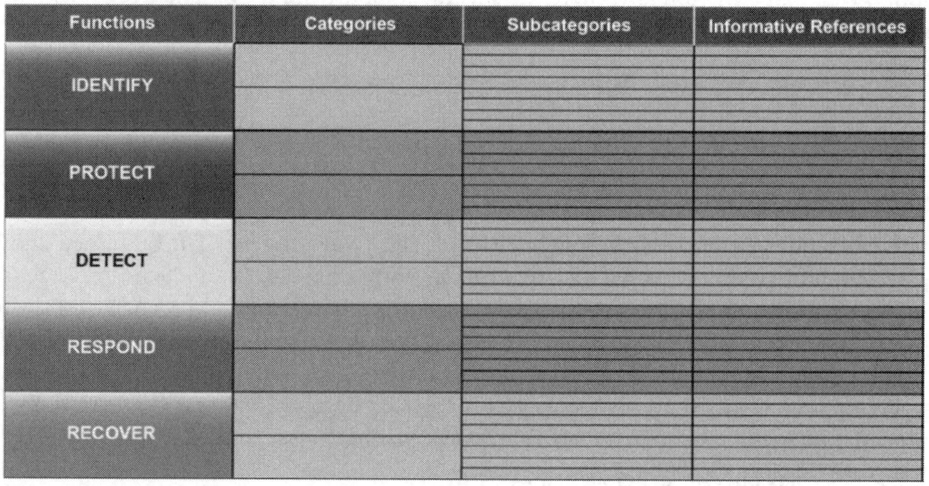

Source: Framework for Improving Critical Infrastructure Cybersecurity, National Institute of Standards and Technology (https://www.nist.gov/sites/default/files/documents/cyberframework/cybersecurity -framework-021214.pdf)

FIGURE 9.4   Asset Management Cybersecurity Framework

Function	Category	Subcategory	Informative References
IDENTIFY (ID)	Asset Management (ID.AM): The data, personnel, devices, systems, and facilities that enable the organization to achieve business purposes are identified and managed consistent with their relative importance to business objectives and the organization's risk strategy.	ID.AM-1: Physical devices and systems within the organization are inventoried	• CCS CSC 1 • COBIT 5 BAI09.01, BAI09.02 • ISA 62443-2-1:2009 4.2.3.4 • ISA 62443-3-3:2013 SR 7.8 • ISO/IEC 27001:2013 A.8.1.1, A.8.1.2 • NIST SP 800-53 Rev. 4 CM-8
		ID.AM-2: Software platforms and applications within the organization are inventoried	• CCS CSC 2 • COBIT 5 BAI09.01, BAI09.02, BAI09.05 • ISA 62443-2-1:2009 4.2.3.4 • ISA 62443-3-3:2013 SR 7.8 • ISO/IEC 27001:2013 A.8.1.1, A.8.1.2 • NIST SP 800-53 Rev. 4 CM-8
		ID.AM-3: Organizational communication and data flows are mapped	• CCS CSC 1 • COBIT 5 DSS05.02 • ISA 62443-2-1:2009 4.2.3.4 • ISO/IEC 27001:2013 A.13.2.1 • NIST SP 800-53 Rev. 4 AC-4, CA-3, CA-9, PL-8
		ID.AM-4: External information systems are catalogued	• COBIT 5 APO02.02 • ISO/IEC 27001:2013 A.11.2.6 • NIST SP 800-53 Rev. 4 AC-20, SA-9
		ID.AM-5: Resources (e.g., hardware, devices, data, time, and software) are prioritized based on their classification, criticality, and business value	• COBIT 5 APO03.03, APO03.04, BAI09.02 • ISA 62443-2-1:2009 4.2.3.6 • ISO/IEC 27001:2013 A.8.2.1 • NIST SP 800-53 Rev. 4 CP-2, RA-2, SA-14
		ID.AM-6: Cybersecurity roles and responsibilities for the entire workforce and third-party stakeholders (e.g., suppliers, customers, partners) are established	• COBIT 5 APO01.02, DSS06.03 • ISA 62443-2-1:2009 4.3.2.3.3 • ISO/IEC 27001:2013 A.6.1.1

Source: Framework for Improving Critical Infrastructure Cybersecurity, National Institute of Standards and Technology (https://www.nist.gov/sites/default/files/documents/cyberframework/cybersecurity -framework-021214.pdf)

TABLE 9.1   NIST Cybersecurity Framework Implementation Tiers

Tier	Risk Management Process	Integrated Risk Management Program	External Participation
Tier 1: Partial	Organizational cybersecurity risk management practices are not formalized, and risk is managed in an ad hoc and sometimes reactive manner.	There is limited awareness of cybersecurity risk at the organizational level and an organization-wide approach to managing cybersecurity risk has not been established.	An organization may not have the processes in place to participate in coordination or collaboration with other entities.
Tier 2: Risk Informed	Risk management practices are approved by management but may not be established as organizational-wide policy.	There is an awareness of cybersecurity risk at the organizational level but an organization-wide approach to managing cybersecurity risk has not been established.	The organization knows its role in the larger ecosystem, but has not formalized its capabilities to interact and share information externally.
Tier 3: Repeatable	The organization's risk management practices are formally approved and expressed as policy.	There is an organization-wide approach to manage cybersecurity risk.	The organization understands its dependencies and partners and receives information from these partners that enables collaboration and risk-based management decisions within the organization in response to events.
Tier 4: Adaptive	The organization adapts its cybersecurity practices based on lessons learned and predictive indicators derived from previous and current cybersecurity activities.	There is an organization-wide approach to managing cybersecurity risk that uses risk-informed policies, processes, and procedures to address potential cybersecurity events.	The organization manages risk and actively shares information with partners to ensure that accurate, current information is being distributed and consumed to improve cybersecurity before a cybersecurity event occurs.

Source: Framework for Improving Critical Infrastructure Cybersecurity, National Institute of Standards and Technology

The NIST Cybersecurity Framework provides organizations with a sound approach to developing and evaluating the state of their cybersecurity programs.

ISO 27001

The International Organization for Standardization (ISO) publishes *ISO 27001*, a standard document titled "Information technology—Security techniques—Information security management systems—Requirements." This standard includes control objectives covering 14 categories:

- Information security policies
- Organization of information security
- Human resource security
- Asset management
- Access control
- Cryptography
- Physical and environmental security
- Operations security
- Communications security
- System acquisition, development, and maintenance
- Supplier relationships
- Information security incident management
- Information security aspects of business continuity management
- Compliance with internal requirements, such as policies, and with external requirements, such as laws

The ISO 27001 standard was once the most commonly used information security standards, but it is declining in popularity outside of highly regulated industries that require ISO compliance. Organizations in those industries may choose to formally adopt ISO 27001 and pursue *certification* programs where an external assessor validates their compliance with the standard and certifies them as operating in accordance with ISO 27001.

Control Objectives for Information and Related Technologies (COBIT)

The *Control Objectives for Information and Related Technologies (COBIT)* is a set of best practices for IT governance developed by the Information Systems Audit and Control Association (ISACA). COBIT divides information technology activities into four domains:

- Plan and Organize
- Acquire and Implement
- Deliver and Support
- Monitor and Evaluate

COBIT addresses each of these four domains of technology by providing five COBIT framework components:

- COBIT framework
- Process descriptions
- Control objectives
- Management guidelines
- Maturity models

Sherwood Applied Business Security Architecture (SABSA)

The *Sherwood Applied Business Security Architecture (SABSA) framework* offers an alternative model for approaching security architecture from a variety of different perspectives that map to architectural layers, shown in Table 9.2.

TABLE 9.2 SABSA architectural layers

View	Architecture layer
Business view	Contextual Security architecture
Architect's view	Conceptual Security architecture
Designer's view	Logical Security architecture
Builder's view	Physical Security architecture
Tradesman's view	Component Security architecture
Service Manager's view	Security Service Management architecture

The SABSA architecture framework is discussed here only because it is specifically listed as a CSA+ exam objective. Neither of the authors of this book, who have four decades of combined cybersecurity experience, have come across this framework in real-world use.

The Open Group Architecture Framework (TOGAF)

While not security-specific, the *Open Group Architecture Framework (TOGAF)* is a widely adopted approach to enterprise architecture. TOGAF divides architecture into four domains:

- *Business architecture* defines governance and organization and explains the interaction between enterprise architecture and business strategy.

- *Applications architecture* includes the applications and systems that an organization deploys, the interactions between those systems, and their relation to business processes.

- *Data architecture* provides the organization's approach to storing and managing information assets.

- *Technical architecture* describes the infrastructure needed to support the other architectural domains.

TOGAF also includes the Architecture Development Method (ADM) shown in Figure 9.5. The ADM describes how an organization might move through the cyclical process of developing its own enterprise architecture.

FIGURE 9.5   TOGAF Architecture Development Model

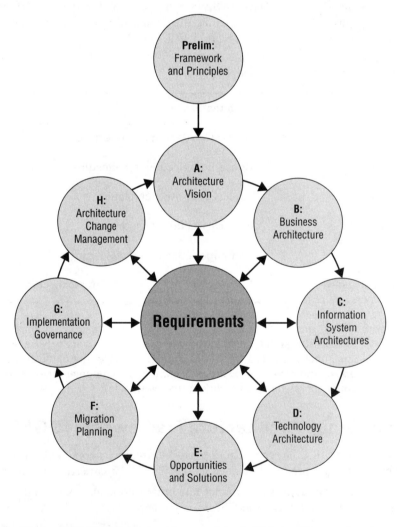

Source: Stephen Marley, NASA /SCI – Architectural Framework Applied Sciences Program, Geosciences Interoperability Office, Stephen Marley NASA /SCI.

Information Technology Infrastructure Library (ITIL)

The *Information Technology Infrastructure Library (ITIL)* is a framework that offers a comprehensive approach to IT service management (ITSM) within the modern enterprise. ITIL covers five core activities:

- Service Strategy
- Service Design
- Service Transition
- Service Operation
- Continual Service Improvement

Figure 9.6 shows how these activities fit together in the ITIL service life cycle. Although it is not widely used as a cybersecurity framework, many organizations choose to adopt ITIL ITSM practices and then include cybersecurity functions within their ITIL implementation.

FIGURE 9.6   ITIL service life cycle

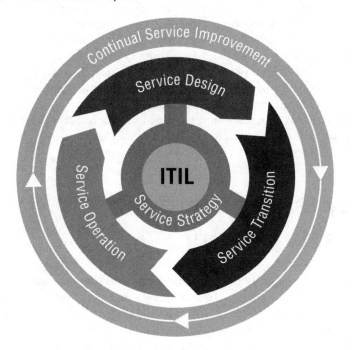

Implementing Policy-Based Controls

Security policy frameworks and the specific security policies adopted by organizations lay out *control objectives* that an organization wishes to achieve. These control objectives are statements of a desired security state, but they do not, by themselves, actually carry out security activities. *Security controls* are specific measures that fulfill the security objectives of an organization. They come in three different categories:

- *Physical controls* are security controls that impact the physical world. Examples of physical security controls include fences, perimeter lighting, locks, fire suppression systems, and burglar alarms.

- *Logical controls* are technical controls that enforce confidentiality, integrity, and availability in the digital space. Examples of logical security controls include firewall rules, access control lists, intrusion prevention systems, and encryption.

- *Administrative controls* are procedural mechanisms that an organization follows to implement sound security management practices. Examples of administrative controls include user account reviews, employee background investigations, log reviews, and separation-of-duties policies.

Organizations should select a set of security controls that meets their control objectives based on the criteria and parameters that they either select for their environment or have imposed on them by outside regulators. For example, an organization that handles sensitive information might decide that confidentiality concerns surrounding that information require the highest level of control. At the same time, they might conclude that the availability of their website is not of critical importance. Given these considerations, they would dedicate significant resources to the confidentiality of sensitive information while perhaps investing little, if any, time and money protecting their website against a denial-of-service attack.

Many control objectives require a combination of physical, logical, and administrative controls. For example, an organization might have the control objective of preventing unauthorized physical access to a facility. They might achieve this goal by implementing locked doors and security guards (physical controls), controlling door access with a strong authentication system that relies on multifactor authentication (logical control), and performing regular reviews of authorized access (administrative control).

Security Control Verification and Quality Control

Quality control procedures verify that an organization has sufficient security controls in place and that those security controls are functioning properly. Every security program should include procedures for conducting regular internal tests of security controls and supplement those informal tests with formal evaluations of the organization's security program. Those evaluations may come in two different forms: audits and assessments.

Audits are formal reviews of an organization's security program or specific compliance issues conducted on behalf of a third party. Audits require rigorous, formal testing of controls and result in a formal statement from the auditor regarding the entity's compliance. Audits may be conducted by internal audit groups at the request of management or by external audit firms, typically at the request of an organization's governing body or a regulator.

Assessments are less formal reviews of security controls that are typically requested by the security organization itself in an effort to engage in process improvement. During an assessment, the assessor typically gathers information by interviewing employees and taking them at their word, rather than preforming the rigorous independent testing associated with an audit.

Summary

Policies form the basis of every strong information security program. A solid policy framework consists of policies, standards, procedures, and guidelines that work together to describe the security control environment of an organization. In addition to complying with internally developed policies, organizations often must comply with externally imposed compliance obligations. Security frameworks, such as the NIST Cybersecurity Framework and ISO 27001, provide a common structure for security programs based on accepted industry best practices. Organizations should implement and test security controls to achieve security control objectives that are developed based on the business and technical environment of the organization.

Exam Essentials

Policy frameworks consist of policies, standards, procedures, and guidelines.   Policies are high-level statements of management intent for the information security program. Standards describe the detailed implementation requirements for policy. Procedures offer step-by-step instructions for carrying out security activities. Compliance with policies, standards, and procedures is mandatory. Guidelines offer optional advice that complements other elements of the policy framework.

Organizations often adopt a set of security policies covering different areas of their security programs.   Common policies used in security programs include an information security policy, an acceptable use policy, a data ownership policy, a data retention policy, an account management policy, and a password policy. The specific policies adopted by any organization will depend on that organization's culture and business needs.

Policy documents should include exception processes.   Exception processes should outline the information required to receive an exception to security policy and the approval authority for each exception. The process should also describe the requirements for compensating controls that mitigate risks associated with approved security policy exceptions.

Organizations face a variety of security compliance requirements.   Healthcare providers must comply with the Health Insurance Portability and Accountability Act (HIPAA). Merchants and credit card service providers must comply with the Payment Card Industry Data Security Standard (PCI DSS). Financial institutions are subject to the Gramm-Leach-Bliley Act (GLBA), whereas public companies must comply with the Sarbanes-Oxley Act (SOX). Educational institutions must follow the Family Educational Rights and Privacy Act (FERPA).

Standards frameworks provide an outline for structuring and evaluating cybersecurity programs. Organizations may choose to base their security programs on a framework, such as the NIST Cybersecurity Framework, ISO 27001, or the IT Infrastructure Library (ITIL). These frameworks sometimes include maturity models that allow an organization to assess its progress. Some frameworks also offer certification programs that provide independent assessments of an organization's progress toward adopting a framework.

Lab Exercises

Activity 9.1: Policy Documents

Match the following policy documents with their descriptions.

Policy	Outlines a step-by-step process for carrying out a cybersecurity activity
Standard	Includes advice based on best practices for achieving security goals that are not mandatory
Guideline	Provides high-level requirements for a cybersecurity program
Procedure	Offers detailed requirements for achieving security control objectives

Activity 9.2: Using a Cybersecurity Framework

Download and read the current version of the NIST Framework for Improving Critical Infrastructure Cybersecurity (`https://www.nist.gov/sites/default/files/documents/cyberframework/cybersecurity-framework-021214.pdf`).

Choose a specific category from the Framework Core that appears in Table 2 at the end of the document. If you are currently employed, describe how your organization addresses each of the subcategories for that function and category. If you are not currently employed, perform the same analysis for an organization with which you are familiar to the best of your ability.

Activity 9.3: Compliance Auditing Tools

The Payment Card Industry Data Security Standard (PCI DSS) includes detailed testing procedures for each one of the standard's requirements.

Download a copy of the current PCI DSS standard from the PCI Security Standards Council website (`https://www.pcisecuritystandards.org/document_library?category=pcidss&document=pci_dss`). Find the section of the standard that includes requirements for password construction (section 8.2.3 in PCI DSS version 3.2).

Describe the testing procedures that an auditor would follow to determine whether an organization is in compliance with this requirement.

Review Questions

1. Joe is authoring a document that explains to system administrators one way that they might comply with the organization's requirement to encrypt all laptops. What type of document is Joe writing?

   A. Policy

   B. Guideline

   C. Procedure

   D. Standard

2. Which one of the following statements is not true about compensating controls under PCI DSS?

   A. Controls used to fulfill one PCI DSS requirement may be used to compensate for the absence of a control needed to meet another requirement.

   B. Controls must meet the intent of the original requirement.

   C. Controls must meet the rigor of the original requirement.

   D. Compensating controls must provide a similar level of defense as the original requirement.

3. What law creates cybersecurity obligations for healthcare providers and others in the health industry?

   A. HIPAA

   B. FERPA

   C. GLBA

   D. PCI DSS

4. Which one of the following is not one of the five core security functions defined by the NIST Cybersecurity Framework?

   A. Identify

   B. Contain

   C. Respond

   D. Recover

5. What ISO standard applies to information security management controls?

   A. 9001

   B. 27001

   C. 14032

   D. 57033

6. Which one of the following documents must normally be approved by the CEO or similarly high-level executive?

    A. Standard

    B. Procedure

    C. Guideline

    D. Policy

7. What SABSA architecture layer corresponds to the designer's view of security architecture?

    A. Contextual security architecture

    B. Conceptual security architecture

    C. Logical security architecture

    D. Component security architecture

8. What law governs the financial records of publicly traded companies?

    A. GLBA

    B. SOX

    C. FERPA

    D. PCI DSS

9. What TOGAF domain provides the organization's approach to storing and managing information assets?

    A. Business architecture

    B. Applications architecture

    C. Data architecture

    D. Technical architecture

10. Which one of the following would not normally be found in an organization's information security policy?

    A. Statement of the importance of cybersecurity

    B. Requirement to use AES-256 encryption

    C. Delegation of authority

    D. Designation of responsible executive

11. Darren is helping the Human Resources department create a new policy for background checks on new hires. What type of control is Darren creating?

    A. Physical

    B. Technical

    C. Logical

    D. Administrative

12. Which one of the following control models describes the five core activities associated with IT service management as service strategy, service design, service transition, service operation, and continual service improvement?

    A. COBIT

    B. TOGAF

    C. ISO 27001

    D. ITIL

13. What compliance obligation applies to merchants and service providers who work with credit card information?

    A. FERPA

    B. SOX

    C. HIPAA

    D. PCI DSS

14. Which one of the following policies would typically answer questions about when an organization should destroy records?

    A. Data ownership policy

    B. Account management policy

    C. Password policy

    D. Data retention policy

15. While studying an organization's risk management process under the NIST Cybersecurity Framework, Rob determines that the organization adapts its cybersecurity practices based on lessons learned and predictive indicators derived from previous and current cybersecurity activities. What tier should he assign based on this measure?

    A. Tier 1

    B. Tier 2

    C. Tier 3

    D. Tier 4

16. Which one of the following security policy framework components does not contain mandatory guidance for individuals in the organization?

    A. Policy

    B. Standard

    C. Procedure

    D. Guideline

17. Tina is creating a set of firewall rules designed to block denial-of-service attacks from entering her organization's network. What type of control is Tina designing?

   A. Logical control

   B. Physical control

   C. Administrative control

   D. Root access control

18. Allan is developing a document that lists the acceptable mechanisms for securely obtaining remote administrative access to servers in his organization. What type of document is Allan writing?

   A. Policy

   B. Standard

   C. Guideline

   D. Procedure

19. Which one of the following is not a common use of the NIST Cybersecurity Framework?

   A. Describe the current cybersecurity posture of an organization.

   B. Describe the target future cybersecurity posture of an organization.

   C. Communicate with stakeholders about cybersecurity risk.

   D. Create specific technology requirements for an organization.

20. Shelly is writing a document that describes the steps that incident response teams will follow upon first notice of a potential incident. What type of document is she creating?

   A. Policy

   B. Standard

   C. Guideline

   D. Procedure

Chapter

10

Defense-in-Depth Security Architectures

THE COMPTIA CYBERSECURITY ANALYST+ EXAM OBJECTIVES COVERED IN THIS CHAPTER INCLUDE:

Domain 4: Security Architecture and Tool Sets

✓ **4.3 Given a scenario, review security architecture and make recommendations to implement compensating controls.**

A well-designed security architecture design seeks to eliminate, or at least minimize, the number of points where a single failure can lead to a breach. The controls that make up each of the layers of security for an organization can include technical controls, administrative controls, and physical controls that prevent, detect, or correct issues.

In the first half of this chapter, we will explore defense-in-depth designs and layered security concepts. We will then look at how those concepts are implemented via network designs, host security models, administrative security tools and techniques, and personnel security practices. Together, these techniques and design elements can create a complete layered security design, resulting in an effective defense-in-depth strategy.

In the second half of this chapter we will analyze security architectures, looking for common flaws like single points of failure, improper control points, or maintenance issues that are likely to result in security issues. We will also discuss how to build a security life cycle for controls to ensure that the controls you implement as part of a design continue to be relevant to the threats that your organization will face in the future.

Understanding Defense in Depth

The foundation of most security designs relies on the concept of defense in depth. In other words, a single defensive measure should not be the only control preventing an attacker (or a mistake!) from creating a problem. Since there are many potential ways for a security breach to occur, a wide range of defenses must be layered together to ensure that a failure in one does not endanger sensitive data, systems, or networks.

Layered Security

One of the most important concepts for defense in depth is the idea of *layered security*. This means that each layer of security adds additional protections that help prevent a hole or flaw in another layer from allowing an attacker in. Figure 10.1 shows a high-level diagram of a sample layered security approach. In this design, data security is at the core where policies, practices, and data classification would be implemented. Each additional layer adds protections, from application layer security that protects the methods used to access the data to endpoint system security like data loss prevention software.

FIGURE 10.1   Layered security network design

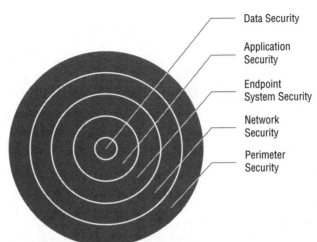

- Data Security
- Application Security
- Endpoint System Security
- Network Security
- Perimeter Security

As you can see, a layered approach can combine technologies that are specifically appropriate to the layer where they reside with technologies that are a fit for multiple layers. Configurations may differ based on the specific needs found at that layer in the security model. For example, data security might require full disk encryption for laptops and mobile devices, while desktops might only leverage data loss prevention software.

 Defense in depth should address all three elements of the CIA triad. Depth in availability can take the form of redundant systems or network devices, multiple network paths and providers, or backup power systems, whereas integrity defenses may include file integrity checking or system configuration validation tools.

Layered security can be complex to design. The interactions between security controls, organizational business needs, and usability all require careful attention during the design of a layered security approach. To meet these requirements, four design models tend to be used as part of a layered security design: uniform protection, protected enclaves, risk or threat analysis–based designs, and information classification–based designs.

Uniform protection provides the same level of protection to all systems or networks. Applying a blanket security design can be attractive because it simplifies the decision and design process, but uniform protection can be expensive if every system needs to be protected at the same high level of security. That cost means that in more complex environments, or in organizations where there are varying levels of security needs, other designs are often used.

Figure 10.2 shows a uniform protection design for a group of workstations. Each receives the same patching, monitoring, software whitelisting, antivirus, and firewall protection. Human resources, finance, and sales all have the same layered security design, which leads to challenges for the salespeople who may not need the same data security protection that the financial team does!

FIGURE 10.2 Uniform protection applied to all systems

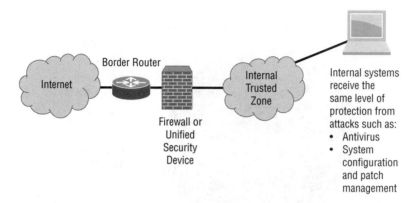

Instead of uniform protection–based designs, some organizations decide to build *protected enclaves*. These can take the form of protected network segments, systems, or physical locations that have additional controls to provide additional protection.

Figure 10.3 provides an example of a protected enclave. In this design example, highly sensitive credit card data is protected in a network enclave, with additional protection applied in the form of a combined security appliance that provides firewall, data loss prevention, and intrusion prevention capabilities that scan all traffic in and out of the network. Additional security is applied to the workstations to ensure that the sensitive data in the enclave remains secure and is properly handled.

FIGURE 10.3 Protected enclave for credit card operations

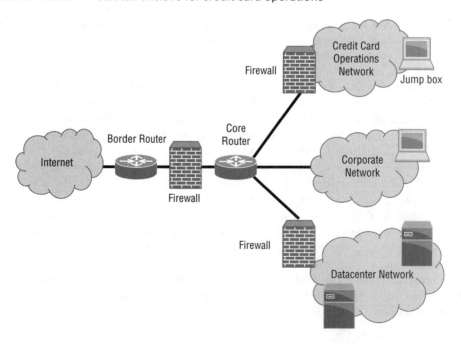

Despite the network-centric focus of these sample diagrams, remember that a complete security design will involve administrative and personnel controls in addition to technical designs and tools.

Another design method is *threat analysis–based design*. This design model reviews potential threat vectors and attempts to address each of them in the design. This can help ensure that only the controls that are needed to address threats are part of the design, thus limiting control costs and maintaining greater usability. The downfall of threat analysis–based design is that it may not handle new or emerging threats without frequent review and updates, and it relies on the threat analysis being accurate.

The final design model, *information-based design* (sometimes called classification-based design), uses information classification, tagging, or other methods to guide the application of security controls. Information classification designs map information protection measures to classes of information. This means that sensitive information as well as systems and networks that handle it will receive more attention in the design, and information that has a low sensitivity level will have fewer or less strict controls. Figure 10.4 shows a network segment designed to handle Top Secret information, with controls specified by the organization's handling requirements. Workstations and systems in the network segment that handles unclassified information are only protected by a firewall and local workstation security policies, whereas the Top Secret classified data is protected by data loss prevention, intrusion detection, a dedicated firewall, and tighter workstation specific policies and practices.

FIGURE 10.4   Data classification–based design

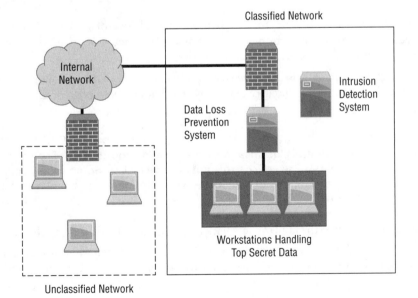

The first step in information-based designs is often to design a classification scheme that fits the organization's needs (and capabilities!). Information classification schemes like the U.S. government's Top Secret, Secret, Confidential, and Restricted classifications have mirrors in the corporate world, often with labels like Restricted, Sensitive, or Business Confidential.

These basic design options are often combined. A company that has public-facing websites, internal servers, high-security research areas, and a corporate network that serves a broad variety of employees might decide on a security architecture using protected enclaves with threat analysis–based designs and then may use information-centric design processes to protect their proprietary data.

Control Types and Classification

Security designs rely on controls that can help prevent, detect, counteract, or limit the impact of security risks. Controls are typically classified based on two categorization schemes: how they are implemented, or when they react relative to the security incident or threat. Classifying controls based on implementation type is done using the following model:

- *Technical controls* include firewalls, intrusion detection and prevention systems, network segmentation, authentication and authorization systems, and a variety of other systems and technical capabilities designed to provide security through technical means.

- *Administrative controls* (sometimes called procedural controls) involve processes and procedures like those found in incident response plans, account creation and management, as well as awareness and training efforts.

- *Physical controls* include locks, fences, and other controls that control or limit physical access, as well as controls like fire extinguishers that can help prevent physical harm to property.

Some control classification schemes add a fourth type of control: legal controls. These are controls put in place by law. Some simply count legal controls as a type of administrative control that is put in place by the legal system.

Classification by when the control acts uses the following classification scheme:

- *Preventive controls* are intended to stop an incident from occurring by taking proactive measures to stop the threat. Preventive controls include firewalls, training, and security guards.

- *Detective controls* work to detect an incident, and to capture information about it, allowing a response like alarms or notifications.

- *Corrective controls* either remediate an incident or act to limit how much damage can result from an incident. Corrective controls are often used as part of an incident response process. Examples of corrective controls include patching, antimalware software, and system restores from backups.

Controls that satisfy a requirement that isn't able to be met by an existing security measure—either because it is too difficult to implement or because it does not fully meet the needs—are known as *compensating controls*. Additional control types that you may occasionally encounter include deterrent controls that warn attackers that they shouldn't attack, directive controls that are intended to lead to a desired outcome, and recovery controls that provide ways to respond to a breach.

Implementing Defense in Depth

Over the next few pages we will examine how to implement defense in depth in network design, host security, policy, process, and standards, and as part of personnel security. When each of these layers is implemented as part of a comprehensive security design that takes into account the benefits and disadvantages of each control, a true defense-in-depth design can be implemented.

Layered Security and Network Design

Implementing layered security for a network relies on a combination of network architecture design, network configuration management, practices, and policies. Common network design models include single firewalls, multi-interface firewalls, and multi-firewall designs. In each of these, networks may be segmented, either logically or physically, to create security boundaries in addition to the boundaries created by firewalls or other security devices. Along with these common architectures, networks that combine onsite networks with outsourced networks and systems are increasingly common.

Segmentation

Network segmentation or compartmentalization is a common element of network design. It provides a number of advantages:

- The number of systems that are exposed to attackers (commonly called the organization's *attack surface*) can be reduced by compartmentalizing systems and networks.

- It can help to limit the scope of regulatory compliance efforts by placing the systems, data, or unit that must be compliant in a more easily maintained environment separate from the rest of the organization.

- In some cases, segmentation can help increase availability by limiting the impact of an issue or attack.

- Segmentation is used to increase the efficiency of a network. Larger numbers of systems in a single segment can lead to network congestion, making segmentation attractive as networks increase in size.

Network segmentation can be accomplished in many ways, but for security reasons, a firewall with a carefully designed ruleset is typically used between network segments with different levels of trust or functional requirements. Network segmentation also frequently relies on routers and switches that support VLAN tagging. In some cases where segmentation is desired and more nuanced controls are not necessary, segmentation is handled using only routers or switches.

The Case for Product Diversity

Product diversity (using products from multiple vendors) is sometimes used to create an additional layer of security. The intent of using diverse products is to eliminate a single point of failure by ensuring that a vulnerability or design flaw found in one product does not make an entire network or system vulnerable to exploit. For example, in a network design, this might mean using Juniper border routers, Cisco core routers, and Palo Alto security devices. If a vulnerability existed in the Cisco core routers, the other devices would be less likely to suffer from the same issue, meaning that attackers should not be able to exploit them, thus potentially limiting the impact of an attack.

Unfortunately, using multiple products rather than settling on a single vendor or product for a solution adds additional overhead and costs for maintenance, training, and support, potentially resulting in more vulnerabilities! The right choice varies from organization to organization and design to design, but diversity may be a useful design choice if your organization is worried about a single vulnerability affecting your entire network, platform, or other environment.

Single Firewall

One of the simplest network designs is a single firewall network design. This design simply places a single firewall between two security zones with different trust levels or functions. Figure 10.5 shows this implemented for a simple internal network with a public-facing (or "world-facing") network segment called the DMZ, where web, email, and DNS servers reside.

FIGURE 10.5   DMZ with a single firewall

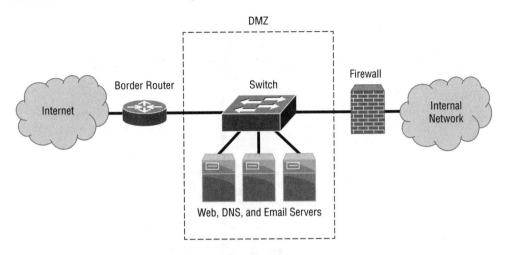

DMZ

Border Router   Switch   Firewall

Internet   Internal Network

Web, DNS, and Email Servers

A demilitarized zone, or *DMZ*, is often used when services or systems need to be exposed to lower trust areas. For many organizations, their DMZ is their public-facing network segment. Since traffic from unknown and untrusted systems enters the DMZ, it is considered less secure, and additional protection is placed between the DMZ and trusted systems. Figure 10.5 shows a DMZ segment between the trusted Internet network and the organization's border router.

We reference firewalls in each of these designs, but some of the same basic design objectives can be met with router access control lists supported by routers or some intelligent routing switches. More advanced network security devices can also replace a dedicated firewall in network designs, so remember that a design may use another device instead of a firewall to meet control objectives.

Multiple Interface Firewalls

Firewalls and other network security devices aren't limited to just one interface, and many designs use multiple interfaces to effectively create many single firewall protected network segments. Figure 10.6 shows a simple example of a protected network and a DMZ both operating behind the same firewall. Different rulesets will be applied to each interface. In this design, the ruleset would likely allow traffic from the Internet to the DMZ for services it provides, but it would prevent inbound Internet traffic from reaching the protected internal network.

FIGURE 10.6 Single firewall service-leg DMZ

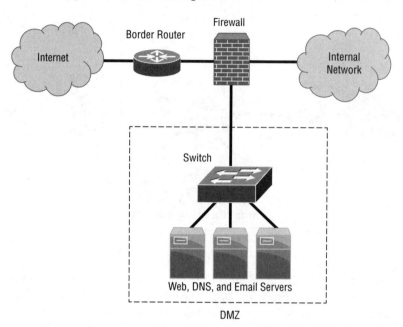

 Multiple interface designs are sometimes called a "service-leg DMZ."

Modern firewalls and network security appliances often have the ability to associate interfaces with virtual firewalls, creating an additional layer of separation between network security zones and thus potentially meeting the need for separation that might have required separate physical devices like those found in multi-firewall designs.

Multi-Firewall

A multi-firewall design like the dual-firewall architecture shown in Figure 10.7 places firewalls at each critical control point. This creates segregated network segments, each of which typically has a different security level. Figure 10.7 shows a typical small corporate network with a firewall protecting a DMZ, and a shielded internal network where the rest of the organization's workstations are protected from Internet traffic.

FIGURE 10.7   Dual-firewall network design

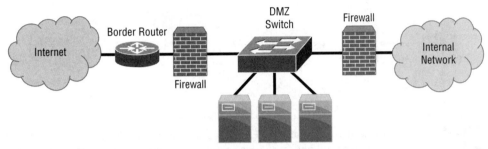

Web, DNS, and Email Servers

This multi-firewall design is logically very similar to the service-leg DMZ design shown in Figure 10.6. In fact, the decision to use separate hardware devices instead of multiple interfaces on a single firewall may come down to financial restrictions:

- A single larger firewall or redundant pair costs more than smaller devices.
- You may require hardware diversity.
- You may need to have different security levels or administrators.
- You must meet compliance requirements that differ from security zone to security zone.

Designs like the architecture shown in Figure 10.7 typically enforce more stringent security requirements as you move deeper into the network, with the most protected network segments behind the most layers of security. Here, the internal network is the most trusted zone, the DMZ is the second most trusted zone, and the Internet-facing border router and firewall are in the most exposed position outside the border firewall.

Secure Network Design and Outsourcing

The increase in the use of cloud and hosted services means that network design often needs to take outsourcing into account. Outsourced services tend to follow one of two designs: remote services or directly connected remote networks.

Remote services host a service entirely on the outsourced vendors' systems and networks. Software and a Service (SaaS) and Platform as a Service (PaaS) solutions both work as remote services. Since the security of outsourced services like these relies on the vendor's security, network security designs that involve remotely hosted services tend to focus on ensuring availability.

Figure 10.8 shows a simplified view of an outsourced service. Since the service itself is outsourced, there is no view into the cloud service itself—all security must be provided by the cloud service provider. Some administrative and technical security options may be available via the configuration and management interface for the cloud service, but choices about network security, server security, and the administrative, procedural, and technical controls that support the underlying systems and networks are handled by the service provider.

FIGURE 10.8 Outsourced remote services via public Internet

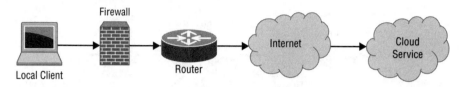

 While control of SaaS and PaaS solutions lies with the vendor, you can take some additional action to help ensure your organization's security. Many cloud vendors offer access to third-party security audit information like a SSAE-16 Type 1 or Type 2 report. In addition, you may want to conduct a security assessment to determine whether the vendor meets your own expected security best practices. Tools like the shared risk assessment tools provided by www.sharedassessments.org can help you conduct an assessment before engaging with a cloud or outsourced IT vendor. While you're at it, you should also ensure that the contract covers any legal or regulatory issues that would impact your outsourced solution.

A *directly connected remote network* is connected "inside" your network's border, possibly into the datacenter itself, and acts as an extension of your trusted network. This design requires the remote network and infrastructure to operate at the same level of trust as your internal secured network. Figure 10.9 shows an example of an Infrastructure as a Service (IaaS) network with a direct point-to-point VPN connection into an onsite secure datacenter network. This connection makes the remote IaaS infrastructure appear as though the systems and services it provides are hosted in your local datacenter.

FIGURE 10.9 VPN-connected remote network design

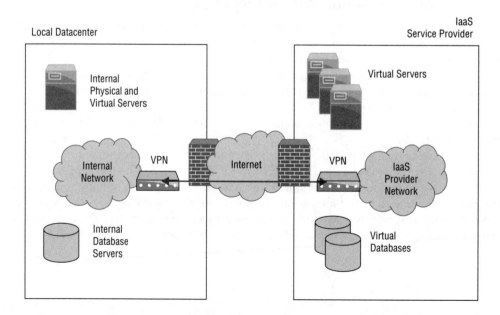

Unlike the infrastructure in the internal network shown in Figure 10.9, the systems and network devices that provide the IaaS environment supplied by the third-party provider are not under your direct control. This means that low-level host security relies on the third party's practices and controls.

When analyzing this type of design, keep in mind the potential for differences in capabilities, management, and incident response processes between your organization and a third-party cloud service. In this model, security issues could occur in either datacenter, and the VPN connection may be a single point of failure. In addition, the underlying infrastructure for the cloud service is unlikely to be visible to your organization, meaning you will have to rely on their security processes to know if there has been an issue.

Layered Host Security

Endpoint systems, whether they are laptops, desktop PCs, or mobile devices, can also use a layered security approach. Since individual systems are often used by individual users for their day-to-day work, they are often one of the most at-risk parts of your infrastructure and can create significant threat if they are compromised.

Layered security at the individual host level typically relies on a number of common security controls:

- Passwords or other strong authentication help ensure that only authorized users access hosts.

- Host firewalls and host intrusion prevention software limit the network attack surface of hosts and can also help prevent undesired outbound communication in the event of a system compromise.

- Data loss prevention software monitors and manages protected data.

- Whitelisting or blacklisting software can allow or prevent specific software packages and applications from being installed or run on the system.

- Antimalware and antivirus packages monitor for known malware as well as behavior that commonly occurs due to malicious software

- Patch management and vulnerability assessment tools are used to ensure that applications and the operating system are fully patched and properly secured.

- System hardening and configuration management that ensures that unneeded services are turned off, that good security practices are followed for operating system–level configuration options, and that unnecessary accounts are not present.

- Encryption, either at the file level or full disk encryption, may be appropriate to protect the system from access if it is lost or stolen or if data at rest needs additional security.

- File integrity monitoring tools monitor files and directories for changes and can alert an administrator if changes occur.

- Logging of events, actions, and issues is an important detective control at the host layer.

The host security layer may also include physical security controls to help prevent theft or undesired access to the systems themselves.

> The CSA+ exam objectives don't spent a significant amount of time on physical security, but you should remember that physical controls are part of a complete security design and that physical security implementation is an important part of threat management for many organizations.

Logging, Monitoring, and Validation

Layered security requires appropriate monitoring, alerting, and validation. Logging systems in a well-designed layered security architecture should ensure that logs are secure and are available centrally for monitoring. Monitoring systems need to have appropriate alert thresholds set and notification capabilities that match the needs of the organization.

Most security designs implement a separate log server, either in the form of a security information and event management (SIEM) device or as a specialized log server. This design allows the remote log server to act as a bastion host, preserving unmodified copies of logs in case compromise and allowing for central analysis of the log data.

In addition to monitoring and logging capabilities, configuration management and validation capabilities are important. Tools like Microsoft's SCCM or Jamf's Jamf Pro offer the ability to set and validate system settings across networks of varying types of devices, thus ensuring that their configurations and installed software match institutional expectations.

> We discussed system logging and network monitoring tools and techniques in more depth in Chapter 6, "Analyzing Symptoms for Incident Response."

Security Data Analytics

Analyzing the information that is gathered by logging and monitoring systems—in addition to integrating firewall logs, system logs, authentication logs, and event logs with data from configuration, patch, and vulnerability management tools as well as other parts of a comprehensive security suite—is a complex task. In some organizations, this is done by *manual review*, with individuals reviewing logs and other data. Unfortunately, when you need to manage larger numbers of devices and have many data sources, the volume of data generated can be too much to handle.

When dealing with large amounts of data or with complex data, using *automated reporting* and automated analysis tools, often found in *security appliances* and various *security suites*, is often the best way of analyzing the data. Collection, analysis, and reporting are key features of security appliances and suites.

Another increasingly popular option is to outsource security analytics and operations to a third party, often as part of a *Security as a Service* (SECaaS) offering. SECaaS providers usually leverage security suites and appliances to capture onsite and hosted data and then use central tools to analyze, report, and alert on issues that they discover.

In each of these three models, critical controls involve the following:

- *Data aggregation and correlation* combines data from multiple sources like syslogs, authentication logs, application logs, event logs, and other logs and statistics in a central location for analysis. It also correlates the information provided from multiple sources to identify events that impact different systems. This capability can be an especially effective detective control for organizations that have differing levels of instrumentation—a well-instrumented system or network control point can identify an event that was missed by another system that does not have the same logging or detection capabilities.

- *Trend analysis* analyzes the state of systems, events, and devices and looks for changes based on trends. Trend analysis can identify unexpected changes that do not match expected growth or decreases, providing useful behavioral insights for security analysis.

- *Historical analysis* leverages data over time, not only to determine what has occurred but also to provide data for trend analysis activities. Historical analysis is also useful when conducting incident response activities since it can provide information about events related to an incident that occurred at some time in the past.

A layered security approach should include multiple methods to capture and analyze data and appropriate monitoring and alerting systems to ensure that appropriate actions are taken when an issue or event is identified. The logs and other data should also be appropriately protected to ensure that they cannot be easily targeted as part of a compromise or exposure.

Cryptography

Both encryption and hashing are critical to many of the controls found at each of the layers we have discussed. They play roles in network security, host security, and data security, and are embedded in many of the applications and systems that each layer depends on. *Cryptography* in the form of encryption and hashing techniques is used to protect data on the wire and at rest, and to validate that data integrity is maintained.

This makes using current, secure encryption techniques, and ensuring that proper key management occurs, critical to a layered security design. When reviewing security designs, it is important to identify where encryption (and hashing) are used, how they are used, and how both the encryption keys and their passphrases are stored. It is also important to understand when data is encrypted and when it is unencrypted—security designs can fail because the carefully encrypted data that was sent securely is unencrypted and stored in a cache or by a local user, removing the protection it relied on during transit.

Support for built in encryption support for many modern computers (particularly business PCs) is provided by Trusted Protection Modules (TPM). They provide dedicated hardware support for cryptographic keys. TPM modules provide three major capabilities:

1. Remote attestation, allowing hardware and software configurations to be verified.

2. Binding which encrypts data.

3. Sealing, which encrypts data and sets requirements for the state of the TPM chip before decryption.

Policy, Process, and Standards

Administrative controls that involve policies, processes, and standards are a necessary layer when looking at a complete layered security design. In addition to controls that support security at the technology layer, administrative controls found in a complete security design include

- Change control

- Configuration management

- Monitoring and response policies

- Personnel security controls

- Business continuity and disaster recovery controls

- Human resource controls like background checks and terminations

Personnel Security

In addition to technical and procedural concerns, the human layer of a design must be considered. Staff need to be trained for the tasks they perform and to ensure that they react appropriately to security issues and threats. Critical personnel controls should be put in place where needed to provide separation of duties and to remove single points of failure in staffing.

A wide variety of personnel controls can be implemented as part of a complete security program, ranging from training to process and human resources–related controls. The most common personnel controls are as follows:

Separation of Duties   When individuals in an organization are given a role to perform, they can potentially abuse the rights and privileges that that role provides. Properly implemented separation of duties requires more than one individual to perform elements of a task to ensure that fraud or abuse do not occur. A typical separation of duties can be found in financially significant systems like payroll or accounts payable software. One person should not be able to modify financial data without being detected, so they should not have modification rights and also be charged with monitoring for changes!

Succession Planning   This is important to ensure continuity for roles, regardless of the reason a person leaves your organization. A departing staff member can take critical expertise and skills with them, leaving important duties unattended or tasks unperformed. When a manager or supervisor leaves, not having a succession plan can also result in a lack of oversight for functions, making it easier for other personnel issues to occur without being caught.

While succession planning is important to an organization's function, it isn't considered a security control in most frameworks. The Cybersecurity Analyst+ body of knowledge specifically mentions it, so make sure you consider the implications of succession planning as part of the critical personnel controls for the exam.

Background Checks   These are commonly performed before employees are hired to ensure that they are suitable for employment with the organization.

Termination   When an employee quits or is terminated, it is important to ensure that their access to organizational resources and accounts is also terminated. This requires reviewing their access and ensuring that the organization's separation process properly handles retrieving any organizational property like laptops, mobile devices, and data. In many organizations, accounts are initially disabled (often by changing the password to one the current user does not know). This ensures that data is not lost and can be accessed by the organization if needed. Once you know that any data associated with the account is no longer needed, you can then delete the account itself.

Cross Training   Cross training focuses on teaching employees skills that enable them to take on tasks that their co-workers and other staff members normally perform. This can help to prevent single points of failure due to skillsets and can also help to detect issues caused by an employee or a process by bringing someone who is less familiar with the task or procedure into the loop. Cross training is commonly used to help ensure that critical capabilities have backups in place since it can help prevent issues with employee separation when an indispensable employee leaves. It is also an important part of enabling other security controls. Succession planning, mandatory vacation, and mandatory vacation are all made easier if appropriate cross training occurs.

Dual Control   Dual control is useful when a process is so sensitive that it is desirable to require two individuals to perform an action together. The classic example of this appears in many movies in the form of a dual-control system that requires two military officers to insert and turn their keys at the same time to fire a nuclear weapon. Of course, this isn't likely to be necessary in your organization, but dual control may be a useful security control when sensitive tasks are involved because it requires both parties to collude for a breach to occur. This is often seen in organizations that require two signatures for checks over a certain value. Dual control can be implemented as either an administrative control via procedures or via technical controls.

Mandatory Vacation   This process requires staff members to take vacation, allowing you to identify individuals who are exploiting the rights they have. Mandatory vacation prevents employees from hiding issues or taking advantage of their privileges by ensuring that they are not continuously responsible for a task.

When mandatory vacation is combined with separation of duties, it can provide a highly effective way to detect employee collusion and malfeasance. Sending one or more employees involved in a process on vacation offers an opportunity for a third party to observe any issues or irregularities in the processes that the employees on vacation normally handle.

🌐 **Real World Scenario**

Outsourcing Your Own Job—Without the Boss Knowing

In 2012, a security team from Verizon identified odd behavior by an employee at a company that they were assessing. The employee's VPN connection was in consistent use, despite the employee being at their desk during the day. When the assessors dug in deeper, they found that the remote access was coming from China—an immediate red flag, especially since the employee in question was on site.

After confronting the employee, they discovered that the employee had outsourced his own job to a third party. His remote replacement accomplished all of the tasks he was assigned, and the employee simply provided daily status updates to his management. As the assessors dug further, they found out that the employee was actually "employed" at multiple other organizations where he worked remotely. In each of those cases, he had outsourced his work as well.

While this scenario isn't common, it is an example of why administrative and technical controls for personnel are important. The company where this was found was not performing geolocation matching for their VPN and authentication systems, which would have shown that their employee was logged in from two distinct locations at the same time—an immediate red flag that might have helped them find the issue. Administrative controls like separation of duties might have also resulted in the company discovering the issue, as the employee was unlikely to be able to fully describe or demonstrate the work that his outsourced replacements had performed.

You can read the complete article about this on CNN's website: www.cnn.com/2013/01/17/business/us-outsource-job-china/.

Outsourcing and Personnel Security

Outsourcing adds an additional set of challenges to personnel security concerns. It creates the potential for a third party to be partially or completely responsible for systems, networks, and data that belongs to your organization owns.

In a cloud hosting environment (SaaS, PaaS, or IaaS), personnel will have control of either the entire application, the platform, or the underlying infrastructure for your organization's outsourced products. This means that the outsourcing organization's personnel policies, procedures, and training are all now part of the security profile you may need to review. Outsourcing other services like software development or other consulting engagements can also create new personnel risks due to outsourced staff following different policies and practices.

Key considerations and questions when reviewing outsourcing include the following:

Proper Vetting   When hiring consultants or other third parties, are they properly vetted, with background checks and internal personnel controls in place?

Access Control   This means access control not only via the application interface, but to underlying systems and networks.

Data Ownership and Control   Is your data encrypted and inaccessible to the outsourced provider? Is it stored in a shared database, filesystem, or other location with other customer data?

Employment Practices   Does the outsourced vendor conduct background checks of their employees? How does it handle employee issues?

Incident Response Processes and Notification Requirements   Will you be notified if there is an incident? When?

Outsourcing relies on trust in the contract between your organization and the vendor, and on their own internal practices. In some cases, you may be able to add additional layers (such as encrypting data stored in IaaS systems), but in many cases you will be limited to what the vendor provides.

Building a Training and Awareness Program

Security awareness is one of the most critical personnel-related controls that an organization can implement. Training programs for security awareness typically focus on matching security knowledge with an individual's role in the organization. Key information found in most programs includes the following:

- The organization's policies related to information security
- Important threats that the organization faces
- Data handling requirements specific to the data the organization or individual handles
- Best practices for passwords, email, remote work, avoiding malware and viruses, secure browsing, and social media usage
- Policies related to technology like bring your own device or organizationally provided devices
- How to report a security issue
- Physical security

Awareness programs must take into account the specific needs of the organization such as compliance requirements, legal and contractual obligations, and the threats that are unique to the organization.

Analyzing Security Architecture

The key to analyzing a security infrastructure for an organization is to identify where defenses are weak, or where an attacker may be able to exploit flaws in architectural design, processes, procedures, or in the underlying technology like vulnerabilities or misconfigurations. Control gaps, single points of failure, and improperly implemented controls are all common issues that you are likely to encounter.

> Penetration testers also perform security architecture analysis when they are working to find ways through an organization's security. It can help to think like a penetration tester (or an attacker!) when you're reviewing a security architecture for flaws.

Analyzing Security Requirements

Security architectures can be analyzed based on their attributes by reviewing the security model and ensuring that it meets a specific requirement. For example, if you were asked to review a workstation security design that used antimalware software to determine if it would prevent unwanted software from being installed, you might identify three scenarios:

Success   Antimalware software can successfully prevent unwanted software installation if the software is known malware or if it behaves in a way that the antimalware software will detect as unwanted.

Failure   It will not detect software that is not permitted by organizational policy but that is not malware.

Failure   It may not prevent unknown malware, or malware that does not act in ways that are typical of known malware.

This type of attribute-based testing can be performed based on a risk assessment and control plan to determine whether the security architecture meets the control objectives. It can also be directly applied to each control by determining the goal of each control and then reviewing whether it meets that goal.

Reviewing Architecture

In addition to a requirement-based analysis method, a number of formal architectural models rely on views, or viewpoints, from which the architecture and controls can be reviewed. Common views that can be taken when reviewing an architecture include the following:

- *Operational views* describe how a function is performed, or what it accomplishes. This view typically shows how information flows but does not capture the technical detail about how data is transmitted, stored, or captured. Operational views are useful for understanding what is occurring and often influence procedural or administrative controls.

- *Technical views* (sometimes called service-oriented, or systems-based, views) focus on the technologies, settings, and configurations used in an architecture. This can help identify incorrect configurations and insecure design decisions. An example of a technical view might include details like the TLS version of a connection, or the specific settings for password length and complexity required for user accounts.

- A *logical view* is sometimes used to describe how systems interconnect. It is typically less technically detailed than a technical view but conveys broader information about how a system or service connects or works. The network diagrams earlier in this chapter are examples of logical views.

Security architecture reviews may need any or all of these viewpoints to provide a complete understanding of where issues may exist.

Formal security frameworks have different views, adding specific viewpoints based on their requirements. The British Ministry of Defense's Architecture Framework (MODAF) uses seven categories: strategic, operational, service oriented, systems, acquisition, technical, and the "all viewpoint," which describes the architecture. The U.S. Department of Defense uses a similar set of views for architectural review: all, capability, data and information, project, services, standards, and systems viewpoints are all considered in the DoD model.

Common Issues

Analyzing security architectures requires an understanding of the design concepts and controls they commonly use as well as the issues that are most frequently encountered in those designs. Four of the most commonly encountered design issues are single points of failure, data validation and trust problems, user issues, and authentication and authorization security and process problems.

Single Points of Failure

A key element to consider when analyzing a layered security architecture is the existence of single points of failure—a single point of the system where, if that component, control, or system fails, the entire system will not work or will fail to provide the desired level of security.

Figure 10.10 shows a fully redundant network design with fault tolerant firewalls, routers, and core switches. Each device communicates with its partner via a heartbeat link, which provides status and synchronization information. If a device's partner fails, it will take over, providing continuity of service. Each device is also cross-linked, allowing any component to send traffic to the devices in front of and behind it via multiple paths, removing a failed wire as a potential point of failure. Similar protections would be in place for power protection, and the devices would typically be physically located in separate racks or even rooms to prevent a single physical issue from disrupting service.

FIGURE 10.10 **FIGURE 10.10**   A fully redundant network edge design

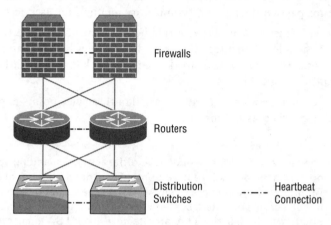

Network and infrastructure design diagrams can make spotting a potential single point of failure much easier. In Figure 10.11, the same redundant network's internal design shows a single point of failure (Point A) at the distribution router and edge switch layers. Here, a failure of a link, the router, or the switches might take down a section of the network, rather than the organization's primary Internet link. In situations like this, a single point of failure may be acceptable based on the organization's risk profile and functional requirements.

FIGURE 10.11   Single points of failure in a network design

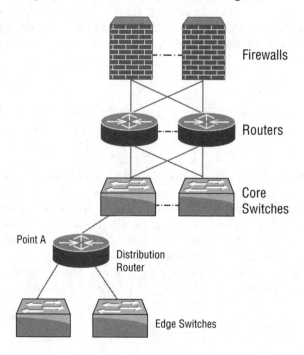

Redundant Layers of Failure

Having a redundant system doesn't guarantee that systems will work. The authors of this book worked with a redundant firewall system that used a heartbeat function for an active/passive pair. In this design, one firewall was always active, and if it failed, the secondary firewall would take over as the active partner. If the primary firewall then resumed function, it would determine that it should then take the passive role, and normal function would continue.

At least, that's how the system was designed. Unfortunately, a software update caused the heartbeat system to fail, resulting in both firewalls determining that their partner was offline. Both firewalls then set themselves to active mode, resulting in network traffic being routed erratically through each firewall as they wrestled for control of the traffic that was supposed to flow through them. Some traffic did make it through, but the failure of the partnering system essentially stopped all traffic into and out of a production datacenter.

In this scenario, the firewall administrators were able to turn off the secondary firewall and then worked to revert it to the software version before the flaw was introduced. They then restored the firewall, failed over to it manually from the primary, and then reverted the broken patch back on the primary firewall to return to a known good state.

The same analysis process can be used to identify issues with applications, processes, and control architectures. A block diagram is created that includes all of the critical components or controls, and the flow that the diagram supports is traced through the diagram. Figure 10.12 shows a sample flow diagram for an account creation process. Note that at point A, an authorized requester files a request for a new account, and at point B, a manager approves the account creation. During process analysis a flaw would be noted if the manager can both request and approve an account creation. If the review at point D is also performed by the manager, this process flaw would be even more severe. This provides a great case for separation of duties as an appropriate and useful control!

FIGURE 10.12   Single points of failure in a process flow

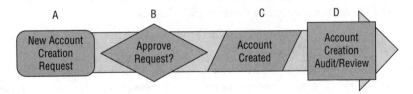

Data Validation and Trust

The ability to trust data that is used for data processing or to make decisions is another area where security issues frequently occur. Data is often assumed to be valid, and incorrect or falsified data can result in significant issues. The ability to rely on data can be enhanced by

- Protecting data at rest and in transit using encryption
- Validating data integrity using file integrity checking tools, or otherwise performing data integrity validation

- Implementing processes to verify data in an automated or manual fashion
- Profiling or boundary checking data based on known attributes of the data

Web application security testers are very familiar with exploiting weaknesses in data validation schemes. Insecure web applications often trust that the data they receive from a page that they generate is valid and then use that data for further tasks. For example, if an item costs $25 and the application pulls that data from a hidden field found in a web form but does not validate that the data it receives matches a value it should accept, an attacker could change the value to $0 and might get the item for free! Validating that the data you receive either matches the specific dataset you expect or is at least in a reasonable range is a critical step in layered security design.

When analyzing data flows, storage, and usage, remember to look for places where data issues could cause high impact failures. Data validation issues at some points in a design can be far more critical to the overall design than it is at other points, making effective control placement extremely important in those locations.

 When assessing data validation and trust controls, it can help to work backward by asking yourself "What would happen if the data were incorrect, or worse, if it an attacker could change it to anything they wanted to?"

Users

Human error is a frequent cause of failure in security architectures. Mistakes, malfeasance, or social engineering attacks that target staff members can all break security designs. Layered security designs should be built with the assumption that the humans who carry out the procedures and processes that it relies on may make mistakes and should be designed to identify and alert if intentional violations occur.

Failures due to users are often limited by

- Using automated monitoring and alerting systems to detect human error
- Constraining interfaces to only allow permitted activities
- Implementing procedural checks and balances like separation of duties and the other personnel controls previously discussed in this chapter
- Training and awareness programs designed to help prepare staff for the types of threats they are likely to encounter

Identifying possible issues caused by users is often useful to brainstorm with experts on the systems or processes. When that isn't possible, reviewing how user actions are monitored and controlled can help point to possible gaps.

A practical example of this type of review occurs in grocery stores where it is common practice to issue a cashier a cash drawer to take to their station. Sometimes, the cashier counts out their own drawer before starting a shift; in other cases they are given a cash drawer with a standard and verified amount of money. During their shift, they are the only users of that drawer, and at the end of the shift, they count out the drawer and have it verified or work with a manager to count it out. If there continued to be loss at grocery store, you might walk through the cashier's tasks, asking them at each step what task they are performing and how it is validated. When you identify an area where an issue could occur, you can then work to identify controls to prevent that issue.

Authentication and Authorization

User credentials, passwords, and user rights are all areas that often create issues in security designs. Common problems include inappropriate or overly broad user rights, poor credential security or management, embedded and stored passwords and keys, as well as reliance on passwords to protect critical systems. Security designs that seek to avoid these issues often implement solutions like

- Multifactor authentication

- Centralized account and privilege management and monitoring

- Privileged account usage monitoring

- Training and awareness efforts

When analyzing a security design for potential authentication and authorization issues, the first step is to identify where authentication occurs, how authorization is performed, and what rights are needed and provided to users. Once you understand those, you can focus on the controls that are implemented and where those controls may leave gaps. Remember to consider technical, process, and human factors!

Cloud computing and other outsourcing models can make security designs even more complex. Fortunately, sample cloud security architecture models have started to become available. NIST, the U.S. National Institute of Standards and Technology, released the NIST Cloud Computing Security Reference Architecture in 2013, providing a useful reference for organizations that need to design or assess cloud security designs. You can find it at http://collaborate.nist.gov/twiki-cloud-computing/pub/ CloudComputing/CloudSecurity/NIST_Security_Reference_Architecture _2013.05.15_v1.0.pdf.

Reviewing a Security Architecture

Reviewing a security architecture requires step-by-step analysis of the security needs that influenced a design and the controls that were put in place. Figure 10.13 shows a high-level design for a web application with a database backend. To analyze this, we can first start with a statement of the design requirements for the service:

> The web application is presented to customers via the Internet, and contains customer business sensitive data. It must be fault-tolerant, secure against web application attacks, and should provide secure authentication and authorization, as well as appropriate security monitoring and system security.

FIGURE 10.13 Sample security architecture

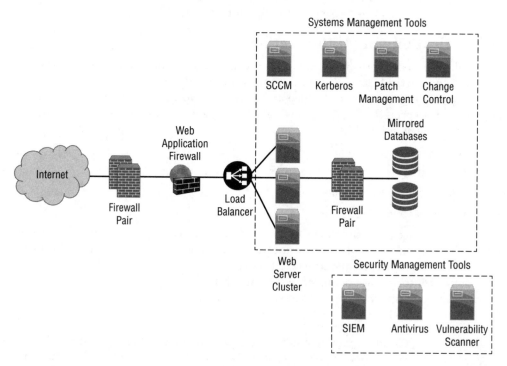

From this, we can review the design for potential flaws. Starting from the left, we will step through each section looking for possible issues. It's important to note that this example won't cover every possible flaw with this design. Instead, this is meant as an example of how a review might identify flaws based on a network logical diagram.

- The Internet connection, as shown, has a single path. This could cause an availability issue.

- There is no IDS or IPS between the Internet and the web server layer. This may be desirable to handle attacks that the WAF and the firewall layer cannot detect.

- The diagram does not show how the network security devices like firewalls and the WAF are managed. Exposure of management ports via public networks is a security risk.

- The web application firewall and the load balancers are shown as clustered devices. This may indicate an availability issue.

- There is no active detection security layer between the web server and the databases. A SQL-aware security device would provide an additional layer of security.

In addition to the information that the logical diagram shows, review of a dataflow diagram, configurations, processes, and procedures would each provide useful views to ensure this design provides an appropriate level of security.

Maintaining a Security Design

Security designs need to continue to address the threats and requirements that they were built to address. Over time, new threats may appear, old threats may stop being a concern, technology will change, and organizational capabilities will be different. That means that they need to be reviewed, improved, and eventually retired.

Scheduled Reviews

A security design should undergo periodical, scheduled reviews. The frequency of the reviews may vary depending on how quickly threats that the organization faces change, how often its systems, networks, and processes change, if regulator or contractual requirements change, and if a major security event occurs that indicates that a review may be needed.

It may seem obvious, but recording the last change date for a security design or program can help track when a review was done. A date in the header of a design file is useful when you are quickly reviewing what has been done.

Continual Improvement

Continual improvement processes (sometimes called CIP or CI processes) are designed to provide incremental improvements over time. A security program or design needs to be assessed on a recurring basis, making a continuous improvement process important to ensure that the design does not become outdated.

Another word frequently used in improvement processes is *kaizen*, a Japanese word that translates as "good change." A kaizen continuous improvement approach is often used in manufacturing and in lean programming and places the responsibility for improvement in the hands of all employees, not just an improvement group or team.

Retirement of Processes

Security processes and policies may become outdated, and instead of updating, they may need to be retired. This is often the case for one of a few reasons:

- The process or policy is no longer relevant.
- It has been superseded by a newer policy or process.
- The organization no longer wants to use the policy or process.

Retirement of processes and policies should be documented and recorded in the document that describes it. Once it a decision has been made, appropriate communication needs to occur to ensure that it is no longer used and that individuals and groups who used the process or policy are aware of its replacement if appropriate.

Summary

Security controls should be layered to ensure that the failure of a control does not result in the failure of the overall security architecture of an organization, system, or service. Layered security designs may provide uniform protection or may implement design choices that place more sensitive systems or data in protected enclaves. It may also use analysis of threats or data classifications as the foundation for design decisions. In any complete security design, multiple controls are implemented together to create a stronger security design that can prevent attacks, detect problems, and allow for appropriate response and recovery in the event that a failure does occur.

Layered security designs often use segmentation and network security devices to separate networks and systems based on functional or other distinctions. Systems also require layered security, and tools like host firewalls, data loss prevention software, antivirus and antimalware software, and system configuration and monitoring tools all providing parts of the host security puzzle. Other common parts of a layered security design include encryption, logging and monitoring, and personnel security, as well as policies, processes, and standards. Attribute-based assessments of security models rely on verifying that a design meets security requirements. Views of the architecture should be used to ensure that the design holds up from multiple perspectives, including operational, technical, and logical paths through the security design. Single points of failure, trust and data validation problems, authentication and authorization issues, and user-related concerns are all important to consider when looking for flaws. All of this means that security designs should undergo regular review and updates to stay ahead of changing needs and new security threats.

Exam Essentials

Defense in depth relies on the idea of layered security. Layered security uses multiple security controls layered together to ensure that a failure in any single control cannot lead to a failure of the system of controls. Controls are classified as administrative, technical, or physical controls, and each control is a detective, preventive, or corrective control. Controls that satisfy a requirement not met by an existing control, or which cover for a flaw in that control, are called compensating controls.

Implementing defense in depth requires designing security in layers. Common designs use segmentation to separate different security levels or areas where security needs differ. Network layered security designs include single firewall, multifirewall, and multiple-interface firewalls. Outsourcing requires additional care due to complex network connections between onsite and offsite systems and devices.

Analyzing security architecture starts with understanding requirements and identifying potential points of failure. Single points of failure are design elements where a single failure can cause the design to fail to function as intended. Other common issues include data validation issues, problems caused by trust and requirements for trust versus whether the data or system can be trusted, user-related failures, and authentication and authorization processes and procedures.

Maintaining layered security designs require continual review and validation.   Scheduled reviews help to ensure that the design has not become outdated. Continual improvement processes keep layered defense designs current while helping to engage staff and provide ongoing awareness. At the end of their life cycle, processes, procedures, and technical designs must be retired with appropriate notification and documentation.

Lab Exercises

Activity 10.1: Review an Application Using the OWASP Application Security Architecture Cheat Sheet

In this exercise you will use the Open Web Application Security Project Application Security Architecture Cheat Sheet to review the security architecture of an application that you are familiar with. If you are not completely familiar with an application infrastructure, you may find it helpful to interview an application administrator or other IT professional who is responsible for application management to complete this exercise.

Part 1: Review the OWASP Application Security Architecture Cheat Sheet

The cheat sheet can be found at https://www.owasp.org/index.php/Application_Security_Architecture_Cheat_Sheet.

Review the cheat sheet, and make sure that you understand all the questions. Some questions may not be relevant. The important part of the exercise at this point is to make sure that you could answer the question. If you're not familiar with the topic area, spend some time researching it.

Part 2: Select an Application You Are Familiar With and Fill Out the Cheat Sheet

Select an application that you have experience with from your professional experience and fill out the cheat sheet. If the application does not fit the question asked, mark it as nonapplicable.

Part 3: Analyze Your Responses to the Cheat Sheet

Use your responses to analyze the application security architecture. Answer the following questions:

1.   Are there controls that are not currently in place that would improve the security design?

2.   Are there single points of failure in the design? What would be required to remediate them?

3. Does the current security architecture match the threats that the application is likely to face? Why or why not?

Activity 10.2: Review a NIST Security Architecture

The following graphic shows the NIST access authorization information flow and its control points in a logical flow diagram as found in NIST SP1800-5b. This NIST architecture uses a number of important information gathering and analytical systems:

- Fathom, a system that provides anomaly detection
- BelManage, which monitors installed software
- Bro, an IDS
- Puppet, an open source configuration management tool that is connected to the organization's change management process
- Snort, an IDS
- WSUS for Windows updates
- OpenVAS, an open source vulnerability management tool
- Asset Central, an asset tracking system
- CA ITAM, which also tracks physical assets
- iStar Edge, a physical access control system

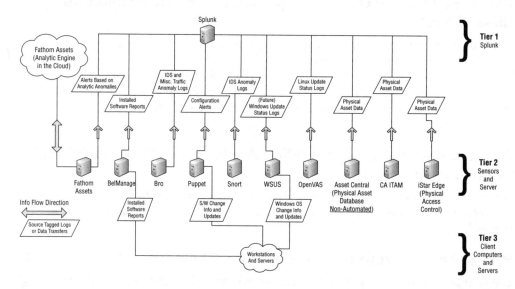

Make note of potential issues with this diagram, marking where you would apply additional controls or where a single failure might lead to systemwide failure. Additional details about the specific systems and capabilities can be found in the NIST ITAM draft at https://nccoe.nist.gov/sites/default/files/library/sp1800/fs-itam-nist-sp1800-5b-draft.pdf.

Activity 10.3: Security Architecture Terminology

Match each of the following terms to the correct description.

Uniform protection	A personnel security control that can help to identify individuals who are exploiting the rights they have as part of their job.
Attack surface	A protected network or location separated from other security zones by protective controls
Administrative controls	A control that remediates a gap or flaw in another control
Protected enclaves	A security design that protects all elements of the environment at the same level using the same tools and techniques
Dual control	The portion of an organization, system, or network that can be attacked
Single point of failure	Controls that include processes and policies
Mandatory vacation	A security control that prevents individuals from performing sensitive actions without a trusted peer reviewing and approving their actions
Compensating control	A part of a system that, if it fails, will cause the failure of the entire system

Review Questions

1. Sue is the manager of a group of system administrators and is in charge of approving all requests for administrative rights. In her role, she files a change request to grant a staff member administrative rights and then approves it. What personnel control would best help to prevent this abuse of her role?

    A. Mandatory vacation

    B. Separation of duties

    C. Succession planning

    D. Dual control

2. Ben wants to ensure that a single person cannot independently access his organization's secure vault. What personnel control is best suited to this need?

    A. Mandatory vacation

    B. Separation of duties

    C. Succession planning

    D. Dual control

3. Lauren's departure from her organization leaves her team without a Linux systems administrator and means they no longer have in-depth knowledge of a critical business system. What should her manager have done to ensure that this issue did not have a significant impact?

    A. Mandatory vacation

    B. Exit interview

    C. Succession planning

    D. HR oversight

4. Ric is reviewing his organization's network design and is concerned that a known flaw in the border router could let an attacker disable their Internet connectivity. Which of the following is an appropriate compensatory control?

    A. An identical second redundant router set up in an active/passive design

    B. An alternate Internet connectivity method using a different router type

    C. An identical second redundant router set up in an active/active design

    D. Place a firewall in front of the router to stop any potential exploits that could cause a failure of connectivity

5. Fred has been assigned to review his organization's host security policies due to a recent theft of a workstation that contained sensitive data. Which of the following controls would best help to prevent a stolen machine from causing a data breach?

    A. Central management

    B. Full disk encryption

    C. Remote wipe capabilities

    D. Machine tracking software

6. A member of Susan's team recently fell for a phishing scam and provided his password and personal information to a scammer. What layered security approach is not an appropriate layer for Susan to implement to protect her organization from future issues?

    A. Multifactor authentication

    B. Multitiered firewalls

    C. An awareness program

    D. A SIEM monitoring where logins occur from

7. Chris is in charge of his organization's Windows security standard, including their Windows XP security standard, and has recently decommissioned the organization's last Windows XP system. What is the next step in his security standard's life cycle?

    A. A scheduled review of the Windows standards

    B. A final update to the standard, noting that Windows XP is no longer supported

    C. Continual improvement of the Windows standards

    D. Retiring the Windows XP standard

8. Example Corporation has split their network into network zones that include sales, HR, research and development, and guest networks, each separated from the others using network security devices. What concept is Example Corporation using for their network security?

    A. Segmentation

    B. Multiple-interface firewalls

    C. Single-point-of-failure avoidance

    D. Zoned routing

9. Which of the following layered security controls is commonly used at the WAN, LAN, and host layer in a security design?

    A. Encryption of data at rest

    B. Firewalls

    C. DMZs

    D. Antivirus

10. In Lauren's initial design for a secure network, she applied the same security controls to every system and network. After reviewing her design, she decided to isolate systems based on their functions and to apply controls to protected network segments for more sensitive data and systems. What two design models did she apply?

    A. Threat analysis–based design, protected enclaves

    B. Uniform protection, threat analysis–based design

    C. Information-based design, uniform protection

    D. Uniform protection, protected enclaves

11. Michelle has been asked to review her corporate network's design for single points of failure that would impact the core network operations. The following graphic shows a redundant network design with a critical fault: a single point of failure that could take the network offline if it failed. Where is this single point of failure?

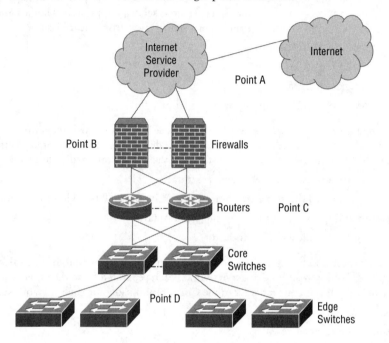

A. Point A

B. Point B

C. Point C

D. Point D

12. During a penetration test of Anna's company, the penetration testers were able to compromise the company's web servers and deleted their log files, preventing analysis of their attacks. What compensating control is best suited to prevent this issue in the future?

A. Using full-disk encryption

B. Using log rotation

C. Sending logs to a syslog server

D. Using TLS to protect traffic

13. Which of the following controls is best suited to prevent vulnerabilities related to software updates?

A. Operating system patching standards

B. Centralized patch management software

C. Vulnerability scanning

D. An IPS with appropriate detections enabled

14. Ben's organization uses data loss prevention software that relies on metadata tagging to ensure that sensitive files do not leave the organization. What compensating control is best suited to ensuring that data that does leave is not exposed?

    A. Mandatory data tagging policies

    B. Encryption of all files sent outside the organization

    C. DLP monitoring of all outbound network traffic

    D. Network segmentation for sensitive data handling systems

15. James is concerned that network traffic from his datacenter has increased and that it may be caused by a compromise that his security tools have not identified. What SIEM analysis capability could he use to look at the traffic over time sent by his datacenter systems?

    A. Automated reporting

    B. Trend analysis

    C. BGP graphing

    D. Log aggregation

16. Angela needs to implement a control to ensure that she is notified of changes to important configuration files on her server. What type of tool should she use for this control?

    A. Anti-malware

    B. Configuration management

    C. File integrity checking

    D. Logging

17. Lauren has recently discovered that the Linux server she is responsible for maintaining is affected by a zero-day exploit for a vulnerability in the web application software that is needed by her organization. Which of the following compensating controls should she implement to best protect the server?

    A. A WAF

    B. Least privilege for accounts

    C. A patch from the vendor

    D. An IDS

18. Mike installs a firewall in front of a previously open network to prevent the systems behind the firewall from being targeted by external systems. What did Mike do?

    A. Reduced the organization's attack surface

    B. Implemented defense in depth

    C. Added a corrective control

    D. Added an administrative control

19. During a security architecture design review, Kathleen notices that there is no written process in place to ensure that systems are returned to their normal state after a compromise. How would this control be classified?

A. A technical, corrective control

B. A corrective, compensatory control

C. An administrative, corrective control

D. A physical, detective control

20. Selah's design for network security is shown in the following graphic. What design model has she used for her network?

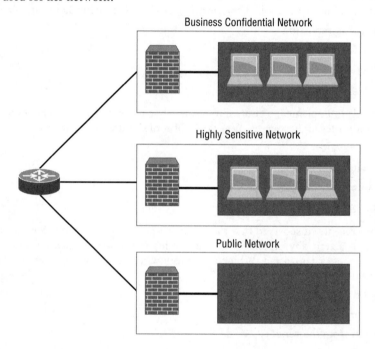

A. Information-based design

B. Threat analysis–based design

C. Protected enclave

D. Uniform protection

Chapter

11

Identity and Access Management Security

THE COMPTIA CYBERSECURITY ANALYST+ EXAM OBJECTIVES COVERED IN THIS CHAPTER INCLUDE:

Domain 4: Security Architecture and Tool Sets

✓ **4.2 Given a scenario, use data to recommend remediation of security issues related to identity and access management.**

Identities—the collection of user information, credentials, rights, roles, group memberships, and other attributes and information about individuals and accounts—are among the most critical assets that an organization owns. Identities, and the access and rights that we grant to them, provide the keys to systems, services, and data, making them targets for both internal and external attackers.

As organizational security has improved, the ability of attackers to simply target unpatched or unprotected systems exposed to the Internet has decreased, making it increasingly necessary for them to obtain accounts to gain and maintain access to their targets. Now, attackers frequently need to have valid user credentials to compromise systems, networks, or services. This means you need to understand both the threats that identity and access systems and technologies face and how to defend against them.

In this chapter, we will explore the major threats to identities, credentials, and the authentication, authorization, and accounting systems behind them. We will look at the ways in which identity can be used as a security layer to provide an important part of a defense-in-depth plan and will review how identity management integrates into a security operations design. Finally, we will discuss federated identities and single sign-on security, an increasingly important element of both cloud services and many organizational support strategies.

Understanding Identity

Identities, or the set of claims made about an individual or account holder that are made about one party to another party (such as a service provider, application, or system), are a key part of authentication, authorization, and trust. The user accounts we use to log in require the ability to uniquely identify individuals and other *subjects* such as services to allow for permissions, rights, group memberships, and attributes to be associated with them.

The attributes associated with an identity include information about a subject and often include their name, address, title, contact information, and other details about the individual. These attributes may be used as part of authentication processes, may be used to populate *directory* information, or could be collected to help meet other organizational needs or business purposes.

Some schemes call out traits and preferences separately from attributes. In those designs, traits are inherent parts of the subject like their hair color, nationality, or birthday. Preferences are based on a person's choices like their favorite color or band.

Identities are used as part the *Authentication*, *Authorization*, and *Accounting* (*AAA*) framework that is used to control access to computers, networks, and services. AAA systems authenticate users by requiring credentials like a username, a password, and possibly a biometric or token-based authenticator. Once individuals have proven who they are, they are then authorized to access or use resources or systems. Authorization applies policies based on the user's identity information and rules or settings, allowing the owner of the identity to perform actions or to gain access to systems. The accounting element of the AAA process is the logging and monitoring that goes with the authentication and authorization. Accounting monitors usage and provides information about how and what users are doing.

Central management of identities normally occurs in identity and access management (IAM) systems. IAM systems are built to create, store, and manage identity information as well as the permissions, groups, and other information needed to support the use of identities. Figure 11.1 shows a high-level view of identity management for an organization. The data to create identities comes from systems of record like the organization's ERP, HR systems, or customer databases. The data is supplied to the identity management systems and services, which provide account creation, provisioning, management, and oversight for the organization. Those systems then offer authentication and authorization services to identity consumers like servers, workstations, services, and third-party service providers.

FIGURE 11.1   A high-level logical view of identity management infrastructure

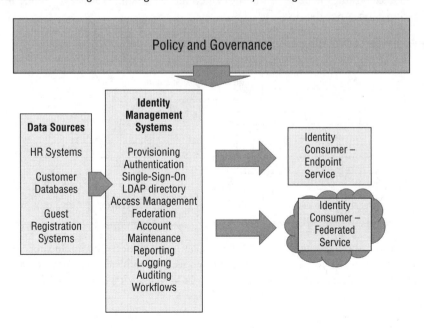

Identity Systems and Security Design

Identity systems provide a number of common functions: identity creation and management, authentication and authorization, and in some cases, federation of identity information to allow use of identities outside of their home organization. To enable this, a number of common technologies are used: directories, authentication services, identity management platforms, and federated identity tools.

> There are many different types of identity-related tools. We have focused on the key elements covered in the Cybersecurity Analyst+ exam, but you may encounter tools or systems that we don't cover here.

Directories

Directory services are used in networks to provide information about systems, users, and other information about an organization. Directory services like *LDAP* (the Lightweight Directory Access Protocol) are commonly deployed as part of an identity management infrastructure and offer hierarchically organized information about the organization. They are frequently used to make available an organizational directory for email and other contact information.

Figure 11.2 shows an example LDAP directory hierarchy for example.com, where there are two organizational units (OUs): security and human resources. Each of those units includes a number of entries labeled with a common name (CN). In addition to the structure shown in the diagram, each entry would have additional information not shown in this simplified diagram, including a distinguished name, an email address, phone numbers, office location, and other details.

FIGURE 11.2   LDAP directory structure

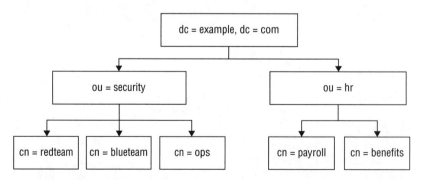

There are a number of open source LDAP server implementations, including OpenLDAP, 389 Directory Server, ApacheDS, and OpenDJ, as well as commercial software like Oracle's Internet Directory, Microsoft's Active Directory, IBM's Security Directory Server, and CA

Directory. Thus, steps required to implement a secure LDAP server will vary, but some of the common considerations remain the same. These include the following:

- Enabling and requiring TLS keeps LDAP queries and authentication secure.

- Setting password storage to use a secure method. LDAP passwords are often stored in plaintext, but additional methods are supported and should be used if possible.

While LDAP implementations vary, OpenLDAP has historically been one of the most common choices. When using OpenLDAP, the SSHA password storage scheme uses a salted SHA hash for password storage. This is stronger than the CRYPT, MD5, SHA, and SASL schemes that OpenLDAP supports. Understanding details of how your specific LDAP server works can make a major difference in how secure it is in practice.

- Using password-based authentication and requiring TLS. LDAP provides three modes of operation: anonymous, unauthenticated, and username/password authenticated. When authenticated sessions are turned on, unauthenticated mode should be disabled to prevent issues with unsecured connections.

- Replication of LDAP servers can help to prevent denial-of-service attacks and other service outages.

- Access control lists for LDAP offer the ability to limit access to specific objects in the directory as well as overall rules for how entries are created, modified, and deleted.

Since directories contain significant amounts of organizational data and may be used to support a range of services, including directory-based authentication, they must be well protected. The same set of needs often means that directory servers need to be publicly exposed to provide services to systems or business partners who need to access the directory information. In those cases, additional security, tighter access controls, or even an entirely separate public directory service may be needed.

One of the most common attacks on web services that use LDAP is LDAP injection, which uses improperly filtered user input via web applications to send arbitrary LDAP queries. Details, and a cheat sheet on how to avoid it, can be found at https://www.owasp.org/index.php/ LDAP_Injection_Prevention_Cheat_Sheet.

Authentication Protocols

Centralized authentication services allow clients to authenticate to a central authentication service, which then supplies verification of the user's identity to the relying system. Central authentication services may also provide authorization information for the user to the relying party, or they may match the identity with their own authorization and rules.

Common authentication protocols include the following:

- *TACACS+*, a Cisco-designed extension to TACAS, the Terminal Access Controller Access-Control System. It uses TCP traffic to provide authentication, authorization, and accounting services. TACACs+ suffers from a number of flaws, including a lack of integrity checking for the data it sends, allowing an attacker with access to the traffic it sends to make arbitrary changes or to use replay attacks against the TACACS+ service. TACACS+ also has encryption flaws that can lead to compromise of the encryption key. This means TACACs+ systems that provide AAA services for network devices should operate on an isolated administrative network if possible.

- *RADIUS*, the Remote Authentication Dial-in User Service, is one of the most common AAA systems for network device, wireless networks, and other services. RADIUS can operate via TCP or UDP and operates in a client-server model. RADIUS sends passwords that are obfuscated by a shared secret and MD5 hash, meaning that its password security is not very strong. RADIUS traffic between the RADIUS network access server and the RADIUS server is typically encrypted using IPSec tunnels or other protections to protect the traffic.

- Unlike TACACS+ and RADIUS, *Kerberos* is designed to operate on untrusted networks and uses encryption to protect its authentication traffic. Users in Kerberos, called principals, are composed of three elements: the primary (frequently the username), the instance (used to differentiate similar primaries), and the realm, which consists of groups of principals. Realms are often separated on trust boundaries and have distinct key distribution centers (KDCs). Figure 11.3 shows the basic Kerberos authentication flow.

FIGURE 11.3   Kerberos authentication flow

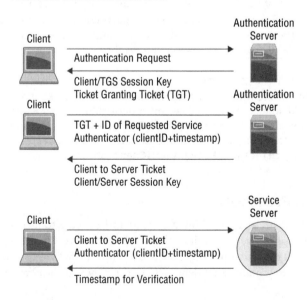

Active Directory uses the Kerberos protocol for authentication. Older versions of Windows relied on NTLM authentication; however, NTLM is outdated and you are unlikely to encounter it in modern environments.

Single Sign-On and Shared Authentication Schemes

Many web applications rely on *single sign-on* systems to allow users to authenticate once and then to use multiple systems or services without having to use different usernames or passwords. *Shared authentication* schemes are somewhat similar to single sign-on and allow an identity to be reused on multiple sites while relying on authentication via a single identity provider. Shared authentication systems require users to enter credentials when authenticating to each site, unlike single sign-on systems.

Common single sign-on technologies include LDAP and *CAS*, the *Central Authentication Service*. Shared authentication technologies include

- *OpenID*, an open source standard for decentralized authentication. OpenID is broadly used by major websites like Google, Amazon, and Microsoft. Users create credentials with an identity provider like Google; then sites (relying parties) use that identity.

- *OAuth*, an open authorization standard. OAuth is used by Google, Microsoft, Facebook, and other sites to allow users to share elements of their identity or account information while authenticating via the original identity provider. OAuth relies on access tokens, which are issued by an authorization server and then presented to resource servers like third-party web applications by clients.

- *OpenID Connect* is a authentication layer built using the OAuth protocol.

- *Facebook Connect*, also known as Login with Facebook, is a shared authentication system that relies on Facebook credentials for authentication.

One of single sign-on's most significant security benefits is the potential to reduce the occurrence of password reuse. This may also reduce the likelihood of credential exposure via third-party sites when users reuse credential sets. In addition, single sign-on is popular due to the potential cost savings from fewer password resets and support calls.

Shared authentication systems share some of the same benefits, allowing users to use their credentials without having to create new accounts on each site, thus reducing password fatigue. In addition, users are typically informed about the types of data that will be released to the relying party, such as email account, contact information, gender, or other personal information. Shared authentication systems do not necessarily provide a single sign-on experience.

Threats to Identity and Access

Identity threats can be broadly classified into a handful of major areas. First, threats to the underlying authentication and authorization systems seek to exploit vulnerabilities in the way that users log in, how their credentials are handled, or how they are authorized.

Second, attackers may also target the account life cycle by creating credentials, preventing them from being removed, or causing them to have greater privileges associated with them. Third, attackers may focus on accounts themselves, either via phishing or compromise of systems where credentials may be stored. Over the next few pages, we will explore attacks on identity repositories and supporting systems, targeting identity management process flaws via the account creation, provisioning, and maintenance process; exploits against identity and authorization systems; how credentials are acquired by attackers; and defenses against these attacks.

Understanding Security Issues with Identities

Identities, including credentials, roles, rights, and permissions, and related data can face a multitude of security issues. The Cybersecurity Analyst+ exam specifically considers six areas:

- *Personnel*-based identity security, which includes training and awareness, as well as threats like insider attacks, phishing, and social engineering

- *Endpoints* and their role in attacks on identity, including capturing credentials via local exploits; screen capture and keyboard capture applications; local administrative rights; and how password stores, tokens, and other credentials are stored on local systems and devices like phones and tablets

- *Servers*-based exploits, which can target the systems that run identity services, or which can attack the servers and send identity and authentication data to AAA services

- *Applications* and *services* that provide, consume, and interact with identity systems

- *Roles*, rights, and permissions that are associated with users or groups

 As you prepare for the exam, remember to consider identity security issues from each of these viewpoints. If you are answering questions about a topic like phishing, you may want to consider multiple controls like a training and awareness program and technical measures, including two-factor authentication, email filtering, and reputation-based sender rules.

Attacking AAA Systems and Protocols

Identity repositories like directory systems, authentication systems, and single-sign-on services are all attractive targets for attackers. Attacks against identity repositories and systems may target the specific software via vulnerabilities or misconfigurations; they can be aimed at the protocol itself or at how the protocol is implemented.

Attacks at the underlying systems, such as denial-of-service attacks and system compromises, are also common, since taking over the host system can provide full control over an authorization system, giving attackers the keys to the entire kingdom. Since there are a multitude of potential attacks against the many types of identity repositories and authorization systems, we will take a brief look at some of the most common protocols and services to gain an understanding of common threats.

LDAP Attacks

LDAP services are used in many organizations for authentication and directory information. This makes them targets for attackers who want to obtain organizational information or to access systems or applications that rely on LDAP-based authentication.

Attacks against LDAP directory servers typically focus on

- Attacks against insecure binding (connection) methods that target unencrypted LDAP traffic, either to capture the traffic or to exploit LDAP as an authentication service

- Improper LDAP access controls that allow attackers to harvest directory information or to make modifications to directory entries that they should not be able to change

- LDAP injection, which exploits web applications that build LDAP queries using user input, allowing attackers to gather additional information or to make changes they should not be authorized to make by operating as the web service

- Denial-of-service attacks, which can disrupt authentication services that rely on LDAP or cause applications and services that rely on LDAP to fail

Each of these attacks can be prevented or mitigated through careful design and implementation of LDAP services and access methods. Requiring secure binding methods, setting appropriate access controls (and verifying them!), using good web application development practices, and designing a scalable LDAP directory service can all reduce the likelihood of LDAP-related security issues.

 Real World Scenario

LDAP as an Attack Tool

In 2016, the Connectionless LDAP service, or CLDAP, was found to be a potential attack vector allowing amplification attacks because it would respond to spoofed addresses, resulting in amplification rates up to 55 times higher than the source traffic. That means that your otherwise innocent appearing LDAP service could DoS your critical infrastructure without an attacker even making it through other network defenses! You can read more about it at www.securityweek.com/ldap-attack-vector-makes-terabit-scale-ddos-attacks-possible.

OAuth, OpenID, and OpenID Connect

OAuth and OpenID are implemented on a per-provider basis, resulting in flaws unique to each party. One of the most common attacks based on this is the use of open redirects. When redirects and forwards are not validated, untrusted user input can be sent to the relying web application, resulting in users being redirected to untrusted sites, allowing phishing scams or permitting attackers to bypass security layers.

    The OpenID Connect implementer's guide can be found at `http://openid.net/connect/` and OAuth 2.0 guides can be found at `https://oauth.net/getting-started/`.

Figure 11.4 shows where this occurs in an OAuth flow. If a user accesses a website that is an open redirect endpoint, it will allow URLs at point A to be any redirect URL, instead of a specific URL associated with that site, and if the site also passes that URL forward at point B, attackers can exploit the authorization flow. Fortunately, this won't cause the account associated with the service provider to be compromised—it only causes issues for the site with the open redirect endpoint, since the redirect can result in the phishing scams and similar issues related to untrusted redirects mentioned above occurring.

FIGURE 11.4   OAuth covert redirects

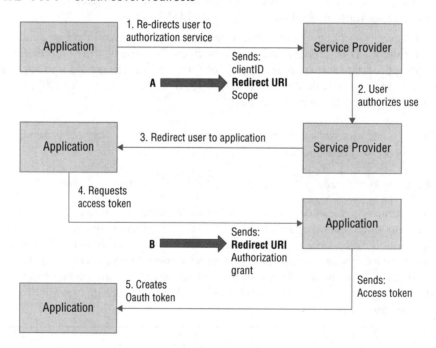

In addition to individual implementation issues, OAuth's broad adoption for cloud services and mobile applications makes it a particularly tempting target for attackers. Poor session management, reliance on a central shared secrets file for OAuth servers, and inadvertent use of plaintext OAuth sessions are all potential issues for OAuth providers.

> ### 🌐 Real World Scenario
>
> **OAuth Security and Threat Models**
>
> OAuth does not set specific requirements for how the backend of OAuth authentication applications interact with third-party applications, leading to issues with single sign-on applications. To read more about recent exposures, visit `https://threatpost.com/oauth-2-0-hack-exposes-1-billion-mobile-apps-to-account-hijacking/121889/`. An in-depth discussion of the OAuth 2.0 threat model can be found in RFC 6819, "OAuth 2.0 Threat Model and Security Considerations," at `https://tools.ietf.org/html/rfc6819`.

Many attacks against OpenID have been aimed at protocol vulnerabilities, including a 2012 discovery related to the ability of attackers to forge OpenID requests in a way that resulted in relying parties allowing arbitrary logins to their services. In addition to protocol attacks, OAuth2 can also be vulnerable to cross-site request forgery (CSRF) attacks, which focus on getting a user to click a link that causes that user's browser to perform an action at that user. OpenID Connect offers additional protections for encryption and signing, which, if properly implemented, can help prevent many of the exploits conducted against OpenID services.

Kerberos

Kerberos relies on a central key distribution center (KDC). Compromise of the KDC would allow an attacker to impersonate any user. Kerberos attacks have received significant attention over the past few years due to local attacks against compromised KDCs resulting in complete compromise of Kerberos authenticated systems. Common Kerberos attacks include the following:

- Administrator account attacks.

- Kerberos ticket reuse, including pass-the-ticket attacks, which allows impersonation of legitimate users for the lifespan of the ticket, and pass-the-key attacks, which reuse a secret key to acquire tickets.

- Ticket granting ticket (TGT) focused attacks. TGTs are incredibly valuable and can be created with extended lifespans. When attackers succeed in acquiring TGTs, the TGTs are often called "golden tickets" because they allow complete access to the Kerberos-connected systems, including creation of new tickets, account changes, and even falsification of accounts or services.

Automated monitoring of authentication and authorization systems can help detect anomalous behaviors like the creation of a golden ticket—a normal ticket generating ticket wouldn't have a lifespan of months or years, making behavior-based monitoring an important part of defense against advanced attackers. Details of this attack can be found here: `https://www.blackhat.com/docs/us-15/materials/us-15-Metcalf-Red-Vs-Blue-Modern-Active-Directory-Attacks-Detection-And-Protection-wp.pdf`.

RADIUS

RADIUS is commonly used for authentication of network devices, including VPNs, network hardware, and similar services. This makes it a tempting target for attackers who want to penetrate the network infrastructure of their targets. RADIUS attacks often focus on

- Session replay of server responses by matching known traffic and replaying previous responses or replaying server responses to authenticate client without valid credentials

- Targeting the RADIUS shared secret, since RADIUS uses a fixed shared secret that can be compromised at the client level

- Denial-of-service attacks aimed to preventing users from authenticating

- Credential-based attacks that rely on the use of a RADIUS-shared secret to brute-force the shared secret given a known password

Using TLS to protect RADIUS authentication instead of relying on the protections built into RADIUS can help mitigate many of these attacks; however, doing so requires consistent implementation throughout an organization.

Active Directory

Active Directory is the core identity store and AAA service for many Windows-centric organizations. That makes AD a popular target for attackers, and the prevalence of Windows workstations in corporate environments means that many exploit tools are built to target both Windows and Active Directory.

Common Active Directory attacks include the following:

- Malware-focused attacks that seek to place credential capturing or exploit-based malware onto Windows systems or AD servers

- Credential theft via phishing or other techniques

- Privilege escalation attacks using known or new Windows exploits

- Service accounts that are an often forgotten element of Active Directory environments and may suffer from both privilege creep and over-permissive rights

- Domain administrator rights that exist for more staff than is necessary, creating more targets for attackers and a greater likelihood that an AD admin account will not be properly maintained or that its password will be exposed

- The use of down-level versions of protocols used in Windows domains like NTLM v1 and LANMAN, NetBIOS, and unsigned LDAP and SMB to capture credentials or to conduct other attacks

Windows domains often include older systems or have settings configured to support them. Combined with the many exploit tools that are aimed at Windows systems, these make Windows domains a tempting target for attackers.

Handling Active Directory GPO Credential Storage

Some specific behaviors of AD and Group Policy are targeted by attackers. Group Policy Preferences can be used to perform a number of actions, but unfortunately, they also store the credentials they use in XML files in the SYSVOL share of every domain controller in the domain. The password storage method used can be easily reversed, making this a significant flaw. The issue is so common that Microsoft provided remediation tools here: `https://support.microsoft.com/en-us/kb/2962486`.

Targeting Account Creation, Provisioning, and Deprovisioning

The steps from account request to creation, provisioning of accounts, maintenance during the life cycle of the account, and the eventual deprovisioning and deletion of the account are known as the account life cycle. Figure 11.5 shows a typical account life cycle, from start to finish.

FIGURE 11.5   A sample account life cycle

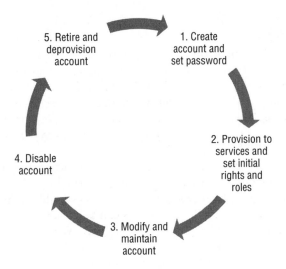

Both internal and external threats target the systems, services, and procedures that make up the account life cycle in order to gain access to accounts, or to gain privileges for the accounts that they already have access to.

The account creation process is an important target for attackers who have either gained access to systems in a trusted environment or are able to use social engineering attacks to persuade someone with appropriate rights to create an account for them. Internal threats may also seek to create accounts for their use to avoid detection.

Once an account exists, attackers will focus on gaining access to it. Social engineering, phishing, and attacks against credential stores and locations where credentials are used and could be compromised in transit or in use are all frequent methods of attack. Compromising credentials can provide the rights and access that the account is provisioned with and may allow attackers to operate in trusted areas where they can attempt attacks that are unlikely to succeed in more protected areas.

Attackers may also focus on accounts that have fallen through the cracks in an identity management system. Major threats from unused or improperly maintained accounts include

- Unused accounts, which attackers can compromise and use without the owner noticing something is amiss.

- Accounts that were not properly deprovisioned and abandoned on systems because they were missed during normal account removal or end-of-life processes. Accounts that are not properly deleted can often indicate an issue with management of the system, and may not be logged or monitored.

- Permissions, group memberships, and other privileges often accrue to accounts during a staff member's employment with an organization and may not be updated properly. Attackers, particularly insider threats, may be able to leverage rights that they, or others, have accrued over time without knowing that they still have them.

Rights and Roles

Maintaining rights, roles, and group memberships is another key element in identity management, and an important feature in identity management systems. User accounts are normally managed using the principle of *least privilege* which states that users should be provided only with the least set of privileges or permissions required to perform their job function. This helps prevent users (or attackers who acquire their credentials) from performing actions that they should not and limits the exposure that they can cause.

Many accounts experience *privilege creep*, or the steady accrual of additional rights over time as account owners change roles, positions, or responsibilities. Privilege creep directly conflicts with the concept of least privilege since accounts should not have rights that aren't required for their current role. Unfortunately, this can be hard to track—new managers may not be aware of the user's old rights, or the user may even be asked to continue to perform their old duties on occasion.

Fortunately, centralized identity management suites provide monitoring and management tools designed to monitor for privilege creep and can be set to identify accounts that end up with excessive privileges or which have privileges beyond what their role requires. Identity management systems like Centrify, Okta, and Ping Identity have account life-cycle maintenance and monitoring features designed to fight this type of issue.

Preventing Common Exploits of Identity and Authorization

There are a few common methods of targeting identity and access management systems as well as the use of identity information, each with common protection methods that can help to remediate them. These include the following

- *Impersonation* attacks occur when an attacker takes on the identity of a legitimate user. Security issues like OAuth open redirects discussed earlier in this chapter can allow impersonation to occur. Preventing impersonation may require stronger session handling techniques like those found in the OWASP session management cheat sheet at `https://www.owasp.org/index.php/Session_Management_Cheat_Sheet`. Other types of impersonation may be prevented by securing session identifiers that attackers might otherwise acquire, either on the local workstation or via the network.

- *Man-in-the-middle* (MiTM) attacks rely on accessing information flow between systems or services. End-to-end encryption of sessions or network links can help reduce the chance of a successful MiTM attack, unless attackers control endpoints or have the encryption keys.

- *Session hijacking* focuses on taking over an already existing session, either by acquiring the session key or cookies used by the remote server to validate the session or by causing the session to pass through a system the attacker controls, allowing them to participate in the session. Much like impersonation and MiTM attacks, securing the data that an attacker needs to acquire to hijack the session, either via encrypting network sessions or links or on the local system, can help limit opportunities for session hijacking.

- *Privilege escalation* attacks focus on exploiting flaws to gain elevated permissions or access. A successful privilege escalation attack can allow a normal or an untrusted user to use administrator or other privileged access. Privilege escalation frequently relies on software vulnerabilities, requiring administrators to ensure that local applications, services, and utilities are not vulnerable.

- *Rootkits* combine multiple malicious software tools to provide continued access to a computer while hiding their own existence. Fighting rootkits requires a full suite of system security practices, ranging from proper patching and layered security design to antimalware techniques like whitelisting, heuristic detection techniques, and malicious software detection tools.

Acquiring Credentials

In addition to attacks against AAA and identity management infrastructure, attacks designed to acquire identities and credentials are common, and they can be easier to accomplish from outside an organization. Attacks against credentials commonly occur in the form of phishing attacks, compromises of other services, and brute-force attacks.

Phishing

Phishing attacks aimed at credentials often use replicas of legitimate authentication portals to trick their victims into entering their username and password. More advanced versions will even replay those entries into the legitimate site to prevent their targets from noticing that their login did not work.

Figure 11.6 shows an example of a phishing email that targets a recipient's PayPal ID. If the potential victim did not notice that the URL was wrong or that the site was not exactly the same as the site they normally log into, they could send their credentials to the attacker.

FIGURE 11.6   Phishing for a PayPal ID

RE: Please confirm your PayPal ID for payment

* LUCROSA support@easytradeapp.com via mailminion.net
to me

@gmail.com,

This is an automatic notice that you
have an incoming PayPal deposit in the
amount of $1,386.28

If you are the account holder at this
email address, please confirm your
PayPal ID now.

===>> Click here to confirm

Your funds will be deposited within
24 hours of confirmation.

Thank you,

- John L.
CEO, Lucrosa Inc

Multifactor authentication can help limit the impact of a successful phishing attack by requiring users to take an additional action and by providing an authenticator with a limited lifespan. User education and training including how to detect phishing and avoiding password reuse are also an important part of anti-phishing defenses.

Compromise of Other Services

Attacking third-party services to obtain passwords that may have been reused is another common threat vector. Attackers who obtain plaintext or recoverable passwords can then reuse those passwords on other accounts the users may have had. Unfortunately, many sites do not use strong password hashing algorithms, allowing attackers to easily crack the hashes for passwords stored using MD5 and other weak mechanisms.

Sites like https://haveibeenpwned.com/ now track major breaches and allow users to check if an email address or username has been exposed in public breaches.

This type of attack means that password reuse is a significant danger, particularly when passwords are used as the only factor for authentication. Breaches of major sites, like the two major Yahoo breaches from 2013 (announced in 2016), have resulted in passwords only minimally protected by MD5 hashes being available for almost a billion potential users. This makes a potential target for exploit any other services those users used that can be matched with their email or other identifiers.

Preventing other sites from being compromised isn't a reasonable expectation for a security professional. That's where technologies like multifactor authentication can provide a useful security layer. Even if users use the same password on multiple sites, their additional factors should remain secure, preventing lost passwords from causing an immediate problem. Training and awareness are still important, since password reuse remains a bad idea.

Brute-Force Attacks

Although having passwords available is preferable for attackers, sites that do not prevent repeated login attempts can still be attacked using brute-force methods by simply attempting to log in using password dictionaries or other brute-force methods. Preventing brute-force attacks requires building in back-off algorithms that prevent repeated logins after failure or other similar solutions like the use of CAPTCHA-style methods to verify that the logins are not being attempted by a script or bot. Some organizations choose to implement account lockout techniques to help with brute-force attacks, although lockouts can increase the workload for support teams unless users have an easy method of unlocking their accounts.

As you might expect, connecting authentication events to your security management and logging tools can help detect brute-force attacks, allowing you to take action to prevent the system or systems that are conducting the brute-force attack from attempting to authenticate. If you are considering this option, be sure to identify appropriate thresholds for what you consider brute force—otherwise you may lock out legitimate but forgetful users!

 CAPTCHA is an acronym for Completely Automated Public Turing test to tell Computers and Humans Apart. CATPCHAs use a variety of methods to try to prevent bots from performing actions, including requiring users to identify numbers, or to differentiate pictures of kittens from pictures of puppies. If you're looking to prevent brute-force web activity, OWASP's "Blocking Brute Force Attacks" guide can offer useful advice: https://www.owasp.org/index.php/Blocking_Brute_Force_Attacks.

Identity as a Security Layer

Identity is a critical part of most defense-in-depth designs. User and service accounts are crucial to controlling access to systems and services and also allow detailed monitoring and auditing of usage. Since rights and permissions are assigned either to roles that accounts are associated with or to individual users, identity is also critical to ensuring that rights management is handled properly.

Identity and Defense-in-Depth

The account life cycle offers a number of opportunities for defense-in-depth designs. While identity management processes will vary from organization to organization, a few critical parts of the identity management life cycle are consistent from a defense-in-depth design perspective. These process requirements occur at the major phases of an account's life cycle:

- Identity creation must ensure that only valid accounts are created and that the correct owner receives the account. At this phase in the account life cycle, it is important to avoid duplicate account creation, to ensure that initial authentication factors are delivered or set securely, and that accounts are added to a central identity management system for monitoring and auditing.

- Account provisioning and rights management needs to be consistent—pockets of unmanaged systems or systems that do not integrate can result in unmanaged accounts. Rights management is typically role based, preventing individual accounts from accruing specialized permissions.

- Account modification and maintenance should track the individual's changing roles and group memberships to prevent privilege creep.

- Account termination needs to ensure that accounts are terminated properly, and that they are removed from all systems that they were provisioned to.

Defense-in-depth for identity should address all three elements of the CIA triad. That means ensuring that credentials and credential stores remain confidential in motion and at rest and that their integrity is monitored to ensure that unauthorized changes do not occur. Availability is also a critical concern—centralized identity and authorization services are wonderful until they allow an entire organization's ability to log in to fail due to a failed service or DoS attack!

Securing Authentication and Authorization

Securing the authentication process requires a combination of technical and procedural elements. Technological controls focus on protecting both the systems that provide authentication services and the traffic between clients and those servers. Providing a secure means of validating the identity of users is also critical, since attackers are more likely to have advanced capabilities that result in them successfully obtaining valid usernames and passwords via phishing, malware, or other means. Figure 11.7 shows a sample authentication flow with security considerations at each point in the flow, including use of TLS, multifactor authentication, and redundant authentication servers. Note that authentication security requires design or process security considerations throughout the flow.

FIGURE 11.7   Authentication security model

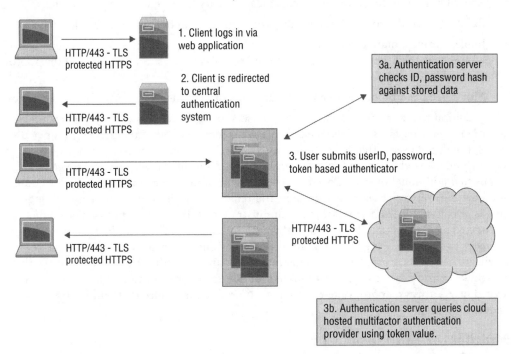

Password management is also a design concern for organizations. Users are asked to remember a large number of passwords, and password reuse is a continuing threat. This means that organizationally sponsored adoption of *password safes* or password storage utilities can have a significant impact on password security. Tools like KeePass, Password Safe, Dashlane, 1Password, and LastPass, as well as enterprise-centric password storage and management tools, can provide a useful means of maintaining distinct passwords without large numbers of support calls.

Moving Beyond Password Complexity Requirements

Password complexity guidelines that included a requirement for specific types of characters and complexity were common until very recently, due in large part to the limited length of passwords supported by many systems. Recommendations for strong passwords have largely changed to be length based, and users are often advised to use a passphrase instead of a password. NIST's SP 800-63-3 "Digital Authentication Guideline" is in draft form right now, but it will reflect major changes in digital authentication standards.

Authorization and Rights Management

Matching users with their rights, roles, and group membership is the next step of identity-based security. Rights management allows *access control* by matching users with the access they should have. Building a rights management security layer relies on the following:

- Building a set of policies that describe what rights are allocated to each role or task

- Implementing a management system to ensure that rights are granted to accounts and groups that need them, and removed from groups and users that do not hold the appropriate role

- Monitoring and reporting to ensure that rights management occurs according to policy

In addition to managing rights for normal users, organizations need to pay particular attention to *privileged user management*, the management of administrative and super-user rights. Privileged users often have the ability to override system policies, to make changes to logging and oversight systems, or to otherwise impact systems in very powerful ways. This means that additional oversight needs to be placed around who can use privileged accounts and how administrative rights are granted and removed. Additional monitoring and logging is also common, and separation of administrative accounts from personal accounts is considered a best practice. This ensures that administrative actions can be logged by requiring users to specifically log into an administrative account or to activate administrative privileges before their use. Since administrative accounts shouldn't be used constantly, this also makes misuse easy to detect by looking for administrative accounts that are constantly logged in. As always, appropriate training is required to make sure that administrators understand this.

Multifactor Authentication

One of the most important security measures put in place to authenticate users is *multifactor authentication (MFA)*. MFA relies on two or more distinct authentication factors like a password, a token or smartcard, a biometric factor, or even the location that the individual is authenticating from. A key part of this is that the factors should be different; two passwords do not make an effective MFA scheme.

MFA relies on a few common types of authentication factors or methods:

- *Knowledge factors* are something you know. Passwords and passphrases are the most common knowledge factors, but authentication systems also sometimes use other data that you may know. Examples include systems that build questions from personal data the organization has about you such as your current mortgage payment, your residence a decade ago, or other things that you will know but that someone else is unlikely to.

- *Possession factors* are something you have. The most common examples of this are authenticator applications, security tokens, and smartcards. Figure 11.8 shows an example of the Google Authenticator application, a smartphone-based onetime password generator tool. Having the application that provides the code is the possession factor when using this type of token.

- *Biometric factors* are something that you are. They include fingerprints, retina scans, voiceprints, and a host of other methods of measuring features of the human body.

- *Location factors*, which are less frequently used, rely on physical location, determined either by where a system or network is located, or by using GPS or other data to verify that you are in a place that is trusted or allowed to access a system.

FIGURE 11.8   Google Authenticator token

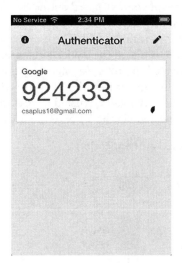

 Since this is a onetime token, it's safe to publish in the book with its associated email address. To access the account, you would need both the current password and the current Google Authenticator code. The authors created a throwaway account for this screenshot anyway!

Context-Based Authentication

A key concept in authentication systems is the idea of context-based authentication. Context-based authentication allows authentication decisions to be made based on information about the user, the system the user is connecting from, or other information that is relevant to the system or organization performing the authentication.

Common data used for context-based authentication includes the following:

- User roles and group memberships related to application or service access

- IP address and/or IP reputation, providing information on whether the remote IP is known to be part of a botnet or other IP range with known bad behavior

- Time of day, often related to a job role or working hours

- Location-based information like their IP address or GPS location

- Frequency of access, which may be combined with behavioral data like keystroke patterns, browsing habits, or other details that can help uniquely identify a user

- Device-based, including information about the web browser in use and other data that can provide a device fingerprint such as its IP address, time zone, screen resolution, cookies or cookie settings, installed fonts, and language.

Figure 11.9 shows an example of context-based authentication flow. A user logs in via the organization's VPN where a network access control (NAC) system profiles the user's device, identifying device-based fingerprint information. The user provides their username and password, which in this example do not match the device—the user has never logged in from it before. Due to this, the user is asked to provide a onetime password code from a security token and is then authenticated, having proven that they are who they say they are. The NAC server records the new device as a valid, trusted device and adds its unique profile to its database, and the user is connected via the VPN to the organization's internal network.

FIGURE 11.9 Context-based authentication

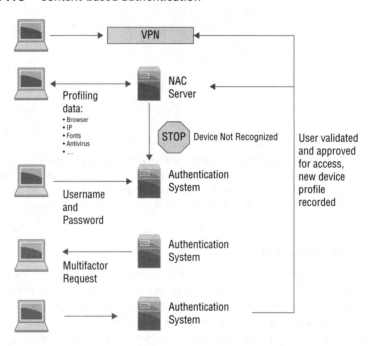

Organizations often use multiple types of contextual information to help to authenticate their users and may use it either in parallel with or in place of other MFA schemes.

Context-based authentication can be combined with multifactor authentication, allowing you to require users to provide enhanced authentication when additional verification is needed or desired.

- *Biometric factors*, sometimes called inherence factors, are something you are. Biometric identifiers include fingerprints, retina scans, voiceprints, and many other potential identifiers.

- A less common but sometimes useful factor is *location-based authentication*, which relies on a trusted method to determine whether a user is connecting from a trusted location. This can be accomplished using GPS data or can sometimes be done in a less secure manner using IP network–based location data.

MFA helps prevent attackers from authenticating using stolen credentials by making it significantly less likely they will have both (or more!) of the factors that are required to authenticate to a user account. If an attacker manages to phish a password or conducts a successful brute-force password guessing attack, they probably won't have access to that individual's cell phone or token or have access to a biometric factor like their fingerprint.

This security advantage means that MFA is increasingly considered a necessary default security control for systems and services that require a greater level of security than a simple password. Major e-commerce, banking, social networks, and other service providers now have two-factor functionality available, and an increasing number are requiring it by default. That doesn't mean that MFA is perfect; a lost phone or token, an insecure method of delivering a second factor, or a backup access method that allows users to bypass the second factor by talking to a support person can all result in a failure of a multifactor system.

The Problem with SMS

You have probably encountered SMS (text message)-based second factors in your daily life—Amazon, among many other major websites, uses it to verify your identity. The idea behind SMS as a second factor is that people will almost always have possession of their phone and that SMS provides a useful second factor when added to a password since it will prevent an attacker who only knows a password from logging in.

Unfortunately, SMS isn't a very secure protocol. In fact, NIST's Special Publication 800-63-3: Digital Authentication Guideline recommends that SMS be deprecated. Not only have successful attacks against SMS-based onetime passwords increased, but there are a number of ways that it can be successfully targeted with relative ease. One of the major areas that this is prevalent is via VoIP systems, where SMS messages are relatively easily stolen, or where the password that an attacker has may have been reused for a given user's account controls, allowing attackers to see SMS messages or redirect them.

Fortunately, reasonable alternatives exist in the form of authenticator applications like Google Authenticator that generate onetime codes on an ongoing basis or by using hardware fobs. Does this mean that SMS will stop being used? Probably not, but it does mean that security professionals need to be aware that SMS probably isn't suitable for high-security environments.

Identity as a Service

Identity as a Service (IDaaS) services provide authentication services, typically as a cloud-hosted service. IDaaS solutions typically provide features that include the following:

- Identity life-cycle management, which consists of technologies and processes to create, provision, and manage identities for systems, services, and even other cloud services

- Directory services, using LDAP, Active Directory, or another directory technology

- Access management with both authentication and authorization capabilities

- Single sign-on support via technologies like Security Assertion Markup Language (SAML) integrations, OAuth, or other standards

- Privileged account management and monitoring

- Reporting, auditing, and other management capabilities to provide oversight and visibility into the identity life cycle

 Identity as a Service can create new security concerns for an organization due to hosting an identity store or an authorization system outside its internal network. Understanding how the IDaaS provider handles and secures identity information, what their incident response practices and notification policy is, and performing due diligence when selecting a provider are all important parts of an IDaaS implementation.

Implementing a cloud-hosted identity service can mean significant changes to internal AAA system designs. Major elements include

- Deciding whether the organization will centralize their directory services or whether internal and third-party hosted directories will both exist

- Similarly, a decision must be made to centralize authentication or to federate multiple authentication and authorization systems

- The location for the organization's authoritative credential store may be local or cloud based

IDaaS is also has significant potential security benefits for organizations either that do not have a strong in-house identity management capability or that need to better integrate with third-party services. In organizations without strong internal identity practices, an IDaaS solution can provide a more secure, better managed, and more capable toolset. Automated monitoring and reporting services can also help identify security issues earlier than might occur with a noncentralized system.

Detecting Attacks and Security Operations

SIEM systems can be used to leverage identity information as well as the other types of security information we have discussed in this book. Using identity information provides the "who" when reviewing events and incidents, and when paired with other SIEM data and event logs, a complete view of what occurred, what the user, service, or account's behavior was, and human or automated analysis can determine whether the actions were appropriate.

Configuring a SIEM or other security monitoring device to look for the following types of events can provide significant security benefits:

- Privileged account usage
- Privilege changes and grants
- Account creation and modification
- Employee termination and terminated account usage
- Account life-cycle management events
- Separation-of-duty violations

Centralizing both IAM and user authentication and authorization systems helps ensure that accounts and privileges are well understood and managed throughout an organization. Attackers who can find a system that uses distinct accounts, or that does not centrally log authentication and authorization events, can far more easily take advantage of that system's isolation without their exploits being detected.

> Much like other security events, detecting identity attacks requires that organizations have well-defined security policies and standards for use of credentials and privileges. Once those are in place, baselines can be set, and anomaly detection can be implemented to sound the alarm when unexpected behaviors occur.

The final layer for any identity-based security system is active monitoring and administration by knowledgeable administrators. Having humans analyze the reports and other information provided by central monitoring and security systems will help identify events that might be missed by automated systems.

Understanding Federated Identity and Single Sign-On

The ability to federate identity, which is the process of linking an identity and its related attributes between multiple identity management systems, has become increasingly common. You have probably already seen or used a federated identity system if you use your Microsoft, Google, Facebook, or LinkedIn accounts to access sites that aren't hosted by those service providers. Each site allows use of their credentials, as well as a set of attributes by third-party sites.

Federated Identity Security Considerations

Federated identities move trust boundaries outside of your own organization, resulting in new concerns when designing, implementing, or using federated identity. This leads to the need to look at federated security from three points of view:

- As an *identity provider (IDP)*, members of a federation must provide identities, make assertions about those identities to relying parties, and release information to relying parties about identity holders. The identities and related data must be kept secure. Identities (and sometimes attributes) have to be validated to a level that fits the needs of the federation, and may have user-level controls applied to their release. In addition, service providers may be responsible for providing incident response coordination for the federation, communication between federation members, or other tasks due to their role in the federation.

- As the *relying party (RP)* or *service provider (SP)*, members of a federation must provide services to members of the federation, and should handle the data from both users and identity providers securely.

- The *consumer* or user of federated services may be asked to make decisions about attribute release, and to provide validation information about their identity claims to the IDP.

Each of these roles appears in Figure 11.10, which shows an example of the trust relationships and authentication flow that are required for federated identities to work.

FIGURE 11.10 Federated identity high-level design

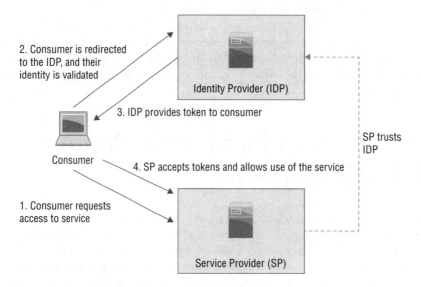

Federated identities can be very useful, but federations are only as strong as their weakest member's security. In 2004, one of the authors of this book was involved in the incident response process between members of a large-scale federation.

A successful hacker used compromised credentials to log into systems at various federation member sites. There, he used the credentials to access systems used for research efforts. Although the credentials he had were not administrative credentials, they did have local system access, allowing the attacker to identify and exploit local privilege escalation flaws. Once he had exploited those flaws, he replaced the ssh daemon running on the systems and captured credentials belonging to other federation members as well as local users. That provided him with enough new credentials to continue his exploits throughout other member sites.

The hacker was eventually tracked back through a series of systems around the world and was arrested after a massive coordinated effort between system administrators, security professionals, and law enforcement. The federation continued to operate, but the hacker's attacks led to additional security controls being put into place to ensure that future attacks of the same nature would be harder.

If you are part of a federation, you should consider how much you trust the organizational security practices and policies of the other federation members. That should drive the rights and access that you provide to holders of federated identities, as well as how you monitor their actions.

If you'd like to read more about this, the U.S. Federal Bureau of Investigation wrote a case study about the event that is available here: https://publish.illinois.edu/kericker/files/2013/09/NCDIR-TR-2008-01.pdf.

Federated Identity Design Choices

Using federated identity creates new security design concerns that you will have to plan and design around. If you are intending to leverage federated identity, the first question to answer is what trust model you want to use with the federated identity provider. Common providers of federated identity include Google, LinkedIn, and Amazon, but a broad range of commercial and private federations exist, including those operated by governments and higher education.

If you are using an existing federated identity provider such as Google, you are likely interested in allowing consumers to bring their own identity, which you will then map internally to your own privilege and rights structures. This model presumes that you do not care that a user is probably who they claim to be—instead, you only care that they own the account they are using.

In federation models that rely on verifiable identities, a greater level of assurance about the user's identity claims is needed, requiring additional trust between the federated identity provider(s) and the relying parties. Examples of this include research federations that have identity vetting and assertion requirements between multiple identity providers within the federation.

Trust decisions will also influence organizational decisions about manual provisioning versus automatic provisioning and deprovisioning. Integration with third-party federated identity services works best when provisioning occurs when users request access with immediate account provisioning occurring once the federated identity has been validated. Manual provisioning provides greater security by allowing for additional oversight but can cause delays for user access.

Provisioning can also involve attribute release, as relying parties in a federation need some basic information for a user account to provide authorization and to contact the user. The amount of information released by an identity provider can vary, from complete attribute release with all data about the account potentially available to very limited release such as the request shown in Figure 11.11.

FIGURE 11.11   Attribute release request for loginradius.com

Figure 11.11 shows an example of an attribute release request for loginradius.com, a site that supports both LinkedIn and Google with federated identities for their users. Implementation decisions for each of these technologies will vary, but design requirements for data handling, storage, and release of attributes are all important.

Similar concerns exist for self-service password resets and other user-initiated account options. Allowing users to change these settings typically results in a lower support load, but it may also allow attackers to use poor security questions or other methods to change user passwords and other data without the user being involved.

Once you have identified the appropriate trust requirements for the identities you intend to use for your federated identities, you will either have to adopt the underlying technologies that they use or select the technology that fits your needs. This is particularly true if you are federating your own organization, rather than using a federated identity provider like LinkedIn or Google. Technologies like SAML, OAuth, OpenID Connect, and Facebook Connect are all potentially part of the solutions you may adopt.

The type of federation you intend to implement also influences the security requirements you can expect, or may require, from federation members, including both identity providers and relying parties. In a loosely bound federation like sites using Google accounts, the underlying security model for Google accounts is not as significant of a concern since any owner of a Google account can typically use services that federate with Google.

In federations that require a higher trust level, vetting of the security practices of both identity providers and relying parties is necessary. Identity providers must validate the identity of the users they support, they must secure their credential store, and they should have a strong handling and notification process in place for security issues that might impact the federation's members. Relying parties need to ensure that their credential handling is properly secured, and that they are meeting any security or operational requirements that the federation presents.

Federated Identity Technologies

Four major technologies serve as the core of federated identity for current federations: SAML, ADFS, OAuth, and OpenID Connect. These technologies provide ways for identity providers to integrate with service providers in a secure manner without having to know details about how the service provider implements their service or their own use of the identity.

Table 11.1 compares OAuth2, OpenID, SAML, and ADFS, including their support for authorization and authentication, some of their most common potential security risks, and how they are often used.

You may wonder why OAuth2 is listed as "partial" for authentication. This is because OAuth2 isn't really an authentication protocol (although there are ways to perform authentication with it) and is typically paired with OpenID Connect to provide a complete solution.

TABLE 11.1 Comparison of federated identity technologies

	SAML	OpenID	OAuth2	ADFS
Authorization	Yes	No	Yes	Yes
Authentication	Yes	Yes	Partial	Yes
Potential Security Risks	Message confidentiality Protocol usage and processing risks Denial of service	Redirect manipulation Message confidentiality Replay attacks CSRF/XSS attacks Phishing	Redirect manipulation Message confidentiality Authorization or resource server impersonation	Token attacks (replay, capture)
Common uses	Enterprise authentication and authorization, particularly in Linux-centric environments	Authentication	API and service authorization	Enterprise authentication and authorization, particularly in Windows-centric environments

SAML

SAML is an XML-based language used to send authentication and authorization data between identity providers and service providers. It is frequently used to enable single sign-on for web applications and services because SAML allows identity providers to make assertions about principals to service providers so that they can make decisions about that user. SAML allows authentication, attribute, and authorization decision statements to be exchanged.

Figure 11.12 shows a very simple sample SAML authentication process. In this flow, a user attempts to use a SAML authenticated service and is referred to the identity provider to authenticate their identity. After a successful login, the browser returns to the relying party with an appropriate SAML response, which it verifies. With these steps done, the user can now use the application they initially wanted to access.

 OWASP provides a comprehensive SAML security cheat sheet at https://www.owasp.org/index.php/SAML_Security_Cheat_Sheet.

FIGURE 11.12   Simple SAML transaction

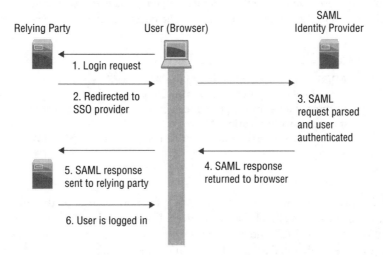

ADFS

Active Directory Federation Services (ADFS) is the Microsoft answer to federation. ADFS provides authentication and identity information as *claims* to third-party partner sites. Partner sites then use *trust policies* to match claims to claims supported by a service, and then it uses those claims to make authorization decisions.

ADFS uses a similar process to an OAuth authentication process:

1. The user attempts to access an ADFS–enabled web application hosted by a resource partner.

2. The ADFS web agent on the partner's web server checks for the ADFS cookie; if it is there, access is granted. If the cookie is not there, the user is sent to the partner's ADFS server.

3. The resource partner's ADFS checks for a SAML token from the account partner, and if it's not found, ADFS performs home realm discovery.

4. Home realm discovery identifies the federation server associated with the user and then authenticates the user via that home realm.

5. The account partner then provides a security token with identity information in the form of claims, and sends the user back to the resource partner's ADFS server.

6. Validation then occurs normally and uses its trust policy to map the account partner claims to claims the web application supports.

7. A new SAML token is created by ADFS that contains the resource partner claims, and this cookie is stored on the user's computer. The user is then redirected to the web application, where the application can read the cookie and allow access supported by the claims.

> ADFS can be controlled using the ADFS MMC snap-in, adfs.msc. The ADFS console allows you to add resource partners and account partners, map partner claims, manage account stores, and configure web applications that support federation. Microsoft provides a useful overview of ADFS at https://msdn.microsoft.com/en-us/library/bb897402.aspx.

OAuth

The OAuth 2.0 protocol provides an authorization framework designed to allow third-party applications to access HTTP-based services. It was developed via the Internet Engineering Task Force (IETF) and supports web clients, desktops, mobile devices, and a broad range of other embedded and mobile technologies, as well as the service providers that they connect to. OAuth provides access delegation, allowing service providers to perform actions for you.

OAuth flows recognize four parties:

Clients   The applications that users want to use

Resource Owners   The end users

Resource Servers   Servers provided by a service that the resource owner wants the application to use

Authorization Servers   Servers owned by the identity provider

Figure 11.13 shows how authentication flows work with OAuth. In this chain, the client is attempting to access a third-party service. The third-party site, which is the consumer, is directed to a service provider to authenticate. To request authentication, the consumer sends a request for a request token. The service provider validates the user's identity, grants a request token, and then directs the consumer back to the service provider. There, the service provider obtains the user authorization and sends the user to the third-party site. The consumer requests an access token, the service provider grants it, and then the consumer can access resources.

OpenID Connect

OpenID Connect is often paired with OAuth to provide authentication. It allows the authorization server to issue to issue an ID token in addition to the authorization token provided by OAuth. This allows services to know that the action was authorized and that the user authenticated with the identity provider.

FIGURE 11.13   OAuth authentication process

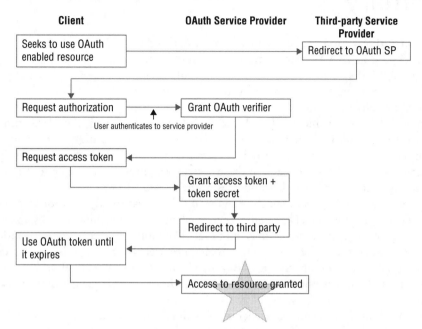

Federation Incident Response

Incident response with federated identities can be a complex topic. The amount of information released by identity providers, service providers, and relying parties will vary due to the contractual agreements (if any!) or the federation operating agreements between them.

Building a response plan for federated identity varies based on the role your organization holds in the federation:

- Identity providers are typically responsible for notifying account owners and may be responsible for notifying relying parties. Incident response policies need to envision compromise of the identity provider itself, as well as what events such as a required password reset for all users would entail.

- Service providers need to determine what their response would be if the identity provider were compromised, as well as a range of smaller incidents, including compromise of their own authorization systems or a limited compromise of accounts provided by the identity provider.

Consumers must consider what the impact would be if their accounts were inaccessible—if they used a Google account for many sites, and Google were compromised or unavailable, what would they do?

As with all incident response policies and procedures, a strong communications plan and testing of the response plan itself, either via practice scenarios or walk-throughs, is strongly recommended.

Summary

Identity and authorization are key elements in a security design. Authentication, authorization, and accounting (AAA) systems are part of an identity and access management (IAM) infrastructure. IAM systems manage user account life cycles, as well as rights and privileges, and provide oversight of identity to ensure that accounts and the rights they have are not misused or abused.

Common AAA systems include LDAP directory servers, Kerberos, RADIUS, and Active Directory. In addition, federated identity systems are increasingly important as organizations connect with cloud-hosted services using onsite and third-party identity and authorization services. Securing each of these systems requires careful configuration and understanding of its security models and uses in the organization.

Attackers target identity and identity systems to gain access to organizational resources and data. They target personnel to acquire their credentials via phishing attacks, malware, and social engineering. At the same time, endpoints like mobile devices and workstations, as well as servers, are targeted for compromise to acquire user IDs, passwords, or even entire identity stores. Applications and services may also be targeted, due to weaknesses in their implementation of authorization or authentication technologies or due to compromised credentials.

Despite the many attacks aimed at identity, it can also provide a useful security layer. Centralized management of authentication and authorization combined with logging and auditing can help prevent attacks, or identify attacks as they occur. Behavioral analysis, policy-based monitoring, and other techniques used in SIEM and other security technologies can be applied to identity systems to detect issues and attacks.

Federated identity adds new complexity to identity-based security design. Federated identity may be as simple as allowing users to bring their own account, thus simplifying account maintenance for the relying organization, but it can also be a complex trust-based relationship with broad attribute release and rights based on those attributes. Responding to federation-based incidents requires an understanding of the trust relationships, privileges, and reporting relationships within the federation.

Exam Essentials

Identities are the core of authentication, authorization, and accounting (AAA) systems. AAA systems authenticate users by using a user ID, password, or other factors. Central management of identities is handled by identity and access management (IAM) systems. IAM systems create, store, manage, and monitor identities and authorization through organizations. Key elements of IAM systems include directories, authentication systems and protocols, single sign-on and shared authentication services, and federated identity systems.

Threats to identities are widespread.   Identity threats target not only the credentials issued to users and services, but also identity management systems, the protocols and applications used to manage and consume identity data, and the account life cycle itself. Personnel are targets of phishing and social engineering attacks, and the roles and privileges they have are targeted for abuse. Malware and compromises target servers, systems, and devices. Applications and services are targeted via misconfigurations, protocol vulnerabilities, design issues, and compromise.

Identity is a critical security layer.   The account life cycle is the core of identity-based security and relies on secure creation, provisioning, maintenance, and removal at the end of the account's life to ensure security. The rights and privileges that accounts are assigned require strong policy-based management and oversight, as well as monitoring to avoid privilege creep. Credential and password management, and the use of multifactor authentication, are important due to increased targeting of credentials by advanced attackers.

Federated identity technologies are broadly used for cloud services and interorganizational authentication and authorization.   Identity providers provide both identities and authentication services to federations. Relying parties and service providers use identities to authorize users to make use of their services or applications. Consumers may use social identities like Google or Facebook credentials to access a broad range of services using protocols like OpenID Connect and OAuth. Incident response in federations requires additional preparation to ensure that new models for reporting, notification, and handling are ready when needed.

Lab Exercises

Activity 11.1: Federated Security Scenario

In this exercise, you will be provided with two different federated identity scenarios. For each, you should research the technology or situation described and then write a written recommendation to handle the issue described.

Part 1: Google OAuth Integration

Example Corp.'s development team has implemented an OAuth integration with Google. The internal development team has written their own libraries for the company's OAuth endpoint and has implemented their server via HTTP between Example Corp.'s servers.

What security issues would you identify with this design, and what fixes would you recommend?

Part 2: High Security Federation Incident Response

Example Corp. is considering using Facebook Login to allow users to bring their own identity for its customer support website. This would remove the need for Example Corp. to handle its own identity management in most cases and is seen as an attractive option to remove expensive user support this type of account.

Answer the following questions:

1. What recommendations and advice would you provide to the implementation team?
2. What should Example Corp.'s incident response plan include to handle issues involving Facebook Login?
3. Does using Facebook Login create more or less risk for Example Corp.? Why?

Part 3: Analyze Your Responses

To analyze your response to Part 1, use the OWASP Authentication cheat sheet found at `https://www.owasp.org/index.php/Authentication_Cheat_Sheet#OAuth`. You will find tips on OAuth and application communications.

To analyze your response to Part 2, review federation-aware incident response policies like `https://spaces.internet2.edu/display/InCFederation/Federated+Security+ Incident+Response` and `https://www.btaa.org/docs/default-source/technology/ federated_security_incident_response.pdf`.

Activity 11.2: Onsite Identity Issues Scenario

In this exercise, you will be provided with two different local identity scenarios. For each, you should research the technology or situation described, and then write a written recommendation to handle the issue described. In Part 3, you will review your answers and look for potential flaws that remain.

Part 1: Emergency Privilege Escalation

At Example Corp., administrative accounts are created and managed using a central identity and access management suite. This suite, as well as the company's central AAA servers, are hosted in redundant datacenters, and site-to-site VPNs normally connect those datacenters to multiple locations around the country.

Example Corp.'s systems engineering department recently dealt with a major Internet connectivity outage, which also resulted in engineers being unable to log into the systems at the sites where they worked. This meant that they were unable to work to fix the issues.

The engineers have requested that you identify a secure way to provide emergency, on-demand privileged access to local servers when the central AAA services are unavailable. You have been asked to provide a solution to central IT management that is both secure and flexible enough to allow authentication for network devices, servers, and workstations.

Part 2: Managing Privilege Creep

A recent audit of Example Corp.'s file shares shows that many long-term employees have significantly broader rights to files and folders than their current roles should allow. In fact, in some cases employees could see sensitive data that could result in negative audit findings in a pending external audit.

How would you recommend that Example Corp. handle both the current issue of privilege creep and the ongoing problem of ensuring that it does not occur in the future without seriously disrupting the company's operations?

Part 3: Review

1. Review your recommendations to ensure that confidentiality, integrity, and availability are maintained. Did you provide a solution that covers each of these three areas?

2. Does your solution cover each of these areas (if appropriate?)
   - Personnel
   - Endpoint devices
   - Servers
   - Services and applications
   - Roles and groups

3. If you were asked to conduct a penetration test of an organization that had implemented your recommendations, how would you approach attacking your solution?

Activity 11.3: Identity and Access Management Terminology

Match each of the following terms to the correct description.

TACACS+	LDAP is deployed in this role.
Identity	An XML-based protocol used to exchange authentication and authorization data.
ADFS	An open standard for authorization used for websites and applications.
Privilege creep	A common AAA system for network devices.
Directory service	This issue occurs when accounts gain more rights over time due to role changes.
OAuth 2.0	The set of claims made about an account holder.
SAML	Microsoft's identity federation service.
RADIUS	A Cisco-designed authentication protocol.

Review Questions

1. Lauren is designing a multifactor authentication system for her company. She has decided to use a passphrase, a time-based code generator, and a PIN to provide additional security. How many distinct factors will she have implemented when she is done?

    A. One

    B. Two

    C. Three

    D. Four

2. What technology is best suited to protecting LDAP authentication from compromise?

    A. SSL

    B. MD5

    C. TLS

    D. SHA1

3. During an incident response process, Michelle discovers that the administrative credentials for her organization's Kerberos server have been compromised and that attackers have issued themselves a TGT without an expiration date. What is this type of ticket called?

    A. A master ticket

    B. A golden ticket

    C. A KDC

    D. A MGT

4. Which of the following technologies is NTLM associated with?

    A. SAML

    B. Active Directory

    C. OAuth

    D. RADIUS

5. Jim was originally hired into the helpdesk at his current employer but has since then moved into finance. During a rights audit, it is discovered that he still has the ability to change passwords for other staff members. What is this issue called?

    A. Rights mismanagement

    B. Least privilege

    C. Permission misalignment

    D. Privilege creep

6. What type of attack occurs when an attacker takes advantage of OAuth open redirects to take on the identity of a legitimate user?

   A. Impersonation

   B. Session hijacking

   C. MiTM

   D. Protocol analysis

7. 2013's Yahoo breach resulted in almost 1 billion MD5 hashed passwords being exposed. What user behavior creates the most danger when this type of breach occurs?

   A. Insecure password reset questions

   B. Use of federated credentials

   C. Password reuse

   D. Unencrypted password storage

8. Authentication that uses the IP address, geographic location, and time of day to help validate the user is known as what type of authentication?

   A. Token based

   B. Context based

   C. NAC

   D. System-data contextual

9. Which of the following is not a common attack against Kerberos?

   A. Administrator account attacks

   B. Ticket reuse attacks

   C. Open redirect based attacks

   D. TGT focused attacks

10. Which of the following technologies is not a shared authentication technology?

   A. OpenID Connect

   B. LDAP

   C. OAuth

   D. Facebook Connect

11. Angela is concerned about attackers enumerating her organization's LDAP directory. What LDAP control should she recommend to help limit the impact of this type of data gathering?

   A. LDAP replication

   B. ACLs

   C. Enable TLS

   D. Use MD5 for storage of secrets

12. What security design is best suited to protect authentication and authorization for a network that uses TACACs+?

   A. Use TACACS+ built-in encryption to protect traffic

   B. Implement TACACS++

   C. Enable accounting services to detect issues

   D. Route management traffic over a dedicated network

13. Jason has user rights on his Linux workstation, but he wants to read his department's financial reports, which he knows are stored in a directory that only administrators can access. He executes a local exploit, which gives him the ability to act as root. What type of attack is this?

   A. Privilege escalation

   B. Zero day

   C. Rootkit

   D. Session hijacking

14. Chris is responsible for monitoring his organization's file shares and security and has discovered that employees are consistently retaining access to files after they change positions. Where should he focus his efforts if his organization's account life cycle matches the following?

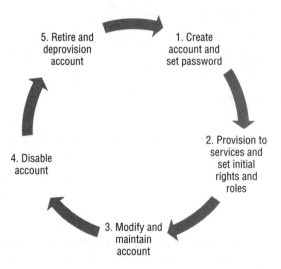

   A. Step 1

   B. Step 2

   C. Step 3

   D. Step 5

15. Which of the following methods is not an effective method for preventing brute-force password guessing attacks via login portals?

    A. CAPTCHAs

    B. Returning an HTTP error

    C. Login throttling

    D. Failed login account lockout

16. Which party in a federated identity service model makes assertions about identities to service providers?

    A. RPs

    B. CDUs

    C. IDPs

    D. APs

17. Which of the following reasons is not a reason to avoid using SMS as a second factor for authentication?

    A. SMS via VoIP is easy to target.

    B. SMS is insecure.

    C. SMS cannot send unique tokens.

    D. VoIP management often uses the same password as the account.

18. Ben's successful attack on an authenticated user required him to duplicate the cookies that the web application put in place to identify the legitimate user. What type of attack did Ben conduct?

    A. Impersonation

    B. MiTM

    C. Session hijacking

    D. Privilege escalation

19. What type of attack can be executed against a RADIUS shared secret if attackers have valid credentials including a known password and can monitor RADIUS traffic on the network?

    A. A brute force attack

    B. A dictionary attack

    C. A pass-the-hash attack

    D. A counter-RADIUS attack

20. Michelle has a security token that her company issues to her. What type of authentication factor does she have?

    A. Biometric

    B. Possession

    C. Knowledge

    D. Inherence

Chapter 12

Software Development Security

THE COMPTIA CYBERSECURITY ANALYST+ EXAM OBJECTIVES COVERED IN THIS CHAPTER INCLUDE:

Domain 4: Security Architecture and Tool Sets

✓ **4.4 Given a scenario, use application security best practices while participating in the Software Development Life Cycle (SDLC).**

Software ranging from customer-facing applications and services to smaller programs, down to the smallest custom scripts written to support business needs, is everywhere in our organizations. The process of designing, creating, supporting, and maintaining that software is known as the software development life cycle (SDLC). As a security practitioner, you need to understand the SLDC and its security implications to ensure that the software your organization uses is well written and secure throughout its lifespan.

In this chapter you will learn about major software development life cycle models and the reasons for choosing them, with examples that include the Waterfall and Spiral models as well as Agile development methods like Scrum and Extreme Programming. Next you will review software development security best practices and guidelines on secure software coding. As part of this, you will see how software is tested and reviewed and how these processes fit into the SDLC. You will learn about code review and inspection methodologies like pair programming and over-the-shoulder code reviews as well as Fagan inspection that can help ensure that the code your organization puts into production is ready to face both users and attackers.

Finally, you will learn how software security testing is conducted during development using code analysis as well as techniques like fuzzing, fault injection, and mutation. In addition, you will examine web application vulnerability and security testing tools and techniques and how they can be applied to protect your organization's data and systems.

Understanding the Software Development Life Cycle

The SDLC describes the steps in a model for software development throughout its life. As shown in Figure 12.1, it maps software creation from an idea to requirements gathering and analysis to design, coding, testing, and rollout. Once software it in production, it also includes user training, maintenance, and decommissioning at the end of the software package's useful life.

Software development does not always follow a formal model, but most enterprise development for major applications does follow most, if not all, of these phases. In some cases, developers may even use elements of an SLDC model without realizing it!

FIGURE 12.1   High-level SDLC view

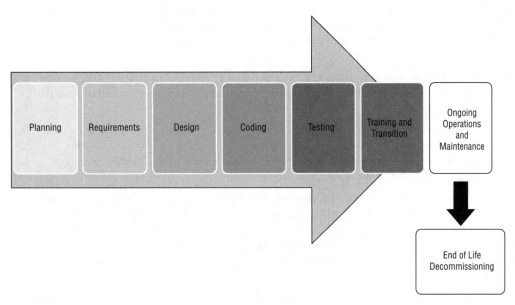

The SDLC is useful for organizations and for developers because it provides a consistent framework to structure workflow and to provide planning for the development process. Despite these advantages, simply picking an SDLC model to implement may not always be the best choice. Each SDLC model has certain types of work and projects that it fits better than others, making choosing an SDLC model that fits the work an important part of the process.

> In this chapter we will refer to the output of the SDLC as "software" or as an "application," but the SDLC may be run for a service, a system, or other output. Feel free to substitute the right phrasing that is appropriate for you.

Software Development Phases

Regardless of which SDLC or process is chosen by your organization, a few phases appear in most SDLC models:

1. The *feasibility* phase is where initial investigations into whether the effort should occur are conducted. Feasibility also looks at alternative solutions and high-level costs for each solution proposed. It results in a recommendation with a plan to move forward.

2. Once an effort has been deemed feasible, it will typically go through an *analysis and requirements definition* phase. In this phase customer input is sought to determine what the desired functionality is, what the current system or application currently does and what it doesn't do, and what improvements are desired. Requirements may be ranked to determine which are most critical to the success of the project.

Security requirements definition is an important part of the analysis and requirements definition phase. It ensures that the application is designed to be secure and that secure coding practices are used.

3. The *design* phase includes design for functionality, architecture, integration points and techniques, dataflows, business processes, and any other elements that require design consideration.

4. The actual coding of the application occurs during the *development* phase. This phase may be involve testing of parts of the software, including *unit testing* (testing of small components individually to ensure they function properly) and *code analysis*.

5. While some testing is likely to occur in the development phase, formal testing with customers or others outside of the development team occurs in the *testing and integration* phase. Individual units or software components are integrated and then tested to ensure proper functionality. In addition, connections to outside services, data sources, and other integration may occur during this phase. During this phase *user acceptance testing* (UAT) occurs to ensure that the users of the software are satisfied with its functionality.

6. The important task of ensuring that the end users are trained on the software and that the software has entered general use occurs in the *training and transition* phase. This phase is sometimes called the acceptance, installation, and deployment phase.

7. Once a project reaches completion, the application or service will enter what is usually the longest phase: *ongoing operations and maintenance*. This phase includes patching, updating, minor modifications, and other work that goes into daily support.

8. The *disposition* phase occurs when a product or system reaches the end of its life. Although disposition is often ignored in the excitement of developing new products, it is an important phase for a number of reasons: shutting down old products can produce cost savings, replacing existing tools may require specific knowledge or additional effort, and data and systems may need to be preserved or properly disposed of.

The order of the phases may vary, with some progressing in a simple linear fashion and others taking an iterative or parallel approach. You will still see some form of each of these phases in successful software life cycles.

Development, Test, and Production—Oh, My!

Many organizations use multiple environments for their software and systems development and testing. The names and specific purposes for these systems vary depending organizational needs, but the most common environments are as follows:

- *Development,* typically used for developers or other "builders" to do their work. Some workflows provide each developer with their own development environment; others use a shared development environment.

- *Test,* an environment where the software or systems can be tested without impacting the production environment. In some schemes, this is preproduction, whereas in others a separate preproduction staging environment is used.

- *Production,* the live system. Software, patches, and other changes that have been tested and approved move to production

Change management processes are typically followed to move through these environments. This provides accountability and oversight and may be required for audit or compliance purposes as well.

Software Development Models

The SDLC can be approached in many ways, and over time a number of formal models have been created to help provide a common framework for development. While formal SDLC models can be very detailed, with specific practices, procedures, and documentation, many organizations choose the elements of one or more models that best fit their organizational style, workflow, and requirements.

Waterfall

The *Waterfall* methodology is a sequential model in which each phase is followed by the next phase. Phases do not overlap, and each logically leads to the next. A typical six-phase Waterfall process is shown in Figure 12.2. In Phase 1, requirements are gathered and documented. Phase 2 involves analysis intended to build business rules and models. In Phase 3, a software architecture is designed, and coding and integration of the software occurs in Phase 4. Once the software is complete, Phase 5 occurs, with testing and debugging being completed in this phase. Finally the software enters an operational phase, with support, maintenance, and other operational activities happening on an ongoing basis.

FIGURE 12.2 The Waterfall SDLC model

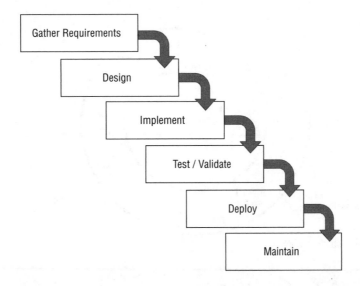

Waterfall has been replaced in many organizations because it is seen as relatively inflexible, but it remains in use for complex systems. Since Waterfall is not highly responsive to changes and does not account for internal iterative work, it is typically recommended for development efforts that involve a fixed scope and a known timeframe for delivery and that are using a stable, well-understood technology platform.

Spiral

The *Spiral* model uses the linear development concepts from the Waterfall model and adds an iterative process that revisits four phases multiple times during the development life cycle to gather more detailed requirements, design functionality guided by the requirements, and build based on the design. In addition, the Spiral model puts significant emphasis on risk assessment as part of the SDLC, reviewing risks multiple times during the development process.

The Spiral model shown in Figure 12.3 uses four phases, which it repeatedly visits throughout the development life cycle:

1. Identification, or requirements gathering, which initially gathers business requirements, system requirements, and more detailed requirements for subsystems or modules as the process continues.

2. Design, conceptual, architectural, logical, and sometimes physical or final design.

3. Build, which produces an initial proof of concept and then further development releases until the final production build is produced.

4. Evaluation, which involves risk analysis for the development project intended to monitor the feasibility of delivering the software from a technical and managerial viewpoint. As the development cycle continues, this phase also involves customer testing and feedback to ensure customer acceptance.

FIGURE 12.3   The Spiral SDLC model

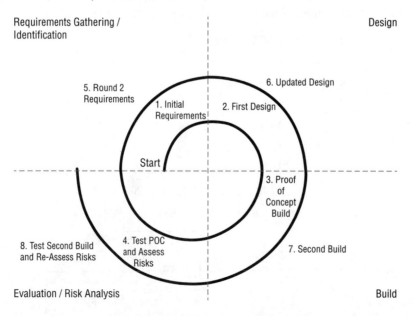

The Spiral model provides greater flexibility to handle changes in requirements as well as external influences such as availability of customer feedback and development staff. It also allows the software development life cycle to start earlier in the process than Waterfall does. Because Spiral revisits its process, it is possible for this model to result in rework or to identify design requirements later in the process that require a significant design change due to more detailed requirements coming to light.

> Because Spiral does not have a defined end, it can result in an infinite loop of customer change requests and clarifications. The same flexibility that makes Spiral useful when tackling projects without completely defined objectives can also be a trap without strong management.

Agile

Agile software development is an iterative and incremental process, rather than the linear processes that Waterfall and Spiral use. Agile is rooted in the Manifesto for Agile Software Development, a document that has four basic premises:

- Individuals and interactions are more important than processes and tools.
- Working software is preferable to comprehensive documentation.
- Customer collaboration replaces contract negotiation.
- Responding to change is key, rather than following a plan.

If you are used to a Waterfall or Spiral development process, Agile is a significant departure from the planning, design, and documentation-centric approaches that Agile's predecessors use. Agile methods tend to break work up into smaller units, allowing work to be done more quickly and with less up-front planning. It focuses on adapting to needs, rather than predicting them, with major milestones identified early in the process but subject to change as the project continues to develop.

Work is typically broken up into short working sessions, called *sprints*, that can last days to a few weeks. Figure 12.4 shows a simplified view of an Agile project methodology with multiple sprints conducted. When the developers and customer agree that the task is done or when the time allocated for the sprints is complete, the development effort is completed.

FIGURE 12.4   Agile sprints

The Agile methodology is based on 12 principles:

- Ensure customer satisfaction via early and continuous delivery of the software.

- Welcome changing requirements, even late in the development process.

- Deliver working software frequently (in weeks rather than months).

- Ensure daily cooperation between developers and businesspeople.

- Projects should be built around motivated individuals who get the support, trust, and environment they need to succeed.

- Face-to-face conversations are the most efficient way to convey information inside the development team.

- Progress is measured by having working software.

- Development should be done at a sustainable pace that can be maintained on an ongoing basis.

- Pay continuous attention to technical excellence and good design.

- Simplicity—the art of maximizing the amount of work not done—is essential.

- The best architectures, requirements, and designs emerge from self-organizing teams.

- Teams should reflect on how to become more effective and then implement that behavior at regular intervals.

These principles drive an SDLC process that is less formally structured than Spiral or Waterfall but that has many opportunities for customer feedback and revision. It can react more nimbly to problems and will typically allow faster customer feedback—an advantage when security issues are discovered.

Agile development uses a number of specialized terms:

- *Backlogs* are lists of features or tasks that are required to complete a project.

- *Planning poker* is a tool for estimation and planning used in Agile development processes. Estimators are given cards with values for the amount of work required for a task. Estimators are asked to estimate, and each reveals their "bid" on the task. This is done until agreement is reached, with the goal to have estimators reach the same estimate through discussion.

- *Timeboxing*, a term that describes the use of timeboxes. Timeboxes are a previously agreed-upon time that a person or team uses to work on a specific goal. This limits the time to work on a goal to the timeboxed time, rather than allowing work until completion. Once a timebox is over, the completed work is assessed to determine what needs to occur next.

- *User stories* are collected to describe high-level user requirements. A user story might be "Users can change their password via the mobile app," which would provide direction for estimation and planning for an Agile work session.

- *Velocity tracking* is conducted by adding up the estimates for the current sprint's effort and then comparing that to what was completed. This tells the team whether they are on track, faster, or slower than expected.

Taking Programming to an Extreme

Extreme programming is a type of Agile development that focuses on shorter development cycles. It often involves other techniques like pair programming, unit testing of every component of the code, and simplifying the management and communications processes around the development effort.

Like each of the SDLC models described here, extreme programming uses a number of phases to organize its work: coding, testing, listening, and designing. It also specifically values communication, simplicity, feedback, respect, and courage.

Ideas that were part of the extreme programming playbook have continued to be used in Agile efforts, and despite other SDLC models growing in popularity, extreme programming is still in use and evolving.

Rapid Application Development

The RAD (Rapid Application Development) model is an iterative process that relies on building prototypes. Unlike many other methods, there is no planning phase; instead, planning is done as the software is written. RAD relies on functional components of the code being developed in parallel and then integrated to produce the finished product. Much like Agile, RAD can provide a highly responsive development environment.

RAD involves five phases, as shown in Figure 12.5.

- *Business modeling*, which focuses on the business model, including what information is important, how it is processed, and what the business process should involve

- *Data modeling*, including gathering and analyzing all datasets and objects needed for the effort and defining their attributes and relationships

- *Process modeling* for dataflows based on the business model, as well as process descriptions for how data is handled

- *Application generation* through coding and use of automated tools to convert data and process models into prototypes

- *Testing and turnover*, which focuses on the dataflow and interfaces between components since prototypes are tested at each iteration for functionality

---

RAD is best suited to development efforts where the application can be modularized and where support for automated code generation exists. It works better for efforts where the ability to handle change is required and where the customer or experts with strong business process domain knowledge are available.

FIGURE 12.5   Rapid Application Development prototypes

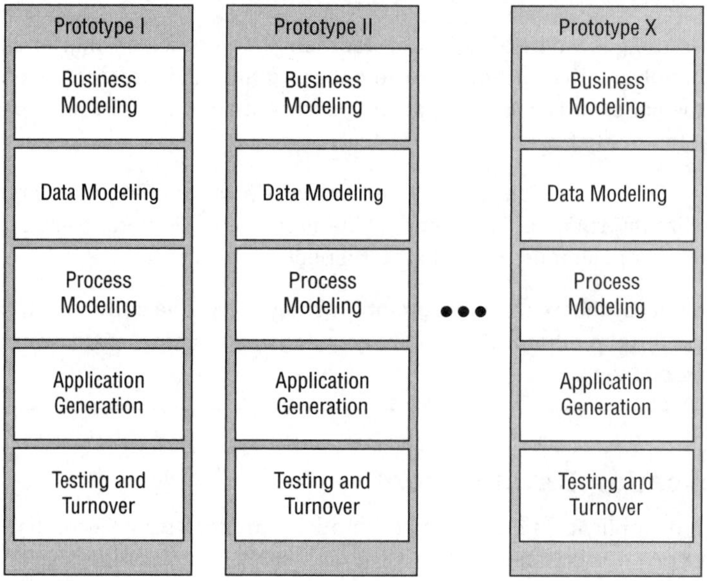

Other Models

While we have discussed some of the most common models for software development, others exist, including:

- The V model, which is an extension of the Waterfall model that pairs a testing phase with each development stage. Each phase starts only after the testing for the previous phase is done. Thus, at the requirements phase the requirements are reviewed (or tested), and at design phase, a test phase for the system design is completed before starting coding.

- The Big Bang SDLC model relies on no planning or process. Instead, it focuses on making resources available and simply starting coding based on requirements as they are revealed. Obviously the Big Bang model doesn't scale, but it is a common model for individual developers working on their own code.

New SDLC models spread quickly and often influence existing models with new ideas and workflows. Understanding the benefits and drawbacks of each SDLC model can help you provide input at the right times to ensure that the software that is written meets the security requirements of your organization.

Designing and Coding for Security

Participating in the SDLC as a security professional provides significant opportunities to improve the security of applications. The first chance to help with software security is in the requirements gathering and design phases when security can be built in as part of the requirements, and then designed in based on those requirements. Later, during the development process, secure coding techniques, code review, and testing can improve the quality and security of the code that is developed.

During the testing phase, fully integrated software can be tested using tools like web application security scanners or penetration testing techniques. This also provides the foundation for ongoing security operations by building the baseline for future security scans and regression testing during patching and updates. Throughout these steps, it helps to understand the common security issues that developers face, create, and discover.

Common Software Development Security Issues

A multitude of development styles, languages, frameworks, and other variables may be involved in the creation of an application, but many of the same security issues are the same regardless of which you use. In fact, despite many development frameworks and languages providing security features, the same security problems continue to appear in applications all the time! Fortunately, a number of common best practices are available that you can use to help ensure software security for your organization.

 Real World Scenario

Removing the Seatbelts and Airbags

A number of years ago, one of the authors of this book was hired to perform a web application security test for a new website. During testing, the website proved to be massively vulnerable to a multitude of common issues, ranging from SQL injection to session hijacking. Many of the issues that were found should have been prevented by default by the web application development environment that the team who built the website was using. In fact, signs pointed to those controls being purposefully removed instead of inadvertently disabled.

When asked about why those controls weren't there, the development team responded that "those controls slowed us down" and "we can build in better security ourselves." In essence, the team had removed every built-in safety feature that they had gotten for free by choosing the development tools they had. The reason that "Leverage Security Frameworks and Libraries" is on the OWASP top 10 controls is to prevent issues like this!

Secure Coding Best Practices

The best practices for producing secure code will vary slightly depending on the application, its infrastructure and backend design, and what framework or language it is written in. Despite that, many of the same development, implementation, and design best practices apply to most applications. These include the following:

- *Have a secure coding policy* to serve as a foundation for secure development practices and standards.

- *Risk assessment* is important to understand what risks the application faces and how to prioritize remediation of those issues. Continuous assessment is recommended for applications using regularly scheduled testing tools that can inform the application risk assessment process.

- *User input validation* helps prevent a wide range of problems, from cross-site scripting to SQL injection attacks.

- *Web application firewalls* can prevent attacks against vulnerable applications and offer a line of defense for applications that don't have an available patch or that cannot be taken offline for patching.

- *Error message management*, particularly ensuring that error messages do not leak information, is important to ensure that attackers can't use error messages to learn about your applications or systems.

- *Database security* at both the application and database can help ensure that data leaks don't occur.

- *Securing sensitive information* by encrypting it or storing it using appropriate secure mechanisms (like password hashes for passwords) helps ensure that a breach of a system does not result in broader issues.

- *Ensuring availability* by performing load and stress testing and designing the application infrastructure to be scalable can prevent outages and may limit the impact of denial-of-service attacks.

- *Monitoring and logging* should be enabled, centralized, and set to identify both application and security issues.

- *Use multifactor authentication* to help limit the impact of credential compromises.

- *Use secure session management* to ensure that user sessions cannot be hijacked by attackers or that session issues don't cause confusion among users.

- *Cookie management* is important for web applications that rely on cookie-based information.

- *Secure all network traffic*—encryption of all traffic is a viable option with modern hardware, and it prevents network-based attacks from easily capturing data that could be sensitive.

Securing Your Application Infrastructure

The Cybersecurity Analyst+ exam objectives mention the Center for Internet Security's system design recommendations and benchmarks, which can be found at `https://learn.cisecurity.org/benchmarks`. The CIS provides extensive configuration benchmarks for web servers, database servers, and web browsers as well as server and desktop operating systems, but they don't currently provide secure coding or SDLC guides.

In the context of the CSA+ exam, the process of securing the underlying infrastructure is important to providing a secure application. This configuration generally occurs as part of the deployment phase in the SDLC, with ongoing security operations occurring as part of the maintenance and operations phase.

One of the best resources for secure coding practices is the Open Web Application Security Project (OWASP). OWASP is the home of a broad community of developers and security practitioners, and it hosts many community-developed standards, guides, and best practice documents, as well as a multitude of open source tools. OWASP provides a regularly updated list of proactive controls that is useful to review not only as a set of useful best practices, but also as a way to see how web application security threats change from year to year.

Here are OWASP's top proactive controls for 2016 with brief descriptions:

Verify for Security Early and Often　Implement security throughout the development process.

Parameterize Queries　Prebuild SQL queries to prevent injection.

Encode Data　Remove special characters.

Validate All Inputs　Treat user input as untrusted and filter appropriately.

Implement Identity and Authentication Controls　Use multifactor authentication, secure password storage and recovery, and session handling.

Implement Appropriate Access Controls　Require all requests to go through access control checks, deny by default, and apply the principle of least privilege.

Protect Data　Use encryption in transit and at rest.

Implement Logging and Intrusion Detection　This helps detect problems and allows investigation after the fact.

Leverage Security Frameworks and Libraries　Preexisting security capabilities can make securing applications easier.

Error and Exception Handling　Errors should not provide sensitive data, and applications should be tested to ensure that they handle problems gracefully.

You can find OWASP's Proactive Controls list at `https://www.owasp.org/index.php/OWASP_Proactive_Controls`, and a useful quick reference guide to secure coding practices is available at `https://www.owasp.org/index.php/OWASP_Secure_Coding_Practices_-_Quick_Reference_Guide`.

In addition to the resources provided by OWASP, SANS maintains a list of the top 25 software errors in three categories:

- *Insecure Interaction Between Components*, which includes issues like SQL and operating system command injection, file upload path issues, cross-site request forgery, and cross-site scripting

- *Risky Resource Management* problems, which deal with buffer overflows, path traversal attacks, and other ways that software fails to properly guard system resources

- *Porous Defenses*, including not using or misuse of defensive techniques like overly permissive rights, hard-coded credentials, missing authorization and authentication, and use of unsalted hashes.

Unfortunately, the SANS/CIS top 25 resource has not been updated since 2011. OWASP's list is regularly updated, but it is web-centric.

Top listings of common controls and problems are useful as a reminder, but understanding the set of controls that are appropriate to your environment is critical. A thorough assessment with developers and other experts who understand not only the business requirements and process but also the development language or framework will help keep your organization secure.

Application Testing

Application testing can be conducted in one of four ways: as a scan using a tool, via an automated vulnerability scanner, through manual penetration testing, or via code review. OWASP's Code Review guide notes that code reviews provide the best insight into all the common issues that applications face: availability, business logic, compliance, privacy, and vulnerabilities. Combining code review with a penetration test based on the code review's output (which then drives further code review, known as a 360 review) can provide even more insight into an application's security.

Information Security and the SDLC

Software defects can have a significant impact on security, but creating secure software requires more than just security scans and reviewing code when it is complete. Information security needs to be involved at each part of the SDLC process.

1. During the *Feasibility phase* security practitioners may be asked to participate in initial assessments or cost evaluations.

2. The *Analysis and Requirements Definition phase* should include security requirements and planning for requirements like authentication, data security, and technical security needs.

3. Security artifacts created during the *Design phase* often include security architecture documentation, dataflow diagrams, and other useful information.

4. The *Development (Implementation) phase* involves security testing of the code, code review, and other development-centric security operations.

5. *Testing and Integration phase* tasks include vulnerability testing and additional code review of the completed product. This also occurs when testing of a completely integrated solution can be conducted to ensure that no security issues show up once components are integrated.

6. While it may not be immediately evident, there is a security aspect to the *Training and Transition phase* as well. User training is part of the security posture of an application, and proper training can help ensure that both the users and administrators of an application are using it correctly.

7. *Operations and Maintenance* activities require ongoing scans, patching, and regression testing when upgrades occur.

8. *Disposition* of the systems and data that the application used when its life is over ensures that the end of operations for the application is not the start of a data breach.

Implementing security controls through the software development life cycle can help ensure that the applications that enter production are properly secured and maintained throughout their life cycle. Being fully involved in the SDLC requires security professionals to learn about the tools, techniques, and processes that development teams use, so be ready to learn about how software is created in your organization.

NIST's "Security Considerations in the System Development Lifecycle" SP 800-64 version 2 covers software development as well as system development. It can be found at http://nvlpubs.nist.gov/nistpubs/ Legacy/SP/nistspecialpublication800-64r2.pdf.

Version Control and Source Code Management

Once the SDLC reaches the development phase, code starts to be generated. That means that the ability to control the version of the software or component that your team is working on, combined with check-in/check-out functionality and revision histories, is a necessary and powerful tool when developing software. Fortunately, version control and *source control management* tools fill that role.

A strong SDLC requires the ability to determine that the code that is being deployed or tested is the correct version and that fixes that were previously applied have not been dropped from the release that is under development. Popular version control systems include Git, Subversion, and CVS, but there are dozens of different tools in use.

Code Review Models

Reviewing the code that is written for an application provides a number of advantages. It helps to share knowledge of the code, and the experience gained in writing is better than simple documentation alone would be since it provides personal understanding of the code and its functions. It also helps detect problems while enforcing coding best practices and standards by exposing the code to review during its development cycle. Finally, it ensures that multiple members of a team are aware of what the code is supposed to do and how it accomplishes its task.

There are a number of common code review processes, including both formal and Agile processes like pair programming, over-the-shoulder, and Fagan code reviews.

OWASP's Code Review guide provides in-depth technical information on specific vulnerabilities and how to find them, as well as how to conduct a code review. It can be found here: https://www.owasp.org/index.php/ Category:OWASP_Code_Review_Project.

Pair Programming

Pair programming is an Agile software development technique that places two developers at one workstation. One developer writes code, while the other developer reviews their code as they write it. This is intended to provide real-time code review, and it ensures that multiple developers are familiar with the code that is written. In most pair programming environments, the developers are expected to change roles frequently, allowing both of them to spend time thinking about the code while at the keyboard and to think about the design and any issues in the code while reviewing it.

Pair programming adds additional cost to development since it requires two full-time developers. At the same time, it provides additional opportunities for review and analysis of the code and directly applies more experience to coding problems, potentially increasing the quality of the code.

Over-the-Shoulder

Over-the-shoulder code review also relies on a pair of developers, but rather than requiring constant interaction and hand-offs, over-the-shoulder requires the developer who wrote the code to explain the code to the other developer. This allows peer review of code and can also assist developers in understanding how the code works, without the relatively high cost of pair programming.

Pass-Around Code Reviews

Pass-around code review, sometimes known as email pass-around code review, is a form of manual peer review done by sending completed code to reviewers who check the code for issues. Pass-around reviews may involve more than one reviewer, allowing reviewers with different expertise and experience to contribute their expertise. Although pass-around reviews allow more flexibility in *when* they occur than an over-the-shoulder review, they don't provide the same easy opportunity to learn about the code from the developer who wrote it that over-the-shoulder and pair programming offer, making documentation more important.

Tool-Assisted Reviews

Tool-assisted code reviews rely on formal or informal software-based tools to conduct code reviews. Tools like Atlassian's Crucible collaborative code review tool, Codacy's static code review tool, and Phabricator's Differential code review tool are all designed to improve the code review process. The wide variety of tools used for code review reflects not only the multitude of software development life cycle options but also how organizations set up their design and review processes.

Choosing a Review Method

Table 12.1 compares the four informal code review methods and formal code review. While specific implementations may vary, these comparisons will generally hold true between each type of code review. In addition, the theory behind each method may not always reflect the reality of how an organization will use it. For example, pair programming is intended to provide the same speed of development as two developers working on their own while increasing the quality of the code. This may be true for experienced programmers who work well together, but lack of training, personality differences, and variation in work styles can make pair programming less effective than expected.

TABLE 12.1   Code review method comparison

	Cost	When review happens	Ability to explain the code	Skill required
Pair programming	Medium	Real time	High	Users must learn how to pair program
Over-the-shoulder	Medium	Real time	High	No additional skill
Pass-around code review	Low/ Medium	Asynchronous	Low	No additional skill
Tool-assisted review	Medium	Tool/process dependent	Typically low	Training to use the tool may be required
Formal code review	High	Asynchronous	Typically low	Code review process training

Formal Code Review

When code requires more in-depth review than the relatively lightweight, Agile processes like pass-around and over-the-shoulder reviews, formal code review processes are sometimes used. As you might imagine from the name, formal code reviews are an in-depth, often time-consuming process intended to fully review code using a team of experts. The primary form of formal code review is Fagan inspection.

Fagan Inspection

Fagan inspection is a form of structured, formal code review intended to find a variety of problems during the development process. Fagan inspection specifies entry and exit criteria for processes, ensuring that a process is not started before appropriate diligence has been performed, and also making sure that there are known criteria for moving to the next phase.

The Fagan inspection process shown in Figure 12.6 shows the six phases of a typical process:

1. Planning, including preparation of materials, attendees, and location

2. Overview, which prepares the team by reviewing the materials and assigning roles such as coder, reader, reviewer, and moderator

3. Preparation, which involves reviewing the code or other item being inspected and documents any issues or questions they may have

4. Meeting to identify defects based on the notes from the preparation phase

5. Rework to resolve issues

6. Follow-up by the moderator to ensure that all issues identified have been found and that no new defects were created during the resolution process

FIGURE 12.6   Fagan code review

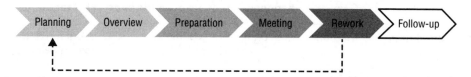

> Fagan inspection and similar formal review processes can sound very expensive, but catching problems early can result in significant savings in time and cost. Fagan code reviews remain relatively rare since many of the "lightweight" review options are easier to implement, offer many of the same benefits, and are far less costly.

Software Security Testing

No matter how well talented the development team for an application is, there will be some form of flaws in the code. Veracode's 2016 metrics for applications based on their testing showed that 61.4 percent of the over 300,000 applications they scanned did not succeed in passing their OWASP Top 10 security issues testing process. That number points to a massive need for software security testing to continue to be better integrated into the software development life cycle.

> Veracode provides a useful yearly review of the state of software security. You can read more of the 2016 report at https://www.veracode.com/sites/default/files/Resources/iPapers/soss-2016/index.html.

A broad variety of manual and automatic testing tools and methods are available to security professionals and developers. Fortunately, automated tools have continued to improve, providing an easier way to verify that code is more secure. Over the next few pages we will review some of the critical software security testing methods and tools.

Analyzing and Testing Code

The source code that is the basis of every application and program can contain a variety of bugs and flaws, from programming and syntax errors to problems with business logic, error handling, and integration with other services and systems. It is important to be able to analyze the code to understand what the code does, how it performs that task, and where flaws may occur in the program itself. This is often done via static or dynamic code analysis, along with testing methods like fuzzing, fault injection, mutation testing, and stress testing. Once changes are made to code and it is deployed, it must be regression tested to ensure that the fixes put in place didn't create new security issues.

Static Code Analysis

Static code analysis (sometimes called source code analysis) is conducted by reviewing the code for an application. Since static analysis uses the source code for an application, it can be seen as a type of white-box testing with full visibility to the testers. This can allow testers to find problems that other tests might miss, either because the logic is not exposed to other testing methods or because of internal business logic problems.

Unlike many other methods, static analysis does not run the program; instead, it focuses on understanding how the program is written and what the code is intended to do. Static code analysis can be conducted using automated tools or manually by reviewing the code— a process sometimes called "code understanding." Automated static code analysis can be very effective at finding known issues, and manual static code analysis helps identify programmer-induced errors.

OWASP provides static code analysis tools for .NET, Java, PHP, C, and JSP, as well as list of other static code analysis tools, at `https://www.owasp.org/index.php/Static_Code_Analysis`.

Dynamic Code Analysis

Dynamic code analysis relies on execution of the code while providing it with input to test the software. Much like static code analysis, dynamic code analysis may be done via automated tools or manually, but there is a strong preference for automated testing due to the volume of tests that need to be conducted in most dynamic code testing processes.

Fuzzing

Fuzz testing, or *fuzzing*, involves sending invalid or random data to an application to test its ability to handle unexpected data. The application is monitored to determine if it crashes, fails, or responds in an incorrect manner. Because of the large amount of data that a fuzz test involves, fuzzing is typically automated, and it is particularly useful for detecting input validation and logic issues as well as memory leaks and error handling. Unfortunately, fuzzing tends to identify only simple problems; it does not account for complex logic or business process issues and may not provide complete code coverage if its progress is not monitored.

Fault Injection

Unlike fuzzing, fault injection directly inserts faults into error handling paths, particularly error handling mechanisms that are rarely used or might otherwise be missed during normal testing. Fault injection may be done in one of three ways:

- Compile-time injection, which inserts faults by modifying the source code of the application

- Protocol software fault injection, which uses fuzzing techniques to send unexpected or protocol noncompliant data to an application or service that expects protocol-compliant input

- Runtime injection of data into the running program, either by inserting it into the running memory of the program or by injecting the faults in a way that causes the program to deal with them

Fault injection is typically done using automated tools due to the potential for human error in the fault injection process.

Mutation Testing

Mutation testing is related to fuzzing and fault injection, but rather than changing the inputs to the program or introducing faults to it, mutation testing makes small modifications to the program itself. The altered versions, or mutants, are then tested and rejected if they cause failures. The mutations themselves are guided by rules that are intended to create common errors as well as to replicate the types of errors that developers might introduce during their normal programing process. Much like fault injection, mutation testing helps identify issues with code that is infrequently used, but it can also help identify problems with test data and scripts by finding places where the scripts do not fully test for possible issues.

Stress Testing and Load Testing

Performance testing for applications is as important as testing for code flaws. Ensuring that applications and the systems that support them can stand up to the full production load they are anticipated to need is part of a typical SDLC process. When an application is ready to be tested, *stress test applications* and *load testing tools* are used to simulate a full application load.

Stress and load testing should typically test for a worst-case scenario. In fact, many organizations load test to the infrastructure's breaking point so that they know what their worst-case scenario is. With automatically scaling applications becoming more common, this is a lot harder to do, so setting a reasonable maximum load to test to is recommended if you have a scalable application or infrastructure.

Stress testing can also be conducted against individual components of an application to ensure that they are capable of handling load conditions. During integration and component testing, fault injection may also be used to ensure that problems during heavy load are properly handled by the application.

Security Regression Testing

Regression testing focuses on testing to ensure that changes that have been made do not create new issues. From a security perspective, this often comes into play when patches are installed or when new updates are applied to a system or application. *Security regression testing* is performed to ensure that no new vulnerabilities, misconfigurations, or other issues have been introduced.

Automated testing using tools like web application vulnerability scanners and other vulnerability scanning tools are often used as part of an automated or semiautomated regression testing process. Reports are generated to review the state of the application (and its underlying server and services) before and after changes are made to ensure that it remains secure.

It isn't uncommon for a vulnerability to be introduced by a patch or fix. Coders who are not following best practices for code commits and other good habits for version control may accidentally put code that was previously fixed back into a new release without noticing the problem. Change control as well as version and source code management practices are critical to preventing this.

Web Application Vulnerability Scanning

Many of the applications our organizations use today are web-based applications, and they offer unique opportunities for testing because of the relative standardization of HTML-based web interfaces. In Chapters 3 and 4, we looked at vulnerability scanning tools like Nessus, Nexpose, and OpenVAS, which scan for known vulnerabilities in systems, services, and, to a limited extend, web applications. Dedicated web application vulnerability scanners provide an even broader toolset specifically designed to identify problems with applications and their underlying web servers, databases, and infrastructure.

Dozens of web application vulnerability scanners are available. Some of the most popular are Acunetix WVS, Arachni, Burp Suite, IBM's AppScan, HP's WebInspect, Netsparker, QualysGuard's Web Application Scanner, and W3AF.

Like many security tools, the gap between vulnerability scanners and web application vulnerability scanners continues to close as products add additional capabilities. Sectoolmarket.com provides a regularly updated price and feature comparison of the major web application scanners at www.sectoolmarket.com/price-and-feature-comparison-of-web-application-scanners-unified-list.html, which can help you understand both the major capabilities and the effectiveness of the major tools on the market.

Web application scanners can be directly run against an application and may also be guided through the application to ensure that they find all of the components that you want to test. Like traditional vulnerability scanners, web application scanning tools provide a report of the issues they discovered when they are done, as shown in Figure 12.7. Additional details, including where the issue was found and remediation guidance, is also typically available by drilling down on the report item.

FIGURE 12.7 Acunetix web application scan vulnerability report

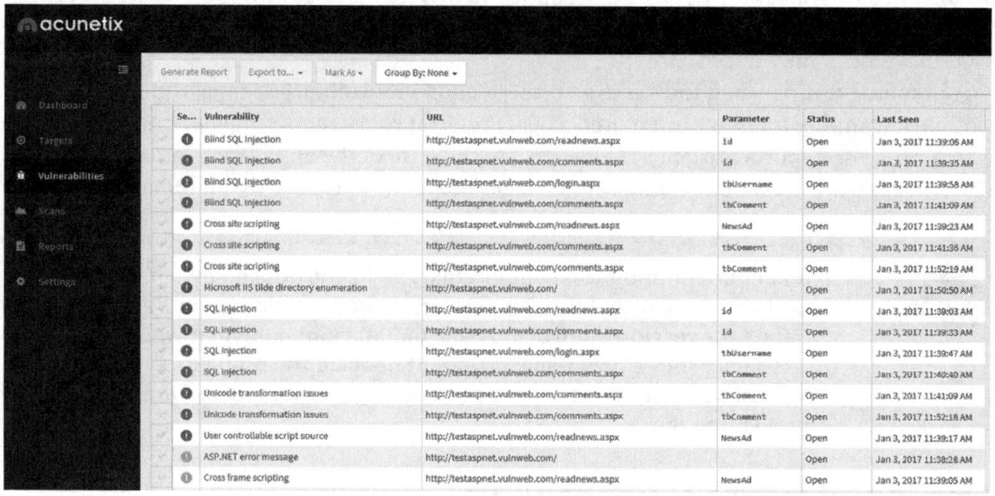

In addition to automated web application vulnerability scanners, manual scanning is frequently conducted to identify issues that automated scanners may not. Manual testing may be fully manual, with inputs inserted by hand, but testers typically use tools called *interception proxies* that allow them to capture communication between a browser and the web server. Once the proxy captures the information, the tester can modify the data that is sent and received.

A web browser plug-in proxy like Tamper Data for Firefox can allow you to modify session values during a live connection, as shown in Figure 12.8. Using an interception proxy to crawl through an application provides insight into both what data the web application uses and how you could attack the application.

There are a number of popular proxy tools ranging from browser-specific plug-ins like Tamper Data and HttpFox to browser-agnostic tools like Fiddler (which runs as a dedicated proxy). In addition, tools like Burp Suite provide a range of capabilities, including application proxies, spiders, web application scanning, and other advanced tools intended to make web application penetration testing easier.

FIGURE 12.8   Tamper Data session showing login data

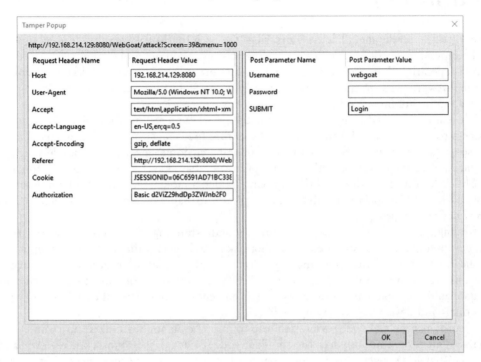

Hiring Third Parties to Test Your Code

While automated scanning is useful, it may also miss business logic issues or other flaws that simple programmatic scanning can't detect. In addition, the ability to look at an application and identify potential flaws that may exist either in the code or in the structure of the application can require human intelligence. Sectoolmarket's 2016 tests shows that even the best of the vulnerability scanners on the market missed items in their benchmarks.

When you need to find the errors that a web application scanner can't, you may want to hire external experts. Companies like WhiteHat Security (https://www.whitehatsec.com/) provide both static and dynamic analysis of applications to identify security issues.

Summary

The software development life cycle describes the path that software takes from planning and requirements gathering to design, coding, testing, training, and deployment. Once software is operational, it also covers the ongoing maintenance and eventual decommissioning of the software. That means that participating in the SDLC as a security professional can have a significant impact on organizational software security.

There are many SDLC models, including the linear Waterfall method, Spiral's iterative process-based design, and Agile methodologies that focus on sprints with timeboxed working sessions and greater flexibility to meet changing customer needs. Other models include Rapid Application Development's iterative prototype-based cycles, the V model with parallel test cycles for each stage, and the Big Bang model, a model without real planning or process. Each SDLC model offers advantages and disadvantages, meaning that a single model may not fit every project.

Coding for information security requires an understanding of common software coding best practices. These include performing risk assessments, validating all user input to applications, ensuring that error messages don't reveal internal information, and securing sessions, traffic, and cookies if they are used. OWASP and other organizations provide up-to-date guidance on common issues as well as current best practices, allowing security professionals and developers to stay up to date.

Security testing and code review can help to improve an application's security and code quality. Pair programming, over-the-shoulder code review, pass-around code reviews, and tool-assisted code reviews are all common, but for formal review Fagan inspection remains the primary, but time-intensive, solution. Security testing may involve static or dynamic code analysis, fuzzing, fault injection, mutation testing, stress or load testing, or regression testing, with each providing specific functionality that can help ensure the security of an application.

Finally, web application security testing is conducted using both automated scanners known as web application vulnerability scanners, and by penetration testers and web application security testing professionals. Much like vulnerability scanning, using application scanning tools provides a recurring view of the application's security profile and monitors for changes due to patches, configuration changes, or other new issues.

Exam Essentials

Software development follows the software development life cycle (SDLC).   SDLC models include Waterfall, Spiral, Agile, and RAD. Each model covers phases like feasibility, requirements gathering, design, development, testing and integration, deployment and training, operations, and eventual decommissioning, although they may not always occur in the same order or at the same time.

Designing information security into applications occurs in each phase of the SDLC. Coding best practices and understanding common software issues are important to prevent security flaws. Version control helps to prevent issues that exist in older code versions from reappearing in new code. Code review models like over-the-shoulder and pair programming, as well as formal review using Fagan inspection, are used to validate the quality and security of code.

Security testing is needed to identify application issues.   The majority of code has critical flaws, making testing a necessity. Static testing targets source code, whereas dynamic testing tests the application itself. Fuzzing, fault injection, mutation testing, stress and load testing, as well as security regression testing are all common testing methods. Web applications are tested using web application vulnerability scanners as well as via manual methods to ensure that they are secure and that no new vulnerabilities have been added by configuration changes or patches.

Lab Exercises

Activity 12.1: Review an Application Using the Owasp Application Security Architecture Cheat Sheet

In this exercise you will use the Acunetix web vulnerability scanner to scan a sample site and then review the data generated.

Part 1: Download and install the Acunetix scanner.

Acunetix provides their Web Vulnerability scanner as a 14-day limited term trial download. You can download it at `www.acunetix.com/vulnerability-scanner/download/`.

Part 2: Select an application and scan it.

When you download the Acunetix scanner, you will receive an email listing Acunetix-hosted vulnerable sites. Select one of these sites, and use the vulnerability scanner to scan it. Once it is complete, review the report that was generated by the scan.

Part 3: Analyze the scan results.

Review the scan results, and answer the following questions.

1. What is the most critical vulnerability? How can it be remediated?

2. What is the most common vulnerability (which occurs most often)? Is there a coding change you would recommend to the developers of this application to prevent it?

3. How would you protect this application if you were not able to change the code?

Activity 12.2: Learn about Web Application Exploits from WebGoat

OWASP in partnership with Mandiant provides the OWASP Broken Web Applications project virtual machine. This VM includes very vulnerable web applications as a VMware VM, including WebGoat, OWASP's web application vulnerability learning environment.

Step 1: Download the VMware VM.

Go to `https://sourceforge.net/projects/owaspbwa/files/1.2/`.

Step 2: Run the VMware VM and start WebGoat.

Run the virtual machine using VMware —you can use the free vSphere Hypervisor from `www.vmware.com/products/vsphere-hypervisor.html`, or the 30-day demo of Workstation Player from `www.vmware.com/products/player/playerpro-evaluation.html`.

Once the VM starts, log in as root with the password **owaspbwa** and run `ifconfig` to determine your system's IP address.

Step 3: Succeed with an attack.

WebGoat includes a multitude of vulnerable web application modules. Select one (or more!) and follow the instructions to attack the application. If you need help, review the WebGoat lesson plans and solutions at `https://www.owasp.org/index.php/Appendix_A:_WebGoat_lesson_plans_and_solutions`, or visit YouTube where you'll find numerous videos that show step-by-step guides to the solutions.

Activity 12.3: SDLC Terminology

Match each of the following terms to the correct description.

Subversion	The first SDLC model, replaced in many organizations but still used for very complex systems
Agile	A formal code review process that relies on specified entry and exit criteria for each phase
Dynamic code analysis	An Agile term that describes the list of features needed to complete a project
Fuzzing	A source control management tool
Fagan inspection	A code review process that requires one developer to explain their code to another developer
Over the shoulder	An SDLC model that relies on sprints to accomplish tasks based on user stories
Waterfall	A code analysis done using a running application that relies on sending unexpected data to see if the application fails
Backlog	A code analysis that is done using a running application

Review Questions

1. Angela's software development team is working on a large-scale control package that will run a nuclear power plant for multiple decades. They want to select an SDLC that fits their needs, which include careful up-front planning and analysis, without any anticipated change during the coding process. What SDLC model should she choose?

    A. Waterfall

    B. Spiral

    C. Agile Scrum

    D. Rapid Application Development

2. During a Fagan code inspection, which process can redirect to the planning stage?

    A. Overview

    B. Preparation

    C. Meeting

    D. Rework

3. Adam is conducting software testing by reviewing the source code of the application. What type of cost testing is Adam conducting?

    A. Mutation testing

    B. Static code analysis

    C. Dynamic code analysis

    D. Fuzzing

4. After a major patch is released for the web application that he is responsible for, Sam proceeds to run his web application security scanner against the web application to verify that it is still secure. What is the term for the process Sam is conducting?

    A. Code review

    B. Regression testing

    C. Stress testing

    D. Whiffing

5. How many phases does the Spiral model cycle through?

    A. Three

    B. Four

    C. Five

    D. Six

6. Charles is worried about users conducting SQL injection attacks. Which of the following solutions will best address his concerns?

    A. Using secure session management

    B. Enabling logging on the database

    C. Performing user input validation

    D. Implementing TLS

7. Susan's team has been writing code for a major project for a year and recently released their third version of the code. During a post-implementation regression test, an issue that was originally seen in version 1 reappeared. What type of tool should Susan implement to help avoid this issue in the future?

    A.   Stress testing

    B.   A WAF

    C.   Pair programming

    D.   Source control management

8. Precompiled SQL statements that only require variables to be input are an example of what type of application security control?

    A.   Parameterized queries

    B.   Encoding data

    C.   Input validation

    D.   Appropriate access controls

9. What process checks to ensure that functionality meets customer needs?

    A.   CNA

    B.   Stress testing

    C.   UAT

    D.   Unit testing

10. What Agile process is used to determine whether application development is occurring at the speed that was expected?

    A.   Velocity tracking

    B.   Speed traps

    C.   Timeboxing

    D.   Planning poker

11. Using TLS to protect application traffic helps satisfy which of the OWASP 2016 best practices?

    A.   Parameterize queries

    B.   Encode data

    C.   Validate all inputs

    D.   Protect data

12. Kristen wants to implement code review but has a distributed team that works at various times during the day. She also does not want to create any additional support load for her team with new development environment applications. What type of review process will work best for her needs?

    A.   Pair programming

    B.   Pass-around

    C.   Over-the-shoulder

    D.   Tool-assisted

13. During which phase would user stories be captured during an Agile sprint in the following graphic?

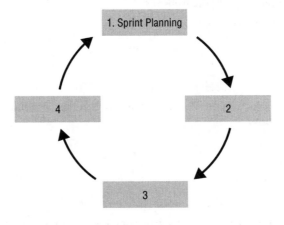

Sprint X

   A. 1
   B. 2
   C. 3
   D. 4

14. Using the Agile sprint process, what step will occur at step 2 in the previous graphic?

   A. Development
   B. Design
   C. Testing
   D. Gathering user stories

15. When is the Agile sprint shown in the previous graphic complete?

   A. After the demonstration
   B. After testing is complete
   C. When customers agree that the task is done
   D. When sprint planning begins for the next sprint

16. What process is used to ensure that an application can handle very high numbers of concurrent users or sessions?

   A. Fuzzing
   B. Fault injection
   C. Mutation testing
   D. Load testing

17. Lauren wants to insert data into the response from her browser to a web application. What type of tool should she use if she wants to easily make manual changes in what her browser sends out as she interacts with the website?

    A. An interception proxy

    B. A fuzzer

    C. A WAF

    D. A sniffer

18. What type of testing focuses on inserting problems into the error handling processes and paths in an application?

    A. Fuzzing

    B. Stress testing

    C. Dynamic code analysis

    D. Fault injection

19. What type of code review requires two programmers, one of whom explains their code to the other developer?

    A. Pair programming

    B. Tool assisted

    C. Over-the-shoulder

    D. Pass-around

20. What term is used to describe high-level requirements in Agile development efforts?

    A. Backlogs

    B. Planning poker

    C. Velocity tracking

    D. User stories

Chapter

13

Cybersecurity Toolkit

THE COMPTIA CYBERSECURITY ANALYST+ EXAM OBJECTIVES COVERED IN THIS CHAPTER INCLUDE:

Domain 4: Security Architecture and Tool Sets

✓ 4.5   Compare and contrast the general purpose and reasons for using various cybersecurity tools and technologies.

Cybersecurity analysts make use of a wide variety of security tools as they perform their duties. Throughout this book, you've already learned many of the roles and responsibilities of a cybersecurity analyst. In this chapter, you will learn about many of the different tools that assist cybersecurity experts with those responsibilities.

Host Security Tools

A broad variety of tools are used to protect local hosts, ranging from antivirus and antimalware tools to system configuration tools and whitelisting utilities. In many cases, these tools are the last technical layer of defense between attackers and workstations, servers, and mobile devices. Understanding the types of tools and how they are used can help you recommend stronger controls and configure better defenses, and it can make incident response and investigation far easier if you know how host security tools work and what information they can provide.

Antimalware and Antivirus

Detecting malicious software has been a key part of defense designs since viruses first became a consistent threat by spreading via floppy disks. Modern software *antivirus* tools have historically focused on Trojans, worms, and viruses, often with a strong signature-based detection capability and frequent updates in their definitions library. Over time, they have added behavior-based detection capabilities to handle unknown threats. *Antimalware* tools tend to focus on exploit tools and the packages used by advanced persistent threat actors, as well as other malware involved in long-term exploit and control of compromised systems. Obviously there is a significant overlap between the two categories, and tools and services exist that blur the lines between both antivirus and antimalware tools.

In many cases, organizations choose to use layered antimalware and antivirus software to have the best chance of detecting a threat. In some designs, antivirus and antimalware tools are present at multiple layers in an organization's security architecture, with detection capabilities built into host-based tools, integrated into email appliances and similar products, or deployed as prat of network layer intrusion detection or prevention systems. In addition, more advanced tools like FireEye's network security appliances actually allow infections to occur on virtual machines, validating the infection before alerting.

Host-based tools like Malwarebytes, shown in Figure 13.1, operate in much the same manner as an antivirus product, including options for central management and reporting functions. SIEM integration is also a common option, allowing detections to be aggregated and used as part of an organization's overall security awareness and management process.

FIGURE 13.1   Malwarebytes Anti-Malware

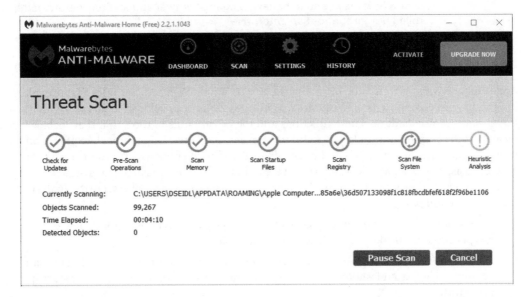

Antivirus and antimalware tools are an important preventive tool in a security analyst's arsenal. It can act as a preventive measure, particularly when deployed in an inline mode via a security appliance or an email gateway. In daily use, host-based antimalware and antivirus software helps to prevent infection during daily use of workstations and devices. It can also be an effective reactive tool when conducting incident response activities by scanning potentially infected or compromised systems for malicious software or components of a rootkit.

EMET

The *Enhanced Mitigation Experience Toolkit (EMET)* provides a set of security mitigation capabilities bundled together to help prevent malware from exploiting vulnerabilities and other attacks. It includes the *Data Execution Prevention (DEP)* feature to prevent the execution of malware loaded into data space in memory; *address space layout randomization (ASLR),* which helps prevent buffer overflow attacks and others that rely on specific knowledge of memory locations; and prevention mechanisms intended to prevent man-in-the-middle certificate attacks.

EMET is supported on all current versions of Microsoft Windows for both PC and servers. It is a free download from Microsoft at https://support.microsoft.com/en-us/kb/2458544. However, EMET is due to reach the end of its life on July 31, 2018.

> EMET can cause problems with applications that rely on data being in a specific order or location in memory. Although EMET is typically deployed centrally, it may need to be tested against critical applications before being rolled out throughout an enterprise.

Sysinternals

The Windows *Sysinternals* Suite includes a variety of Windows specific utilities that provide insight into underlying parts of Windows operating systems or provide specific functionality that is not typically built in. These functions and the broad range of tools that they include mean that the Sysinternals tools are useful for preventive, collective, analytical, exploit, and forensics purposes. Sysinternals can be downloaded and used either as a full suite, on a tool-by-tool basis, or via Windows Sysinternals Live at https://live.sysinternals.com.

The suite includes a number of tools that can be very useful to a cybersecurity analyst, including the following:

- AccessEnum, which enumerates the access on a system, providing a good view of who has permissions to files, directories, and other objects.

- AutoRuns, a utility that shows what programs start at login or system boot. This can be useful when troubleshooting some adware, malware, or other problematic startup programs.

- *Process Explorer*, a tool that shows the files, DLLs, Registry keys, and other objects in use by each process.

- PsTools, a set of command-line utilities with a broad range of functions, including process information and start/stop capabilities, event log dumping, password changes, and many others.

- SDelete, a secure file deletion utility.

- ShareEnum, a tool that analyzes shares and their permissions.

- Sysmon, which is often used for intrusion detection and forensic analysis for its ability to monitor processes and their activity in a searchable and easily viewable manner.

- ProcDump, which provides process dumping for memory and error analysis.

- TCPView, a tool for socket-level visibility for analyzing network-connected services.

Process Explorer, shown in Figure 13.2, shows an excellent example of the type of visibility that Sysinternals tools can provide. In addition to the service name, it shows CPU, memory, process ID, description, and software provider detail. By clicking on a process, you can drill down into additional capabilities such as killing processes, restarting them, dumping them, or even checking them against known malware via VirusTotal.

FIGURE 13.2   Sysinternals Process Explorer

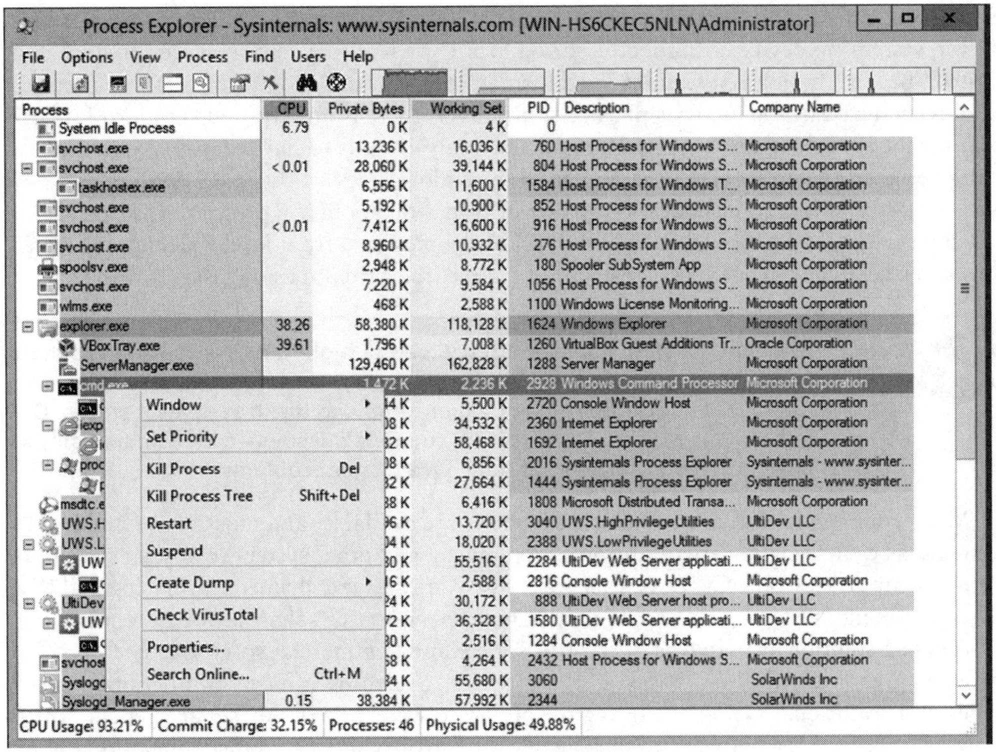

The combination of powerful utilities and a focus on command line–friendly tools makes the Sysinternals suite handy for security analysts who work with Windows systems. When used in combination with PowerShell, the Sysinternals tools can provide deep insight into processes, network access, rights, and permissions as well as a plethora of other information. In addition, they can provide the ability to take a broad range of actions both locally and remotely on Windows desktops, laptops, and servers.

Monitoring and Analysis Tools

The analytical tasks that are at the core of the Cybersecurity Analyst+ exam rely on capturing and analyzing data, primarily for collective and analytical purposes, although at times the data they gather is also used for forensic or other purposes. The monitoring tools that can acquire data, export it, and provide insights into what occurred are also involved in almost every part of organizational security efforts in some way. Their capabilities and functions vary, but each type of tools described next should have a place in your information security toolkit.

Syslog

Syslog is a standard for logging and is designed to allow logs to be created on an endpoint server, system, or device, and then be stored locally or sent to a central server or storage system. Because syslog is a standardized format, logs sent in syslog format can be more readily analyzed by log analysis packages. However, there is no required standard for content for the actual log message itself, requiring analysis tools to have plug-ins, modules, or rules designed to handle syslog data from each vendor or device that they analyze.

Syslog contains specific codes to provide information about the program that logs a given message (the facility); the severity level of the message, from level 7 debugging messages to level 0 emergency messages; and of course, the actual message that is being sent.

 Event and system logs are often wiped or modified by attackers. It's therefore critical to use a central system logging system that is heavily secured to prevent attackers from wiping or removing the log copies it stores. Central system logging can also help you detect issues—a system that stops talking to the syslog server may have bigger problems.

Many commercial and open source syslog tools are available, and most Linux and Unix systems, as well as many network devices, appliances, and other systems can send syslog-formatted messages. The Cybersecurity Analyst+ exam specifically mentions syslog and Kiwi Syslog, although syslog-ng and rsyslog are popular open source solutions for system logging.

A syslog solution available as both open source and commercial software, *syslog-ng* provides greater capabilities than traditional syslog. Syslog-ng offers a number of advantages over traditional syslog, including the ability to write to a database, greater support for how messages are formatted, and message flow control. These capabilities mean that many administrators install syslog-ng when they need to centralize syslog data.

Kiwi Syslog, shown in Figure 13.3, is a commercial syslog server tool sold by SolarWinds. In addition to centralizing logs, it provides the ability filter, display, and alert on log events, as well as support for event-driven actions. You can buy it from www.kiwisyslog.com.

FIGURE 13.3 Kiwi Syslog

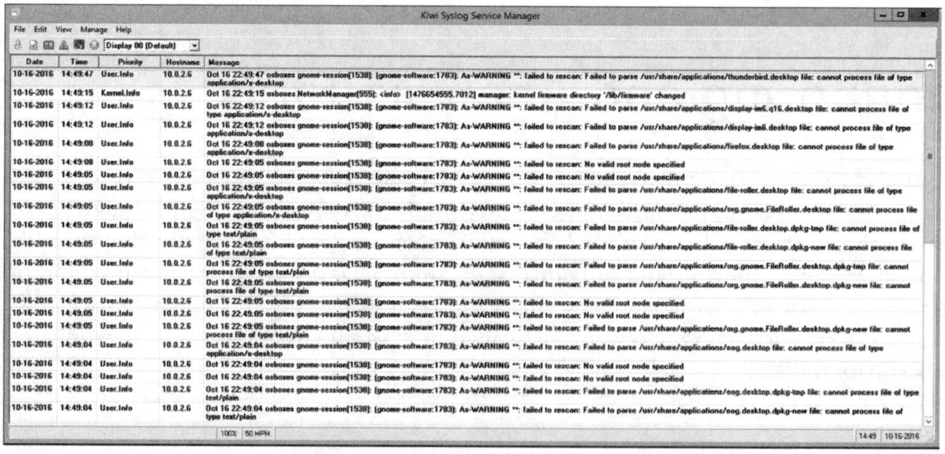

![Kiwi Syslog Service Manager screenshot showing a table of log entries with Date, Time, Priority, Hostname, and Message columns]

Security Information and Event Management (SIEM)

Security professionals are often faced with the challenge of handling a massive volume of event logs, security logs, network flow data, SNMP information, and a variety of other information. The need to store, correlate, and analyze all of this information led to the creation of security information and event management tools, or *SIEM* software and appliances.

> You may see tools called SIM, or security information management tools, or SEM, security event management tools. These describe different approaches to security data. Many vendors have moved to the combined SIEM space, but some continue to specialize in event logs (SIM) or threat analysis and event management, including security operations, incident response, and threat analysis (SEM). Picking the right tool is important, so make sure you know what your organization is buying—and what capabilities you need.

SIEM systems covered include ArcSight, QRadar, Splunk, AlienVault, and AlienVault's open source SIM, OSSIM.

Splunk

Splunk is a tool designed to provide large-scale data collection and analysis capabilities for a broad range of data types. It supports many common types of logs, making Splunk a favorite tool for analysts who are faced with massive amounts of data that needs to be searched, visualized, or otherwise used. Due to its ability to combine multiple types of data, it is also useful for incident response as well as daily security operations activities. Splunk's search interface, shown in Figure 13.4, automatically indexes data, providing easy drill-down searches through datasets, including time-based visualization and other tools.

AlienVault

AlienVault's Universal Security Manager (USM) provides SIEM functionality as well as asset discovery, vulnerability scanning and assessment, behavior (heuristic) analysis capabilities, and IDS capabilities. Figure 13.5 shows the security module of the AlienVault console, which is representative of the top-level analysis view typically found in SIEM consoles. Each segment allows drill-down reporting, and additional analysis and reporting capabilities can be used to help with security operations.

Figure 13.6 demonstrates SIEM analysis using drill-down and filtering capabilities. The ability to consolidate multiple devices or types of devices in a single view is critical to the broad visibility that a SIEM can provide.

FIGURE 13.4 Splunk

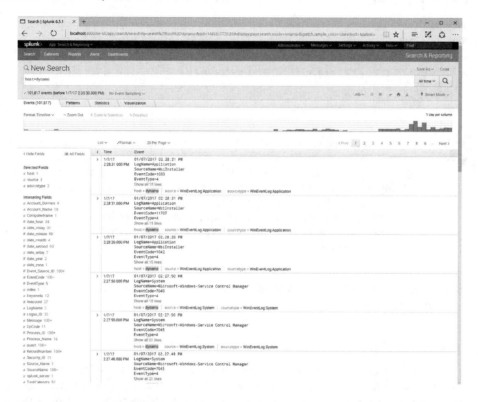

FIGURE 13.5 AlienVault SIEM

FIGURE 13.6   AlienVault SIEM drill-down

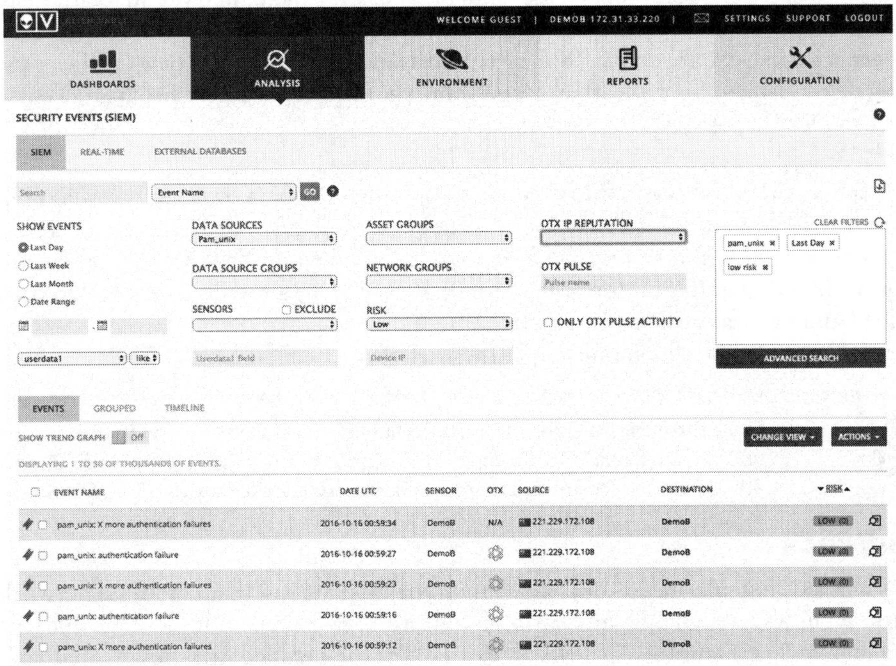

OSSIM

AlienVault offers OSSIM, an open source SIEM that integrates a number of open source tools to provide security information and event management capabilities, including

- OpenVAS for vulnerability scanning
- Suricata for network-based IDS
- Nagios for monitoring
- OSSEC for host-based IDS
- Munin for traffic analysis
- FProbe for NetFlow generation

OSSIM also provides correlation, reporting, and alerting capabilities that are typical of a SIEM product. OSSIM also plugs into AlienVault's Open Threat Exchange to provide IP reputation functionality.

Network Monitoring

Networks drive modern organizations. Whether data traverses the public Internet, travels between cellular and satellite-based wireless systems, or is sent between systems on internal networks, understanding the network traffic and the state of the devices that carry it can make the difference between successful defense of an organization and falling victim to attacks. At their most basic level, these tools simply measure network traffic and whether routers, switches, and other network gear are online. In their more advanced incarnations, they can help predict outages, detect denial-of-service attacks, and show you when unexpected behavior occurs.

Cacti

Cacti is a network graphing tool that runs on top of RRDtool (a data logging and graphing system) to allow recurring, time-based data collection and analysis. In operation, Cacti polls network devices and systems on a regular basis, collecting that data and then enabling it to be displayed in graphical form. It can pull SNMP data, allowing it to be used to create CPU load and network utilization graphs.

You can download Cacti at www.cacti.net.

Even though the Cybersecurity Analyst+ exam objectives include Cacti, you're more likely to run into other tools in most environments. Cacti is relatively dated compared to many of its competitors, despite a 2016 update.

SolarWinds

SolarWinds's Orion provides a centralized monitoring platform that combines network monitoring, flows, system and application monitoring, and support for storage and virtualization monitoring. Figure 13.7 shows an example of the detailed drill-downs that you can configure in Orion, with a view of an Active Directory server in the SolarWinds demonstration environment with an added window showing current processes running.

FIGURE 13.7 SolarWinds's Orion

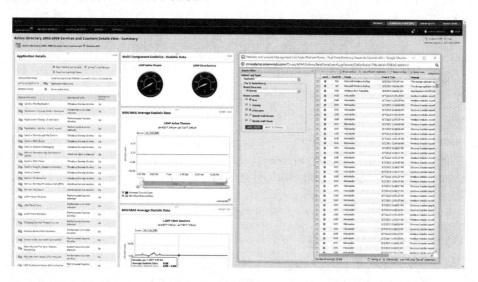

Combined monitoring tools like Orion are incredibly useful for security operations and incident response activities because they can provide in-depth insight into the state of systems, networks, and devices. In addition, the ability to centrally search through logs provides a much faster way to access event data.

Visualization, reporting, and analytics tools built into central monitoring and alerting tools can be leveraged to provide information security functionality by monitoring for security events, by looking for specific log entries, or simply by using the dashboards they provide to monitor for anomalies.

SolarWinds provides a variety of monitoring and management tools at www.solarwinds.com.

> You can find additional information on Nagios, SolarWinds, and similar tools in Chapter 6, "Analyzing Symptoms for Incident Response."

NetFlow Analyzer

ManageEngine's NetFlow Analyzer is a commercial network flow analyzer tool that provides graphical views of network bandwidth usage and other flow-related information. NetFlow Analyzer is also available as a free product that can monitor up to two interfaces, providing a useful free tool option if you want to try out netflow monitoring. You can download NetFlow Analyzer at https://www.manageengine.com/products/netflow/.

Nagios

Nagios is a monitoring tool available as both an open source product called Nagios Core and a commercial version. It provides monitoring of services, system resources, and support for monitoring a wide variety of other devices, services, and tools via a plug-in architecture. It provides an easy-to-use web interface for analysis and reporting, and it can alert on issues identified by its monitoring capabilities. Nagios is one of the most popular monitoring tools, and both the commercial and open source versions can be found at https://www.nagios.org/.

MRTG

Multi Router Traffic Grapher (MRTG) is a network monitoring tool that leverages SNMP to monitor traffic on network connections. MRTG is open source under the GNU GPL and can be downloaded at http://oss.oetiker.ch/mrtg/.

> We provided examples earlier in the book using PRTG. Although MRTG is a great open source tool and is part of the CSA+ recommended list of tools, a more fully featured tool like PRTG can provide useful capabilities beyond those that MRTG has.

Scanning and Testing Tools

Attackers understand that finding a way into an organization that they are targeting means finding an exposed service, a misconfigured or open system, or a vulnerable application. To do that, they use scanning and testing tools like these to identify potential targets. Security practitioners use many of the same tools to perform proactive scans, allowing them to work to secure systems and to identify flaws before attackers can exploit them.

Network Scanning

Network scanning is commonly conducted as part of reconnaissance activities to determine what systems, devices, and services exist on a network. Scanning is also part of the day-to-day security operations for many organizations, where it is used to test systems before they are placed into production and to verify that their configuration has not changed on a recurring basis.

Many security tools integrate a network scanning function, but the most commonly used network scanning tool is *nmap*, the network mapper. Nmap is a command-line utility that provides port scanning, operating system and service identification, as well as general network mapping. It provides features intended to allow it to scan through firewalls and other common network security devices, and it provides many different scanning and analysis features.

The nmap.org site has extensive documentation of these and all of the other nmap flags. If you make nmap part of your practice, you should learn the most common nmap flags that make sense for your use of the tool using the excellent nmap reference guide.

You can download nmap for Windows, MacOS, and Linux from nmap.org. In addition, nmap is available through the built-in package manager tools for most Linux distributions. The Kali Linux security toolkit we use throughout the examples in the book also comes with both nmap and Zenmap built in.

In the example in Figure 13.8, a vulnerable system was scanning using no ping (-P0), operating system identification was turned on (-0), and the scan was set to use TCP SYN scan (-sS). A limited range of possible ports 1–9000 was scanned, and the T4 option was used to select one of nmap's five levels of aggression—in this case, level 4, the second highest. Finally, the target IP address was set.

For a detailed discussion of network scanning using nmap, see Chapter 2, "Reconnaissance and Intelligence Gathering."

Vulnerability Scanning

Vulnerability scanners probe networks, systems, and applications for the presence of known vulnerabilities and provide detailed reporting and remediation plans that are valuable to cybersecurity analysts. Chapter 3, "Designing a Vulnerability Management Program," and Chapter 4, "Analyzing Vulnerability Scans," provided detailed coverage of vulnerability scanning in general and covered the use of network vulnerability scanners in particular. As you fill out your cybersecurity toolkit, you will want to have both a network vulnerability scanner and a web application scanner available for use. Vulnerability scanners are often leveraged for preventive scanning and testing and are also found in penetration testers toolkits where they help identify systems that testers can exploit. This also means they're a favorite tool of attackers!

FIGURE 13.8   Nmap

Network Vulnerability Scanning

The following tools are examples of network vulnerability scanners and were discussed in detail in Chapters 3 and 4:

- Tenable's *Nessus* is a well-known and widely respected network vulnerability scanning product that was one of the earliest products in this field.

- Qualys's *QualysGuard* is a more recently developed commercial network vulnerability scanner that offers a unique deployment model using a Software-as-a-Service (SaaS) management console to run scans using appliances located both in on-premises data-centers and in the cloud.

- Rapid7's *Nexpose* is another commercial vulnerability management system that offers capabilities similar to those of Nessus and QualysGuard.

- The open source *OpenVAS* offers a free alternative to commercial vulnerability scanners.

These four products are the network vulnerability scanners that you are required to know for the Cybersecurity Analyst+ exam. Many other examples of network vulnerability scanners are on the market today, and every mature organization should have at least one scanner in their toolkit. Many organizations choose to deploy two different vulnerability scanning products in the same environment as a defense-in-depth control.

Microsoft Baseline Security Analyzer (MBSA)

Microsoft offered the Microsoft Baseline Security Analyzer (MBSA) as a Windows-specific security tool for many years. This tool was limited in scope, as it worked only with Windows systems and only checked for missing security patches.

Although Microsoft has not made any official announcement about MBSA, it appears that the product is no longer supported. Microsoft released the most recent version of MBSA in 2013, and it does not support newer operating systems, including Windows 10 and Windows Server 2016.

The CSA+ objectives do include MBSA as a tool that CSA+ candidates must know, so you should be familiar with it. However, this tool is no longer commonly used in enterprise IT environments.

Web Application Scanning

Web application scanners are specialized tools used to examine the security of web applications. These tools test for web-specific vulnerabilities, such as SQL injection, cross-site scripting (XSS), and cross-site request forgery (CSRF) vulnerabilities. They work by combining traditional network scans of web servers with detailed probing of web applications using such techniques as sending known malicious input sequences and fuzzing in attempts to break the application.

Nikto is the only web application scanning tool that is required knowledge for the CSA+ exam. It is an open source tool that is freely available for anyone to use. As shown in Figure 13.9, it uses a command-line interface and is somewhat difficult to use.

FIGURE 13.9 Nikto web application scanner

```
 Scripting (XSS). http://www.cert.org/advisories/CA-2000-02.html.
+ /servlet/org.apache.catalina.ContainerServlet/<script>alert('Vulnerable')</script>: Apache-Tomcat is vulnerab
le to Cross Site Scripting (XSS) by invoking java classes. http://www.cert.org/advisories/CA-2000-02.html.
+ /servlet/org.apache.catalina.Context/<script>alert('Vulnerable')</script>: Apache-Tomcat is vulnerable to Cro
ss Site Scripting (XSS) by invoking java classes. http://www.cert.org/advisories/CA-2000-02.html.
+ /servlet/org.apache.catalina.Globals/<script>alert('Vulnerable')</script>: Apache-Tomcat is vulnerable to Cro
ss Site Scripting (XSS) by invoking java classes. http://www.cert.org/advisories/CA-2000-02.html.
+ /servlet/org.apache.catalina.servlets.WebdavStatus/<script>alert('Vulnerable')</script>: Apache-Tomcat is vul
nerable to Cross Site Scripting (XSS) by invoking java classes. http://www.cert.org/advisories/CA-2000-02.html.
+ /nosuchurl/><script>alert('Vulnerable')</script>: JEUS is vulnerable to Cross Site Scripting (XSS) when reque
sting non-existing JSP pages. http://securitytracker.com/alerts/2003/Jun/1007004.html
+ /~/<script>alert('Vulnerable')</script>.aspx?aspxerrorpath=null: Cross site scripting (XSS) is allowed with .
aspx file requests (may be Microsoft .net). http://www.cert.org/advisories/CA-2000-02.html
+ /~/<script>alert('Vulnerable')</script>.aspx: Cross site scripting (XSS) is allowed with .aspx file requests
(may be Microsoft .net). http://www.cert.org/advisories/CA-2000-02.html
+ /~/<script>alert('Vulnerable')</script>.asp: Cross site scripting (XSS) is allowed with .asp file requests (m
ay be Microsoft .net). http://www.cert.org/advisories/CA-2000-02.html
+ /node/view/666\"><script>alert(document.domain)</script>: Drupal 4.2.0 RC is vulnerable to Cross Site Scripti
ng (XSS). http://www.cert.org/advisories/CA-2000-02.html.
+ /mailman/listinfo/<script>alert('Vulnerable')</script>: Mailman is vulnerable to Cross Site Scripting (XSS).
Upgrade to version 2.0.8 to fix. http://www.cert.org/advisories/CA-2000-02.html.
+ OSVDB-27095: /bb000001.pl<script>alert('Vulnerable')</script>: Actinic E-Commerce services is vulnerable to C
ross Site Scripting (XSS). http://www.cert.org/advisories/CA-2000-02.html.
+ OSVDB-54589: /a.jsp/<script>alert('Vulnerable')</script>: JServ is vulnerable to Cross Site Scripting (XSS) w
hen a non-existent JSP file is requested. Upgrade to the latest version of JServ. http://www.cert.org/advisorie
s/CA-2000-02.html.
+ /<script>alert('Vulnerable')</script>.thtml: Server is vulnerable to Cross Site Scripting (XSS). http://www.c
ert.org/advisories/CA-2000-02.html.
+ /<script>alert('Vulnerable')</script>.shtml: Server is vulnerable to Cross Site Scripting (XSS). http://www.c
ert.org/advisories/CA-2000-02.html.
+ /<script>alert('Vulnerable')</script>.jsp: Server is vulnerable to Cross Site Scripting (XSS). http://www.cer
t.org/advisories/CA-2000-02.html.
+ /<script>alert('Vulnerable')</script>.aspx: Cross site scripting (XSS) is allowed with .aspx file requests (m
ay be Microsoft .net). http://www.cert.org/advisories/CA-2000-02.html.
```

Most organizations do use web application scanners, but they choose to use commercial products that offer advanced capabilities and user-friendly interfaces. While there are dedicated web application scanners, such as Acunetix, on the market, many firms use the web application scanning capabilities of traditional network vulnerability scanners, such as Nessus, QualysGuard, and Nexpose. Figure 13.10 shows an example of Nessus used in a web scanning role.

FIGURE 13.10   Nessus web application scanner

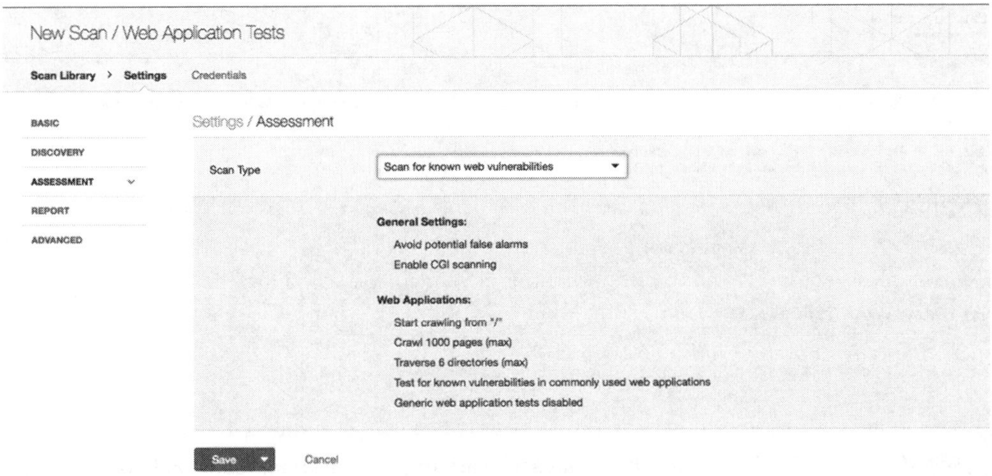

Exploit Frameworks

Packaging exploits and then using them can be quite challenging, particularly for those who are not experts in the technologies, systems, or services that the exploits target. Historically, that meant that each exploit had to be independently packaged or required a custom delivery tool. The *Metasploit* framework changed that by integrating exploit packages, delivery methods, remote shells, and other tools into a single framework.

Metasploit allows exploit developers to build Metasploit-compatible packages and then release them knowing that they will work with other Metasploit modules. To use a Metasploit exploit, you just need to know the target, the exploit, and what you want to have Metasploit deliver if the exploit succeeds.

Figure 13.11 shows Metasploit's simple menuing system with an exploit selected and ready to be delivered.

Metasploit's catalog of exploits can serve as a useful metric for the availability of compromise code. Monitoring when an exploit is released for use with Metasploit provides information about when attacks using that exploit have become almost trivial. If you haven't fixed systems that are susceptible to that exploit by the time it is available via Metasploit, you're an easy target!

FIGURE 13.11   Metasploit Console

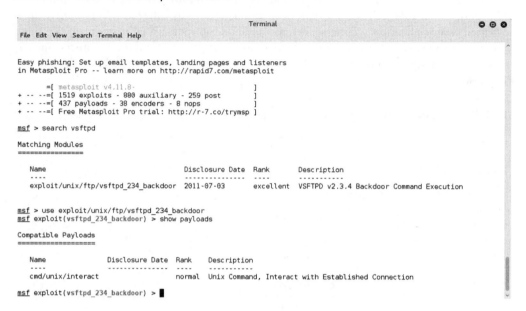

The Cybersecurity Analyst+ exam objectives specifically call out Nexpose's relation to exploit frameworks. This connection is important because Metasploit can be integrated with vulnerability scanning tools like Nexpose and Nessus, allowing you to import hosts, lists of open ports, and other information to then use with your exploits.

Password Cracking and Recovery

The first step when cracking or recovering passwords is to acquire them. That means dumping passwords from a password store or recovering them from a database or other storage location. A number of tools are designed to help with acquisition of passwords, including *fgdump*, *pwdump*, and *SAMdump2*.

Once you have acquired passwords, it helps to determine how they are stored. In some cases, it is trivial to check the hashed passwords to determine if they're hashed with a commonly used hash like MD5 or SHA1. If a more complex method was used, you'll have to either check the code used to create the stored passwords or perform extensive reverse engineering to determine what was done. That technique is well beyond the scope of this book, so we'll stick to cracking passwords encoded in well-known ways like those found in Windows and passwords stored in MD5 hashes.

Password cracking tools are frequently used in both exploit and forensic activities. Forensic analysts may need to recover passwords to access encrypted files or drives.

Penetration testers may use them to analyze password files or hashes they acquire, providing useful ways to access other systems or accounts.

Password and Hash Cracking Tools

John the Ripper is an open source tool designed to crack passwords and hashes, including Linux, Windows, Kerberos, and other frequently used password hashing methods. It supports a number of modes of operation, allowing its cracking process to be set based on how much information you have about the passwords such as word lists or password complexity requirements or limitations.

Figure 13.12 shows John being run against a set of sample hashes from an MD5 hashed password file. Within just a few minutes John returned valid passwords.

FIGURE 13.12   John the Ripper

```
root@demo:~/Downloads/John demo/cmiyc_2012_password_hash_files# john --wordlist=rockyou.txt hashes-3.des.txt
Using default input encoding: UTF-8
Loaded 10290 password hashes with 3741 different salts (descrypt, traditional crypt(3) [DES 128/128 AVX-16])
Press 'q' or Ctrl-C to abort, almost any other key for status
superman          (rhond.joseph)
chocolat          (jacksojo)
password          (pamel.smith)
nicholas          (moraleke)
qwertyui          (memiller)
metallic          (steph.shaw)
sebastia          (patria)
volleyba          (smithka)
portugal          (smithm)
rockstar          (sandrr)
barcelon          (fredf)
cocacola          (melanl)
lollypop          (snelson)
starwars          (carlo.garcia)
anderson          (rodrigul)
gorgeous          (brendc)
remember          (sue.reed)
```

Details of how to use John the Ripper, including examples and suggestions for the order of cracking attempts, can be found at www.openwall.com/john/.

Cain and Abel is a multifunction password recovery and cracking tool for Windows. Unfortunately, the last update to Cain and Abel occurred in 2014, and it isn't clear that it will receive major updates soon. Cain & Abel remains a powerful Windows tool for password recovery and hash cracking, but it may not succeed against modern systems. It provides a wide range of password cracking capabilities, including

- Password dumping tools
- Hash cracking for NTLM and NTLMv2 hashes, MD5, SHA1 and SHA2 hashes, MySQL and Microsoft SQL hashes, and a variety of other common password and data storage hashes
- VoIP phone decoding capabilities
- A network sniffing and over-the-wire password capture tool
- A wide variety of other security tools

Cain and Abel can be found at www.oxid.it/cain.html.

Ophcrack is an open source password cracking tool that relies on rainbow tables to quickly look up hashes to return their original value. With a large set of rainbow tables that are suited to the hash and password length used, almost any hashed password can be looked up in a very short period of time. For this reason, Ophcrack (and other rainbow table–based hash cracking solutions) are much quicker than brute-force or wordlist password crackers. Their limitation is that they can only crack passwords for which they have a valid lookup entry.

Due to their capabilities, many hash cracking and password recovery tools are flagged as malware by some antivirus tools. If you download these tools, you may have to disable your antivirus software or tell your browser to disable security protections.

Network Security Tools

Network security tools help organizations build strong network perimeters, detect and block potential network attacks, and monitor network traffic for signs of suspicious or problematic activity. Firewalls, IDS, IPS, HIPS, and web proxy systems are primarily used as preventive tools, whereas packet capture and network command-line tools are often used for analytical and collective purposes. In some cases, packet capture and command-line tools are also used as part of exploit toolkits, where they can provide useful insights into network traffic and network-connected systems.

Firewalls

Firewalls are the first line of defense from a network security perspective. In Chapter 1, "Defending Against Cybersecurity Threats," you learned the role that firewalls play in building strong network perimeters and segmenting networks of varying security levels.

Cybersecurity analysts must know how to design and implement the rules that govern firewall activity. This includes designing specific rules that allow activity associated with enterprise information systems and understanding that the firewall's default deny rule will block any traffic that is not explicitly allowed.

Many different firewall platforms are available to modern enterprises. Figure 13.13 shows an example of the rule configuration interface for a Check Point firewall.

As you prepare for the CSA+ exam, you should be familiar with the major providers of network firewalls. Check Point and *Palo Alto* are companies that specialize in firewalls. Traditional networking companies, including *Cisco* and *Juniper*, also produce dedicated firewalls and incorporate firewall capabilities into their other networking products.

Network Intrusion Detection and Prevention

Intrusion detection and prevention systems play an important role in protecting networks by monitoring for signs of malicious activity. *Intrusion detection systems (IDSs)* installed on a network monitor all network traffic passing a sensor location and use pattern recognition and/or behavior analysis to detect potentially malicious traffic. When an IDS detects a suspicious situation, it alerts administrators to conduct further investigation.

FIGURE 13.13   Check Point firewall console

No.	Hits	Name	Source	Destination	VPN	Service	Action	Track	Install On	Time	Comment
1	89M	Web Servers to SQL	SVR-Mercury, SVR-Centurion	SVR-Ironman, SVR-Littleboy, SVR-Miamsql01	Any Traffic	MS-SQL-Server, MS-SQL-Server,	accept	None	Policy Targets	Any	DMZ Webservers access to internal SQL Servers
2	72K	DMZ backups	SVR-Pixhana, DMZ-MIAMI	SVR-Pixhana, DMZ-MIAMI	Any Traffic	Appassure1, Appassure2, https	accept	None	Policy Targets	Any	Access for backup server to back up every DMZ server.
3	150K	Web access to BrandBox	Any	SVR-Galatian	Any Traffic	https, http	accept	None	Policy Targets	Any	
4	54K	BrandBox Reverse Proxy	SVR-Galatian	SVR-BrandBox	Any Traffic	https, http	accept	None	Policy Targets	Any	
5	90K	Kaspersky Cellphone App	Any	SVR-ezekiel01, SVR-ezekiel02	Any Traffic	Kaspersky, Kaspersky2, Kaspersky3	accept	None	Policy Targets	Any	Kaspersky cellphone application. Same physical server with 2 IP addresses
6	243K	RDP public	Any	Any	Any Traffic	websenseWEB	accept	None	Policy Targets	Any	RDP-public ips
7	30K	Office Cameras	Any	SVR-MiamiCam	Any Traffic	Cameras, Cameras2, Cameras3	accept	None	Policy Targets	Any	Access to ... internal and external
8	20K	Access to SmartDashboard	Administrators		Any Traffic	Any	accept	Log	Policy Targets	Any	Allow access to Checkpoint's Administration HTTPS page
9	9		Any		Any Traffic	Any	drop	None	Policy Targets	Any	Drop access to ...
10	17M	Connection between MIA and NY	INTERNAL-VLAN, NY-NetworkALL	NY-NetworkALL, INTERNAL-VLAN	Any Traffic	Any	accept	None	Policy Targets	Any	Connection between all networks in Miami and New York.
11	2K	VoIP IPPONE Toolbar	INTERNAL-VLAN	ws.ioncom.net	Any Traffic	ipfone	accept	Log	Policy Targets	Any	Access For IPFone Toolbar
12	55K	Support VPN users	VLAN-14-Inform, OfficeMode	OfficeMode, VLAN-14-Inform	Any Traffic	Any	accept	Log	Policy Targets	Any	
13	132h	Open Access (Everything)	Open Access	Any	Any Traffic	Any	accept	None	Policy Targets	Any	All Traffic from the inside going out.
14	8M	Limited Open Access	Limited-Open-/	Any	Any Traffic	Direct-Internet	accept	None	Policy Targets	Any	Allow nodes full access to the internet and other protocols as well.
15	10M	Access to our Sites and Conf	Any	Web-Servers, SVR-Sonexis02	Any Traffic	WebServices	accept	Log	Policy Targets	Any	Allows access to our websites and Conferencing Server from External and Internal
16	8M	Access to OWA	Any	OWA-Servers	Any Traffic	OWAServices	accept	Log	Policy Targets	Any	Allows access for OWA Access from External and Internal
17	209K	Internal to External Services	INTERNAL-VLAN	Any	Any Traffic	BI-Allowed-Ser	accept	Log	Policy Targets	Any	Allows internal users access to the specific services in this rule
18	2M	Access for SMTP	Any	SMTP-Servers	Any Traffic	smtp	accept	Log	Policy Targets	Any	Allows email communication
19	6K	Access to Spam Dashboard	Any	SVR-BrandMail, SVR-Brandmail	Any Traffic	SpamControl-V, SMTPS	accept	Log	Policy Targets	Any	Allows access to Spam Dashboard web login so employees can check their spam.
20	2	Deny Access from VPN to MIACAM	VPN-Employees	SVR-MiamiCam	RemoteAccess	Any	drop	Log	Policy Targets	Any	Deny's VPN users to access the camera server.

Intrusion prevention systems (IPSs) go beyond the passive responses of an IDS and allow the system to take proactive action in the event of a potential security breach. For example, administrators may configure an IPS to block future connections from systems identified as engaging in brute-force password attacks, vulnerability scans, or other malicious activity.

> While there was once a distinction between IDS and IPS technology, modern intrusion technology generally supports both modes. That said, the CompTIA Cybersecurity Analyst+ curriculum treats these as two different topics, so you should be prepared to distinguish between the passive action of an IDS and the active response of an IPS.

Many intrusion detection and prevention systems are available on the commercial market today. *Snort* was one of the earliest intrusion detection systems, first developed in 1998 and still used today. It uses a community-curated set of rules to identify patterns of known malicious activity. Snort was originally created as an open source IDS/IPS, which was later commercially developed by *Sourcefire* as their FirePower tool. Cisco Systems acquired Sourcefire in 2013 and began incorporating FirePower technology into Cisco security products.

Bro is another open source intrusion detection and prevention system developed by Vern Paxson at the University of California, Berkeley. Bro works by performing protocol analysis on network connections and also finds significant use as a network analysis and forensic tool. Figure 13.14 shows an example of Bro's connection logging capabilities.

FIGURE 13.14 Bro intrusion detection and prevention system

```
#set_separator  ,
#empty_field    (empty)
#unset_field    -
#path    conn
#open    2016-09-25-20-51-28
#fields ts       uid       id.orig_h       id.orig_p       id.resp_h       id.resp_p       proto    service duration          o
rig_bytes        resp_bytes        conn_state      local_orig      local_resp      missed_bytes    history orig_pkts         o
rig_ip_bytes     resp_pkts         resp_ip_bytes   tunnel_parents
#types  time     string    addr      port      addr      port      enum      string   interval          count    count    string bool b
ool     count    string    count     count     count     count     set[string]
1474836683.377265         CMo8KU3ziIFt6PLnIb         98.220.1.103    46374    172.30.0.57     22       tcp      ssh      0.37094
8       1533     2059      SF        -         -         0         ShAdDaFf        15       2325     13       2743     (empty)
1474836684.330720         CH7Pnv2UcZi3WdfWji         98.220.1.103    42760    172.30.0.57     22       tcp      ssh      0.36815
4       1533     2059      SF        -         -         0         ShDaAdFf        15       2325     13       2743     (empty)
1474836685.240912         C3ST3sLISZLHtNuV5          98.220.1.103    40230    172.30.0.57     22       tcp      ssh      0.35444
6       1533     2059      SF        -         -         0         ShADadFf        15       2325     12       2691     (empty)
1474836683.706477         CsbxAc3L4qTQOV5rZb         172.30.0.57     38913    172.30.0.2      53       udp      dns      0.00080
9       43       91        SF        -         -         0         Dd        1        71       1        119      (empty)
1474836683.707394         CUOTGa3lJd865Lz1Ue         172.30.0.57     48345    172.30.0.2      53       udp      dns      0.00062
3       52       68        SF        -         -         0         Dd        1        80       1        96       (empty)
1474836683.746749         CDOCQx2hjfhroZ0MXe         172.30.0.57     45311    172.30.0.2      53       udp      dns      0.00097
7       104      172       SF        -         -         0         Dd        2        160      2        228      (empty)
1474836684.655082         CvMVZs4o4zFcmTV0ri         172.30.0.57     40198    172.30.0.2      53       udp      dns      0.00077
9       43       91        SF        -         -         0         Dd        1        71       1        119      (empty)
1474836684.655953         CvVJGo4mFApE4YqUj5         172.30.0.57     38733    172.30.0.2      53       udp      dns      0.00064
9       52       68        SF        -         -         0         Dd        1        80       1        96       (empty)
1474836684.697226         C7L68vMy6bYAsAPk5          172.30.0.57     43767    172.30.0.2      53       udp      dns      0.00114
9       104      172       SF        -         -         0         Dd        2        160      2        228      (empty)
1474836685.554087         CZEX5P19Nw8lg5e456         172.30.0.57     58584    172.30.0.2      53       udp      dns      0.00078
7       43       91        SF        -         -         0         Dd        1        71       1        119      (empty)
1474836685.554980         CbaLjL1BDCq3uk2Uj8         172.30.0.57     49540    172.30.0.2      53       udp      dns      0.00065
0       52       68        SF        -         -         0         Dd        1        80       1        96       (empty)
1474836685.593986         C0Wf1i1XaoP2TDk8w8         172.30.0.57     34829    172.30.0.2      53       udp      dns      0.00086
5       104      172       SF        -         -         0         Dd        2        160      2        228      (empty)
1474836729.380644         Ckp05h1oOYQ5qKGj42         98.220.1.103    43193    172.30.0.57     22       tcp      ssh      0.59194
1       1533     2059      SF        -         -         0         ShDaAdFf        16       2389     14       2995     (empty)
--More--(45%)
```

Host Intrusion Prevention

Host intrusion prevention systems (HIPSs) perform actions similar to their network counterparts, seeking to identify and block potentially malicious network traffic. They differ in their scope. While network IPS technology seeks to filter all traffic crossing a network chokepoint, HIPS resides on and protects a single host. Due to many issues with the configuration and management of HIPS technology, most organizations tend not to use traditional HIPS approaches on their systems.

One branch of HIPS technology that is more widely used is *file integrity monitoring* software. These tools, including the popular Tripwire package, build a table of hash values for all files resident on a protected computer system and then monitor files for unexpected changes in those hash values. When properly tuned, file integrity monitoring software can provide early warning of system compromises. This software is so reliable that its use is mandated for credit card processing systems by the Payment Card Industry Data Security Standard (PCI DSS), which states in requirement 11.5 that organizations must

> Deploy a change detection mechanism (for example, file integrity monitoring tools) to alert personnel to unauthorized modification (including changes, additions and deletions) of critical system files, configuration files, or content files; and configure the software to perform critical file comparisons at least weekly.

Packet Capture

Packet capture tools provide cybersecurity analysts with valuable insight into the communications that take place over a network. These tools run on a system connected to the network in *promiscuous mode*. Promiscuous mode instructs the network interface to capture *all* packets that pass by on the network, not just those addressed to the system. Depending on the system's vantage point, it may capture a significant amount of network traffic. Systems used to capture network traffic may also be attached to a *span port* on a switch that is designed to receive copies of traffic sent to all other ports on the switch.

Wireshark is the most popular packet capture tool. Available for all major operating systems, Wireshark provides a graphical user interface that makes it easy to apply filters to captured traffic; reassemble TCP, UDP, and HTTP streams; and search through captured packets for specific desired information. Figure 13.15 shows an example of Wireshark in action. Each line in the top third of the Wireshark window shows the details of an individual packet; the other two portions of the screen provide details on the contents of that packet.

FIGURE 13.15 Wireshark packet captures

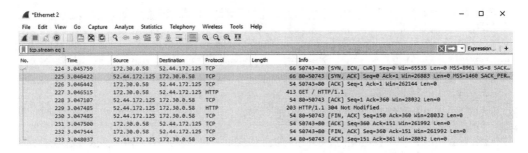

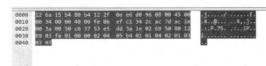

Cybersecurity analysts should be deeply familiar with the use of packet capture tools, including Wireshark and tcpdump. They should also know how to interpret the results. If you are not familiar with these tools, you should learn more about them by reading a book such as Laura Chappell's *Wireshark 101: Essential Skills for Network Analysis* (Laura Chappell University, 2013). There is no substitute, however, for hands-on experience using these tools in a cybersecurity environment.

While Wireshark is the most popular packet capture tool, many other tools also provide this same capability. One common alternative is the *tcpdump* command-line packet capture tool, shown in Figure 13.16. This tool, available on all major operating systems, provides a clean way to capture traffic easily from the command line.

FIGURE 13.16   tcpdump packet captures

```
● ● ●                              ⬚ mchapple — -bash — 139×49
Mikes-Mac-mini:~ mchapple$ sudo tcpdump -i en1
tcpdump: verbose output suppressed, use -v or -vv for full protocol decode
[listening on en1, link-type EN10MB (Ethernet), capture size 262144 bytes
16:52:45.106982 IP 10.0.1.201.ipp > 10.0.1.77.52730: Flags [R.], seq 0, ack 1285087891, win 0, length 0
16:52:45.107361 IP 10.0.1.77.52731 > 10.0.1.201.ipp: Flags [SEW], seq 4212382519, win 65535, options [mss 1460,nop,wscale 5,nop,nop,TS val
1104744370 ecr 0,sackOK,eol], length 0
16:52:45.111209 IP6 2601:245:c101:54f6:1cf9:4aae:38a4:897.56462 > 2601:245:c101:54f6:3612:98ff:fe00:8727.domain: 59359+ PTR? 201.1.0.10.in-
addr.arpa. (41)
16:52:45.111462 IP 10.0.1.201.ipp > 10.0.1.77.52731: Flags [R.], seq 0, ack 4212382520, win 0, length 0
16:52:45.111799 IP 10.0.1.77.52732 > 10.0.1.201.ipp: Flags [SEW], seq 1842530049, win 65535, options [mss 1460,nop,wscale 5,nop,nop,TS val
1104744374 ecr 0,sackOK,eol], length 0
16:52:45.113463 IP6 2601:245:c101:54f6:3612:98ff:fe00:8727.domain > 2601:245:c101:54f6:1cf9:4aae:38a4:897.56462: 59359 NXDomain 0/0/0 (41)
16:52:45.114366 IP6 2601:245:c101:54f6:1cf9:4aae:38a4:897.56623 > 2601:245:c101:54f6:3612:98ff:fe00:8727.domain: 62958+ PTR? 77.1.0.10.in-a
ddr.arpa. (40)
16:52:45.115945 IP 10.0.1.201.ipp > 10.0.1.77.52732: Flags [R.], seq 0, ack 1842530050, win 0, length 0
16:52:45.116273 IP 10.0.1.77.52733 > 10.0.1.201.ipp: Flags [SEW], seq 1611759023, win 65535, options [mss 1460,nop,wscale 5,nop,nop,TS val
1104744378 ecr 0,sackOK,eol], length 0
16:52:45.117139 IP6 2601:245:c101:54f6:3612:98ff:fe00:8727.domain > 2601:245:c101:54f6:1cf9:4aae:38a4:897.56623: 62958 NXDomain 0/0/0 (40)
16:52:45.119007 IP6 2601:245:c101:54f6:1cf9:4aae:38a4:897.51872 > 2601:245:c101:54f6:3612:98ff:fe00:8727.domain: 56438+ PTR? 7.9.8.0.4.a.8.
3.e.a.a.4.9.f.c.1.6.f.4.5.1.0.1.c.5.4.2.0.1.0.6.2.ip6.arpa. (90)
16:52:45.120434 IP 10.0.1.201.ipp > 10.0.1.77.52733: Flags [R.], seq 0, ack 1611759024, win 0, length 0
16:52:45.120863 IP6 2601:245:c101:54f6:3612:98ff:fe00:8727.domain > 2601:245:c101:54f6:1cf9:4aae:38a4:897.51872: 56438 NXDomain 0/0/0 (90)
16:52:45.120878 IP 10.0.1.77.52734 > 10.0.1.201.ipp: Flags [S], seq 3942032670, win 65535, options [mss 1460,nop,wscale 5,nop,nop,TS val 11
04744382 ecr 0,sackOK,eol], length 0
16:52:45.121578 IP6 2601:245:c101:54f6:1cf9:4aae:38a4:897.49159 > 2601:245:c101:54f6:3612:98ff:fe00:8727.domain: 9986+ PTR? 7.2.7.8.0.0.e.f
.f.f.8.9.2.1.6.3.6.f.4.5.1.0.1.c.5.4.2.0.1.0.6.2.ip6.arpa. (90)
16:52:45.126044 IP 10.0.1.201.ipp > 10.0.1.77.52734: Flags [R.], seq 0, ack 3942032671, win 0, length 0
16:52:45.126437 IP 10.0.1.77.52735 > 10.0.1.201.ipp: Flags [SEW], seq 3507703142, win 65535, options [mss 1460,nop,wscale 5,nop,nop,TS val
1104744387 ecr 0,sackOK,eol], length 0
16:52:45.130647 IP 10.0.1.201.ipp > 10.0.1.77.52735: Flags [R.], seq 0, ack 3507703143, win 0, length 0
16:52:45.131042 IP 10.0.1.77.52736 > 10.0.1.201.ipp: Flags [SEW], seq 2894567839, win 65535, options [mss 1460,nop,wscale 5,nop,nop,TS val
1104744391 ecr 0,sackOK,eol], length 0
16:52:45.136121 IP 10.0.1.201.ipp > 10.0.1.77.52736: Flags [R.], seq 0, ack 2894567840, win 0, length 0
16:52:45.136532 IP 10.0.1.77.52737 > 10.0.1.201.ipp: Flags [SEW], seq 3119359010, win 65535, options [mss 1460,nop,wscale 5,nop,nop,TS val
1104744396 ecr 0,sackOK,eol], length 0
16:52:45.140689 IP 10.0.1.201.ipp > 10.0.1.77.52737: Flags [R.], seq 0, ack 3119359011, win 0, length 0
16:52:45.141149 IP 10.0.1.77.52738 > 10.0.1.201.ipp: Flags [SEW], seq 868865502, win 65535, options [mss 1460,nop,wscale 5,nop,nop,TS val 1
104744400 ecr 0,sackOK,eol], length 0
16:52:45.145295 IP 10.0.1.201.ipp > 10.0.1.77.52738: Flags [R.], seq 0, ack 868865503, win 0, length 0
16:52:45.145706 IP 10.0.1.77.52739 > 10.0.1.201.ipp: Flags [SEW], seq 57343648, win 65535, options [mss 1460,nop,wscale 5,nop,nop,TS val 11
04744404 ecr 0,sackOK,eol], length 0
16:52:45.149931 IP 10.0.1.201.ipp > 10.0.1.77.52739: Flags [R.], seq 0, ack 57343649, win 0, length 0
16:52:45.150366 IP 10.0.1.77.52740 > 10.0.1.201.ipp: Flags [SEW], seq 3551317811, win 65535, options [mss 1460,nop,wscale 5,nop,nop,TS val
1104744408 ecr 0,sackOK,eol], length 0
16:52:45.154449 IP 10.0.1.201.ipp > 10.0.1.77.52740: Flags [R.], seq 0, ack 3551317812, win 0, length 0
16:52:45.154836 IP 10.0.1.77.52741 > 10.0.1.201.ipp: Flags [S], seq 1914292298, win 65535, options [mss 1460,nop,wscale 5,nop,nop,TS val 11
04744412 ecr 0,sackOK,eol], length 0
16:52:45.157541 IP6 2601:245:c101:54f6:3612:98ff:fe00:8727.domain > 2601:245:c101:54f6:1cf9:4aae:38a4:897.49159: 9986 NXDomain 0/0/0 (90)
16:52:45.160974 IP 10.0.1.201.ipp > 10.0.1.77.52741: Flags [R.], seq 0, ack 1914292299, win 0, length 0
```

Both Wireshark and tcpdump are open source tools available for free. Many commercial products, including Network General's line of tools, provide similar functionality. Most of these tools provide the ability to write captured packets into a PCAP file, which uses a standardized format to exchange data between network analysis tools.

Aircrack-ng provides similar capabilities dedicated specifically to wireless networks. It also allows administrators to test the security and configuration of WiFi networks.

Command-Line Network Tools

Cybersecurity analysts should be familiar with many common command-line network tools. These simple tools are the staples of any cybersecurity toolkit and allow for basic troubleshooting and investigation. They are available on all major operating systems.

Netstat

Netstat provides a listing of all Internet connections to or from a machine and offers information on their current state. Figure 13.17 shows a sample of netstat output.

FIGURE 13.17   Netstat output

```
Mikes-Mac-mini:Documents mchapple$ netstat
Active Internet connections
Proto Recv-Q Send-Q  Local Address          Foreign Address        (state)
tcp4      0      0   10.0.1.77.50984        54.239.31.83.https     ESTABLISHED
tcp6      0      0   2601:245:c101:54.51156 ord30s31-in-x0e..https ESTABLISHED
tcp6      0      0   2601:245:c101:54.54869 ord36s02-in-x03..http  ESTABLISHED
tcp6      0      0   2601:245:c101:54.54848 ord36s04-in-x0e..https ESTABLISHED
tcp6      0      0   2601:245:c101:54.60629 ord30s22-in-x0e..https ESTABLISHED
tcp4      0      0   10.0.1.77.59512        74.112.184.86.https    ESTABLISHED
tcp6      0      0   2601:245:c101:54.56894 ord30s31-in-x0e..https ESTABLISHED
tcp6      0      0   2601:245:c101:54.56871 ord36s02-in-x0e..https ESTABLISHED
tcp4     31      0   10.0.1.77.56323        server-52-84-59-.https CLOSE_WAIT
tcp4      0      0   10.0.1.77.54421        ec2-52-7-36-215..https CLOSE_WAIT
tcp6      0      0   2601:245:c101:54.54766 ord36s02-in-x0e..https ESTABLISHED
tcp4      0      0   10.0.1.77.49432        www.evernote.com.https ESTABLISHED
tcp6      0      0   2601:245:c101:54.54613 ord30s25-in-x0a..https CLOSE_WAIT
tcp4      0      0   10.0.1.77.63156        107.152.24.197.https   CLOSE_WAIT
tcp4      0      0   10.0.1.77.61441        74.112.184.85.https    CLOSE_WAIT
tcp4      0      0   10.0.1.77.61373        74.112.184.85.https    CLOSE_WAIT
tcp6      0      0   2601:245:c101:54.53387 ord30s31-in-x0a..https CLOSE_WAIT
tcp6      0      0   2601:245:c101:54.52964 ord30s31-in-x0d..https CLOSE_WAIT
tcp4      0      0   10.0.1.77.56458        162.125.34.129.https   ESTABLISHED
tcp6      0      0   2601:245:c101:54.56197 ord31s21-in-x0d..https CLOSE_WAIT
tcp6      0      0   2601:245:c101:54.52920 ord30s25-in-x0a..https CLOSE_WAIT
tcp6      0      0   fe80::41:dba5:74.black fe80::64c6:5e14:.29345 ESTABLISHED
tcp6      0      0   fe80::41:dba5:74.1024  fe80::64c6:5e14:.1024  ESTABLISHED
tcp6      0      0   2601:245:c101:54.52756 ord31s21-in-x01..https CLOSE_WAIT
tcp6      0      0   2601:245:c101:54.52749 ord31s21-in-x01..https CLOSE_WAIT
tcp6      0      0   2601:245:c101:54.52686 ord30s26-in-x01..https CLOSE_WAIT
tcp4      0      0   10.0.1.77.52598        ec2-52-3-14-160..https ESTABLISHED
tcp4      0      0   10.0.1.77.52597        ec2-52-3-14-160..https ESTABLISHED
tcp6      0      0   2601:245:c101:54.50848 ord30s31-in-x0d..https CLOSE_WAIT
tcp6      0      0   2601:245:c101:54.50847 ord37s03-in-x0a..https CLOSE_WAIT
tcp6      0      0   2601:245:c101:54.49964 ord36s01-in-x0a..https CLOSE_WAIT
tcp6      0      1   2601:245:c101:54.49962 jl-in-x7d.1e100..jabbe ESTABLISHED
tcp4     37      0   10.0.1.77.49941        107.152.25.197.https   CLOSE_WAIT
tcp4      0      0   10.0.1.77.49936        74.112.185.182.https   CLOSE_WAIT
tcp6      0      0   2601:245:c101:54.49770 jm-in-xbc.1e100..5228  ESTABLISHED
tcp4      0      0   10.0.1.77.49752        ntt-3.lastpass.c.https ESTABLISHED
tcp4      0      0   10.0.1.77.49614        17.188.132.72.5223     ESTABLISHED
tcp4      0      0   10.0.1.77.49379        17.249.76.31.5223      ESTABLISHED
tcp4      0      0   10.0.1.77.61285        ec2-52-44-172-12.ssh   TIME_WAIT
udp4      0      0   10.0.1.77.60782        *.*
udp6      0      0   2601:245:c101:54.51784 ord30s31-in-x0e..https
udp6      0      0   2601:245:c101:54.51783 ord30s31-in-x0e..https
udp4      0      0   *.56506                *.*
```

Ping

Ping gives administrators the ability to verify whether a remote system is alive on the network and answering requests. The system initiating a ping request sends an ICMP Echo

Request packet and the target system may choose to respond with an ICMP Echo Reply packet. Not all systems respond to ping requests, so failing to receive a response does not necessarily mean that the system is down. Figure 13.18 shows the results of pinging a live system that responds to ICMP Echo Request packets.

FIGURE 13.18 Ping

```
Mikes-Mac-mini:Documents mchapple$ ping www.chapple.org
PING www.chapple.org (72.167.232.145): 56 data bytes
64 bytes from 72.167.232.145: icmp_seq=0 ttl=53 time=57.796 ms
64 bytes from 72.167.232.145: icmp_seq=1 ttl=53 time=56.529 ms
64 bytes from 72.167.232.145: icmp_seq=2 ttl=53 time=58.353 ms
64 bytes from 72.167.232.145: icmp_seq=3 ttl=53 time=57.787 ms
64 bytes from 72.167.232.145: icmp_seq=4 ttl=53 time=58.054 ms
64 bytes from 72.167.232.145: icmp_seq=5 ttl=53 time=57.634 ms
64 bytes from 72.167.232.145: icmp_seq=6 ttl=53 time=62.177 ms
64 bytes from 72.167.232.145: icmp_seq=7 ttl=53 time=58.157 ms
64 bytes from 72.167.232.145: icmp_seq=8 ttl=53 time=56.852 ms
64 bytes from 72.167.232.145: icmp_seq=9 ttl=53 time=58.975 ms
64 bytes from 72.167.232.145: icmp_seq=10 ttl=53 time=58.551 ms
^C
--- www.chapple.org ping statistics ---
11 packets transmitted, 11 packets received, 0.0% packet loss
round-trip min/avg/max/stddev = 56.529/58.260/62.177/1.408 ms
Mikes-Mac-mini:Documents mchapple$
```

Traceroute

Traceroute provides an idea of the network path between two systems. It includes information about all systems between the source and destination that are willing to supply such information. This can be a valuable tool in identifying problematic nodes in a connection. In addition, the DNS names reported by intermediate nodes can also give clues to a system's geographic location and ownership. Figure 13.19 shows traceroute in action.

FIGURE 13.19 Traceroute

```
Mikes-Mac-mini:~ mchapple$ traceroute comcast.com
traceroute to comcast.com (69.252.80.75), 64 hops max, 52 byte packets
 1  10.0.1.1 (10.0.1.1)  2.155 ms  2.025 ms  1.139 ms
 2  96.120.24.121 (96.120.24.121)  14.384 ms  10.443 ms  11.850 ms
 3  te-0-5-0-17-sur02.mishawaka.in.sbend.comcast.net (68.87.204.53)  13.234 ms  11.367 ms  9.946 ms
 4  te-0-7-0-3-sur01.mishawaka.in.sbend.comcast.net (69.139.235.249)  15.946 ms
    te-0-7-0-1-sur01.mishawaka.in.sbend.comcast.net (69.139.235.241)  12.016 ms  8.581 ms
 5  te-1-7-0-2-ar01.area4.il.chicago.comcast.net (162.151.36.53)  15.779 ms
    te-1-0-0-4-ar01.area4.il.chicago.comcast.net (68.87.211.105)  19.532 ms
    te-2-2-0-11-ar01.area4.il.chicago.comcast.net (162.151.36.61)  15.274 ms
 6  be-33491-cr02.350ecermak.il.ibone.comcast.net (68.86.91.165)  16.626 ms  15.246 ms  16.994 ms
 7  be-10305-cr02.newyork.ny.ibone.comcast.net (68.86.85.201)  31.593 ms  39.069 ms  35.003 ms
 8  be-7922-ar03.ivyland.pa.panjde.comcast.net (68.86.93.174)  37.905 ms  38.187 ms  36.837 ms
 9  ae100-ur12-d.newcastlerdc.de.panjde.comcast.net (68.85.159.146)  36.829 ms  40.446 ms  38.173 ms
10  urlrw01.cable.comcast.com (69.252.80.75)  39.747 ms  37.992 ms  38.030 ms
Mikes-Mac-mini:~ mchapple$
```

The traceroute command is abbreviated tracert on Windows systems.

ifconfig

The ifconfig command provides detailed configuration information about the network interfaces on a system. This includes both Ethernet and IP addresses as well as information about the network settings configured by the administrator. Figure 13.20 provides an example of *ifconfig* output from a Mac.

FIGURE 13.20   ifconfig

```
Mikes-Mac-mini:~ mchapple$ ifconfig
lo0: flags=8049<UP,LOOPBACK,RUNNING,MULTICAST> mtu 16384
        options=1203<RXCSUM,TXCSUM,TXSTATUS,SW_TIMESTAMP>
        inet 127.0.0.1 netmask 0xff000000
        inet6 ::1 prefixlen 128
        inet6 fe80::1%lo0 prefixlen 64 scopeid 0x1
        nd6 options=201<PERFORMNUD,DAD>
gif0: flags=8010<POINTOPOINT,MULTICAST> mtu 1280
stf0: flags=0<> mtu 1280
en0: flags=8863<UP,BROADCAST,SMART,RUNNING,SIMPLEX,MULTICAST> mtu 1500
        options=10b<RXCSUM,TXCSUM,VLAN_HWTAGGING,AV>
        ether 98:5a:eb:cf:5d:21
        nd6 options=201<PERFORMNUD,DAD>
        media: autoselect (none)
        status: inactive
en1: flags=8863<UP,BROADCAST,SMART,RUNNING,SIMPLEX,MULTICAST> mtu 1500
        ether 78:9f:70:7a:63:56
        inet6 fe80::c04:d54a:4a38:fab7%en1 prefixlen 64 secured scopeid 0x5
        inet 10.0.1.77 netmask 0xffffff00 broadcast 10.0.1.255
        inet6 2601:245:c101:54f6:1cf9:4aae:38a4:897 prefixlen 64 autoconf secured
        inet6 2601:245:c101:54f6:b0b3:d875:df5d:69b2 prefixlen 64 deprecated autoconf temporary
        inet6 2601:245:c101:54f6:9d2e:4a3b:3c03:8fb3 prefixlen 64 deprecated autoconf temporary
        inet6 2601:245:c101:54f6:91c4:2844:1c7:97d0 prefixlen 64 deprecated autoconf temporary
        inet6 2601:245:c101:54f6:46a:838f:27b2:b2e1 prefixlen 64 deprecated autoconf temporary
        inet6 2601:245:c101:54f6:f877:aa73:2726:daad prefixlen 64 autoconf temporary
        nd6 options=201<PERFORMNUD,DAD>
        media: autoselect
        status: active
```

The ifconfig command does not exist on Windows systems, which use ipconfig in its place.

Nslookup

Nslookup provides the ability to perform manual DNS queries to troubleshoot connections on Windows systems, allowing users to learn more about systems during a cybersecurity investigation. Figure 13.21 shows the output from a basic DNS lookup performed using nslookup.

FIGURE 13.21   nslookup

```
Mikes-Mac-mini:~ mchapple$ nslookup www.chapple.org
Server:     2601:245:c101:54f6:3612:98ff:fe00:8727
Address:    2601:245:c101:54f6:3612:98ff:fe00:8727#53

Non-authoritative answer:
Name:   www.chapple.org
Address: 72.167.232.145
```

Dig is a similar tool that has largely replaced nslookup for Linux and macOS. Dig provides a little more detail than nslookup and is the DNS lookup tool of choice for many cybersecurity analysts. Figure 13.22 provides an example of dig output.

FIGURE 13.22   dig

```
Mikes-Mac-mini:~ mchapple$ dig www.chapple.org

; <<>> DiG 9.8.3-P1 <<>> www.chapple.org
;; global options: +cmd
;; Got answer:
;; ->>HEADER<<- opcode: QUERY, status: NOERROR, id: 60051
;; flags: qr rd ra; QUERY: 1, ANSWER: 1, AUTHORITY: 0, ADDITIONAL: 0

;; QUESTION SECTION:
;www.chapple.org.                IN      A

;; ANSWER SECTION:
www.chapple.org.        3193    IN      A       72.167.232.145

;; Query time: 5 msec
;; SERVER: 2601:245:c101:54f6:3612:98ff:fe00:8727#53(2601:245:c101:54f6:3612:98ff:fe00:8727)
;; WHEN: Sun Oct 30 17:23:09 2016
;; MSG SIZE  rcvd: 49

Mikes-Mac-mini:~ mchapple$ █
```

Web Proxies

Proxy servers play an important role in many network security architectures. Web proxies act as intermediaries between clients and web servers. Systems configured to use a web proxy server send all web requests to the proxy server rather than directly reaching out to the web servers hosting the requested site. The proxy server then initiates the connection to the remote web server on behalf of the original client, receives the requested information, and relays it to the client, as shown in Figure 13.23.

FIGURE 13.23   Proxy servers act as intermediaries for network communications.

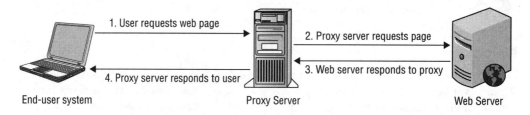

End-user system   Proxy Server   Web Server

1. User requests web page
2. Proxy server requests page
3. Web server responds to proxy
4. Proxy server responds to user

At first glance, proxy servers may seem like an unnecessary redundancy. After all, end-user systems could easily reach out directly to web servers without requiring an intermediary. However, proxy servers can provide two important benefits over direct connections:

Proxy servers provide an opportunity to perform content filtering.   The proxy serves as a choke point for all outbound web requests. If the proxy server receives a request for content that violates the organization's acceptable use policy, the proxy may block the request.

Proxy servers may perform caching of frequently requested content.   If users on a network request the same sites repeatedly, the proxy server may temporarily cache that content and answer user requests directly without reaching out to the remote web server. This improves the response time for users and decreases bandwidth consumption.

When an organization chooses to use proxy servers, administrators must configure all systems on the network to use the proxy server. This may be done by altering the network settings on individual systems, as shown in Figure 13.24, or it may be automated by applying configuration policies to multiple systems automatically, such as by using Group Policy Objects on a Windows network.

FIGURE 13.24   Configuring a web proxy

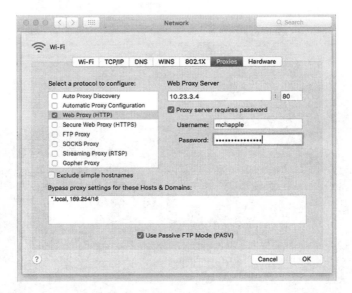

It is important that administrators also carefully configure the network firewall settings to block users from bypassing the proxy server. This may be done by blocking outbound HTTP and HTTPS connections that originate from any system other than the proxy server or other hosts that are authorized to bypass the proxy server.

When most people refer to "proxy servers," they are referring specifically to web proxies that proxy HTTP and HTTPS requests. Proxies can actually relay any application protocol if they are configured to do so.

Cybersecurity analysts should also be aware that proxy servers can play a detrimental role as well. Many public proxy servers are available on the Internet, such as the one shown in Figure 13.25. These proxy servers are intended to allow users to bypass content filtering policies on their local networks by relaying requests through an anonymizing proxy. Security administrators seeking to enforce a content filtering policy should also block the use of known proxy servers.

FIGURE 13.25   Kproxy.com public anonymizing proxy

OpenSSL

Transport Layer Security (TLS) and the Secure Sockets Layer (SSL) provide encryption services for web servers, virtual private networks, and many other forms of encrypted network communication. The majority of servers implementing TLS and SSL do so by using an open source library called *OpenSSL*. This library is available for all major operating systems and is very commonly used on production systems. Cybersecurity analysts may download the most recent copy of OpenSSL from the project's website at www.openssl.org.

TLS vs. SSL

In October 2014, security researchers discovered a vulnerability called Padding Oracle On Downgraded Legacy Encryption (POODLE) that affected all existing implementations of SSL. In the aftermath of this attack, security experts recommend against using SSL in secure environments and instead suggest that all encrypted network communications use TLS.

However, just to keep things confusing, many security professionals still use the term SSL to refer to this style of encryption, even when they are really talking about TLS! To be safe, when you hear someone use the phrase "SSL encryption," you should verify that they are actually referring to TLS and are not planning to use the insecure SSL protocol.

Web Application Security Tools

The web hosts many, if not most, of the applications that organizations use around the world, and those same web applications are often exposed to the world to allow easier access for staff. Attackers look for the best and most prevalent targets, meaning that web applications and the systems and services that run behind them are major targets. Tools like web application firewalls, web application vulnerability scanners (which we covered earlier in the chapter), interception proxies, and fuzzers are all part of the toolset required to test and maintain secure web applications.

Web Application Firewalls

Web application firewalls (WAFs) are purpose-built devices, software, or services that provide content and protocol-aware firewall and technical protections for web applications. They are protective devices, and they provide defenses against common types of attacks using rulesets and specialized capabilities aimed at web applications such as SQL injection, cross-site scripting, and inspection capabilities for SSL, JSON, and other web-centric technologies. In addition, WAFs can be used to provide protection against zero-day attacks that are not patched but that have known attack profiles by building custom rules that address the exploit.

Major vendors of commercial web application firewalls include Akamai's Kona Site Defender, CloudFlare's cloud WAF offerings, F5's ASM, Fortinet's FortiWeb, Imperva's SecureSphere and Incapsula products, Radware's AppWall, among others, as well as open source solutions like NAXSI and ModSecurity. The market is complicated by similarities and capability overlap with next-generation firewalls, web application vulnerability scanners, load balancing and SSL termination systems, as well as niche players and tools with specialized coverage aimed at specific issues.

Figure 13.26 shows a firewall log entry for ModSecurity. The ability to quickly add rules that can detect and prevent web application attacks with relatively simple syntax provides a flexible protection layer for applications.

A web application firewall is increasingly a necessity for enterprise security due to the steady growth of web applications as a default means of delivering services combined with the broad range of attacks against web applications that organizations face on a daily basis. Many organizations choose to implement WAF technology to provide an additional security layer beyond traditional IDS/IPS and firewalls, particularly if they have internal application developers or rely on web-based applications that they host for critical business purposes.

FIGURE 13.26 ModSecurity firewall log entry

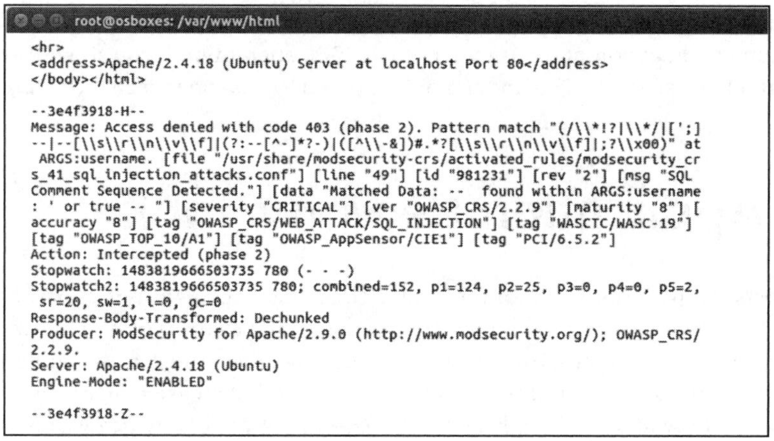

```
root@osboxes: /var/www/html
<hr>
<address>Apache/2.4.18 (Ubuntu) Server at localhost Port 80</address>
</body></html>

--3e4f3918-H--
Message: Access denied with code 403 (phase 2). Pattern match "(/\\*!?|\\*/|[';]
--|--[\\s\\r\\n\\v\\f]|(?:--[^-]*?-)|([^\\-&])#.*?[\\s\\r\\n\\v\\f]|;?\\x00)" at
 ARGS:username. [file "/usr/share/modsecurity-crs/activated_rules/modsecurity_cr
 s_41_sql_injection_attacks.conf"] [line "49"] [id "981231"] [rev "2"] [msg "SQL
 Comment Sequence Detected."] [data "Matched Data: --  found within ARGS:username
 : ' or true -- "] [severity "CRITICAL"] [ver "OWASP_CRS/2.2.9"] [maturity "8"] [
 accuracy "8"] [tag "OWASP_CRS/WEB_ATTACK/SQL_INJECTION"] [tag "WASCTC/WASC-19"]
 [tag "OWASP_TOP_10/A1"] [tag "OWASP_AppSensor/CIE1"] [tag "PCI/6.5.2"]
Action: Intercepted (phase 2)
Stopwatch: 1483819666503735 780 (- - -)
Stopwatch2: 1483819666503735 780; combined=152, p1=124, p2=25, p3=0, p4=0, p5=2,
 sr=20, sw=1, l=0, gc=0
Response-Body-Transformed: Dechunked
Producer: ModSecurity for Apache/2.9.0 (http://www.modsecurity.org/); OWASP_CRS/
2.2.9.
Server: Apache/2.4.18 (Ubuntu)
Engine-Mode: "ENABLED"

--3e4f3918-Z--
```

If you are planning to implement a web application firewall, make sure you consider whether it can integrate with your existing tools—many have the ability to receive data from web application vulnerability scanners and to plug into SIEM systems, allowing them to have a better understanding of what they are protecting as well as the organization's overall security posture.

WAF as a Service

In addition to traditional deployment models that focused on WAF appliances or software, web application firewalls are available as a service. CloudFlare, Radware, and Amazon's AWS environment as well as other vendors offer the ability to simply subscribe to a WAF service and then redirect your traffic through their systems. This allows organizations to add WAF capabilities without the effort of maintaining the underlying systems. As you might imagine, managed WAF services are also available for organizations that want to completely hand off the management of the service.

Interception Proxies

Interception proxies are valuable tools for penetration testers and others seeking to evaluate the security of web applications. As such, they can be classified as exploit tools. They run on the tester's system and intercept requests being sent from the web browser to the web server before they are released onto the network. This allows the tester to manually manipulate the request to attempt the injection of an attack.

In Chapter 12, "Software Development Security," you learned about the use of the Firefox Tamper Data extension as an application proxy. There are other tools that fulfill this same purpose and are browser-independent. For example, Figure 13.27 shows the popular open source Zed Attack Proxy (ZAP). ZAP is a community development project coordinated by the Open Web Application Security Project (OWASP). Users of ZAP can intercept requests sent from any web browser and alter them before passing them to the web server.

FIGURE 13.27   Zed Attack Proxy (ZAP)

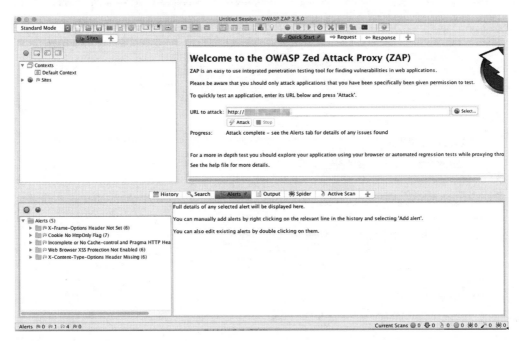

The Burp Proxy, shown in Figure 13.28, is another option available to cybersecurity analysts seeking an interception proxy. It is part of a commercial web application security toolkit called the Burp Suite from PortSwigger. While the full Burp Suite requires a paid license, Burp Proxy is currently available as part of a free edition of the product.

The open source Vega web application security suite also includes an interception proxy capability. For more information on Vega, see https://subgraph.com/vega/.

Fuzzers

Interception proxies allow web application testers to manually alter the input sent to a web application in an attempt to exploit security vulnerabilities. *Fuzzers* are automated testing tools that rapidly create thousands of variants on input in an effort to test many more input combinations than would be possible with manual techniques. Their primary use is as a preventive tool to ensure that software flaws are identified and fixed.

FIGURE 13.28   Burp Proxy

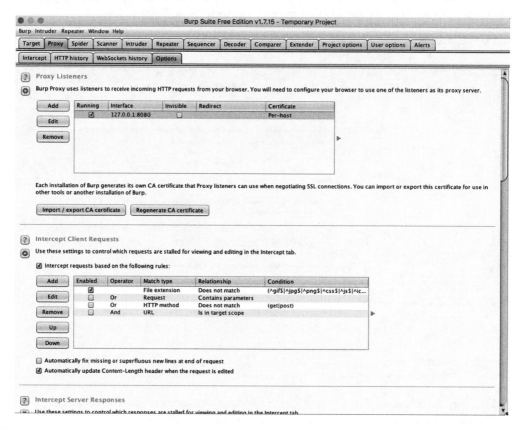

CSA+ candidates should be familiar with two specific fuzzing suites. First, the *Peach Fuzzer* is a commercial product that performs fuzz testing against many different testing environments. These include files, network protocols, embedded devices, proprietary systems, drivers, and Internet of Things (IOT) devices. The CSA+ body of knowledge also mentions the *Untidy* fuzzer. Untidy was once a stand-alone fuzzer designed to work against XML but is now part of the Peach Fuzzer toolkit.

The CSA+ curriculum also mentions that students should be familiar with the fuzzing tools available in the *Microsoft Security Development Lifecycle (SDL)*. These included the *MiniFuzz* file fuzzer and the *SDL Regex Fuzzer* that work on regular expressions. Although CSA+ candidates are required to be familiar with these tools, they are no longer available from Microsoft.

Forensics Tools

Forensic tools give cybersecurity analysts the ability to investigate cybersecurity incidents, obtain evidence, and document the chain of custody for that evidence. The use of proper forensic tools is critical to the integrity of cybersecurity investigations and the admissibility of digital forensic evidence in court.

Hashing

Hash algorithms play an important role in forensic analysis. As discussed in Chapter 7, "Performing Forensic Analysis," forensic analysts use hash algorithms to create digital fingerprints of files, drives, and other data sources when they are first collected as evidence. They may later repeat this hashing process to confirm that the evidence was not tampered with between the time of collection and the time of analysis or the time of introduction into evidence in court.

The two major hash functions used by forensic analysts are *Message Digest 5 (MD5)* and the *Secure Hash Algorithm (SHA)*. Tools that implement each of these hash functions are available as a command-line tool that is provided as a standard component of most Linux distributions. To generate the MD5 hash value for a file using the *md5sum* command, simply use the following syntax:

```
md5sum <filename>
```

Similarly, to find the SHA hash for a file, use the *shasum* command with this syntax:

```
shasum <filename>
```

Figure 13.29 shows an example of the shasum tool in use in a terminal window. The first command displays a file containing the first stanza of the "Star Spangled Banner." The second command uses shasum to determine that the SHA hash value for this file is

FIGURE 13.29   shasum

```
b9d3700e6d64f6cc672bac8116be000ea3dd3e0
```

The next command displays a slightly modified version of the file with a new line added at the end. Finally, the fourth command uses shasum to compute the SHA hash value for the modified file, which is

```
da4b15408b2f284f299a53afdddd35c47f74121f
```

It is important to recognize here that the hash value changed completely from one file to the next. It is not possible to determine from two hash values what changed between two versions of the file or the extent of those changes. Even changing a single character in the file will yield a dramatically different hash value.

 This section describes the MD5 hash function because it is included on the Cybersecurity Analyst+ exam. However, it is very important to note that cryptographers recently discovered significant flaws in MD5 and it is no longer considered secure for use. SHA is a much preferred alternative.

Imaging

The ability to create a forensic image is a crucial part of the forensic process. Forensic images must be created in a way that creates a provably identical image on a bit-by-bit level of the original through hashing, they cannot change the original due to the creation process, and they need to be handled in a documented and secure manner to remove the potential for tampering or mistakes.

There are three major forensic image formats, although other formats exist for specific programs or needs:

- *RAW,* bit-by-bit copies of the original format. Metadata is sometimes acquired along with RAW images and stored separately
- *AFF,* the Advance Forensic Format, an open, extensible forensic format for disk images and metadata
- *E01,* EnCase's file format, which is commonly used for law enforcement investigations

Stand-alone imaging utilities are available:

- *dd,* the disk duplicator utility and a broad range of offshoots with specific forensic capabilities like dc3dd, dcfldd, and others. The dd utility is built into most Linux and Unix systems, and advanced forensic versions are available for download either as part of forensic suites or as independent tools.
- *OSFClone,* a free, bootable imaging tool that produces images in AFF and dc3dd formats. It is available from www.osforensics.com/tools/create-disk-images.html.
- *FTK Imager,* FTK's portable imaging utility, which can be downloaded at http://accessdata.com/product-download.

If you want to see dd or FTK imager in action, simply flip back to Chapter 7.

There are many options when it comes to drive imaging, so selecting an imaging utility that fits your organization's needs is important. You should focus on the file format, portability, and compatibility that you need, as well as the usability and fit to your process that the tool provides.

Forensic Suites

Forensic suites combine multiple forensic tools and capabilities into a full forensic investigation package. They typically allow image creation, investigation tracking, file carving and search tools, reporting mechanisms, and a variety of specialized tools allowing decryption, password recovery, and other forensic support capabilities.

Figure 13.30 shows an example of FTK in use to review email recovered as part of a forensic investigation using an image of a system. The ability to view, label, and search from a single interface is a powerful capability during complex investigations.

FIGURE 13.30   FTK email viewer

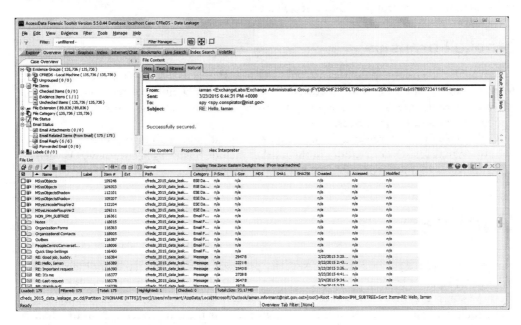

Popular forensic suites include the following:

- *EnCase,* Guidance Software's commercial forensic suite, provides a GUI-driven full forensic suite. It provides support for workflows, searches, and scalable processing for large datasets (https://www.guidancesoftware.com/encase-forensic).

- *FTK,* the Forensic Toolkit, is a complete commercial forensic suite provided by Access-Data. FTK provides a broad variety of investigation tools via a GUI environment and is designed to allow scaling by using multiple systems (http://accessdata.com/solutions/digital-forensics/forensic-toolkit-ftk/).

- *SANS SIFT,* the SANS Investigative Forensics Toolkit, is a toolkit built using open source tools and is based on Ubuntu Linux. It supports multiple disk image formats and provides log timeline, file carving, and other useful forensic capabilities (https://digital-forensics.sans.org/community/downloads).

- *The Sleuth Kit & Autopsy* are a pair of tools that provide broad forensic capabilities. Autopsy is a GUI-based program that provides forensic image analysis capabilities, and the Sleuth Kit is a command line–based toolkit for image analysis and file recovery. Autopsy is based on the Sleuth Kit tools (https://www.sleuthkit.org/).

- *Helix 3 Enterprise and Pro* are a pair of commercial forensic tools. Helix 3 Enterprise provides additional incident response and e-discovery features, and Helix 3 Pro is focused on forensics, providing a suite of open source forensic tools in a bootable format.

In addition to their use during traditional forensic investigations, forensic suites are continuing to add significant antimalware capabilities, making them even more useful during investigations of compromised and infected systems.

Mobile Forensics

Some mobile forensics capabilities are built in, or available as add-ons to traditional forensics suites. In addition, products like Cellebrite's UFED mobile forensics tools provide dedicated mobile forensics features designed to capture, analyze, and report on data from phones and other mobile devices.

Cellebrite's mobile forensic offerings can be found at www.cellebrite.com/Mobile-Forensics. Other vendors in the market include Susteen's SecureView, Oxygen's Forensic Analyst, and Elcomsoft's Mobile Forensic Bundle.

Summary

Numerous tools are available to cybersecurity professionals as they build out their toolkits. In this chapter, you learned about many of the available options with a particular focus on those covered by the CSA+ exam objectives. It is important to remember that many, many tools are available that fulfill the same purpose as the tools described in this chapter. As you build your toolkit, your focus should not be so much on using the specific tools described in this (or any other) book but rather on ensuring that you select an array of tools that meet all of your cybersecurity objectives.

Appendix A

Answers to the Review Questions

Chapter 1: Defending Against Cybersecurity Threats

1. B. The three primary objectives of cybersecurity professionals are confidentiality, integrity, and availability.

2. B. In this scenario, Tommy identified a deficiency in the security of his web server that renders it vulnerable to attack. This is a security vulnerability. Tommy has not yet identified a specific risk because he has not identified a threat (such as a hacker) that might exploit this vulnerability.

3. C. The NIST risk assessment process says that organizations should identify threats before identifying vulnerabilities or determining the likelihood and impact of risks.

4. D. Widespread infrastructure failures, such as those affecting the power grid or telecommunications circuits, are considered man-made disasters and fall under the category of environmental threats.

5. A. Adversarial threat analysis requires examining the capability of the threat source, the intent of the threat source, and the likelihood that the threat will target the organization.

6. D. In an availability attack, the attacker disrupts access to information or a service by legitimate users. In this attack, the attacker disrupted access to the organization's website, violating the principle of availability.

7. D. Penetration tests are an example of an operational security control. Encryption software, network firewalls, and antivirus software are all examples of technical security controls.

8. A. Any action that an organization takes to reduce the likelihood or impact of a risk is an example of risk mitigation. In this case, Paul chose to implement a technical control—a network firewall—to mitigate the likelihood of a successful attack.

9. B. Network access control (NAC) solutions are able to verify the security status of devices before granting them access to the organization's network. Devices not meeting minimum security standards may be placed on a quarantine network until they are remediated.

10. D. The Remote Access Dial-In User Service (RADIUS) is an authentication protocol used for communications between authenticators and the authentication server during the 802.1x authentication process.

11. A. Any device that wishes to join an 802.1x network must be running an 802.1x supplicant that can communicate with the authenticator before joining the network.

12. D. The Secure HTTP (HTTPS) protocol uses TCP port 443 for communications between web browsers and the web server.

13. A. Next-generation firewalls (NGFWs) incorporate contextual information about users, applications, and business processes in their decision-making process.

14. B. Port 23, used by the Telnet protocol, is unencrypted and insecure. Connections should not be permitted to the jump box on unencrypted ports. The services running on ports 22 (SSH), 443 (HTTPS), and 3389 (RDP) all use encryption.

15. A. Administrators may use Group Policy Objects (GPOs) to control a wide variety of Windows settings and create different policies that apply to different classes of system.

16. A. During the planning phase of a penetration test, the testers should confirm the timing, scope, and authorization for the test in writing.

17. A. After the completion of the discovery phase, penetration testers first seek to gain access to a system on the targeted network and then may use that system as the launching point for additional attacks.

18. A. The red team plays the role of the attacker and uses reconnaissance and exploitation tools to attempt to gain access to the protected network.

19. D. Sandboxing is an approach used to detect malicious software based on its behavior rather than its signatures. Sandboxing systems watch systems and the network for unknown pieces of code and, when they detect an application that has not been seen before, immediately isolate that code in a special environment known as a sandbox where it does not have access to any other systems or applications.

20. B. Web application firewalls (WAFs) are specialized firewalls designed to protect against web application attacks, such as SQL injection and cross-site scripting.

Chapter 2: Reconnaissance and Intelligence Gathering

1. D. DNS zone transfers provide a method to replicate DNS information between DNS servers, but they are also a tempting target for attackers due to the amount of information that they contain. A properly secured DNS server will only allow zone transfers to specific, permitted peer DNS servers. DNSSEC is a suite of DNS security specifications, AXR is a made up term (AXFR is the zone transfer command), and DNS registration is how you register a domain name.

2. C. Nmap's operating system identification flag is -o. This enables OS detection. -A also enables OS identification and other features. -osscan with modifiers like -limit and -guess set specific OS identification features. -os and -id are not nmap flags.

3. B. Traceroute (or tracert on Windows systems) is a command-line tool that uses ICMP to trace the route that a packet takes to a host. Whois and nslookup are domain tools, and routeview is not a command-line tool.

4. B. Exif (Exchangeable Image Format) data often includes location and camera data, allowing the images to be mapped and identified to a specific device or type of camera.

5. A. Log level 0 is used for emergencies in Cisco's logging level scheme. Log level 7 is for debugging information and is at the bottom of the scale.

6. C. IPX connections are not shown by netstat. IPX is a non-IP protocol. Active TCP connections, executables that are associated with them, and route table information are all available via netstat.

7. D. Although it is possible that a system named "db1" with a hostname "sqldb1" is not a Microsoft SQL server, the most likely answer is that it is a MS-SQL server.

8. B. Microsoft Windows security logs can contain information about files being opened, created, or deleted if configured to do so. Configuration and httpd logs are not a type of Windows logs, and system logs contain information about events logged by Windows components.

9. D. The Internet Assigned Numbers Authority manages the global IP address space. ARIN is the American Registry for Internet Numbers, WorldNIC is not an IP authority, and NASA tackles problems in outer space, not global IP space.

10. C. Metadata purging removes hidden information about a file like the creator, creation time, system used to create the file, and a host of other information. The other answers are made up.

11. C. Heuristic analysis focuses on behaviors, allowing a tool using it to identify malware behaviors instead of looking for a specific package. Trend analysis is typically used to identify large-scale changes from the norm, and it is more likely to be useful for a network than for a single PC. Regression analysis is used in statistical modeling.

12. B. Registering manually won't prevent DNS harvesting, but privacy services are often used to prevent personal or corporate information from being visible via domain registrars. CAPTCHAs, rate limiting, and blacklisting systems or networks that are gathering data are all common anti-DNS harvesting techniques.

13. D. The axfr flag indicates a zone transfer in both the dig and host utilities.

14. C. A packet capture can't provide plausible deniability, as it provides evidence of action. Packet capture is often used to document work, including the time that a given scan or process occurred, and it can also be used to provide additional data for further analysis.

15. D. Operating system detection often uses TCP options support, IP ID sampling, and window size checks, as well as other indicators that create unique fingerprints for various operating systems. Service identification often leverages banners since TCP capabilities are not unique to a given service. Fuzzing is a code testing method, and application scanning is usually related to web application security.

16. B. Netflow is a Cisco network protocol that collects IP traffic information that allows analysis of traffic flow and volume. Netstat provides information about local connections, which applications have made them, and other useful local system information. Libpcap is the Linux packet capture library and would not be used alone. pflow is a made-up term.

17. B. Zone transfers are intended to allow DNS database replication, but an improperly secured DNS server can also allow third parties to request a zone transfer, exposing all of their DNS information. Traceroute is used to determine the path and latency to a remote host, whereas dig is a useful DNS query tool. DNS sync is a made-up technical term.

18. A. The Internet Archive maintains copies of sites from across the Internet, and it can be used to review the historical content of a site. WikiLeaks distributes leaked information, whereas the Internet Rewinder and TimeTurner are both made-up names.

19. B. Social media can be a treasure trove of personal information. Company websites and forums are usually limited in the information they provide, and Creepy is a geolocation tool that gathers data from social media and geotagging.

20. C. Whois provides information that can include the organization's physical address, registrar, contact information, and other details. Nslookup will provide IP address or hostname information, whereas host provides IPv4 and IPv6 addresses as well as email service information. Traceroute attempts to identify the path to a remote host as well as the systems along the route.

Chapter 3: Designing a Vulnerability Management Program

1. C. The Federal Information Security Management Act (FISMA) requires that federal agencies implement vulnerability management programs for federal information systems.

2. D. The Federal Information Security Management Act (FISMA) requires vulnerability management programs for all federal information systems, regardless of their assigned impact rating.

3. A. An asset inventory supplements automated tools with other information to detect systems present on a network. The asset inventory provides critical information for vulnerability scans.

4. D. PCI DSS requires that organizations conduct vulnerability scans on at least a quarterly basis, although many organizations choose to conduct scans on a much more frequent basis.

5. B. QualysGuard, Nessus, and OpenVAS are all examples of vulnerability scanning tools. Snort is an intrusion detection system.

6. A. PCI DSS requires that organizations conduct vulnerability scans quarterly, which would have Bethany's next regularly scheduled scan scheduled for June. However, the standard also requires scanning after any significant change in the payment card environment. This would include an upgrade to the point-of-sale system, so Bethany must complete a new compliance scan immediately.

7. D. Credentialed scans only require read-only access to target servers. Renee should follow the principle of least privilege and limit the access available to the scanner.

8. C. Common Product Enumeration (CPE) is an SCAP component that provides standardized nomenclature for product names and versions.

9. D. Internal scans completed for PCI DSS compliance purposes may be conducted by any qualified individual.

10. C. The Federal Information Security Management Act (FISMA) requires that government agencies conduct vulnerability scans. HIPAA, which governs hospitals and doctors' offices, does not include a vulnerability scanning requirement, nor does GLBA, which covers financial institutions.

11. C. Control enhancement number 4 requires that an organization determine what information about the system is discoverable by adversaries. This enhancement only applies to FISMA high systems.

12. B. The organization's risk appetite is its willingness to tolerate risk within the environment. If an organization is extremely risk averse, it may choose to conduct scans more frequently to minimize the amount of time between when a vulnerability comes into existence and when it is detected by a scan.

13. D. Scan schedules are most often determined by the organization's risk appetite, regulatory requirements, technical constraints, business constraints, and licensing limitations. Most scans are automated and do not require staff availability.

14. B. If Barry is able to limit the scope of his PCI DSS compliance efforts to the isolated network, then that is the only network that must be scanned for PCI DSS compliance purposes.

15. C. Ryan should first run his scan against a test environment to identify likely vulnerabilities and assess whether the scan itself might disrupt business activities.

16. C. While reporting and communication are an important part of vulnerability management, they are not included in the life cycle. The three life-cycle phases are detection, remediation, and testing.

17. A. Continuous monitoring incorporates data from agent-based approaches to vulnerability detection and reports security-related configuration changes to the vulnerability management platform as soon as they occur, providing the ability to analyze those changes for potential vulnerabilities.

18. B. Systems have a moderate impact from a confidentiality perspective if the unauthorized disclosure of information could be expected to have a serious adverse effect on organizational operations, organizational assets or individuals.

19. A. The Common Vulnerability Scoring System (CVSS) provides a standardized approach for measuring and describing the severity of security vulnerabilities. Jessica could use this scoring system to prioritize issues raised by different source systems.

20. B. While any qualified individual may conduct internal compliance scans, PCI DSS requires the use of a scanning vendor approved by the PCI SSC for external compliance scans.

Chapter 4: Analyzing Vulnerability Scans

1. B. Although the network can support any of these protocols, internal IP disclosure vulnerabilities occur when a network uses Network Address Translation (NAT) to map public and private IP addresses but a server inadvertently discloses its private IP address to remote systems.

2. C. The *authentication metric* describes the authentication hurdles that an attacker would need to clear to exploit a vulnerability.

3. C. An access complexity of "low" indicates that exploiting the vulnerability does not require any specialized conditions.

4. D. If any of these measures is marked as C, for Complete, it indicates the potential for a complete compromise of the system.

5. D. Version 3.0 of CVSS is currently available but is not as widely used as the more common CVSS version 2.0.

6. B. The CVSS exploitability score is computed using the access vector, access complexity, and authentication metrics.

7. C. Vulnerabilities with a CVSS score higher than 6.0 but less than 10.0 fall into the High risk category.

8. A. A false positive error occurs when the vulnerability scanner reports a vulnerability that does not actually exist.

9. B. It is unlikely that a database table would contain information relevant to assessing a vulnerability scan report. Logs, SIEM reports, and configuration management systems are much more likely to contain relevant information.

10. A. Microsoft discontinued support for Windows Server 2003, and it is likely that the operating system contains unpatchable vulnerabilities.

11. D. Buffer overflow attacks occur when an attacker manipulates a program into placing more data into an area of memory than is allocated for that program's use. The goal is to overwrite other information in memory with instructions that may be executed by a different process running on the system.

12. B. In October 2016, security researchers announced the discovery of a Linux kernel vulnerability dubbed Dirty COW. This vulnerability, present in the Linux kernel for nine years, was extremely easy to exploit and provided successful attackers with administrative control of affected systems.

13. D. Telnet is an insecure protocol that does not make use of encryption. The other protocols mentioned are all considered secure.

14. D. TLS 1.1 is a secure transport protocol that supports web traffic. The other protocols listed all have flaws that render them insecure and unsuitable for use.

15. B. Digital certificates are intended to provide public encryption keys, and this would not cause an error. The other circumstances are all causes for concern and would trigger an alert during a vulnerability scan.

16. D. In a virtualized data center, the virtual host hardware runs a special operating system known as a *hypervisor* that mediates access to the underlying hardware resources.

17. A. VM escape vulnerabilities are the most serious issue that can exist in a virtualized environment, particularly when a virtual host runs systems of differing security levels. In an escape attack, the attacker has access to a single virtual host and then manages to leverage that access to intrude on the resources assigned to a different virtual machine.

18. B. Intrusion detection systems (IDSs) are a security control used to detect network or host attacks. The Internet of Things (IoT), supervisory control and data acquisition (SCADA) systems, and industrial control systems (ICS) are all associated with connecting physical world objects to a network.

19. D. In a cross-site scripting (XSS) attack, an attacker embeds scripting commands on a website that will later be executed by an unsuspecting visitor accessing the site. The idea is to trick a user visiting a trusted site into executing malicious code placed there by an untrusted third party.

20. A. In a SQL injection attack, the attacker seeks to use a web application to gain access to an underlying database. Semicolons and apostrophes are characteristic of these attacks.

Chapter 5: Building an Incident Response Program

1. D. A former employee crashing a server is an example of a computer security incident because it is an actual violation of the availability of that system. An intruder breaking into a building may be a security event, but it is not necessarily a computer security event unless he or she performs some action affecting a computer system. A user accessing a secure file and an administrator changing a file permission settings are examples of security events but are not security incidents.

2. A. Organizations should build solid, defense-in-depth approaches to cybersecurity during the preparation phase of the incident response process. The controls built during this phase serve to reduce the likelihood and impact of future incidents.

3. C. A security information and event management (SIEM) system correlates log entries from multiple sources and attempts to identify potential security incidents.

4. C. The definition of a medium functional impact is that the organization has lost the ability to provide a critical service to a subset of system users. That accurately describes the situation that Ben finds himself in. Assigning a low functional impact is only done when the organization can provide all critical services to all users at diminished efficiency. Assigning a high functional impact is only done if a critical service is not available to all users.

5. C. The containment protocols contained in the containment, eradication, and recovery phases are designed to limit the damage caused by an ongoing security incident.

6. D. National Archives General Records Schedule (GRS) 24 requires that all federal agencies retain incident handling records for at least three years.

7. C. In a proprietary breach, unclassified proprietary information is accessed or exfiltrated. Protected critical infrastructure information (PCII) is an example of unclassified proprietary information.

8. A. The Network Time Protocol (NTP) provides a common source of time information that allows the synchronizing of clocks throughout an enterprise.

9. A. An organization's incident response policy should contain a clear description of the authority assigned to the CSIRT while responding to an active security incident.

10. D. A web attack is an attack executed from a website or web-based application—for example, a cross-site scripting attack used to steal credentials or redirect to a site that exploits a browser vulnerability and installs malware.

11. A. CSIRT members do not normally communicate directly with the perpetrator of a cybersecurity incident.

12. A. The incident response policy provides the CSIRT with the authority needed to do their job. Therefore, it should be approved by the highest possible level of authority within the organization, preferably the CEO.

13. A. Detection of a potential incident occurs during the detection and analysis phase of incident response. The other activities listed are all objectives of the containment, eradication, and recovery phase.

14. C. Extended recoverability effort occurs when the time to recovery is unpredictable. In those cases, additional resources and outside help are typically needed.

15. D. An attrition attack employs brute-force methods to compromise, degrade, or destroy systems, networks, or services—for example, a DDoS attack intended to impair or deny access to a service or application or a brute-force attack against an authentication mechanism.

16. C. Lessons-learned sessions are most effective when facilitated by an independent party who was not involved in the incident response effort.

17. D. Procedures for rebuilding systems are highly technical and would normally be included in a playbook or procedure document rather than an incident response policy.

18. B. An impersonation attack involves the replacement of something benign with something malicious—for example, spoofing, man-in-the-middle attacks, rogue wireless access points, and SQL injection attacks all involve impersonation.

19. C. Incident response playbooks contain detailed step-by-step instructions that guide the early response to a cybersecurity incident. Organizations typically have playbooks prepared for high-severity and frequently occurring incident types.

20. A. The event described in this scenario would not qualify as a security incident with measurable information impact. Although the laptop did contain information that might cause a privacy breach, that breach was avoided by the use of encryption to protect the contents of the laptop.

Chapter 6: Analyzing Symptoms for Incident Response

1. B. The df command will show you a system's current disk utilization. Both the top command and the ps command will show you information about processes, CPU, and memory utilization, whereas lsof is a multifunction tool for listing open files.

2. C. Perfmon provides the ability to gather detailed usage statistics for many items in Windows. Resmon monitors CPU, memory, and disk usage, but does not provide information about things like USB host controllers and other detailed instrumentation. Statmon and winmon are not Windows built-in tools.

3. D. Flow data provides information about the source and destination IP address, protocol, and total data sent and would provide the detail needed. Syslog, resmon, and WMI data is all system log information and would not provide this information.

4. A. Network access control (NAC) can be set up to require authentication. Port security is limited to recognizing MAC addresses, making it less suited to preventing rogue devices. PRTG is a monitoring tool, and NTP is the network time protocol.

5. A. A monitoring threshold is set to determine when an alarm or report action is taken. Thresholds are often set to specific values or percentages of capacity.

6. C. Active monitoring is focused on reaching out to gather data using tools like ping and iPerf. Passive monitoring using protocol analyzers collects network traffic and router-based monitoring using SNMP, and flows gather data by receiving or collecting logged information.

7. A. Beaconing activity (sometimes called heartbeat traffic) occurs when traffic is sent to a botnet command and control system. The other terms are made up.

8. C. Log analysis, flow monitoring, and deploying an IPS are all appropriate solutions to help detect denial-of-service attacks. iPerf is a performance testing tool used to establish the maximum bandwidth available on a network connection.

9. D. Hardware vendor ID codes are part of MAC addresses and can be checked for devices that have not had their MAC address changed. It is possible to change MAC addresses, so relying on only the MAC address is not recommended.

10. B. Locating a rogue AP is often best done by performing a physical survey and triangulating the likely location of the device by checking its signal strength. If the AP is plugged into the organization's network, nmap may be able to find it, but connecting to it is unlikely to provide its location (or be safe!). NAC would help prevent the rogue device from connecting to an organizational network but won't help locate it.

11. A. System Center Configuration Manager provides non-real-time reporting for disk space. Resmon, perfmon, and SCOM can all provide real-time reporting, which can help to identify problems before they take a system down.

12. B. The best way to deal with memory leaks is to patch the application or service. If a patch is not available, restarting the service or the underlying operating system is often the only solution. Buffer overflow and stack smashing prevention both help deal with memory-based attacks rather than memory leaks, and monitoring can help identify out-of-memory conditions but don't directly help deal with a memory leak.

13. A. A blacklisting application or tool can allow Jack to specifically prevent specific files or applications from being installed. SCCM could be used uninstall files, and SCOM could be used to monitor machines for files, but neither is as well suited. Whitelisting works in the opposite manner by listing allowed files.

14. C. The most likely answer is that the link has failed. Incorrectly set sampling rates will not provide a good view of traffic, and a DDoS attack is more likely to show large amounts of traffic. SNMP is a monitoring tool and would not result in flow data changing.

15. B. SNMPv3 adds encryption, authentication, and user account support, providing significantly better security than previous versions.

16. B. The `service --status` command is a Linux command. Windows service status can be queried using `sc`, the Services snap-in for the Microsoft Management Console, or via a PowerShell query.

17. D. Protocol analysis, using heuristic (behavior)-based detection capabilities, and building a network traffic baseline are all common techniques used to identify unexpected network traffic. Beaconing occurs when a system contacts a botnet command and control system, and is likely to be a source of unexpected traffic.

18. C. SNMP will not typically provide specific information about a system's network traffic that would allow you to identify outbound connections. Flows, sniffers (protocol analyzers), and an IDS or IPS can all provide a view that would allow the suspect traffic to be captured.

19. A. Whitelisting software prevents software that is not on a preapproved list from being installed. Blacklists prevent specific software from being installed, whereas heuristic and signature-based detection systems focus on behavior and specific recognizable signatures respectively.

20. B. The `top` command in Linux provides an interactive interface to view CPU utilization, memory usage, and other details for running processes. `df` shows disk usage, `tail` displays the end of a file, and `cpugrep` is a made-up command.

Chapter 7: Performing Forensic Analysis

1. B. dd creates files in RAW, bit-by-bit format. EN01 is the EnCase forensic file format, OVF is virtualization file format, and ddf is a made-up answer.

2. B. Slack space is the space that remains when only a portion of a cluster is used by a file. Data from previous files may remain in the slack space since it is typically not wiped or overwritten. Unallocated space is space on a drive that has not been made into part of a partition. Outer space and non-Euclidean space are not terms used for filesystems or forensics.

3. C. Event logs do not typically contain significant amounts of information about file changes. The Master File Table and file indexes (INDX files) both have specific information about files, whereas volume shadow copies can help show differences between files and locations at a point in time.

4. C. Write blockers ensure that no changes are made to a source drive when creating a forensic copy. Preventing reads would stop you from copying the drive, drive cloners may or may not have write blocking capabilities built in, and hash validation is useful to ensure contents match but don't stop changes to the source drive from occurring.

5. C. USB Historian provides a list of devices that are logged in the Windows Registry. Frederick can check the USB device's serial number and other identifying information against the Windows system's historical data. If the device isn't listed, it is not absolute proof, but if it is listed, it is reasonable to assume that it was used on the device.

6. D. Core dumps and hibernation files both contain an image of the live memory of a system, potentially allowing encryption keys to be retrieved from the stored file. The MFT provides information about file layout, and the Registry contains system information but shouldn't have encryption keys stored in it. There is no hash file or encryption log stored as a Windows default file.

7. A. Timelines are one of the most useful tools when conducting an investigation of a compromise or other event. Forensic tools provide built-in timeline capabilities to allow this type of analysis.

8. D. Since Danielle did not hash her source drive prior to cloning, you cannot determine where the problem occurred. If she had run MD5sum prior to the cloning process as well as after, she could verify that the original disk had not changed.

9. D. The Volatility Framework is designed to work with Windows, macOS, and Linux, and it provides in-depth memory forensics and analysis capabilities. LiME and fmem are Linux tools, whereas DumpIt is a Windows-only tool.

10. D. Windows installer logs are typically kept in the user's temporary app data folder. Windows does not keep install log files, and System32 does not contain an Installers directory.

11. B. Windows crash dumps are stored in `%SystemRoot%\MEMORY.DMP` and contain the memory state of the system when the system crash occurred. This is her best bet for gathering the information she needs without access to a live image. The Registry and system restore point do not contain this information, and WinDbg is a Windows debugger, not an image of live memory.

12. D. Manual access is used when phones cannot be forensically imaged or accessed as a volume or filesystem. Manual access requires that the phone be reviewed by hand, with pictures and notes preserved to document the contents of the phone.

13. A. CCleaner is a PC cleanup utility that wipes Internet history, destroys cookies and other cached data, and can impede forensic investigations. CCleaner may be an indication of intentional anti-forensic activities on a system. It is not a full disk encryption tool or malware packer, nor will it modify MAC times.

14. B. Unallocated space is typically not captured during a live image, potentially resulting in data being missed. Remnant data from the tool, memory and drive contents changing while the image is occurring, and malware detecting the tool are all possible issues.

15. D. Jeff did not create the image and cannot validate chain of custody for the drive. This also means he cannot prove that the drive is a copy of the original. Since we do not know the checksum for the original drive, we do not have a bad checksum or a hash mismatch— there isn't an original to compare it to. Anti-forensics activities may have occurred, but that is not able to be determined from the question.

16. A. Imaging the system while the program is live has the best probability of allowing Jeff to capture the encryption keys or decrypted data from memory. An offline image after the system is shut down will likely result in having to deal with the encrypted file. Brute-force attacks are typically slow and may not succeed, and causing a system crash may result in corrupted or nonexistent data.

17. C. Windows stores information about programs that run when Windows starts in the Registry as Run and RunOnce Registry keys, which run each time a user logs in. INDX files and the MFT are both useful for file information, and volume shadow copies can be used to see point-in-time information about a system.

18. A. Ben is maintaining chain-of-custody documentation. Chris is acting as the validator for the actions that Ben takes, and acts as a witness to the process.

19. D. While AES does have a hashing mode, MD5, SHA1, and built-in hashing tools in FTK and other commercial tools are more commonly used for forensic hashes.

20. B. The df tool will show you a system's current disk utilization. Both the top and the ps tools will show you information about processes, CPU, and memory utilization, and lsof is a multifunction tool for listing open files.

Chapter 8: Recovery and Post-Incident Response

1. A. The containment, eradication, and recovery phase of incident response includes active undertakings designed to minimize the damage caused by the incident and restore normal operations as quickly as possible.

2. C. NIST recommends using six criteria to evaluate a containment strategy: the potential damage to resources, the need for evidence preservation, service availability, time and resources required (including cost), effectiveness of the strategy, and duration of the solution.

3. C. In a segmentation approach, the suspect system is placed on a separate network where it has very limited access to other networked resources.

4. B. In the isolation strategy, the quarantine network is directly connected to the Internet or restricted severely by firewall rules so that the attacker may continue to control it but not gain access to any other networked resources.

5. D. In the removal approach, Alice keeps the systems running for forensic purposes but completely cuts off their access to or from other networks, including the Internet.

6. A. Sandboxes are isolation tools used to contain attackers within an environment where they believe they are conducting an attack but, in reality, are operating in a benign environment.

7. C. Tamara's first priority should be containing the attack. This will prevent it from spreading to other systems and also potentially stop the exfiltration of sensitive information. Only after containing the attack should Tamara move on to eradication and recovery activities. Identifying the source of the attack should be a low priority.

8. D. CompTIA includes patching, permissions, security scanning, and verifying logging/ communication to monitoring in the set of validation activities that cybersecurity analysts should undertake in the aftermath of a security incident.

9. C. Understanding the root cause of an attack is critical to the incident recovery effort. Analysts should examine all available information to help reconstruct the attacker's actions. This information is crucial to remediating security controls and preventing future similar attacks.

10. C. Lynda should consult the flowchart that appears in Figure 8.7. Following that chart, the appropriate disposition for media that contains high security risk information and will be reused within the organization is to purge it.

11. B. New firewall rules, if required, would be implemented during the eradication and recovery phase. The validation phase includes verifying accounts and permissions, verifying that logging is working properly, and conducting vulnerability scans.

12. D. The primary purpose of eradication is to remove any of the artifacts of the incident that may remain on the organization's network. This may include the removal of any malicious code from the network, the sanitization of compromised media, and the securing of compromised user accounts.

13. B. There are many potential uses for written incident reports. First, it creates an institutional memory of the incident that is useful when developing new security controls and training new security team members. Second, it may serve as an important record of the incident if there is ever legal action that results from the incident. These reports should be classified and not disclosed to external parties.

14. D. Malware signatures would not normally be included in an evidence log. The log would typically contain identifying information (e.g., the location, serial number, model number, hostname, MAC addresses and IP addresses of a computer), the name, title and phone number of each individual who collected or handled the evidence during the investigation, the time and date (including time zone) of each occurrence of evidence handling, and the locations where the evidence was stored.

15. D. Even removing a system from the network doesn't guarantee that the attack will not continue. In the example given in this chapter, an attacker can run a script on the server that detects when it has been removed from the network and then proceeds to destroy data stored on the server.

16. A. The data disposition flowchart in Figure 8.7 directs that any media containing highly sensitive information that will leave the control of the organization must be destroyed. Joe should purchase a new replacement device to provide to the contractor.

17. B. Incident reports should include a chronology of events, estimates of the impact, and documentation of lessons learned, in addition to other information. Incident response efforts should not normally focus on uncovering the identity of the attacker, so this information would not be found in an incident report.

18. D. NIST SP 800-61 is the *Computer Security Incident Handling Guide*. NIST SP 800-53 is *Security and Privacy Controls for Federal Information Systems and Organizations*. NIST SP 800-88 is *Guidelines for Media Sanitization*. NIST SP 800-18 is the *Guide for Developing Security Plans for Federal Information Systems*.

19. A. Resetting a device to factory state is an example of a data clearing activity. Data purging activities include overwriting, block erase, and cryptographic erase activities when performed through the use of dedicated, standardized device commands.

20. A. Only removal of the compromised system from the network will stop the attack against other systems. Isolated and/or segmented systems are still permitted access to the Internet and could continue their attack. Detection is a purely passive activity that does not disrupt the attacker at all.

Chapter 9: Policy and Compliance

1. B. The key word in this scenario is "one way." This indicates that compliance with the document is not mandatory, so Joe must be authoring a guideline. Policies, standards, and procedures are all mandatory.

2. A. PCI DSS compensating controls must be "above and beyond" other PCI DSS requirements. This specifically bans the use of a control used to meet one requirement as a compensating control for another requirement.

3. A. The Health Insurance Portability and Accountability Act (HIPAA) includes security and privacy rules that affect healthcare providers, health insurers, and health information clearinghouses.

4. B. The five security functions described in the NIST Cybersecurity Framework are identify, protect, detect, respond, and recover.

5. B. The International Organization for Standardization (ISO) publishes ISO 27001, a standard document titled "Information technology—Security techniques—Information security management systems—Requirements."

6. D. Policies require approval from the highest level of management, usually the CEO. Other documents may often be approved by other managers, such as the CISO.

7. C. The logical security architecture corresponds to the designer's view in the SABSA model. The contextual architecture is the business view, the conceptual architecture is the architect's view, and the component architecture is the tradesman's view.

8. B. The Sarbanes-Oxley (SOX) Act applies to the financial records of publicly traded companies and requires that those companies have a strong degree of assurance around the IT systems that store and process those records.

9. C. In the TOGAF model, the data architecture provides the organization's approach to storing and managing information assets.

10. B. Security policies do not normally contain prescriptive technical guidance, such as a requirement to use a specific encryption algorithm. This type of detail would normally be found in a security standard.

11. D. Administrative controls are procedural mechanisms that an organization follows to implement sound security management practices. Examples of administrative controls include user account reviews, employee background investigations, log reviews, and separation of duties policies.

12. D. The Information Technology Infrastructure Library (ITIL) is a framework that offers a comprehensive approach to IT service management (ITSM) within the modern enterprise. ITIL covers five core activities: Service Strategy, Service Design, Service Transition, Service Operation, and Continual Service Improvement.

13. D. The Payment Card Industry Data Security Standard (PCI DSS) provides detailed rules about the storage, processing, and transmission of credit and debit card information. PCI DSS is not a law but rather a contractual obligation that applies to credit card merchants and service providers.

14. D. The data retention policy outlines what information the organization will maintain and the length of time different categories of information will be retained prior to destruction.

15. D. The description provided matches the definition of a Tier 4 (Adaptive) organization's risk management practices under the NIST Cybersecurity Framework.

16. D. Guidelines are the only element of the security policy framework that are optional. Compliance with policies, standards, and procedures is mandatory.

17. A. Logical controls are technical controls that enforce confidentiality, integrity, and availability in the digital space. Examples of logical security controls include firewall rules, access control lists, intrusion prevention systems, and encryption.

18. B. Standards describe specific security controls that must be in place for an organization. Allan would not include acceptable mechanisms in a high-level policy document, and this information is too general to be useful as a procedure. Guidelines are not mandatory, so they would not be applicable in this scenario.

19. D. The NIST Cybersecurity Framework is designed to help organizations describe their current cybersecurity posture, describe their target state for cybersecurity, identify and prioritize opportunities for improvement, assess progress, and communicate with stakeholders about risk. It does not create specific technology requirements.

20. D. Procedures provide checklist-style sets of step-by-step instructions guiding how employees should react in a given circumstance. Procedures commonly guide the early stages of incident response.

Chapter 10: Defense-in-Depth Security Architectures

1. B. Separation of duties would prevent Sue from both requesting and approving a change. Although this would not prevent her from having an employee make the request, it would stop her from handling the entire process herself. Mandatory vacation might help catch this issue if it were consistent but does not directly solve the problem. Succession planning identifies employees who might fill a role in the future, and dual control requires two people to work together to perform an action, neither of which is appropriate for this issue.

2. D. Ben's best option is dual control, which requires two individuals to collaborate to perform an action. This might take the form of independent access codes, both of which are required to access a secure vault. Mandatory vacation, succession planning, and separation of duties do not directly prevent an individual from gaining independent access to a secure location.

3. C. Succession planning can help to ensure that employee departures do not result in critical skillsets and knowledge being inaccessible. Exit interviews may identify tasks or skills but won't ensure that skills and knowledge are already prepared before an employee leaves. Mandatory vacation and HR oversight do not address this issue.

4. B. Ric's best option is to implement backup Internet connectivity using a different make and model of router. This reduces the chance of the same exploit being able to take down both types of device while removing the single point of failure for connectivity. Adding a second identical router in either active/active or active/passive mode does not work around the flaw since an attacker could immediately repeat the attack to take down the matching router. A firewall might help, but in many cases attacks against routers take place on a channel that is required for the router to perform its function.

5. B. Fred's best option is to employ full disk encryption. Without a valid login, a thief would find that all data on the system was encrypted. Remote wipe capabilities and machine tracking software would provide helpful additional capabilities, but both rely on the system connecting to a network after it is stolen. Central management is useful for reporting machine state and might even help locate a machine if it was reconnected to a network, but it does not protect the data the machine contains.

6. B. A multitier firewall is least likely to be an effective security control when Susan's organization deals with compromised credentials. Multifactor authentication would require the attacker to have the second factor in addition to the password, an awareness program may help Susan's employees avoid future scams, and a SIEM monitoring for logins that are out of the ordinary may spot the attacker logging in remotely or otherwise abusing the credentials they obtained.

7. D. Retirement is the last step at the end of the life cycle for a standard or process. Of course this means that if the process is retired, a final update to it is not needed! The standards for other, currently maintained operating systems should undergo regular scheduled review, and staff who support them may participate in a continuous improvement process to keep the standards up to date.

8. A. Example Corporation is using network segmentation to split their network up into security zones based on their functional requirements. They may use multiple-interface firewalls for this, and they may try to avoid single points of failure, but the question does not provide enough information to know if that is the case. Finally, zoned routing is a made up term—zone routing is an actual technical term, but it is used for wireless networks.

9. B. Firewalls are commonly used to create network protection zones, to protect network borders, and at the host level to help armor the host against attacks. Encryption at rest is most frequently used at the host layer, whereas DMZs are typically used at the edge of a network for publicly accessible services. Antivirus is sometimes used at each layer but is most commonly found at the host layer.

10. D. Lauren's initial design provided uniform protection. Her redesign placed systems into protected enclaves based on their sensitivity. If she had used threat analysis–based design, she would have considered threat vectors to build her design. An information-based design would have applied protections based on information classification or control requirements.

11. A. This diagram shows two potential single points of failure, but only one that meets Michelle's goals: the single connection to the Internet from the ISP is an immediate concern at Point A. Point D shows single connections to each edge switch, which would result in the devices connected to that switch failing, but that would not result in the impact to the core network that Michelle is concerned about. Points B and C both have fully redundant network devices with heartbeat connections.

12. C. Sending logs to a remote log server or bastion host is an appropriate compensating control. This ensures that copies of the logs exist in a secure location, allowing them to be reviewed if a similar compromise occurred. Full-disk encryption leaves files decrypted while in use and would not secure the log files from a compromise, whereas log rotation simply means that logs get changed out when they hit a specific size or timeframe. TLS encryption for data (including logs) in transit can keep it private and prevent modification but wouldn't protect the logs from being deleted.

13. B. While each of the items listed can help as part of a comprehensive security architecture, using centralized patch management software will typically have the largest impact in an organization's handling of vulnerabilities related to software updates. Vulnerability scanning can help detect issues, and an IPS with the appropriate detections enabled may help prevent exploits, but both are less important than patching itself. Similarly, standards for patching help guide what is done but don't ensure that the patching occurs.

14. B. Since Ben must assume that data that leaves may be exposed, his best option is to enforce encryption of files that leave the organization. Mandatory data tagging and DLP monitoring can help catch data that is accidentally sent, and network segmentation can help reduce the number of points he has to monitor, but encryption is the only control that can have a significant impact on data that does leave.

15. B. Trend analysis using historical data will show James what his network traffic's behavior has been. James may notice an increase since a new storage server with cloud replication was put in, or he may notice that a DMZ host has steadily been increasing its outbound traffic. Automated reporting might send an alarm if it has appropriate thresholds set, and log aggregation is the foundation of how a SIEM gathers information, but neither will individually give James the view he needs. BGP is a routing protocol, and graphing it won't give James the right information either.

16. C. File integrity checking tools like Tripwire can notify an administrator when changes are made to a file or directory. Angela can implement file integrity monitoring for her critical system files, thus ensuring she is warned if they change without her knowledge. Antimalware tools only detect behaviors like those of malware and may not detect manual changes or behaviors that don't match the profile they expect. Configuration management tools can control configuration files but may not note changes that are made, and logging utilities often don't track changes to files.

17. A. A web application firewall can provide protection against unknown threats and zero-day exploits by restricting attacks based on behavior or by implementing custom protection based on known exploit behavior. A patch from the vendor is often not immediately available, an IDS cannot stop an attack—at best it will report the attack—and least privilege for accounts may limit the impact of an attack but won't stop it.

18. A. Mike reduced the organization's attack surface. This occurs when the number of potential targets are reduced. Since the question describes only one security activity, we don't know that defense in depth has been implemented. The firewall may be a corrective control, but the question does not specify that it is there as part of a response or to deal with a specific problem, and firewalls are technical controls rather than administrative controls.

19. C. The control Kathleen identified as missing would be an administrative (process) control that acts in a corrective manner to ensure that remediation occurs. It is nontechnical and not a physical control. It also does not make up for a flaw in other controls and is thus not a compensatory control.

20. A. Retirement is the last step at the end of the life cycle for a standard or process. If the process is retired, a final update to it is not needed! The standards for other, currently maintained operating systems should undergo regularly scheduled review, and staff who support them may participate in a continuous improvement process to keep the standards up to date.

Chapter 11: Identity and Access Management Security

1. B. While it may seem like Lauren has implemented three different factors, both a PIN and a passphrase are knowledge-based factors and cannot be considered distinct factors. She has implemented two distinct factors with her design. If she wanted to add a third factor, she could replace either the password or the PIN with a fingerprint scan or other biometric factor.

2. C. LDAP authentication occurs in plaintext, requiring TLS to protect the communication process. SSL is outdated, and both MD5 and SHA1 are useful for hashing but not for protecting authentication traffic.

3. B. The nightmare scenario of having her a compromised Kerberos server that allows attackers to issue their own ticket granting tickets, known as golden tickets, would result in attackers being able to create new tickets, perform account changes, and even create new accounts and services. A KDC is a Kerberos key distribution center; MGT and master tickets were both made up for this question.

4. B. The NT LAN Manager security protocols are associated with Active Directory. SAML, OAuth, and RADIUS do not use NTLM.

5. D. Privilege creep occurs as staff members change roles but their rights and permissions are not updated to match their new responsibilities. This violates the concept of least privilege. Rights mismanagement and permission misalignment are both terms made up for this question.

6. A. OAuth redirect exploits are a form of impersonation attack, allowing attackers to pretend to be a legitimate user. Session hijacking would take advantage of existing sessions, whereas man-in-the-middle (MiTM) attacks take advantage of being in the path of communications. Protocol analysis is a networking term used when reviewing packet contents.

7. C. Breaches of passwords stored in easily recoverable or reversible formats paired with user IDs or other identifying information create significant threats if users reused passwords. Attackers can easily test the passwords they recover against other sites and services. Poor password reset questions are a threat even without a breach, and unencrypted password storage is an issue during breaches, but this type of breach is enabled by poor storage, rather than a result of the breach. Use of federated credentials is not a critical concern in cases like this.

8. B. Context-based authentication allows authentication decisions to be made based on information about the user, the system they are using, or other data like their geographic location, behavior, or even time of day. Token-based authentication uses a security token to generate a onetime password or value, and NAC is network access control, a means of validating systems and users that connect to a network. System-data contextual is a made-up answer for this question.

9. C. Common attacks against Kerberos include attacks aimed at administrative accounts, particularly those that attempt to create a ticket granting ticket. Ticket reuse attacks are also common. Open redirect–based attacks are associated with OAuth rather than Kerberos.

10. B. LDAP is sometimes used for single sign-on but is not a shared authentication technology. OpenID Connect, OAuth, and Facebook Connect are all examples of shared authentication technologies.

11. B. LDAP access control lists (ACLs) can limit which accounts or users can access objects in the directory. LDAP replication may help with load issues or denial-of-service attacks, TLS helps protect data in transit, but MD5 storage for secrets like passwords is a bad idea!

12. D. TACACS+ should be run on an isolated management network to protect it from attackers. It does not provide built-in encryption, TACACS++ does not exist, and while enabling auditing features is a good idea, it won't stop attacks from occurring.

13. A. Jason's exploit is a form of privilege escalation, which uses a flaw to gain elevated privileges. Local users have a far greater ability to attempt these attacks in most organizations, since flaws that are only exploitable locally often get less attention from administrators than those that can be exploited remotely. A zero-day attack would use previously unknown flaws to exploit a system, rootkits are aimed at acquiring and maintaining long-term access to systems, and session hijacking focuses on taking over existing sessions.

14. C. Chris has identified a problem with the maintenance and modification processes his organization uses. He should review how employee accounts are reviewed and how changes are requested when employees change positions in the organization.

15. B. CAPTCHAs, login throttling, and locking out accounts after a set number of failed logins are all useful techniques to stop or delay brute-force password guessing attacks. Some sites also use unique URLs, or limit the IP ranges that systems can authenticate from. Returning an HTTP error actually works in the attacker's favor, as they can key off of that error to try their next login attempt!

16. C. Identity providers, or IDPs, make assertions about identities to relying parties and service providers in a federation. CDUs and APs are not terms used in federated identity designs.

17. C. NIST SP 800-63-3 recommends that SMS be deprecated due to issues with VoIP including password reuse and the ability to redirect SMS sent via VoIP calls. In addition, SMS itself is relatively insecure, allowing attackers with the right equipment to potentially intercept it. The good news is that SMS can send unique tokens—they're just text!

18. C. Ben successfully conducted a session hijacking attack by copying session information and using the existing session. If he had impersonated a legitimate user, it would have been an impersonation attack, while a MiTM attack would require being in the flow of traffic between two systems or services. Privilege escalation attacks focus on acquiring higher levels of privilege.

19. A. RAIDUS shared secrets can be brute forced if attackers can gain access to a known password and can monitor traffic on the network. A dictionary attack is a type of attack used against passwords, pass-the-hash attacks attempt to reuse previously used hashes to authenticate, and counter-RADIUS attacks is a made-up term.

20. B. Michelle's security token is an example of a possession factor, or "something you have." A password or PIN would be a knowledge factor or "something you know," while a fingerprint or retina scan would be a biometric, or inherence factor.

Chapter 12: Software Development Security

1. A. Waterfall continues to be useful in complex software development efforts where requirements are well documented and careful planning is required. Spiral would fit better if risks were likely to change during the development effort, whereas Agile Scrum is well suited to changing requirements. Rapid Application Development's prototype model is not a good fit for controlling a nuclear reactor!

2. D. During the rework stage of Fagan inspection, issues may be identified that require the process to return to the planning stage and then proceed back through the remaining stages to re-review the code.

3. B. Adam is conducting static code analysis by reviewing the source code. Dynamic code analysis requires running the program, and both mutation testing and fuzzing are types of dynamic analysis.

4. B. Sam is conducting a regression test, which verifies that changes have not introduced new issues to his application. Code review focuses on the application code, whereas stress testing verifies that the application will perform under load or other stress conditions. Whiffing isn't a term used in this type of review.

5. B. The Spiral model cycles through four phases: requirements gathering, design, build, and evaluation/risk analysis.

6. C. Charles should perform user input validation to strip out any SQL code or other unwanted input. Secure session management can help prevent session hijacking, logging may provide useful information for incident investigation, and implementing TLS can help protect network traffic, but only input validation helps with the issue described.

7. D. A source control management tool like Subversion or Git can help prevent old code from being added to current versions of an application. Developer practices still matter, but knowing what version of the code you are checking in and out helps! Stress testing would help determine whether the application can handle load, a WAF or web application firewall can protect against attacks, but neither would resolve this issue. Pair programing might detect the problem, but the question specifically asks for a tool, not a process.

8. A. A parameterized query (sometimes called a prepared statement) uses a prebuilt SQL statement to prevent SQL-based attacks. Variables from the application are fed to the query, rather than building a custom query when the application needs data. Encoding data helps to prevent cross-site scripting attacks, as does input validation. Appropriate access controls can prevent access to data that the account or application should not have access to, but they don't use precompiled SQL statements.

9. C. User acceptance testing (UAT) is the process of testing to ensure that the users of the software are satisfied with its functionality. Stress testing verifies that the application will perform when under high load or other stress, and unit testing validates individual components of the application. CNA is not a term associated with application development.

10. A. Velocity tracking calculates the actual speed based on accomplishments versus the estimated work from the sprint planning effort. Timeboxing is used to limit the time spent on an effort, while planning poker is used for estimation. Speed traps are not a term associated with the Agile methodology.

11. D. TLS satisfies the "protect data" best practice by ensuring that network traffic is secure. Parameterizing queries uses prebuilt SQL, while encoding data removes control characters that could be used for cross-site scripting attacks and other exploits. Validating all inputs requires treating all user input as untrusted.

12. B. Pass-around reviews normally rely on email to move code between developers. In Kristen's case, a pass-around review will exactly meet her needs. Pair programming and over-the shoulder review both require developers to work together, whereas tool-assisted reviews require implementation of a tool to specifically support the review.

13. A. During an Agile sprint user stories are gathered during sprint planning.

14. A. During an Agile sprint, development typically comes after sprint planning. Sprint planning may involve gathering user stories, and design may be part of the planning process. Testing occurs after development.

15. C. Agile sprints are considered done after the customer agrees that the task is complete or the time allocated for the sprint is complete. Demonstrations may result in further customer feedback, and testing is conducted prior to the demonstration. Sprint planning for the next sprint is not necessarily bound to the completion of the first sprint, but typically follows rather than running in parallel due to a desire to keep resources focused on the tasks they are working on.

16. D. Load testing is used to validate the performance of an application under heavy loads like high numbers of concurrent user sessions. Fuzzing, mutation testing, and fault injection are all types of code review and testing.

17. A. Interception proxies are designed to allow testers to intercept, view, and modify traffic sent from web browsers and are often used for penetration testing and web application security testing. Fuzzers are used for application testing by sending invalid data to the application, a WAF is a web application firewall, and a sniffer is useful for monitoring traffic, but not for modifying web traffic in a live, easy-to-use manner.

18. D. Fault injection directly inserts faults into the error handling paths for an application to verify how it will handle the problem. Stress testing focuses on application load, dynamic code analysis describes any type of live application testing, and fuzzing sends invalid data to applications to ensure that they can deal with it properly.

19. C. Over-the-shoulder code reviews use a pair of developers to perform peer code review, one of whom explains their code to the other. Pair programming also uses two developers but allows the developers to swap roles between writing code and observing and strategizing. Tool-assisted review uses a code review tool, whereas pass-around review uses email or other methods to send code to others for review.

20. D. User stories are collected to describe high-level user requirements in Agile development efforts. Backlogs are lists of features and tasks that are needed to finish the project, whereas planning poker is an estimation method and velocity tracking is used to measure progress versus expectations.

Appendix
B

Answers to the Lab Exercises

Chapter 1: Defending Against Cybersecurity Threats

Solution to Activity 1.4: Security Tools

Firewall	Filters network connections based upon source, destination, and port
Decompiler	Attempts to recover source code from binary code
Antivirus	Scans a system for malicious software
NAC	Determines what clients may access a wired or wireless network
GPO	Deploys configuration settings to multiple Windows systems
Hash	Creates a unique fingerprint of a file
Honeypot	System intentionally created to appear vulnerable
WAF	Protects against SQL injection attacks

Chapter 2: Reconnaissance and Intelligence Gathering

Solution to Activity 2.3: Intelligence Gathering Tools

Route to a system	Traceroute
Open services via a network	Nmap
IP traffic flow and volume	Netflow
Organizational contact information associated with domain registration	Whois
Connections listed by protocol	Netstat
Zone transfer	Dig
Packet capture	Wireshark
Social media geotagging	Creepy

Chapter 4: Analyzing Vulnerability Scans

Solution to Activity 4.2: Security Tools

The CVSS vector for the IKE Aggressive Mode Pre-Shared Key vulnerability shown in Figure 4.20 is CVSS2#AV:N/AC:L/Au:N/C:P:/I:N/A:N. Breaking this down piece-by-piece gives us:

- **AV:N** indicates that an attacker may exploit the vulnerability remotely over a network. This is the most serious value for this metric.
- **AC:L** indicates that exploiting the vulnerability does not require any specialized conditions. This is the most serious value for this metric.
- **Au:N** indicates that attackers do not need to authenticate to exploit the vulnerability. This is the most serious value for this metric.
- **C:P** indicates that a successful exploitation of this vulnerability would yield partial access to information. This is the middle value for this metric.
- **I:N** indicates that a successful exploitation of this vulnerability would have no integrity impact. This is the least serious value for this metric.
- **A:N** that a successful exploitation of this vulnerability would have no availability impact. This is the least serious value for this metric.

The CVSS vector for the POODLE vulnerability shown in Figure 4.21 is CVSS2#AV:N/ AC:M/Au:N/C:P/I:N/A:N. Breaking this down piece-by-piece gives us:

- **AV:N** indicates that an attacker may exploit the vulnerability remotely over a network. This is the most serious value for this metric.
- **AC:M** indicates that exploiting the vulnerability requires somewhat specialized conditions. This is the middle value for this metric.
- **Au:N** indicates that attackers do not need to authenticate to exploit the vulnerability. This is the most serious value for this metric.
- **C:P** indicates that a successful exploitation of this vulnerability would yield partial access to information. This is the middle value for this metric.
- **I:N** indicates that a successful exploitation of this vulnerability would have no integrity impact. This is the least serious value for this metric.
- **A:N** indicates that a successful exploitation of this vulnerability would have no availability impact. This is the least serious value for this metric.

Based upon this CVSS analysis, the first vulnerability in Figure 4.20 is slightly more serious. They have identical CVSS vectors except for the Access Complexity metric. This means that the IKE vulnerability does not require specialized conditions to exploit, while the POODLE vulnerability does require "somewhat specialized" conditions.

Chapter 5: Building an Incident Response Program

Solution to Activity 5.1: Incident Severity Classification

The functional impact of this incident is high because the organization has lost the ability to sell products to customers. This fits the definition of the "organization is no longer able to provide some critical services to any users."

The economic impact of this incident is high. The organization expects to lose $2,000,000 per day. This fits the definition of the high category: "The organization expects to experience a financial impact of $500,000 or more."

The recoverability effort of this incident is extended. The organization has exhausted all internal resources and is seeking a consultant to assist. This fits the extended category definition of "Time to recovery is unpredictable; additional resources and outside help are needed."

The information impact of this incident is none. The attack described in this scenario is a denial-of-service attack, and there is no indication of the compromise of sensitive information. This fits the none category definition of "No information was exfiltrated, changed, deleted or otherwise compromised."

Solution to Activity 5.2: Incident Response Phases

Activity	Phase
Conducting a lessons-learned review session	Post-Incident Activity
Receiving a report from a staff member about a malware infection	Detection and Analysis
Upgrading the organization's firewall to block a new type of attack	Preparation
Recovering normal operations after eradicating an incident	Containment, Eradication, and Recovery
Identifying the attacker(s) and attacking system(s)	Containment, Eradication, and Recovery

Activity	Phase
Interpreting log entries using a SIEM to identify a potential incident	Detection and Analysis
Assembling the hardware and software required to conduct an incident investigation	Preparation

Chapter 6: Analyzing Symptoms for Incident Response

Solution to Activity 6.3: Security Tools

Flows	A set of packets passing from a source system to a destination system in a given time interval
Resmon	A Windows tool that monitors memory, CPU, and disk usage
iPerf	A tool for testing the maximum available bandwidth for a network
PRTG	A network management and monitoring tool that provides central visibility into flows and SNMP data for an entire network
Beaconing	Traffic sent to a command and control system by a PC that is part of a botnet
SNMP	A protocol for collecting information like status and performance about devices on a network
top	A Linux command that displays processes, memory utilization, and other details about running programs
Perfmon	A Windows tool that monitors a wide range of devices and services, including energy, USB, and disk usage

Chapter 7: Performing Forensic Analysis

Solution to Activity 7.2: Conduct the NIST Rhino Hunt

You can find a complete answer to the NIST Rhino hunt from Activity 7.2 at `https://www.cfreds.nist.gov/dfrws/DFRWS2005-answers.pdf`.

Solution to Activity 7.3: Security Tools

dd	A Linux tool used to create disk images
md5sum	Used to determine whether a drive is forensically sound
Volatility Framework	A memory forensics and analysis suite
FTK	A full-featured forensic suite
Eraser	A drive and file wiping utility sometimes used for anti-forensic purposes
Write blocker	A device used to prevent forensic software from modifying a drive while accessing it
WinDBG	A tool used to review Windows memory dumps
Forensic drive duplicator	A device used to create a complete forensic image and validate it without a PC

Chapter 8: Recovery and Post-Incident Response

Solution to Activity 8.1: Incident Containment Options

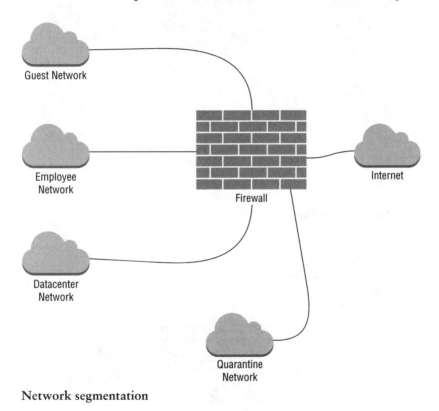

Network segmentation

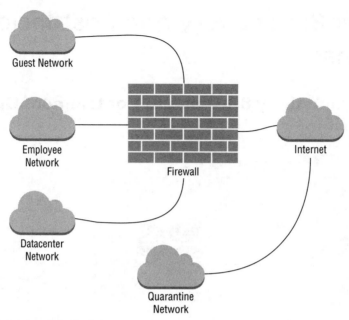

Network isolation

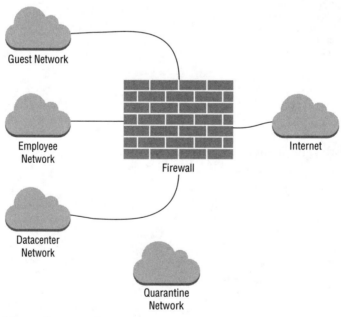

Network removal

Solution to Activity 8.2: Incident Response Activities

Patching	Validation
Sanitization	Eradication
Lessons learned	Post-Incident Activities
Reimaging	Eradication
Secure disposal	Eradication
Isolation	Containment
Scanning	Validation
Removal	Containment
Reconstruction	Eradication
Permission verification	Validation
User account review	Validation
Segmentation	Containment

Solution to Activity 8.3: Sanitization and Disposal Techniques

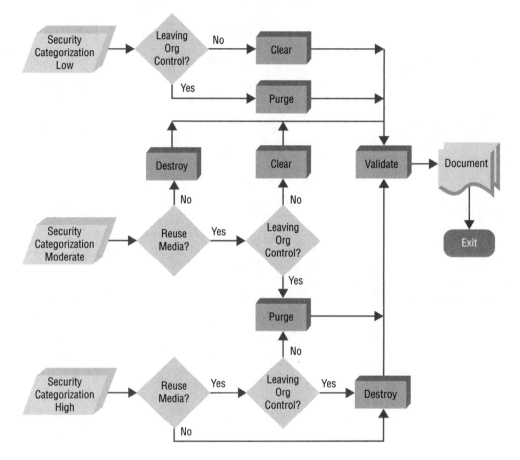

Chapter 9: Policy and Compliance

Solution to Activity 9.1: Policy Documents

Policy	Provides high-level requirements for a cybersecurity program
Standard	Offers detailed requirements for achieving security control objectives
Guideline	Includes advice based on best practices for achieving security goals that are not mandatory
Procedure	Outlines a step-by-step process for carrying out a cybersecurity activity

Solution to Activity 9.3: Compliance Auditing Tools

The testing procedures for PCI DSS requirement 8.2.3 instruct auditors to inspect system configuration settings and verify that the user password/passphrase requirements are set to require a minimum length of at least seven characters and to require that passwords contain both alphabetic and numeric characters.

Chapter 10: Defense-in-Depth Security Architectures

Solution to Activity 10.3: Security Architecture Terminology

Uniform protection	A security design that protects all elements of the environment at the same level using the same tools and techniques
Attack surface	The portion of an organization, system, or network that can be attacked
Administrative controls	Controls that include processes and policies
Protected enclaves	A protected network or location separated from other security zones by protective controls
Dual control	A security control that prevents individuals from performing sensitive actions without a trusted peer reviewing and approving their actions
Single point of failure	A part of a system that, if it fails, will cause the failure of the entire system
Mandatory vacation	A personnel security control that can help to identify individuals who are exploiting the rights they have as part of their job
Compensating control	A control that remediates a gap or flaw in another control

Chapter 11: Identity and Access Management Security

Activity 11.1: Federated Security Scenario

Part 1: You should identify two major problems: use of HTTP, rather than HTTPS, and the development team's creation of their own Oauth libraries.

Part 2: Answers may vary but should include detail similar to:

1. What recommendations and advice would you provide to the implementation team?

   The implementation team should use open source or Facebook-provided libraries and code and should follow recommended best practices for implementation. Secure connections should be required for all authentication and authorization traffic.

   A strong answer might also reference the OWASP Facebook development guide at https://www.owasp.org/index.php/Facebook

2. What should Example Corp.'s incident response plan include to handle issues involving Facebook Login?

   Responses will vary but should take into account the fact that Example Corp. will now be relying on a third party and will need to know how to contact Facebook, what they will do if Facebook is compromised, and how individual account issues will be handled.

3. Does using Facebook Login create more or less risk for Example Corp.? Why?

   Responses will vary but should take into account use of a third-party authentication service and lack of control of accounts versus the utility of a third-party service provider.

Activity 11.2: Onsite Identity Issues Scenario

Part 1: You should suggest solutions involving local authentication with appropriate monitoring, logging, and management to ensure that local accounts are secure.

Part 2: You should suggest a central identity and access management system to centrally manage credentials and rights, and administrative policies and controls that ensure that roles and rights are updated when users change positions or roles.

Part 3: Answers are left to your own analysis of your work.

Solution to Activity 11.3: Identity and Access Management Terminology

TACACs+	A Cisco-designed authentication protocol.
Identity	The set of claims made about an account holder.

ADFS	Microsoft's identity federation service.
Privilege creep	This issue occurs when accounts gain more rights over time due to role changes.
Directory service	LDAP is deployed in this role.
OAuth 2.0	An open standard for authorization used for websites and applications.
SAML	An XML-based protocol used to exchange authentication and authorization data.
RADIUS	A common AAA system for network devices.

Chapter 12: Software Development Security

Solution to Activity 12.3: Security Tools

Subversion	A source control management tool
Agile	An SDLC model that relies on sprints to accomplish tasks based on user stories
Dynamic code analysis	A code analysis that is done using a running application
Fuzzing	A code analysis done using a running application that relies on sending unexpected data to see if the application fails
Fagan inspection	A formal code review process that relies on specified entry and exit criteria for each phase
Over the shoulder	A code review process that requires one developer to explain their code to another developer
Waterfall	The first SDLC model, replaced in many organizations but still used for very complex systems
Backlog	An Agile term that describes the list of feature needed to complete a project

Index

Note to the Reader: Throughout this index **boldfaced** page numbers indicate primary discussions of a topic. *Italicized* page numbers indicate illustrations.

J

M

T

X-Y-Z

Comprehensive Online Learning Environment

Register on Sybex.com to gain access to the comprehensive online interactive learning environment and test bank to help you study for your CompTIA Cybersecurity Analyst (CSA+) certification.

The online test bank includes:

- **Assessment Test** to help you focus your study to specific objectives
- **Chapter Tests** to reinforce what you learned
- **Practice Exams** to test your knowledge of the material
- **Digital Flashcards** to reinforce your learning and provide last-minute test prep before the exam
- **Searchable Glossary** gives you instant access to the key terms you'll need to know for the exam

Go to http://www.wiley.com/go/sybextestprep to register and gain access to this comprehensive study tool package.

30% off On-Demand IT Video Training from ITProTV

ITProTV and Sybex have partnered to provide 30% off a Premium annual or monthly membership. ITProTV provides a unique, custom learning environment for IT professionals and students alike, looking to validate their skills through vendor certifications. On-demand courses provide over 1,000 hours of video training with new courses being added every month, while labs and practice exams provide additional hands-on experience. For more information on this offer and to start your membership today, visit http://itpro.tv/sybex30/.